AF505742

The Illuminated Window

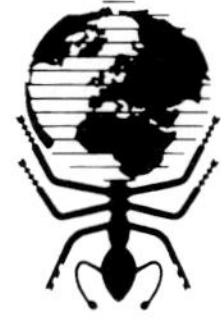

The Illuminated Window

Stories across Time

Virginia Chieffo Raguin

REAKTION BOOKS

'The world is charged with the grandeur of God.
It will flame out, like shining from shook foil'
Gerard Manley Hopkins, 'God's Grandeur', 1877

Published by Reaktion Books Ltd
Unit 32, Waterside
44–48 Wharf Road
London N1 7UX, UK
www.reaktionbooks.co.uk

First published 2023
Copyright © Virginia Chieffo Raguin 2023

Printed and bound in India by Replika Press Pvt. Ltd

A catalogue record for this book is available from the British Library

ISBN 978 1 78914 793 3

Contents

—

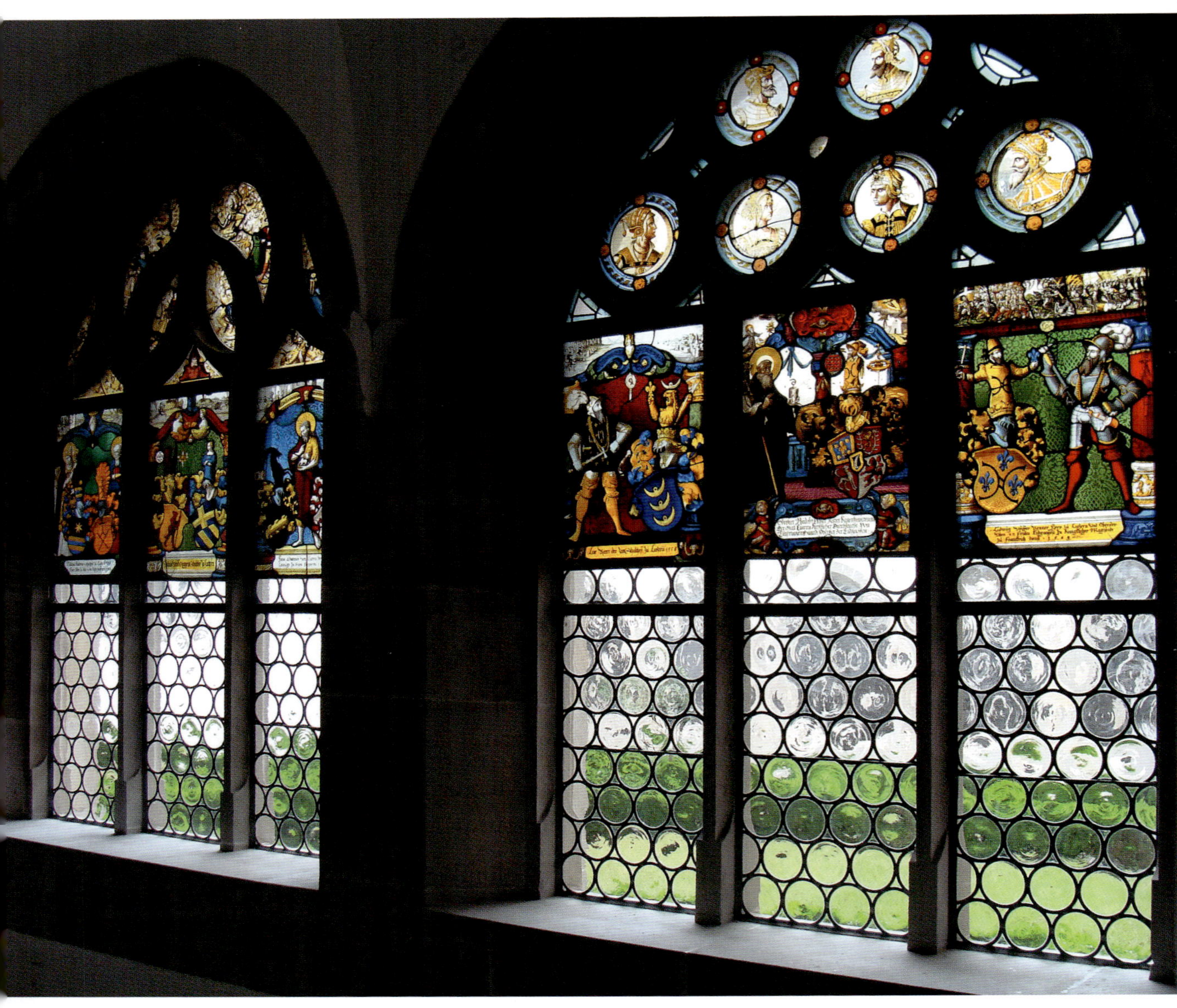

1 Cloister, Benedictine abbey of Muri, Switzerland, West V and VI, 1566–9.

Introduction: Patrons and Process

—

Rather than a chronological survey, this study focuses on selected monuments, enabling the viewer to become engaged in the moment of their creation and the motivations of their patrons. Unlike viewing art in museums, stained glass is almost always encountered in its original setting. Our experience of the window is very different from perusing a collection of isolated paintings silhouetted against a neutral space, a situation where we often struggle to reconstruct the context within which these works first achieved meaning. We, of course, bring our own contemporary sensibilities to every encounter. When we enter a building, such as the cathedrals of Cologne or Chartres, or the parish church of Fairford, the architecture is a frame, not only for the windows but for our own bodies as they move through space. We become keenly aware, for example in the cathedral at Canterbury, how the first viewers experienced the evocation of the power of the martyred bishop, Thomas. In vignette after vignette, they saw his healing actions, aiding villagers, heads of state, the professed religious, foreign visitors, children, elders and males and females equally.

A window is created not only by the artist, but through the collaborative tension between the physical site, the programme desired by the patron, the concern for its legibility for the spectator, the technological possibilities of the medium and the prevailing style of the era. We see the donor panel develop in Switzerland, responding to the Swiss desire for an object to commemorate reciprocal dependencies. Of small size, these windows were ubiquitous in town halls, law courts and guild halls, as well as sites of worship. They were an art of exchange, proclaiming friendships and obligations (illus. 1). In the modern era, Harvard University erected a multi-use hall, dining room, lecture hall and passageway to commemorate the sacrifice of so many in the American Civil War. Harvard's programme is self-reflective, commemorating, as well, a privileged education, depicting past heroes in science, art, exploration, religion and government, made accessible to the present.

In many ways, the experience of windows evokes the ethos of much contemporary art. Many artists work collaboratively and engage in site-specific installations. They frequently emphasize the distinct nature of materials. We need only turn to the popularity of installation art or 'environments' pioneered by Kurt Schwitters's Merzbau from the 1930s. Christo and Jeanne-Claude's ability to engage others in both constructing and experiencing large-scale, if temporary, environmental change, is paralleled by the buildings in this study. The spectator's experience changes over time with variations of light and movement through space, and with the activities/spectacles designed for these spaces.

It is hoped that this series of studies will encourage the reader to peruse the text in any order, starting with what first engages attention, as something new, or something familiar. References to other chapters and their concepts are interspersed through the text, encouraging the reader to review, compare and contemplate.

The Materials

The windows studied here, with some exceptions, utilize paint, composed of a low-firing, essentially clear, glass-flux and opaque metallic oxides, generally iron or copper. This is mixed with a binder and then applied with a brush to the surface of the glass in a wide range of painting styles. We can still look to the treatise written in the early twelfth century by a monk under the pseudonym of Theophilus for a basic understanding of the steps required to fabricate a window. Theophilus was a metalworker but he reassures the reader that he had diligently learned from experts in painting on glass to construct his treatise. He pays particular attention to techniques of applying paint, telling the glass painter to take the pigment and 'smear it about with the brush in such a way that . . . the glass is made transparent in the part where you normally make highlights in a painting, such as for faces around the eyes, nostrils, and chin and on bare feet and hands.' Theophilus also wrote about stickwork, or the process of removing the paint (done easily before firing) with the pointed handle of a brush to make 'circles and branches with flowers and leaves . . . as is done in the case of painted letters [in manuscripts]'.[1] This technique is illustrated by the Swiss shield with the red clover discussed later in this chapter (see illus. 9).

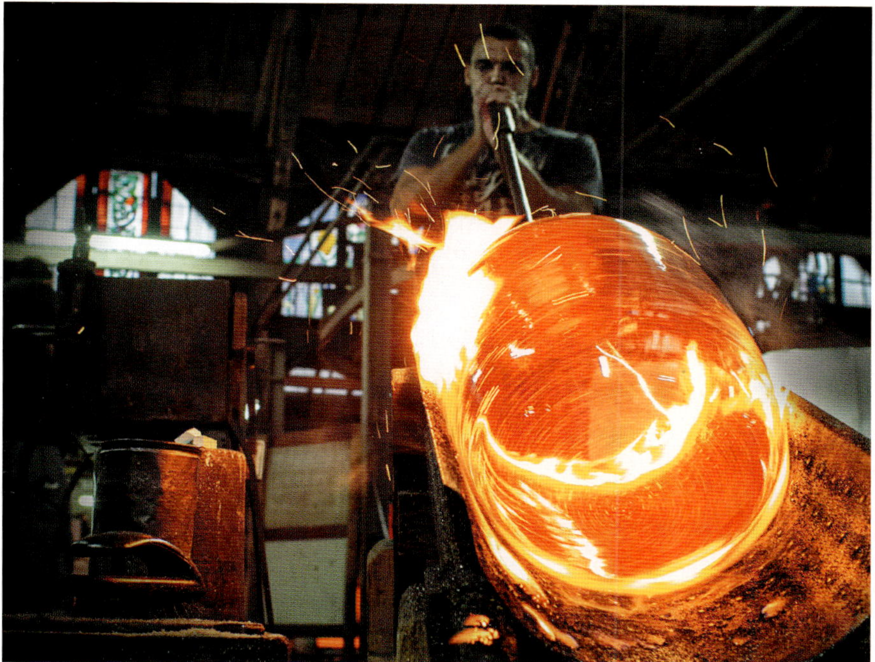

2 Mouth-blown glass manufacture, Glashütte Lamberts, Waldsassen, Germany.

We also have contemporary producers of glass whose accounts provide fascinating insights into the process. Glashütte Lamberts, Waldsassen, Germany is highly respected for making traditional mouth-blown glass. The raw materials of quartz sand, sodium carbonate and limestone are carefully measured before being mixed in ceramic pots. The mixture, melted at high temperatures, 1,400°C (2,552°F), would normally be completely clear but can be tinted by the addition of precise amounts of iron, copper, nickel and other metal alloys as well as silver and gold. Then follows the blowing of glass, during which the production temperature of 1,100°C (2,012°F) is maintained. In a carefully choreographed process, several individuals work together to handle the successive stages. The starter dips the blowpipe into the pot and keeps it constantly rotating. The motion thus gathers the molten glass onto the end of the pipe. The starter repeats this procedure several times until the quantity required has been reached. In this process one craftsperson lifts the pipe in and out of the pot of molten glass and onto wooden moulds. By means of rotating motions and simultaneous blowing, the starter works the gob through the different sizes of moulds to give it the appropriate shape. The gob at this stage is only slightly inflated by the starter, who then passes the blowpipe on to the master. Now comes the most exacting part of the process. While rotating the balloon in the steel trough, the master blows

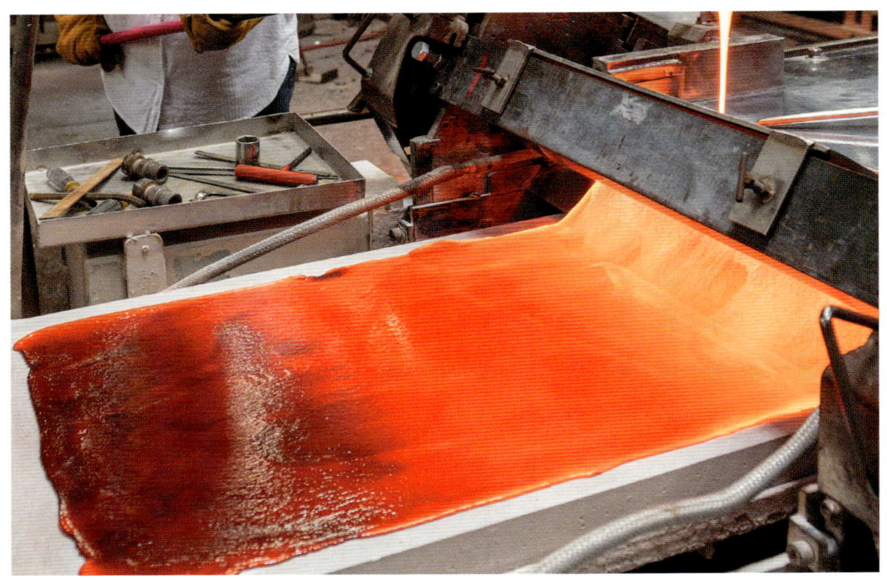

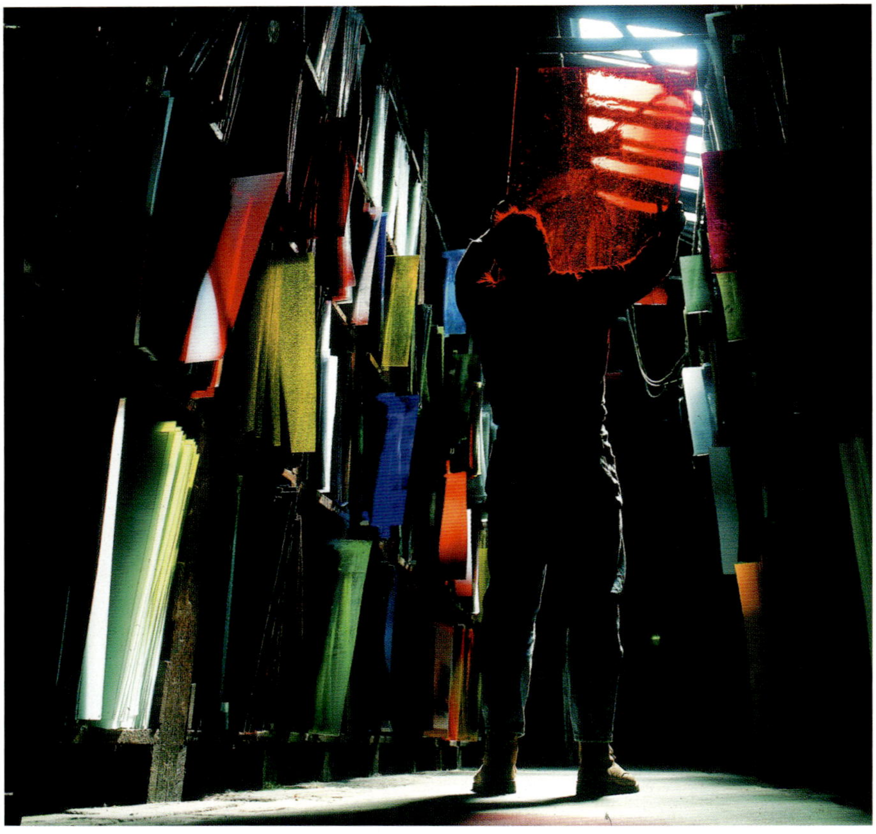

3 Rolled glass, Bullseye Glass Co., Portland, Oregon.
4 Selection of glass sheets, Glashütte Lamberts, Waldsassen, Germany.

it up to full size, giving it the desired shape and structure (illus. 2). During this time, which can take up to ten minutes, the cylinder goes back and forth into the 'glory hole', a small kiln, in order to keep the glass hot enough to manipulate.

The glass becomes a red-hot cylindrical balloon. It is then cut open at one end and dilated by means of metal scissors by the assistant. After a transfer again to the glory hole so that the glass regains the proper temperature, the same procedure takes place at the other end, the one closest to the pipe. In this way a well-proportioned glass cylinder comes into existence. If molten glass is cooled too rapidly, it undergoes an uneven temperature distribution (tension) throughout the material. This can result in cracks in the glass, or a weakness in the structure that leads to cracks later. To prevent this, the cylinder is placed in an annealing lehr, a long oven with a mechanized system to ensure a controlled temperature gradient. Travelling through the oven on a continuous belt, the glass takes over an hour to cool to room temperature. The cooled cylinder is scored lengthwise. After being returned to the kiln, the cylinder can then be opened to lie flat. The sheet is then cooled slowly by travelling through another annealing lehr. It thus loses its inherent tensions so that it can be easily cut by the artist fabricating a window. Molten glass can also be processed through rollers to produce a sheet (illus. 3). That also must be slowly cooled in a similar annealing lehr to diminish internal tensions. The cooled and hardened sheets are then stored on racks. The selection process can often seem as if one could hold beams of light in one's hands (illus. 4).

The Leaded Window in History

Sheets of glass, both blown and cast, had been used architecturally since Roman times. This ancient glass was set into wooden frames or moulded and carved stucco or plaster. When or where the idea of using strips of lead to hold glass pieces together was first employed is not recorded, but lead's malleability and strength greatly increased the variety of possible shapes available to artists, giving them greater creative freedom. Excavations at Jarrow, England, a site dating from the seventh to the ninth centuries, have yielded strips of lead and unpainted glass cut to specific shapes. Taking these shapes and making an image – the German term for stained glass is *Glasmalerei* (glass painting) – begins with the artist's sketch. In medieval times this was known as the *vidimus*, Latin for 'we have seen.' Understandably, few of these contract sketches have survived. A late sixteenth-century pen-and-ink drawing for a window by Hans Jacob Plepp (illus. 5), for example, contains only a portion of the design; there is no

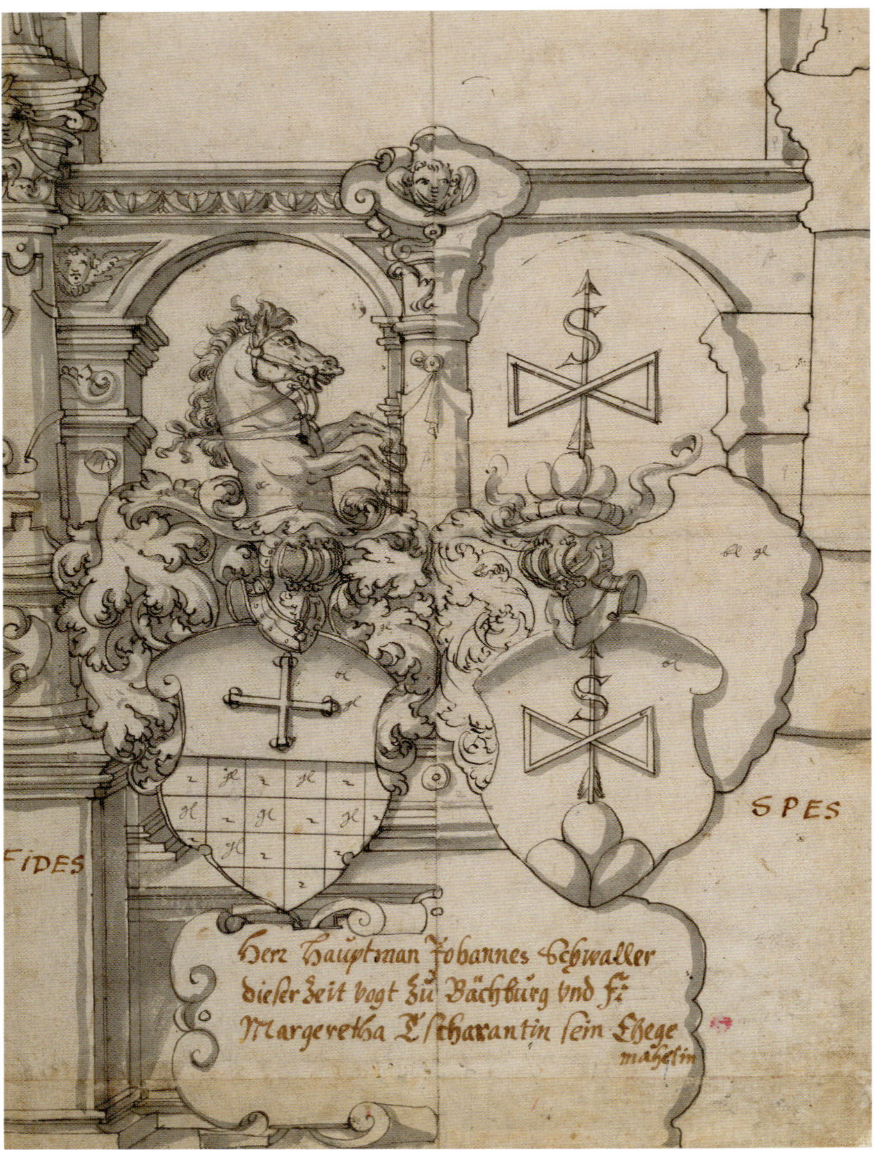

5 Hans Jacob Plepp, *Stained-Glass Design with Two Coats of Arms,*
c. 1590–95, now at the J. Paul Getty Museum, Los Angeles.

need to repeat drawings of elaborate architectural decoration once an exem-
plar is produced. In the inscription panel, we read the text: 'Captain Johannes
Schwaller, current governor of Bächburg [Bechburg] and Margaretta Tscharant,
his wife.' We do not see the calligraphy as it will be rendered in the cartouche.
The allegorical virtues are named, not drawn, *Fides* (Faith) and *Spes* (Hope).
Arguably, the client had been shown for approval other drawings of these stock

figures in Swiss glass of that era. The sketch is then enlarged into a full-scale pattern called a cartoon. The cartoon is also used to create the patterns given to the glazier, who cuts the required segments from the selected sheets of glass, the colour of which has been produced during the molten process described above.

Adhering the Paint

A glass painter, as described by Theophilus, then intervenes to paint the elements that carry the image, such as faces, drapery or decorative designs. Close inspection reveals significant artistic individuality enjoyed by the painters. It has been possible to identify multiple painters with different techniques within a single workshop. A single designer may have created a series of figures, but different painters executed them, some favouring shades of tonal wash and others linear systems of hatching and cross-hatching. Collaboration is truly essential for the window. For example, the English painter Edward Burne-Jones created many designs for windows produced by William Morris, pioneer of the Arts and Crafts movement, but he delegated the painting to others.

Differences in period styles, of course, are evident. The torso of one of the dead rising from the tomb, dated about 1200 and associated with windows from Notre-Dame Cathedral, Paris (illus. 6), displays bold draughtsmanship typical of the era. Head, torso and both arms are a single piece of glass. The artist painted both the back and the front of the glass, creating an enhanced sense of three-dimensionality. Broad stokes of the brush in a medium tone define the curvature of the ribs and the sternum. Fully saturated paint accents the hair, chin and facial features as well as the division between pectorals and abdomen. A contemporary artist, Kiki Smith (illus. 7), applies paint in ways that would be familiar to her predecessors over centuries. The base tone is achieved through a light, uniform wash, over which she applies darker strokes until, ultimately, she adds fine marks with a thin brush. During the process, paint can also be removed using a stick or a needle to achieve highlights, mentioned by Theophilus.

The sections of glass are subsequently fired in a kiln to fuse the painted details with the surface of the coloured glass, thus achieving permanence over the centuries. The fired sections are then joined by malleable lead elements called cames. The cames are soldered at their joints and caulked to make them watertight. These leaded sections are then set into a larger iron framework and fitted into the stone or wood of the window opening.

A highly important innovation appeared in architectural glass around the beginning of the fourteenth century: silver stain, the only true 'stain' in stained

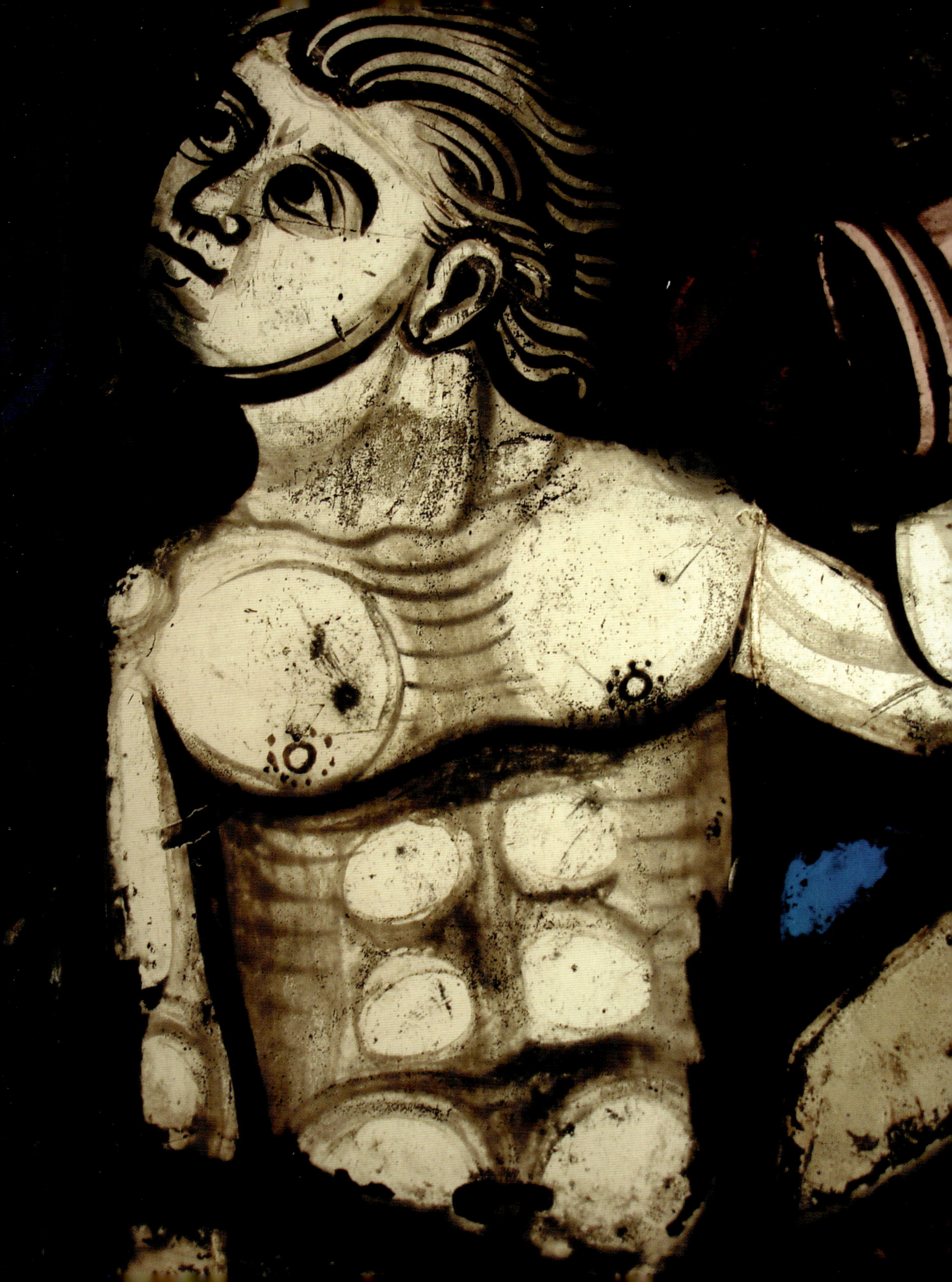

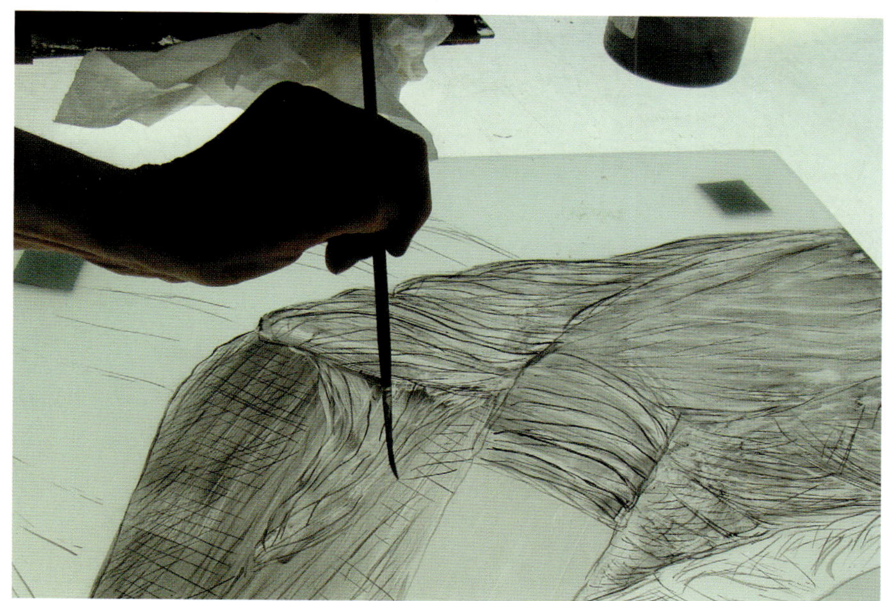

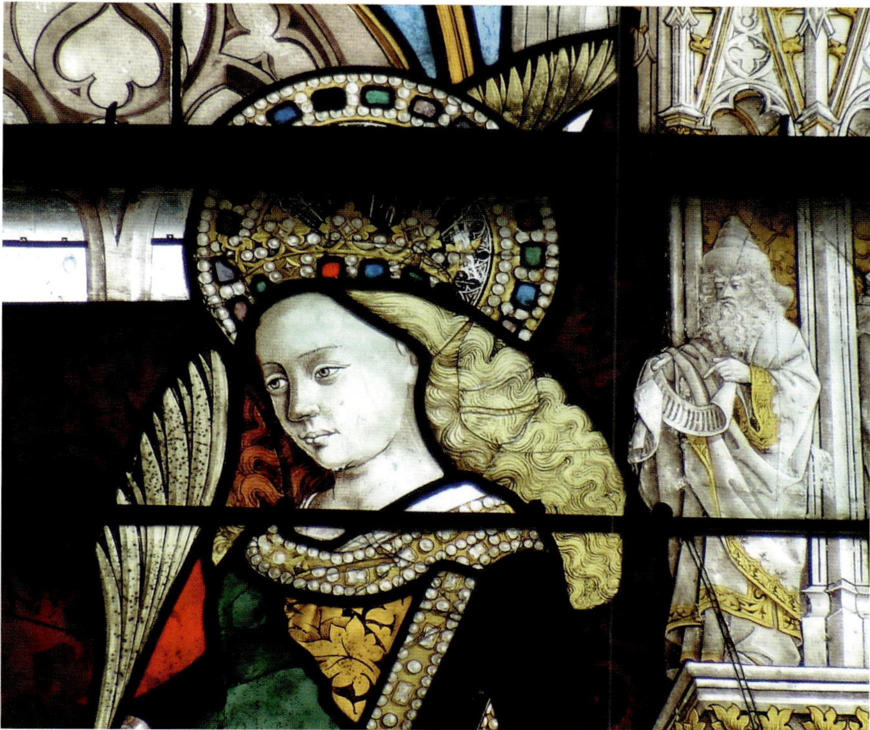

6 Last Judgement (detail), dead rising, c. 1200, associated with the style of the panels of St Matthew in the South Rose, cathedral of Notre-Dame, Paris, transferred before 1848 to the Sainte-Chapelle, then to the Cluny Museum, Paris.

7 Kiki Smith, painting glass for Lodestar, Pace Gallery, New York City, 2010.

8 Detail of St Barbara from the Annunciation window of Jacques Coeur, c. 1448–50, Bourges Cathedral, France, bay 25.

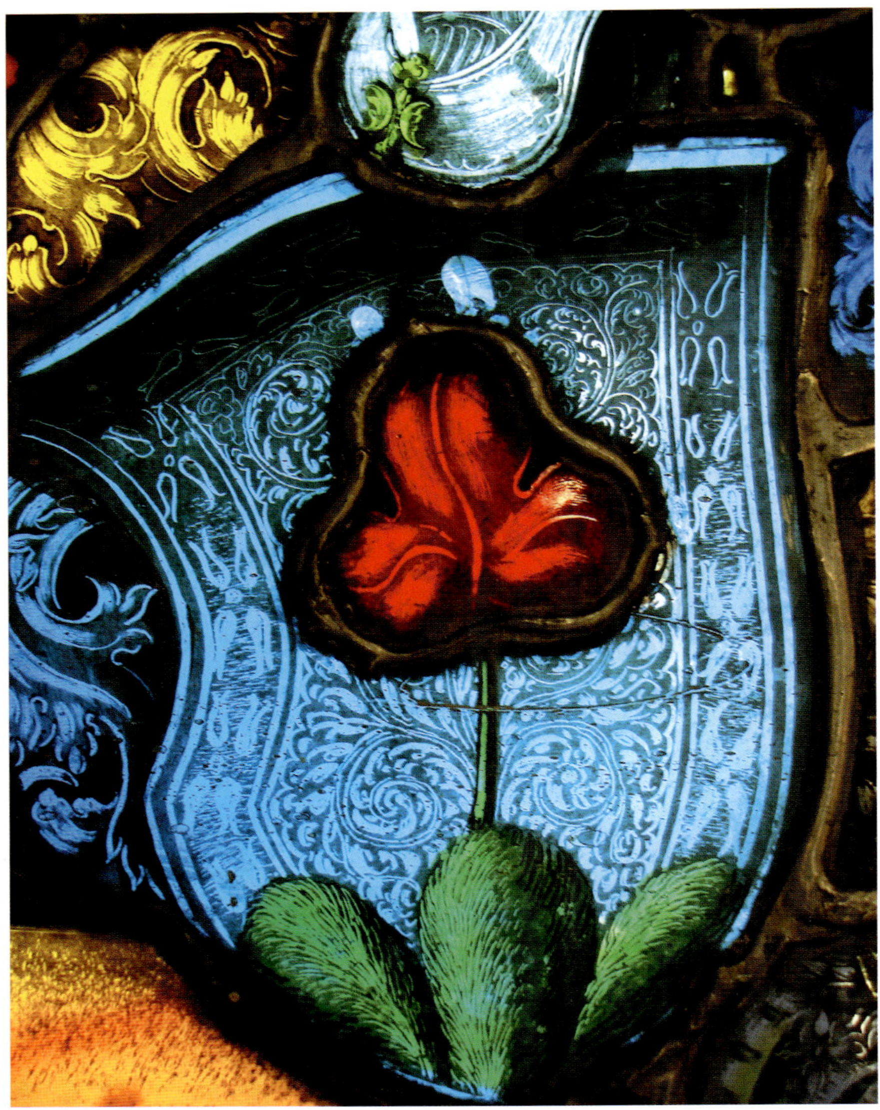

9 Workshop of Carl von Egeri, detail of inserted glass from the
Arms of Fridolin Kleger with the Figure of Lucretia, 1561, now
at the J. Paul Getty Museum, Los Angeles.

glass. In colouring the glass, a silver oxide in an opaque medium is applied, usually
to the back of the glass, and fired. During the firing, silver ions migrate into
the glass. They are suspended within the glass network rather than fused onto
the surface, as is the glass paint. After firing, the opaque medium is removed
from the glass, revealing a transparent yellow that can vary from a pale yellow
to a deep orange. An example appears in the window given by Jacques Coeur,

financial minister to King Charles VII, dated about 1448–50, in a chapel of Bourges Cathedral (illus. 8). Different yellows appear in the pot-metal glass and the silver stain that define St Barbara's flowing hair, the pearl-strewn borders of her robe and the gold decorating the architecture and statue on the right.

Commensurate with the immense wealth of the donor, the Bourges window also shows the technique of the *chef-d'œuvre*. Artisans developed impressive skills in glass cutting; here an interior section of glass is removed and glass of another colour is inserted and held by a lead. We know from contracts that such techniques greatly increased the cost of a window. Barbara's halo bristles with many coloured gems. A Swiss panel from a century later displays a shield with a blue background and an insert of a red clover (illus. 9). The clover springs from three green mounds achieved by the application of silver stain to the blue glass. The only major addition to this repertoire was the use of enamel paint, popular from the seventeenth century. Enamels are intensely coloured ground-up glass suspended in a liquid medium that are painted onto glass, most often of a light tint. They are fused onto the glass surface and thus frequently appear on the reverse of the glass as a slightly raised layer. While they are not opaque, they lack the transparency of pot-metal glass. The windows in this study demonstrate the ceaselessly inventive creation within this fascinating medium, at once object, architecture element and testimony of social consensus.

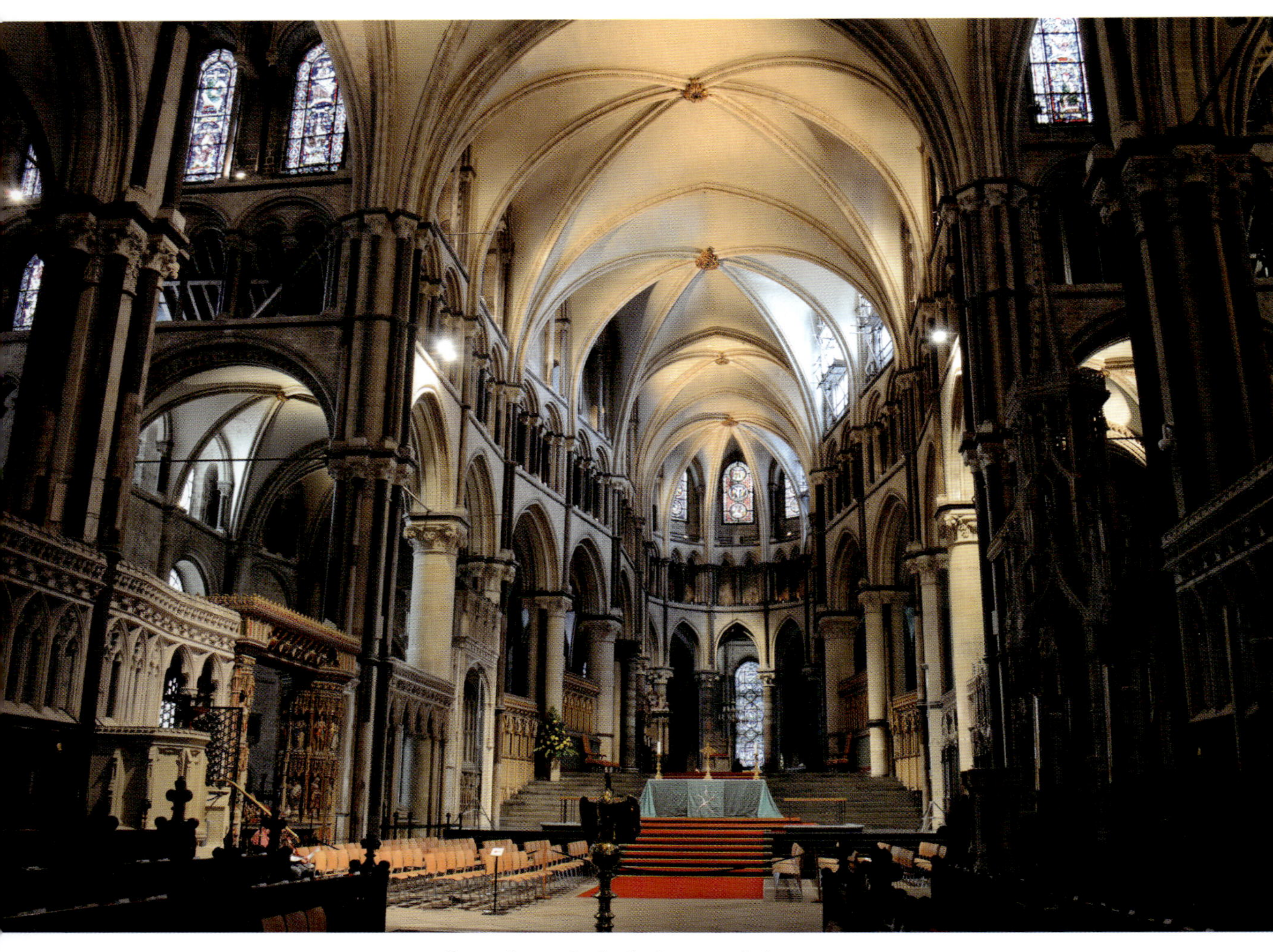

10 Canterbury Cathedral, view of choir,
Trinity Chapel, and transepts, completed 1184.

I

Canterbury:
A Martyr's Tomb
and Its Cathedral

—

Canterbury Cathedral in Kent (illus. 10 and 11), part of a World Heritage site, was founded in 597 by the Benedictine monk Augustine of Canterbury, previously abbot of St Andrew's Monastery in Rome. The original church was destroyed by fire and Lanfranc, the first Norman archbishop, and his successors rebuilt the church from 1070 to 1126, largely after the model of Saint-Étienne, in Caen. The cathedral's choir was enlarged after a devastating fire of 1174 and the nave reconstructed in the late fourteenth century. Canterbury's history and its glass reveal much about medieval relationships between monastic life and the administration of a diocese as well as between Church and State. Long associated with one of the great works of English literature, Chaucer's late fourteenth-century *Canterbury Tales*, the site exemplifies the economic and social importance of pilgrimage.

Cathedral and Monastery

Canterbury developed in an unusual situation since it was both a monastic foundation of Benedictines and the seat of the archbishop. Monasticism had long influenced the development of European society. Living apart from society began as a practice of hermits, located in areas of the eastern Mediterranean in the late third to early fourth centuries. As they began to attract followers, they developed systems conducive to communal life. In early Europe, reciprocity ordered relationships and religious practice was viewed as a viable element of exchange. Prayers were necessary, not simply for rituals associated with births, deaths and marriages, but for daily petitions for good health or favourable weather, and certainly in times of stress as with prayers for victory in battle or alleviation of pestilence. Those who could devote their lives exclusively to prayer were believed to be more effective in their petitions, and thus could speak to God for others. Monastic foundations soon entered the lives of cities, ultimately becoming a significant economic, social and intellectual force. In the West, Benedict of Nursia (c. 480–547), who had withdrawn to the wilderness in southern Italy, founded twelve monasteries, the most important being Montecassino. The *Rule of St Benedict*, compiled in the first half of the sixth century, set out a long-lived plan for communal and individual prayer, duties of the abbot, injunctions against private ownership and rules for celibacy.

Relics and Pilgrimage

Even before the late twelfth century and the development of pilgrimages to the tomb of the assassinated archbishop, Thomas Becket, Canterbury venerated relics. Although the cloistered areas of monasteries were forbidden to all except the professed, most monastic churches welcomed pious visitors to venerate their shrines and relics. The visits were a significant source of revenue, since the pilgrims left gifts in honour of the saints. These practices have their origins in the belief that Christ possesses two natures, divine and human, and that his human nature died and rose from the dead, a tangible promise of the resurrection of the dead for all his followers. As Peter Brown states:

> In believing in the resurrection of the dead, Jews and Christians could envision that one day the barriers of the universe would be broken … The joining of Heaven and Earth was made plain even by the manner in which contemporaries designed and described the shrines of the saints. Filled with great candelabra, their dense clusters of lights mirrored in shimmering mosaic and caught in the gilded roof, late Roman *memoriae* brought the still light of the Milky Way to within a few feet of the grave.[1]

Christians characterized the dead as those who 'slept in Christ' and treated them as members of the extended Christian community. Unlike practices in the classical world, where the dead were seen as unclean, and buried outside the city walls, burial places were clustered around, in and under places of worship and these grew up over the sites of significant graves. The custom received official sanction when, in 319–22, the emperor Constantine built the basilica

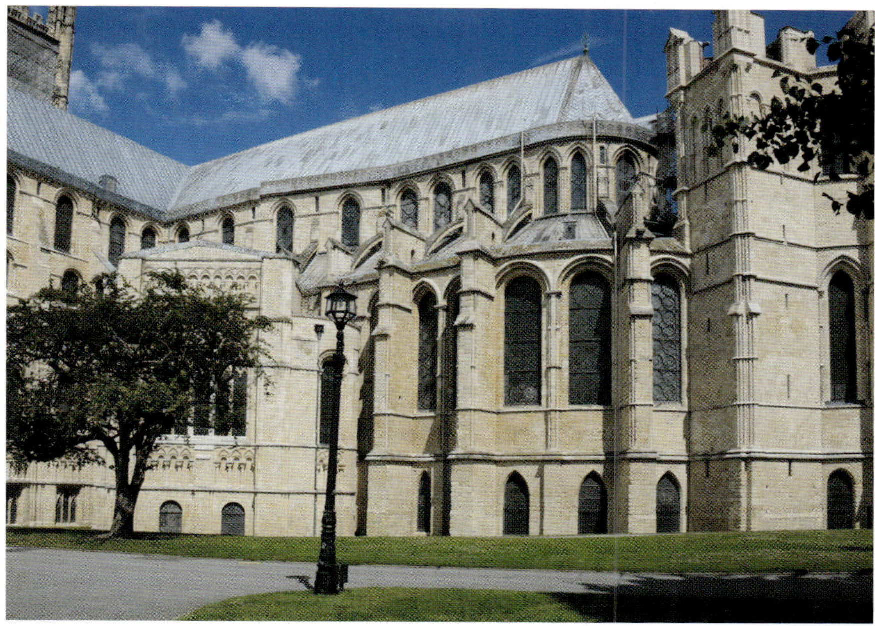

11 Canterbury Cathedral, Trinity Chapel, exterior, completed 1184.

of St Peter in Rome over a cemetery assumed to contain the grave of the first pope. Medieval tradition believed that subsequently St Helena, the emperor's mother, journeyed to Jerusalem and unearthed the cross on which Christ died. Constantine supported the building of the Church of the Holy Sepulchre in 325–6 to enshrine both the place of Christ's death and his tomb.

Early pilgrims to these sites wished to return with a tangible souvenir of the pilgrimage. Relics for the pilgrim might be a stone from the Holy Land, water from a well or even a piece of cloth or a statue that touched Christ's tomb. A sixth-century painted box now in the Vatican (Treasury of the Chapel of the Sancta Sanctorum, Lateran Palace, Rome Cat. 61883.2.1-2) contains bits of soil and stones as souvenirs of places in the Holy Land. The interior of the lid depicts the Nativity, Christ's Baptism in the Jordan, the Crucifixion, Holy Women at the Tomb and the Ascension, serving as a meditational summary of the pilgrim's experience. The faithful did not believe that the actual presence of the holy person remained in such relics (bones, clothes worn or elements of martyrdom, such as the stones used to kill the first martyr, St Stephen), but that these things would act as conduits to grace. These mementos were invariably encased in the most elaborate housing available to the owner.

Heroic Christians, the great confessors and martyrs, were widely venerated. The enthusiasm for welcoming the saints can be seen in the 396 celebrations of the arrival of relics from Rome to the French city of Rouen. A local cleric, Victricius, speaking for the Christian community, stated: 'Give me these temples of Saints . . . If a light touch of the hem of the Saviour's garment could cure, then there is no doubt that these dwelling places of Martyrdom [the Relics] carried in our arms, will cure us.' Here Victricius refers to the Gospel story of Christ healing the woman with the issue of blood who touched his robe (Luke 8:43–8), arguing that the saints who imitated Christ's virtues were also delegated Christ's power to heal. He continues, 'But we have nothing to fear. Here is a multitude of Saints who come to us . . . Victory is certain when one fights with such companions in arms and with Christ as Commander.'[2] These ideas encouraged the partition of bodies to allow the sacred 'aura' to be shared among a growing community. For the founding of Canterbury in 597, according to the monk and historian Bede (673–735), the pope provided Augustine with 'all the things needful for the worship and service of the church, namely, sacred vessels, altar linen, church ornaments, priestly and clerical vestments, relics of the holy Apostles and martyrs and also many books.'[3]

Thomas Becket

Canterbury's greatest 'relic', a martyred archbishop, came much later. Thomas Becket was born in about 1119 in London. Both his parents were of Norman descent, his father a small landowner or very possibly a knight. His early education was at Merton Priory, an Augustinian foundation, located about 13 kilometres (8 mi.) south of the present Buckingham Palace. His education, for the time, was not extensive, very probably at Merton, an upper-level school in London. Apparently, his father, Gilbert Becket, ran into money problems and his son was compelled to earn his living as a clerk, ultimately in the service of Theobald of Bec, Archbishop of Canterbury. In Theobald's service, Thomas visited Rome on several missions; the archbishop also sent him to study canon law in Bologna and in Auxerre. In 1154, Theobald appointed him to the post of Archdeacon of Canterbury as well as to several other ecclesiastical offices. The quality of his work brought him to the attention of Henry II, who made him Lord Chancellor in 1155. Seven years later, in 1162, Becket succeeded Theobald as Archbishop of Canterbury. His resignation of the office of Lord Chancellor began the profound estrangement between Becket and Henry. We have every indication that Becket was highly personable and an extremely efficient manager, something that ingratiated him with the king. Becket's prioritization of his service to the Church over the Crown resulted in the king organizing a council of ecclesiastics at his palace in Clarendon in 1164. Henry insisted that the authority of secular courts also extended to Britain's clergy. Becket refused to sign the document. Ultimately Becket was forced to flee to France, where he and several of his clergy sought protection in the Cistercian abbey at Pontigny and later in the city of Sens. After papal intervention, Becket was persuaded to return to Canterbury in 1170. He continued to protest against what he saw as Henry's overreaching of clerical authority, in particular the coronation of the heir apparent, Henry the Young King (r. 1170–83). Henry's expressions of frustration apparently inspired four knights to confront the archbishop in Canterbury. On 29 December 1170, they entered the church in the evening, prior to the service of Vespers, as contemporaneous accounts record, ultimately slicing off the top of Becket's head so that his brains fell to the pavement.

Barely two years after the assassination, Becket was canonized by Pope Alexander III on 21 February 1173. Such speed was unprecedented. Alexander also excommunicated both Henry and the four knights. The subsequent resolution of these issues involved, as is so often the case, ancillary power struggles. Three of Henry II and Eleanor of Aquitaine's four sons were joined by Eleanor in a rebellion against the king that lasted for eighteen months. During the

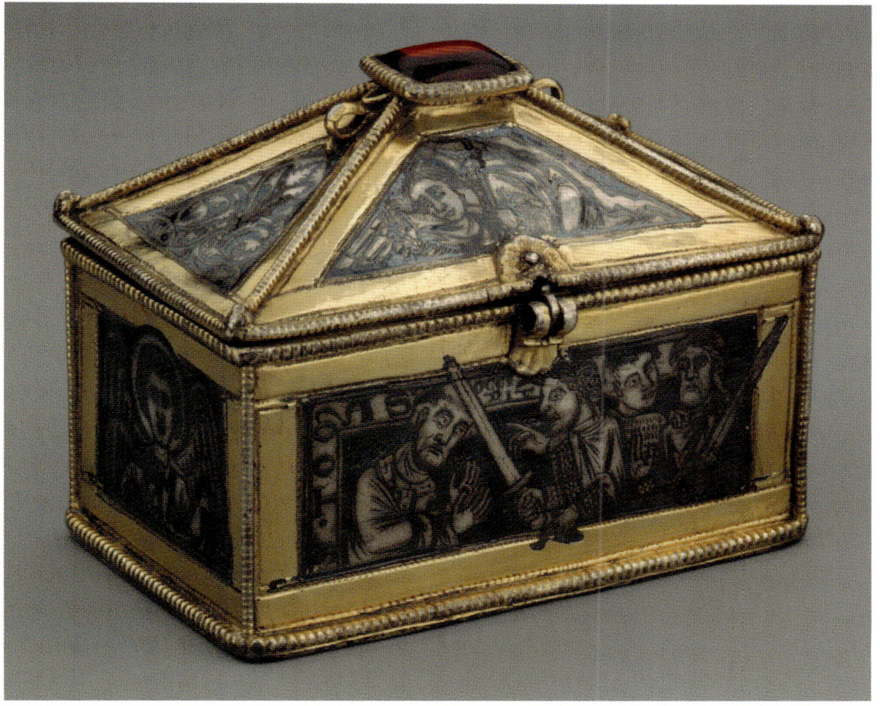

12 Reliquary casket with scenes from the martyrdom of St Thomas Becket, England, *c.* 1173–80, now at the Metropolitan Museum of Art.

struggle, Henry did public penance at Becket's tomb in Canterbury. The four knights sought forgiveness from the pope, who enjoined them to perform service in the Holy Land for fourteen years.

The martyrdom was quickly commemorated in text and image. One of the earliest appears on a tiny reliquary box produced in England before 1180 (illus. 12). One side of the box shows the saint attacked by three knights, inscribed in Latin, 'Thomas is killed', while on the opposite side, his body lies in state. The object is of precious materials, silver with gold gilt. Possibly a few years earlier, an inserted miniature in the Harley Psalter may be one of the best-known depictions.[4] Four knights are shown, including one whose sword cuts the arm of the eyewitness, the monk Edward Grim who later wrote a biography of Becket. The scene also appears in a psalter, created before 1185 in the abbey of St-Pierre in Corbie, 16 kilometres (10 mi.) north of the city of Amiens.[5] The abbey had been founded in the seventh century and become an important centre of manuscript production. Becket's appearance in a French book is testimony to the widespread importance of the event. Similar early representations have been noted in Spain and Italy. A clergyman was struck dead while at prayer. Knights, whose oaths included the defence of the Church, had invaded the space of sanctuary. Sanctuary was a concept well known since the early Middle Ages. It was a means of ensuring protection for the helpless against rash acts of violence. Thus the knights violated not only their oaths made before God but a time-honoured legal precedent.

The monks were quick to exploit the situation. We must remember the power play between religious and secular rulers at this time. In an age of hereditary power, the Church was an essential counterbalance as its celibate clergy did not produce descendants, a situation that promoted stability in administrative and educational institutions. Each monastic foundation was poised to find means to ensure its continuation. A heroic martyr was valued and Becket quickly entered a select group of saints venerated as great English heroes. We see this in the Huntingfield Psalter.[6] Produced in Oxford between 1212 and 1220, the psalter shows four early Christian martyrs, starting with the stoning of Stephen (Acts 7:54–60). The following page introduces the list of English saints, starting with Becket attacked by four mailed knights, witnessed by Grim. Becket was therefore given precedence over the following saint, the ninth-century King Edmund, who, with Edward the Confessor, was then venerated as the patron saint of England.

Fire and Rebuilding

All this history is embodied in both the architecture and the imagery of the present cathedral. After Becket's death, the building was devasted by fire on 5 September 1174. Gervase of Canterbury, a monastic historian, opened his chronicle with a description. Vivid and emotional, it speaks of the heat melting the lead roof until it reached the interior, the monks and laypersons rushing to the scene with cries of 'Vae, vae, ecclesia ardet' (Woe, woe, the church is burning) and relics rescued before the shrines were destroyed. He includes details of the many tombs of sainted predecessors and a lengthy description of Becket. Reconstruction began a year later. Gervase describes how the first architect, William of Sens, who had introduced progressive French aesthetics, was disabled by a fall from scaffolding in 1178, returning to France a year later. His successor, William the Englishman, continued his work. By 1184, in place of the old, square-ended eastern chapel, we find the present Trinity Chapel, a broad extension with an ambulatory, designed to house Becket's yet unbuilt shrine. A further chapel, circular in plan, housed additional relics of Becket, widely believed to have included the top of his skull, struck off during his assassination. This latter chapel became known as the 'Corona' or 'Becket's Crown'.

Madeline Caviness, the most eminent scholar of the glass, has provided a comprehensive reconstruction of what the windows would have been like originally since they have suffered serious losses and rearrangement of panels. The subject-matter in the windows added after the fire allows us to see the purposeful design devised by the inhabitants of the building. In the choir, an area reserved for the exclusive use of the monks, the windows display complex theological expositions, quite different from the narrative simplicity of Becket's miracles. The Benedictine monks who managed the cathedral had a long tradition of intense meditative practice. With lives dedicated to intellectual pursuits, including theology and history, as well as prayer, they demanded windows that would constantly intrigue.

The upper parts of the newly refurbished church were united in a great programme illustrating the ancestors of Christ (illus. 13). The original group numbered 86 figures of which 43 survive today. The issue is not simple, as both Luke and Matthew offer extensive genealogies agreeing on the ancestors from Abraham to David, but differing radically afterwards. Matthew has 27 generations whereas Luke has 42. Today the figures are grouped in the multi-tiered windows of the west wall and of the southwest transept. Renowned for their majestic presence and tension-filled poses, the windows have frequently been

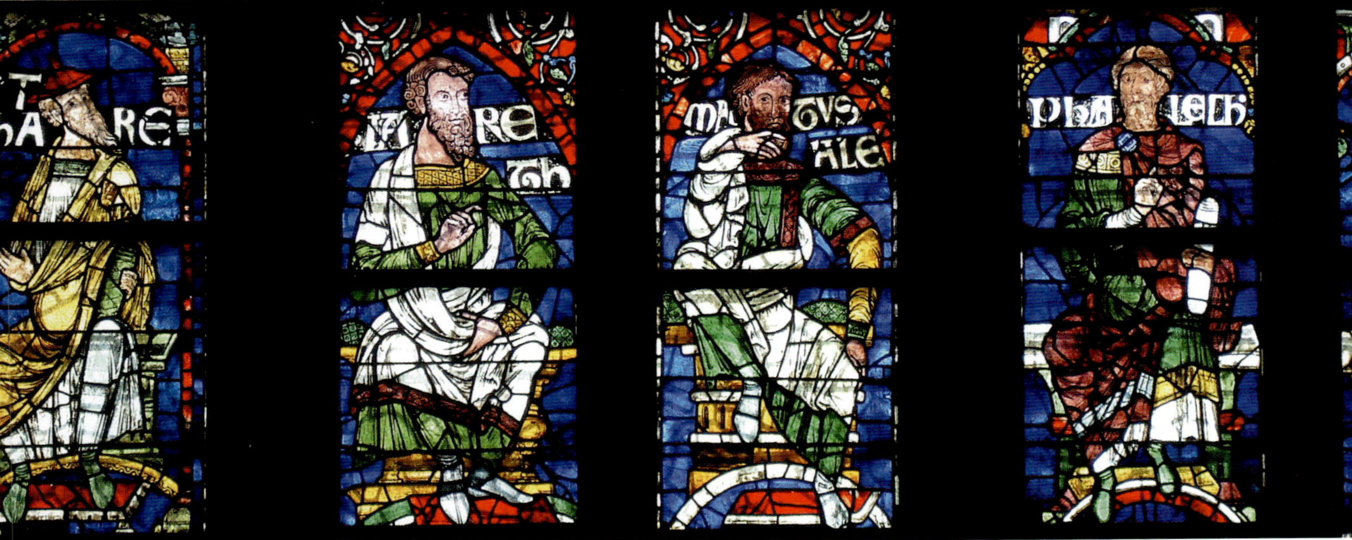

13 Ancestors of Christ: Thara (n.xiv), Jared (n.xxii), Methuselah (n.xxi),
Phalec (n.xvi) and Ragau (n.xvi), Canterbury Cathedral, 1178–80,
now southwest transept.

cited as important examples of Romanesque art. A selection of figures repositioned in the southwest transept includes the ancestors named in the Gospel
of Luke (3:23–38), starting with God, then Adam, continuing through Thara
twenty-first, Jared seventh, Methuselah ninth, Phalec seventeenth and Ragau
the eighteenth generation. The first three have been preserved almost intact;
the face of Phalec is a restoration. These great seated figures originally always
illuminated the liturgical areas during all canonical prayers, save for in the dead
of winter.

As Caviness has pointed out, their meaning would depend on the background of the viewer. Seated in their choir stalls, the monks could see this vast
array appearing as a transcending choir of glassy brilliance, singing in harmony
with their flesh-and-blood choir below. During the performance of the communal liturgy by the monks, the repetitions of genealogies sung throughout
Christmas liturgies could easily be experienced as a heraldic proclamation of
titles. To the secular viewer, especially the landed nobility, the windows could
have evoked the concepts of primogeniture and inheritance descending to a
single male in each generation. At the time the windows were made, several
manuscripts included lengthily illustrated charts of the descendants of Adam
and Eve through various biblical characters, most frequently Abraham. One of
the most cherished of medieval themes, the Tree of Jesse (Isaiah 11:1–2), received

its iconic form in the mid-twelfth century with abbot Suger's stained glass at Saint-Denis, showing a recumbent figure at the bottom and a vine growing upwards. Entwined in the branches are the ancestors of Christ, culminating in the Virgin and Christ.

Monastic Erudition and the Typological Windows

Typology, elaborate discourses on the relationship between the Old Testament and the New, dominated the subject-matter. The windows became famous in the Middle Ages, attested by manuscripts from the thirteenth to the fifteenth century that recorded their lengthy Latin inscriptions. Although this kind of study was well known, especially in monastic circles, Canterbury's twelve typo-logical windows constituted the longest cycle for its time. They were distributed in the choir, transepts and the presbytery, seven on the north and five on the south. An additional window, the central window in the Corona that focused on the Redemption, may be considered the culminating point of the series. The windows all differ in their medallion structure as well as in the number of types and antitypes. We might even surmise that their creation was not the work of a single monk planning out a comprehensive programme, but rather the output of multiple collaborators. The series testifies to an environment supporting an energetic community of scholars both designing and viewing the windows over time. In each, we find references to the broader themes of the authority of the Church, including over secular rulers, praise for those who have recognized Christ and reflections on the final destiny of the human soul.

One of the simplest is the Second Typological window (illus. 14), which survives in place. In a series of horizontal rows of three medallions, the New Testament narrative is in the centre, starting with the Three Kings travelling to Judea and ending with the Massacre of the Innocents (now lost). At the top, the Three Kings point to the star that leads them on their journey (Matthew 2:1–12). To the left is the prophet Balaam and to the right Isaiah. Like the Magi, Balaam is mounted and points to the star. The Latin text reads: 'A Star shall come out of Jacob; a Sceptre shall rise out of Israel' (Numbers 24:17). Isaiah stands, also gesturing to the star with the text: 'The Gentiles shall come to thy light and kings to the brightness of thy rising' (Isaiah 60:3). Both Balaam and Isaiah were familiar prototypes for Christ's birth. The level below shows the Magi being interrogated by Herod, who sought to discover the birthplace of a future rival. The panel to the left shows Moses leading the Israelites out of Egypt, repudiating Pharoah just as the Magi turn away from Herod. The theme

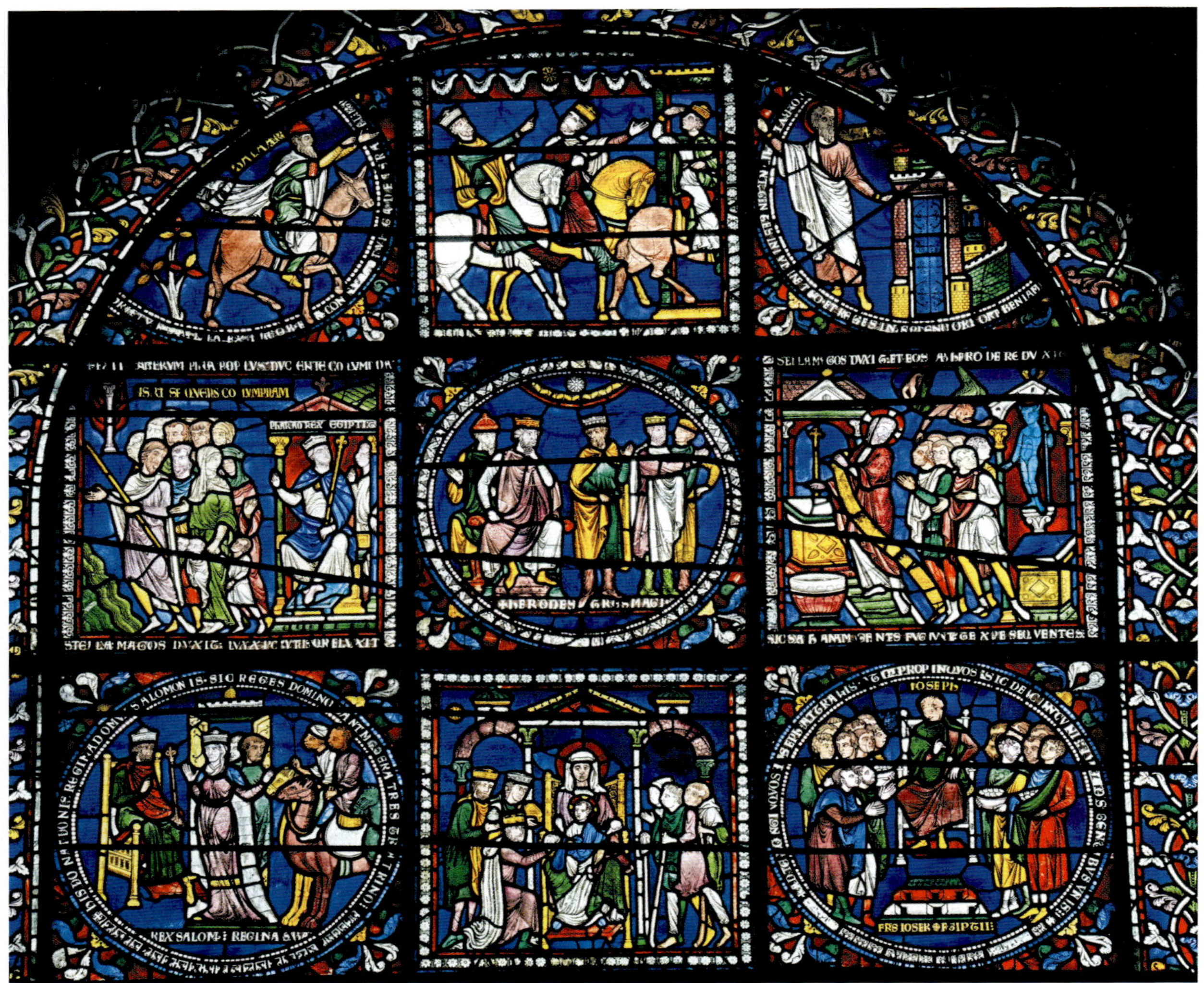

14 Second Typological window, Nativity of Christ, 1178–80, n.xv.

of light continues, with the inscription: 'The people come out of tribulation
lead by the pillar.' Exodus (13:21) relates that the 'Lord went before them by day
in a pillar of cloud to lead the way, and by night in a pillar of fire'. To the right,
we find a unique representation: Christ leads the faithful away from paganism, symbolized by a statue of a nude male set on a column. Above, a winged
demon tries vainly to lead them back. The third level presents more traditional
parallels. The Three Magi and three shepherds adore the Christ child, seated
on Mary's lap. To the left and right are Old Testament stories of the honouring
of wisdom: the Queen of Sheba visits Solomon (1 Kings 10:1–13), and Joseph's
brothers seek his help during a famine (Genesis 42–3).

The Sixth Typological (illus. 15) window presents more challenges for the uninitiated. Its seven extant panels are grouped, out of order, at the bottom of the Second Typological window. Its original construction involved variously shaped rectangles displaying the Parable of the Sower in the central column and on the sides both biblical and historical exemplars of those who respond to God's call and those who reject it. Christ's parable describes a farmer sowing seeds; some fall on the path and the birds eat them, some fall on rocky ground and cannot thrive, some fall on soil full of weeds that choke the seed, and some fall on good soil and yield a hundredfold (Luke 8:5–15, and in Matthew and Mark). In the original window, to the left of the Sower whose seed 'fell upon a rock' was originally the panel of the three Pharisees turning away from Jesus. That panel is now in the centre of the second row from the bottom of window. Christ appears as a supplicating figure, isolated as he moves forwards, seeking to communicate his words to those rejecting him. The inscription reads *Semen rore carens expers radices et arens svun qvi credvnt tentantvr siq' recedvnt* (Seed lacking dew, having no root and dry, these are those who believe, are tempted and thus fall back). The two images now flanking this scene are not contrasts, but complementary expositions of faithfulness. On the right are the three virtuous states of virginity, continence and marriage, represented by three men standing under arches. On the left is Ecclesia (Church) with the three sons of Noah: Shem, Ham and Japheth. The inscription at the top reads: *Vna fides natis ex his tribus- e[s]t Deitatis* (From these three sons is one faith in the Godhead).

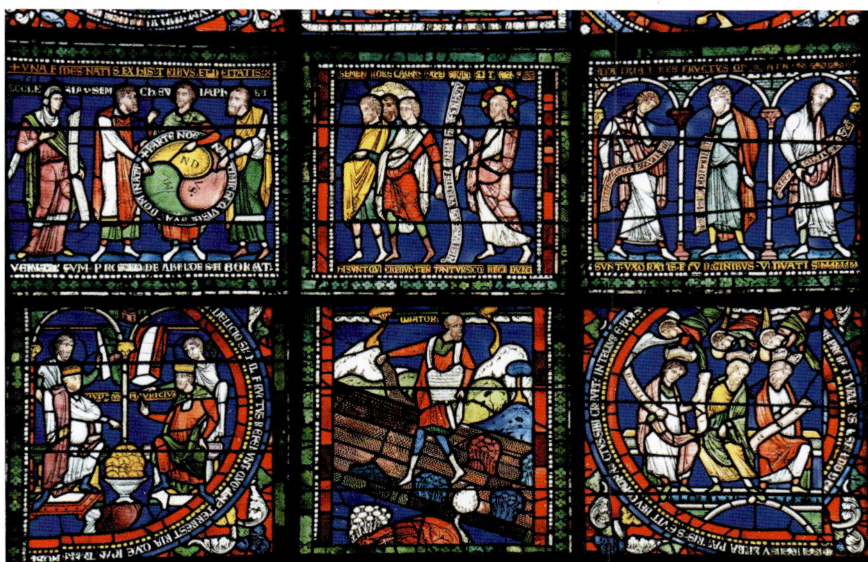

15 Sixth Typological window, Parable of the Sower, 1178–80, n.xv.

Genesis (9–11) recounts how, after the flood, the whole earth spoke one language. Noah's sons hold a representation of the world, with their three separate kingdoms distinguished by green, ochre or mauve.

On the bottom tier, the Roman emperors Julian and Maurice flank an image from the parable of the Sower, who casts seed on fertile ground. The contrast is one of virtue and vice. The Roman emperors sit enthroned in a palace with servants, gesturing towards the pile of gold coins at their feet. The damaged inscription has been translated as 'These thorny ones are the rich and extravagant; they bear naught of fruit since they seek earthly things.' The historic figures are contrasted to righteous men from scripture, Daniel, Job and Noah, on the right. The three, each with identifying banderols, are symbolic of unwavering faith, fortitude during adversity and energetic engagement to work for the good. Three angels descend to crown their labours. These are certainly not topics that could have been easily understood by most of the travellers in Chaucer's *Canterbury Tales*.

The Second Typological window was executed by the same artist responsible for the ancestor figure of Methuselah. The dignified seated figure of Herod, who lifts his hand to his chin as he ponders the Magi's information or the dynamic swirls of draperies clothing the fleeing Israelites, is reminiscent of the power seen in Methuselah. The artist responsible for the Sixth Typological window moves away from this *gravitas* inspired by classical statuary to favour more elegant compositions, often with the figures aligned in the foreground. His body types are tall and slender, exemplified by the three men in the Virtuous States. The panel is in an excellent state of preservation, except for the head of the figure representing the state of marriage, on the right. We observe a singularly graceful fall of draperies, especially in the youthful figure of Virginity as he strides forward, the drapery tight on his knee and falling in scoop folds between his legs.

Windows on the theme of Becket's miracles (illus. 16), in contrast to the typological series, are far better preserved. They constitute the theme of the Trinity Chapel, where the saint's remains were translated in 1220. Indeed, the windows can only be understood in their relationship to Becket's shrine. From the beginning, it was clear that the monks had planned the extension of the church with its Trinity Chapel and Corona as a site of veneration. Many of the windows were in place by 1207, when the monks faced another crisis. Canterbury

16 Children saved from illness and a collapsed building,
1213–15/1220, Trinity Chapel, s.vii.

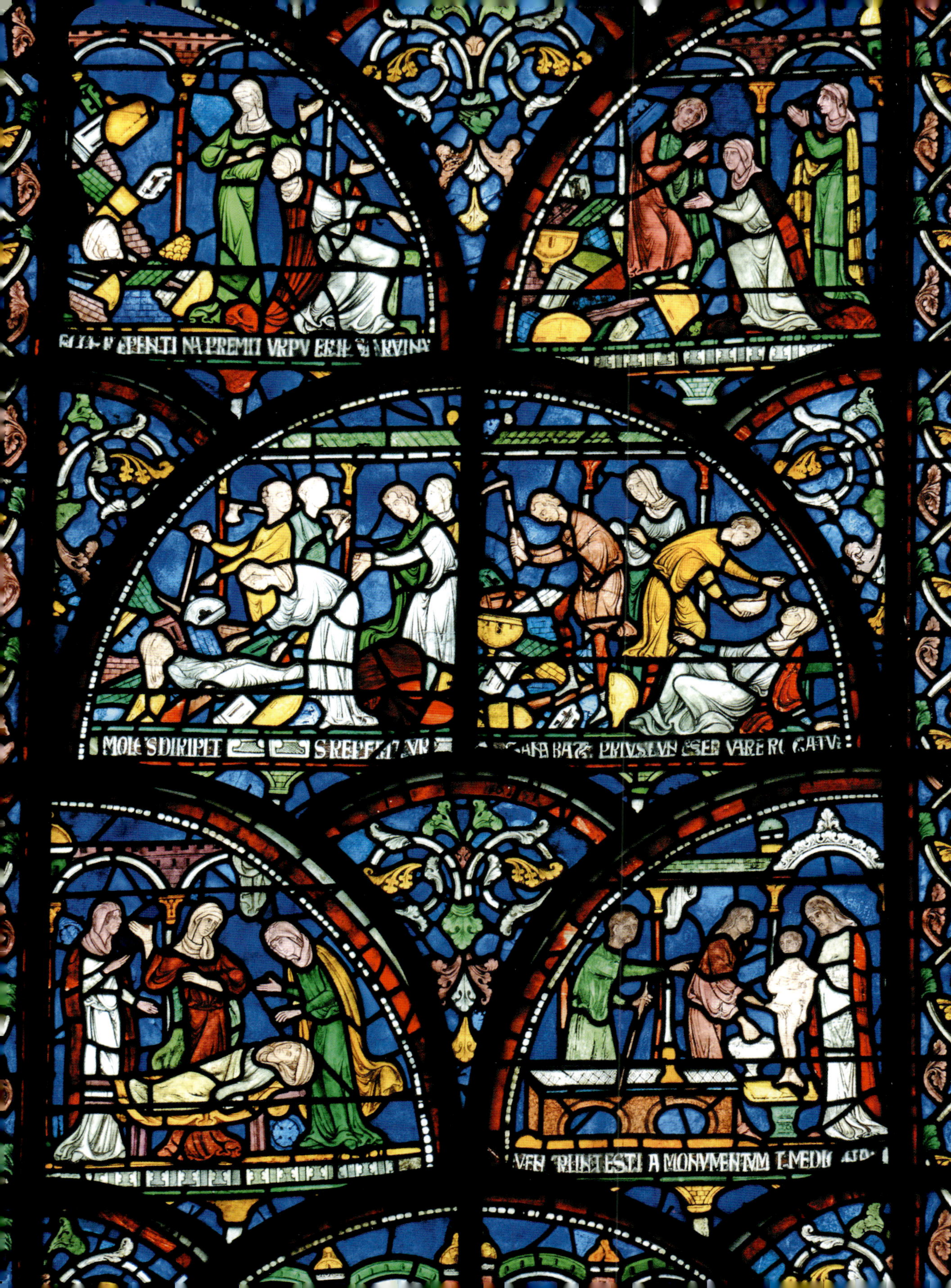

R A REPENTI NA PREMIT URPU EEIL SARVINA
MOL S DIRIPIT   S REPLEAT UR
ABBATU PRIUS EUN ESER VARE ROGATU
VEN RUNT ESTI A MONUMENTVM T MEDIU

became embroiled in a controversy involving the English barons, Pope Innocent III and King John, which ultimately forced John to grant his seal to the Magna Carta (15 June 1215). In 1207, Stephen Langdon had been chosen archbishop. He was an English theologian who had distinguished himself though a brilliant career in Paris. The king refused to accept the election and expelled the monks, who took refuge in France, as had Becket some forty years earlier, only returning in 1213. Langdon remained steadfast in support of political liberty through John's reign, and that of Henry II. It was Langdon who supervised the completion of the shrine, engaging Elías of Dereham, who was a member of the monks' household, and Walter of Colchester. The events were recorded by Matthew of Paris, the English chronicler writing in 1240–53.

Becket's Shrine

We have both verbal and visual records of Becket's shrine before it was destroyed on the orders of Henry VIII. Henry's break with the pope in 1534 was accompanied by a move against the veneration of the saints and against the religious orders, such as the Benedictine monks who managed the shrine. The king appropriated the lands held by the monks, distributing them to loyal nobility. Confiscating Becket's shrine in 1538 significantly increased the royal coffers. The shrine was large and, like many reliquaries of this time, constructed as a house elevated on columns. A pilgrim's badge (illus. 17), dating to about 1350–1400, gives a reasonable approximation of the form. The most common token for pilgrims to acquire was a badge to be worn on the pilgrim's hat or bag, or to be pinned to an outer garment. Made of an alloy of tin and lead, and cast in moulds, they were accessible to the ordinary person who had travelled to the site. In this way the badges had a dual purpose, first as a personal keepsake for pilgrims to recall their journey and, second, to announce to the world that the wearer had visited a particular shrine.

Several windows show details of the shrine; one of the most complete and intact, save for the head of Thomas, shows Becket emerging from his casket to effect cures (illus. 18). Lifted on arches, the brilliant yellow casket is covered with incised decoration. On the floor below lies a man in bed, experiencing the vision. He is presumably either Benedict or William, the two monks who composed prose accounts of Becket's miracles in 1172–4. Desiderius Erasmus, the Dutch humanist scholar, wrote a critique of pilgrimages after visiting Canterbury and seeing Becket's golden shrine. *A Pilgrimage for Religion's Sake* of 1526 was quickly translated into English. As the shrine was fitted with a lid that could be

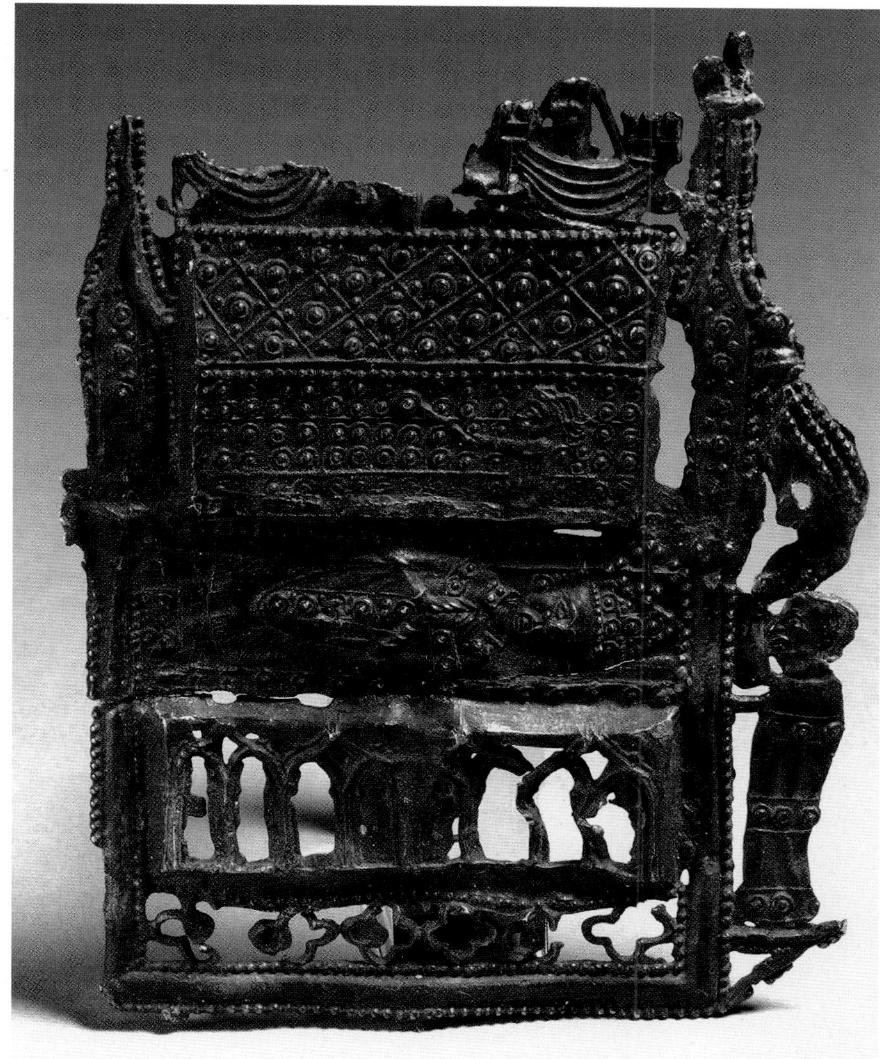

17 Pilgrim's badge of the Shrine of St Thomas Becket at Canterbury,
England, 1350–1400, now at the Metropolitan Museum of Art.

raised and lowered by ropes to hide it from casual view, Erasmus describes the
showmanship when the lid was lifted to reveal the gem-encrusted casket.

> Even the most insignificant part was all in gold; everything did
> shine, and scintillate as if hit with lightning. It was strewn with a
> multitude of precious stones; some were bigger than a goose egg.
> Diverse monks stood there with great reverence and when the cover
> was taken away, we all knelt down and worshipped. The prior with

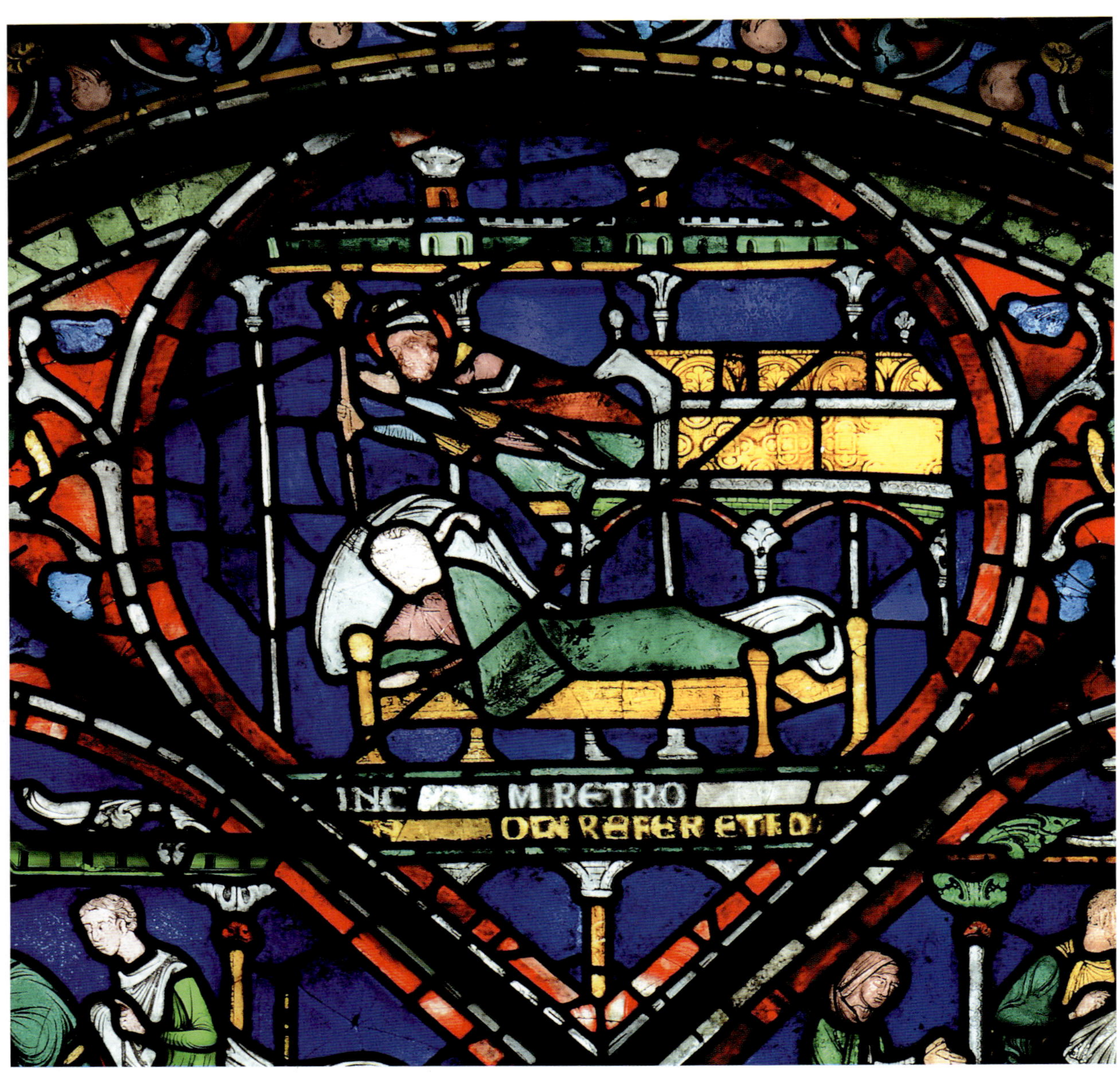

18 Vision at the Shrine of Thomas Becket, Trinity Chapel, 1213–15/1220, n.II.

a white rod pointed out every stone, adding the French name, the value and the donor of the gift, for the most important stones were given by princes.[7]

Becket's Miracle Windows

Installed in 1185–1207 and 1213/15–20 the windows promulgated Becket's cult, a tradition that formed the basis for Chaucer's *Canterbury Tales*, noting the journey's purpose as: *The hooly blisful martir for to seke/ That hem hath holpen when that they were seeke*. In an extraordinary diversity of armature designs, the windows recount different miracles from all classes of society. Scene after scene shows the martyred archbishop, who intervenes to rescue someone from drowning, to resurrect another and to effect a wide manner of cures of madness, suffocation, haemorrhaging or mutilation, in people as diverse as a nun from Cologne, the king of France and a naughty child from a neighbouring town. Caviness demonstrated that the twelve windows represent a conflation of Becket's miracles compiled by Benedict and William, the two monks of the

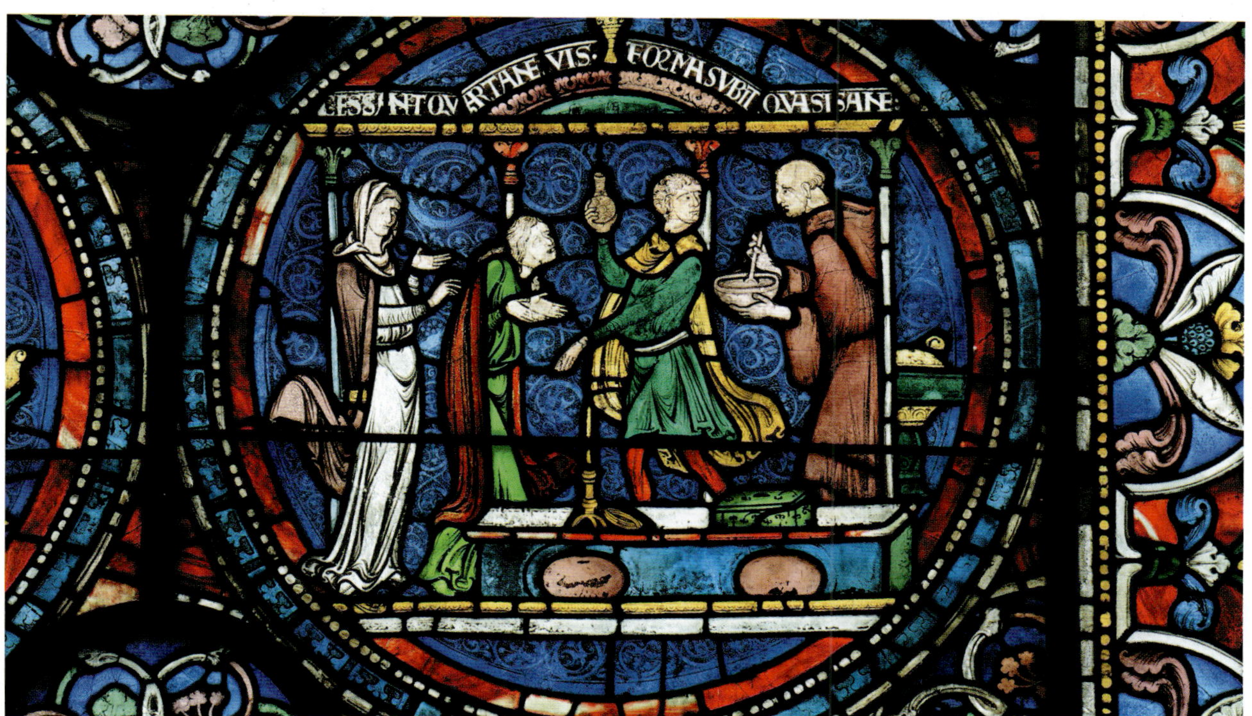

19 Etheldreda, a young woman of Canterbury, second from left, is given the miraculous effusion of the blood of St Thomas and is cured of Quartan fever, 1185–1207, Trinity Chapel, n.IV.

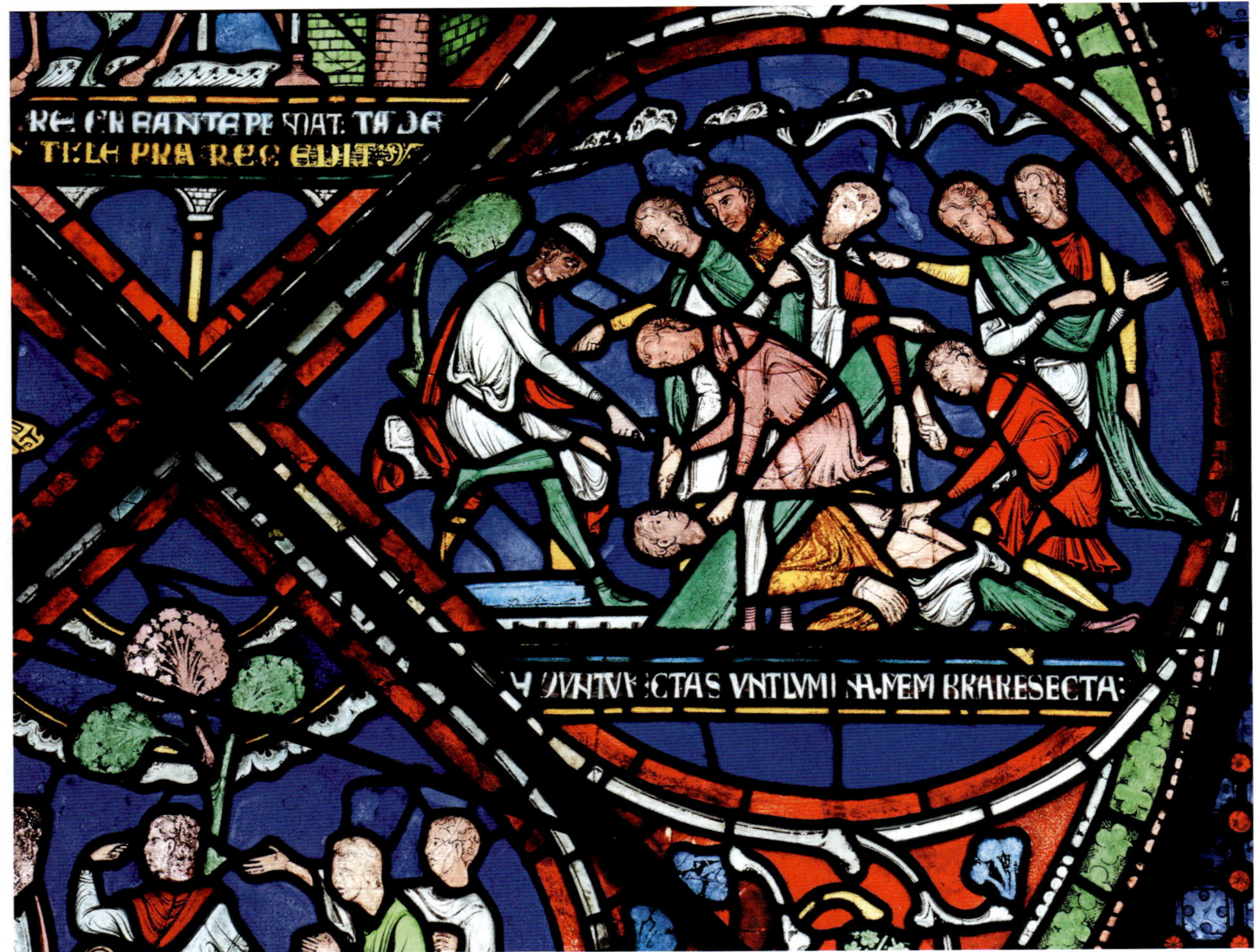

20 A knight, Eilward of Westoning, blinded and castrated,
1213–15/1220, Trinity Chapel, n.III.

cathedral. The miracles are often grouped by type, such as resurrections to
teach the validity of the belief in the Resurrection. The windows made claims
for the power of the God through his saints as superior to lay medicine. Thus
Abbot Hugh of Jervaulx is cured when a monk pushes aside a layman physician and approaches the sick bed. Etheldreda, a local woman from Canterbury,
had suffered from fever. She is depicted receiving the miraculous effusion from
the tomb, described as Becket's blood (illus. 19). The effusion was mixed with
water that was administered to the ailing at the tomb and distributed in tiny
ampules. The robes of the monk on the right, and his mixing bowl and the
woman on the far left, are restored but the area showing Etheldreda and the
man with the flask is intact. The window is distinctive for its detailed painting,

in particular the stick-work removing the basic wash to create the damascene effect of the backgrounds.

In contrast to the highly individualized episodes in the typological windows, Becket's miracles frequently show compositional and thematic similarities. In one showing episodes of healing (illus. 16), a medallion pattern engages the eye with an alternation of joined and opposing quarter circles. The upper-right and lower-left medallions of the illustrated detail, however, are new. We recognize two children in distress, one, already ill, crushed by a sudden fall of masonry. Vivid depiction shows the rubble, a man with a pickaxe trying to clear it away, a fainting mother and a rescued child. In the following episode a child is standing on a pedestal, close to Becket's tomb and being washed by two women. All the Miracle windows are framed by lush decorative borders. Interlacing foliage in a variety of formats conveys a sense of unity, no matter how many or different the miracles.

In a clear statement of the superiority of clerical institutions, the knight, Eilward of Westoning, is brought before a judge, unjustly punished with blinding and castration. The episode plays out over five scenes, set in the lower middle of the window. Eilward, his garments flying and his hands bound, is brought before a magistrate. The medallion on the right shows the punishment (illus. 20). The magistrate (his upper body is new) sits, directing seven men who pin Eilward to the ground under a plank of wood. He is then blinded and castrated. The inscription reads: '[his] eyes were put out; [his] members mutilated.' In a third

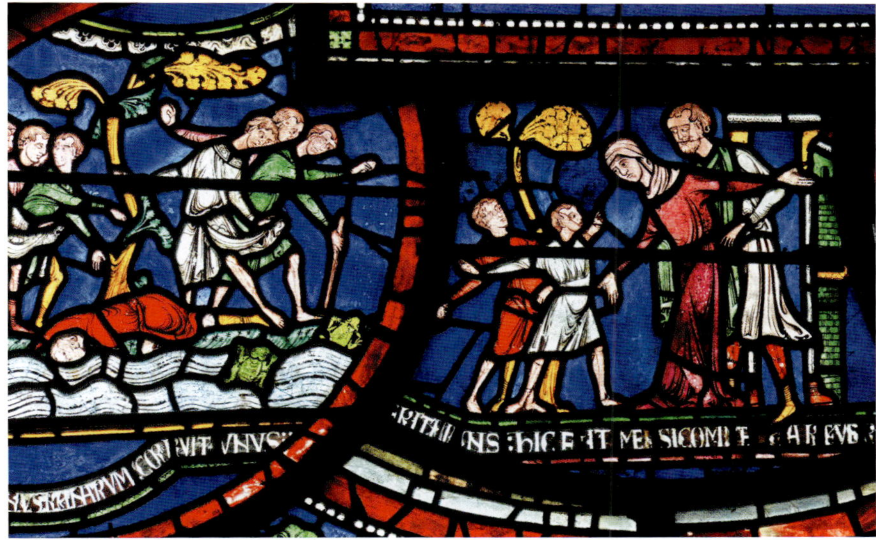

21 'Naughty Bobby' of Rochester falling into the Medway, 1213–15/1220, Trinity Chapel, n.II.

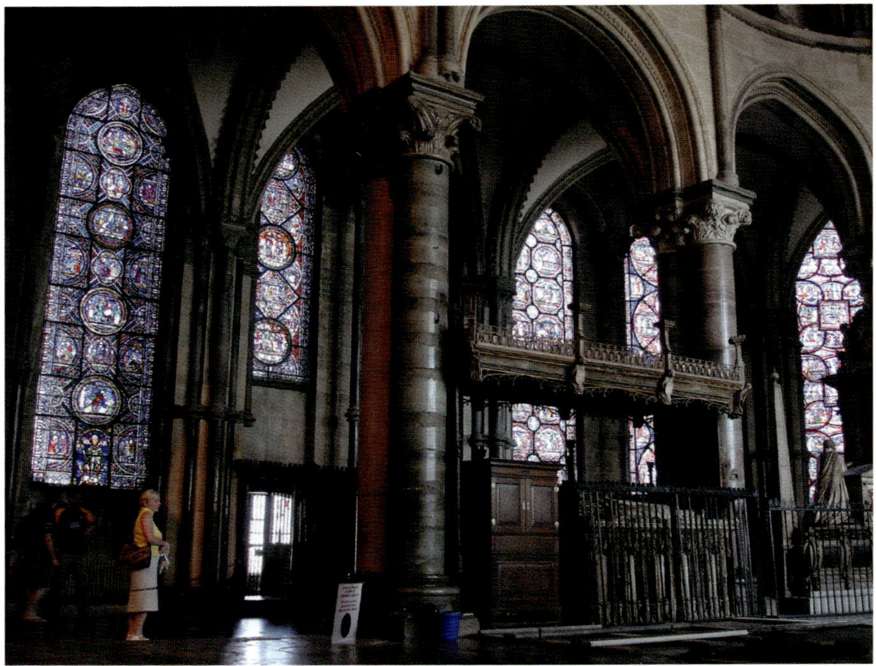

22 Visitors viewing windows, interior of Trinity chapel, north wall, n. III–n. v.

medallion below, cured through Thomas's intersession, Eilward gives alms to a crippled man at his feet, a mark of prosperity, and points to his restored eyes. An additional scene includes the text: 'His [members] are restored and swell up and gradually grow again.'

An episode of a boy saved from drowning is probably a conflation of several stories. Benedict records a Rodbertulus (Bobby) of Rochester, a town about 48 kilometres (30 mi.) northwest of Canterbury, who nearly drowned when he fell into the Medway while he and his companions were throwing stones at frogs (illus. 21). The inscription reads: 'As he rushes to the death of the frogs, one boy falls headlong in.' In the adjacent scene where Bobby's friends inform his distraught parents, the upper part of the body of the mother and the lower part of the father's tunic are also modern. The inscription reads 'The comrades of the drowned boy return to the house.'

The windows are an arresting display, a seemingly endless reiteration of the power of the martyr to intercede for his petitioners (illus. 22). The sheer brilliance of the multiple patterns – angular petals radiating from squares, circles divided in quadrants, canted squares and half circles, fan-shaped successions, quatrefoils within circles, alterations of circles and diamonds – reinforce the multiplicity of cures. Just as preachers developed sermons for specific purposes for an audience of laity, it is probable that the monks who led the pilgrims around the Trinity Chapel explained the individual miracles. Pilgrim literature in the later Middle Ages, such as Margery Kempe's account of her visit to the Holy Sepulchre in 1414, describes the Franciscans leading pilgrims and pointing out the sites: 'Then the friars lifted up a cross and led the pilgrims about from one place to another where Our Lord had suffered his pain and his Passion, every man and woman holding a wax candle in her hand. And the friars always, as they went about, told them what Our Lord suffered in every place.'[8] Innumerable images from medieval times show such processions led by a cross, usually held before the leader. We should always be aware that religions, however transcendent their aspirations, are practised socially.

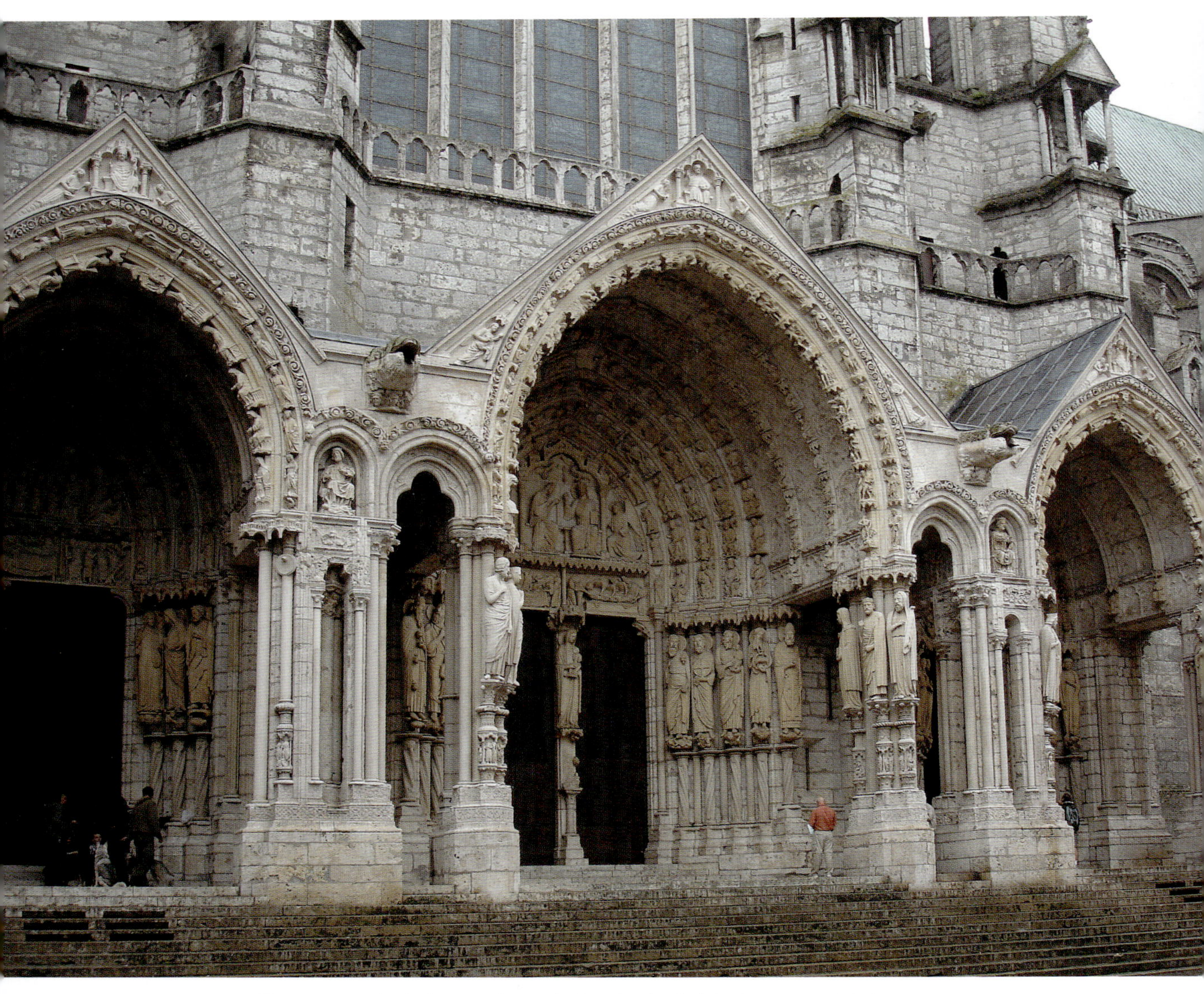

23 Chartres Cathedral, portal, north facade: (right) Judgement of Solomon
and the story of Job; (centre) Dormition and Coronation of the Virgin Mary;
(left) Nativity, *c.* 1230.

2

Chartres: Representations in an Iconic Gothic Programme

—

The great Gothic cathedrals amaze us today and their construction engages our curiosity. How were they planned, financed and executed? At that time, all power on earth was thought to find its legitimacy in God's sovereignty. This was the dominant understanding in theology and in politics, and it served the interests of both the secular and religious leaders to mutually reinforce their claims of authority. Written documentation of the building process is sparce so that we rely a great deal on the evidence of the monuments themselves. Chartres Cathedral shows a wealth of so-called donor portraits of nobility and of commoners. Yet, how are these representations to be interpreted? We may believe that the Church strove to demonstrate its universality – from high to low ranks of society and across the professions: 'There is one body, but it has many parts. But all its many parts make up one body. We were all given the same Spirit to drink. So the body is not made up of just one part. It has many parts' (1 Corinthians 12:12–14). Even with such a noble motivation, how exactly were these 'many parts' involved? Exploration leads to fascinating, if far from conclusive, revelations.

Funding the Enterprise

Building on our contemporary experience of fundraising, we assume that a representation implies the specific volition and financing of a donor. Harvard University, for example, retains minutes of deliberations concerning subject-matter, funding and choice of artist for the classes who donated windows to its Memorial Hall between 1879 and 1902. However, we are also familiar with entrepreneurial enthusiasm. Whatever the enterprise, its backers strive to demonstrate its value to a broad spectrum of people. Since antiquity, we find documentation by rulers of widespread approval for building projects that motivated the governed to freely offer their labour. Suger, Abbot of Saint-Denis, wrote in around 1144 that when suitable columns had been quarried for the abbey church 'both our pious neighbours, nobles and common folk alike, would tie their arms, chests, and shoulders to ropes and, acting like draft animals, drew the columns up' (*De Consecratione* II). At the same time, Robert of Torigni (*c.* 1110–1186), Abbot of Mont-Saint-Michel, wrote of the 'cult of the carts' at Chartres, as it was later named by the art historian Arthur Kingsley Porter. 'At Chartres men began, with their own shoulders, to drag the wagons loaded with stone, wood, grain, and other material to the workshop of the church.'[1] In 1145, Hugh, Archbishop of Rouen, wrote to Theodore, Bishop of Amiens, describing how the citizens of Chartres had pulled construction carts. Hugh then added that, in his own diocese, people pull 'their wagons with their own shoulders in humility and silence and present their offering'.[2]

Thematic Unity of Sculpture and Windows

Chartres was a small town, although centred amid the fertile region of the Beauce, famous for its production of wheat and rye. It was built at a time when most economic activity was by bartering, manufacturing was a cottage industry and trade guilds such as those we meet in fifteenth-century York did not exist. The town's ability to attract funding has often been associated with its position as a pilgrimage site. Its treasured relic of the Virgin's tunic had been miraculously saved from the devasting fire of 1194 that destroyed all but the building's west facade. Rivalling the cathedrals of Paris, Reims or Bourges, Chartres was swiftly rebuilt; first the nave, then the choir and finally the transepts. Throughout the building, sculpted and painted images enunciate theological priorities and spatial hierarchies. All was planned together; stained-glass windows were produced as each section of the building was nearing completion.

The noble 'parts' as mentioned in 1 Corinthians are often clear; for example, the rose windows in the transepts on the north show the Capetian monarchy and, on the south, the House of Dreux, controlling the Duchy of Brittany. The sculpture of the north facade (illus. 23) was completed about 1230, and the glass five years later. Three deeply recessed portals framing the three doors lead to the cathedral. The narrative theme is the Old Testament prefiguring the New. On the west, the portal shows the Judgement of Solomon and the story of Job.

Flanking the door are figures including Joseph, Judith and the Queen of Sheba. The Birth of Christ is depicted on the eastern portal. The central door is dedicated to the Dormition (Death) and then Coronation of the Virgin Mary in heaven, a theme inspired by the Old Testament Song of Songs, whose text reappeared in Marian hymns: 'Thou art all fair, O my love, and there is not a spot in thee' (4:7). The statues flanking the central door depict patriarchs, priests and prophets. St Anne holding the infant Virgin Mary appears on the central post of the main portal, a theme inspired by the presence of a relic of the head of the saint taken in 1204 as booty during the Fourth Crusade and the sacking of Constantinople. Display of hereditary power extended to the interior, where the window repeats the image of Anne and also carries the insignia of the royal house of France and that of the queen mother, Blanche of Castile. The role of the monarchy in augmenting the power of the state and protecting the Church is implicit throughout the programme.

North Facade: Royal Successes in Image and Deed

France had vastly increased its territory during the rule of Philip II, named Philip Augustus, who reigned from 1180 to 1223. In 1214, at the Battle of Bouvines, he defeated the House of Plantagenet. Although the story is complex, the Plantagenets can be thought of as having controlled the 'Angevin Empire' from the marriage of Eleanor of Aquitaine to the English king, Henry II, in 1152. In addition to England, the territory comprised roughly half of France, extending from Normandy to the border with Spain. After the battle, King John of England was forced to sign the Magna Carta. Philip focused on consolidating his gains, as he had earlier by negotiating the dynastic succession of the dukes of Brittany, a theme in the window in the south transept. During Philip's reign, much of the structure of Paris as we know it had begun to be established: the cathedral of Notre-Dame, except for the north and south transepts, was completed; the great market of Les Halles was inaugurated; the palace of the Louvre was begun; and the University of Paris received its charter. Philip was succeeded by his son Louis VIII (1187–1226), who had been active in his father's achievements, but whose reign only lasted from 1223 to 1226. In 1200, at the age of twelve, Louis had married Blanche of Castile (1188–1252), the daughter of Alfonso VIII (r. 1158–1214), renowned for his defeat of the Almohad Caliphate at the Battle of Las Navas de Tolosa in 1212, by which the Christian kingdoms took the initiative for Spain's *Reconquista*. Louis and Blanche, who survived her husband by 26 years, had thirteen children, seven of them reaching adulthood.

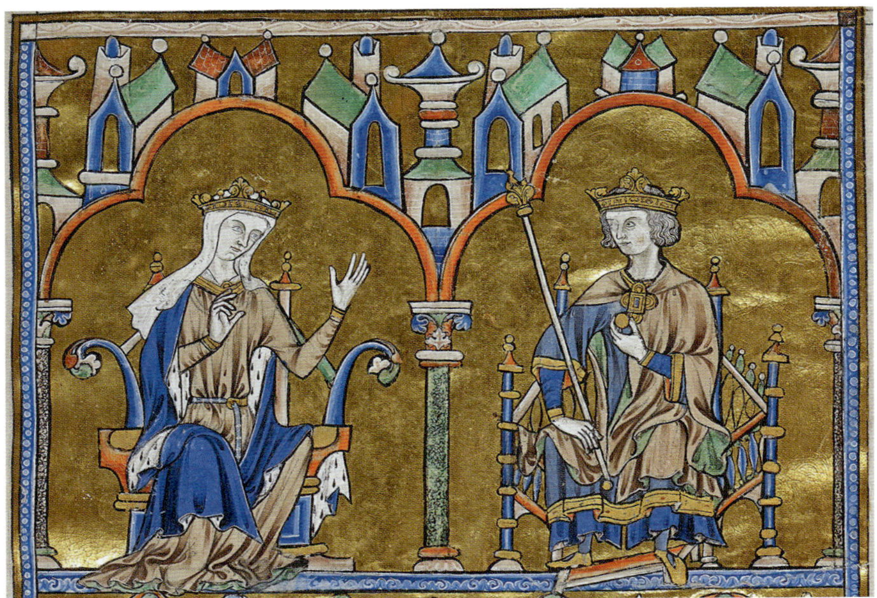

24 Blanche of Castile and Louis IX, moralized Bible, 1227–34,
Paris, now at the Morgan Library and Museum, New York.

At the death of his father, and at the age of twelve, Louis IX (1214–1270) was
crowned in the city of Reims. His mother Blanche ruled the kingdom as regent
for eight years until his majority in 1234. She was considered a close advisor for
the remaining eighteen years of her life. Portraits of Blanche and Louis appear
in a moralized Bible (illus. 24) executed in Paris between 1227 and 1234, during
regency. The Bible may have been designed as a gift to the cathedral of Toledo,
where the main portion of the manuscript now resides. In the north transept
glass at Chartres (illus. 25), we see the arms of Blanche, yellow three-towered
castles on a red ground (gules a triple-towered castle or) and the Capetian coat
of arms borne by Louis, yellow fleur-de-lis on a blue ground (azur semé-de-
lys or). Its programme continues the exploration of the Old Testament as a
precursor to the New that was articulated in the portal sculpture. In the rose,
the Virgin and Child are surrounded by twelve kings of Judah, secular rulers,
and twelve prophets, religious leaders. The lancet windows below continue references to royalty and priesthood. Flanking the image of St Anne carrying the
Virgin Mary stand Melchizedek over Nebuchadnezzar, King David over Saul,
King Solomon over Jeroboam and Aaron over Pharaoh. Significantly, kings,
rather than priests, stand closest to St Anne.

The programme affirms both ecclesiastic and dynastic authority and triumph over adversaries. For the clergy, Melchizedek blesses Abraham, who

brought him bread and wine after his victories. Abraham subsequently gave the priest one-tenth of everything (Genesis 14:18–20), a concept welcomed by Chartres' clergy to emphasize the obligation to tithe one-tenth of one's income to the Church. Nebuchadnezzar was a king of Babylon, who in 586 BCE conquered Judah, destroyed Jerusalem and initiated the 'Babylonian captivity' of the Jews (Jeremiah 27–9). The window shows Nebuchadnezzar before the statue of gold, silver, bronze, iron and clay, which he saw in a dream. Daniel was able to interpret this as a prophecy of the kingdoms to follow Nebuchadnezzar (Daniel 2). Aaron was the brother of Moses and High Priest, who shared the triumph over

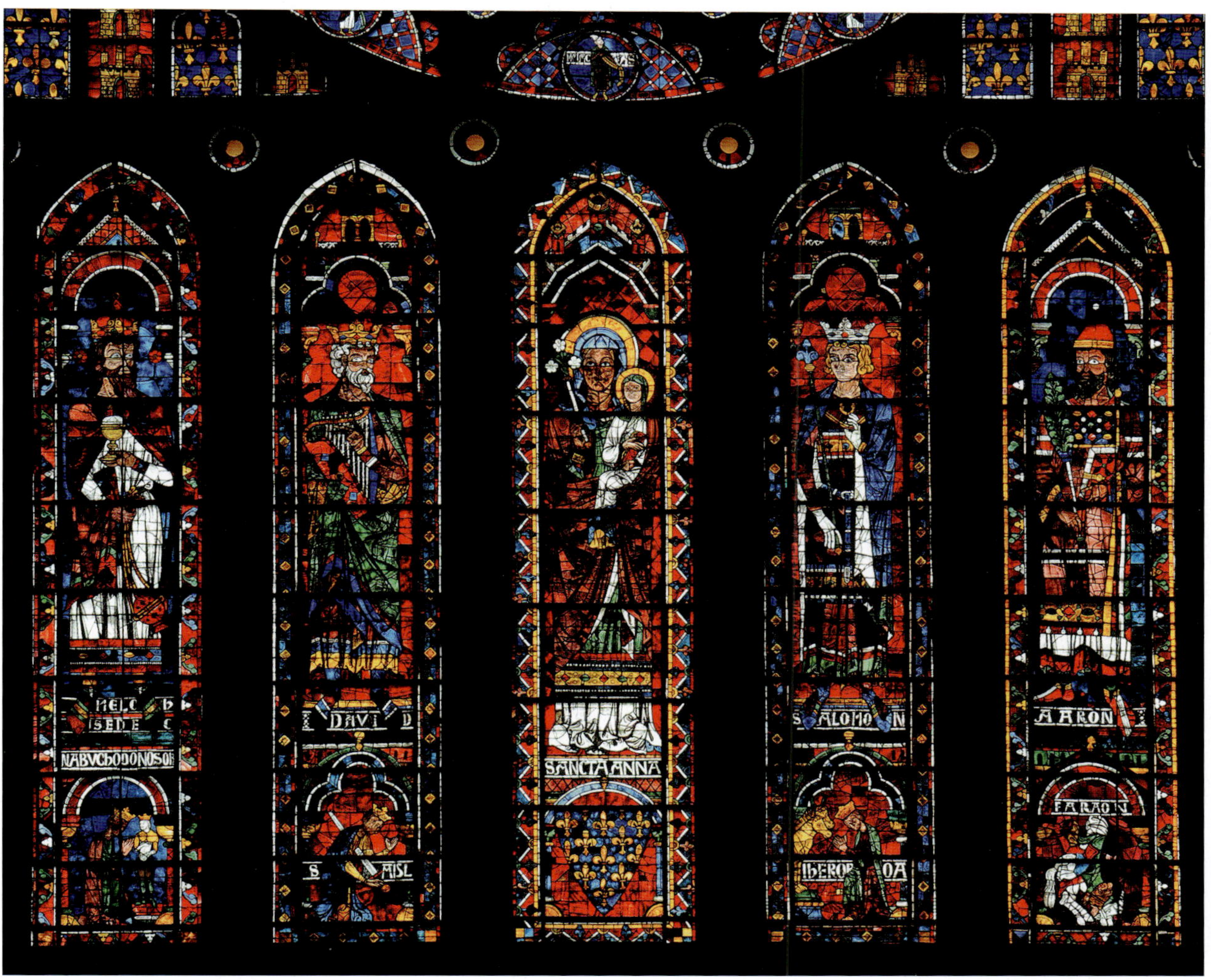

25 North transept (121), detail of lancets: (centre) St Anne carrying the Virgin Mary over the Capetian coat of arms; flanking her (left) Melchizedek over Nebuchadnezzar and King David over Saul, (right) King Solomon over Jeroboam and Aaron over Pharaoh, *c.* 1235.

Pharaoh and the exodus from Egypt (Exodus 8:15). The exemplars of secular rulership include David, who stands in the place of honour on St Anne's right (viewer's left). David had been threatened by King Saul but escaped; later, Saul, after defeat in battle, fell on his sword and eventually David became king (I Samuel 31; II Samuel 5). During the thirteenth century, the Church attributed the Book of Psalms to King David. He is recorded as having played the harp to soothe the dark humour of King Saul, and the harp was a traditional accompaniment to poetry, such as the Psalms. Thus the window affirms the king's legacy for the clergy as the Psalms constituted a principal element of their daily prayers. Solomon, given his reputation for wisdom (I Kings 3:7–28), was usually represented as a mature man. Here, however, he is youthful with a blond bob and smooth jaw. Like the portrait of Louis in the moralized Bible, Solomon wears a three-pointed crown, holds a sceptre surmounted by a fleur-de-lis in his right hand and lifts his left hand towards his throat. It is highly probable that this is a portrait of the young Louis IX, at that time about 21 years of age. Below him, Jeroboam, a rebellious Jew at the time of Solomon, is shown as an idolater, worshipping golden bovines (I Kings 11–14). Louis, early in his life, gained a reputation for personal piety. He became the only French king to be canonized.

Our contemporary culture has relegated religious and secular authority to separate spheres. In thirteenth-century France, they were far more entwined. Both engaged in reciprocal power plays. Kings generally were deferred to concerning the choice of bishops. They, however, received their authority through a ritual consecration administered by a bishop. In France it was the archbishop of Reims. The hierarchy of the Church was invariably recruited from the ranks of the nobility, although many, like the gifted abbot Suger of Saint-Denis, were of the lesser nobility who rose to prominence through personal endeavour.

South Facade: The House of Dreux-Bretagne

From the north face we turn towards the south (illus. 26) and find a window of some five to ten years earlier. The rose presents Christ surrounded by the 24 elders of the Apocalypse, a complement to the 24 Old Testament kings and prophets on the north. The lancets below show the Virgin and Child flanked by four evangelists over four prophets: Jeremiah carrying Luke, Isaiah carrying

26 South transept (122), rose with Christ surrounded by the 24 elders of the Apocalypse above lancets (left to right): Jeremiah carrying Luke, Isaiah carrying Matthew, the Virgin and Child over the Dreux-Bretagne coat of arms, Ezekiel carrying John and Daniel carrying Mark, 1221–30.

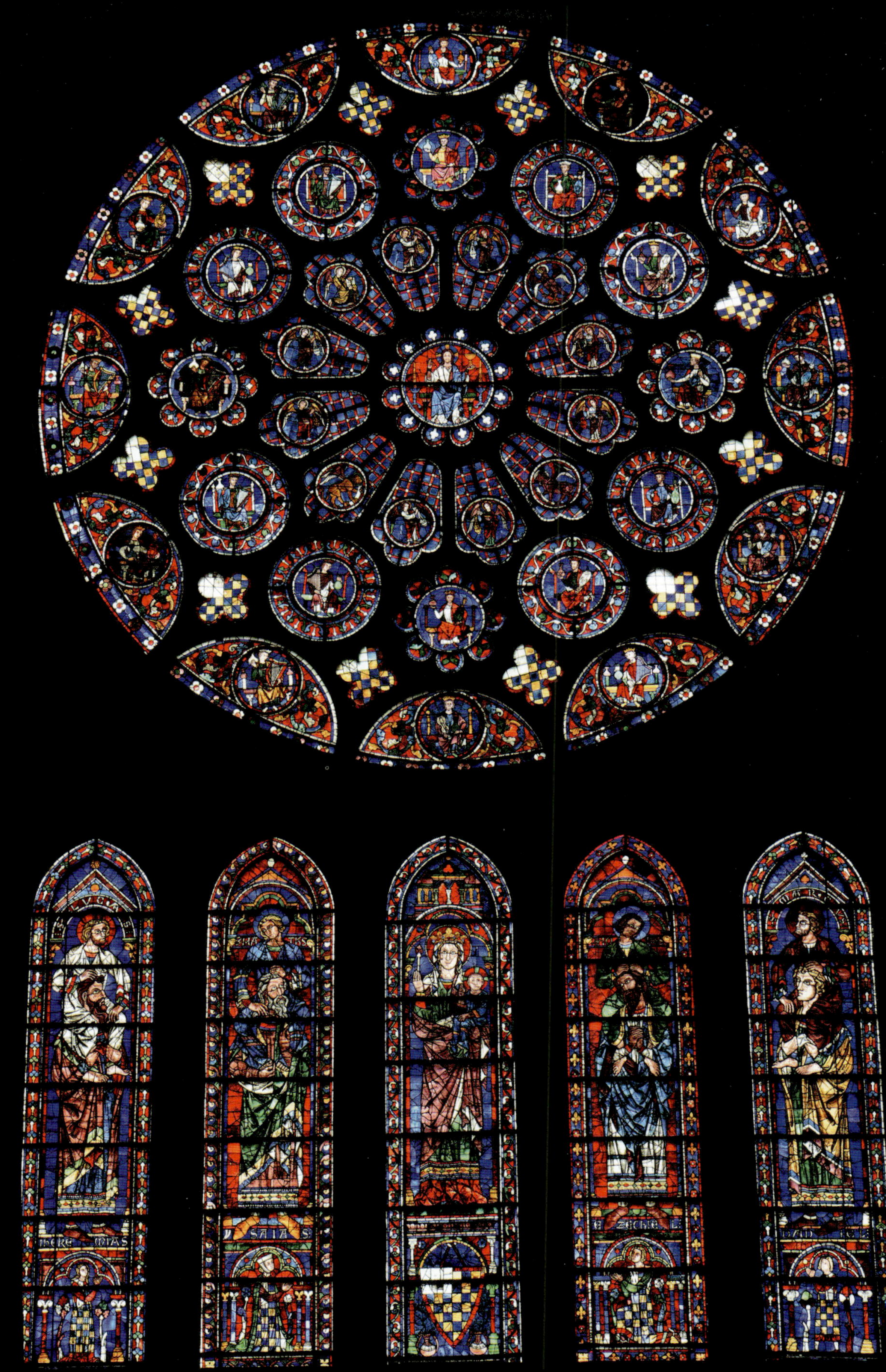

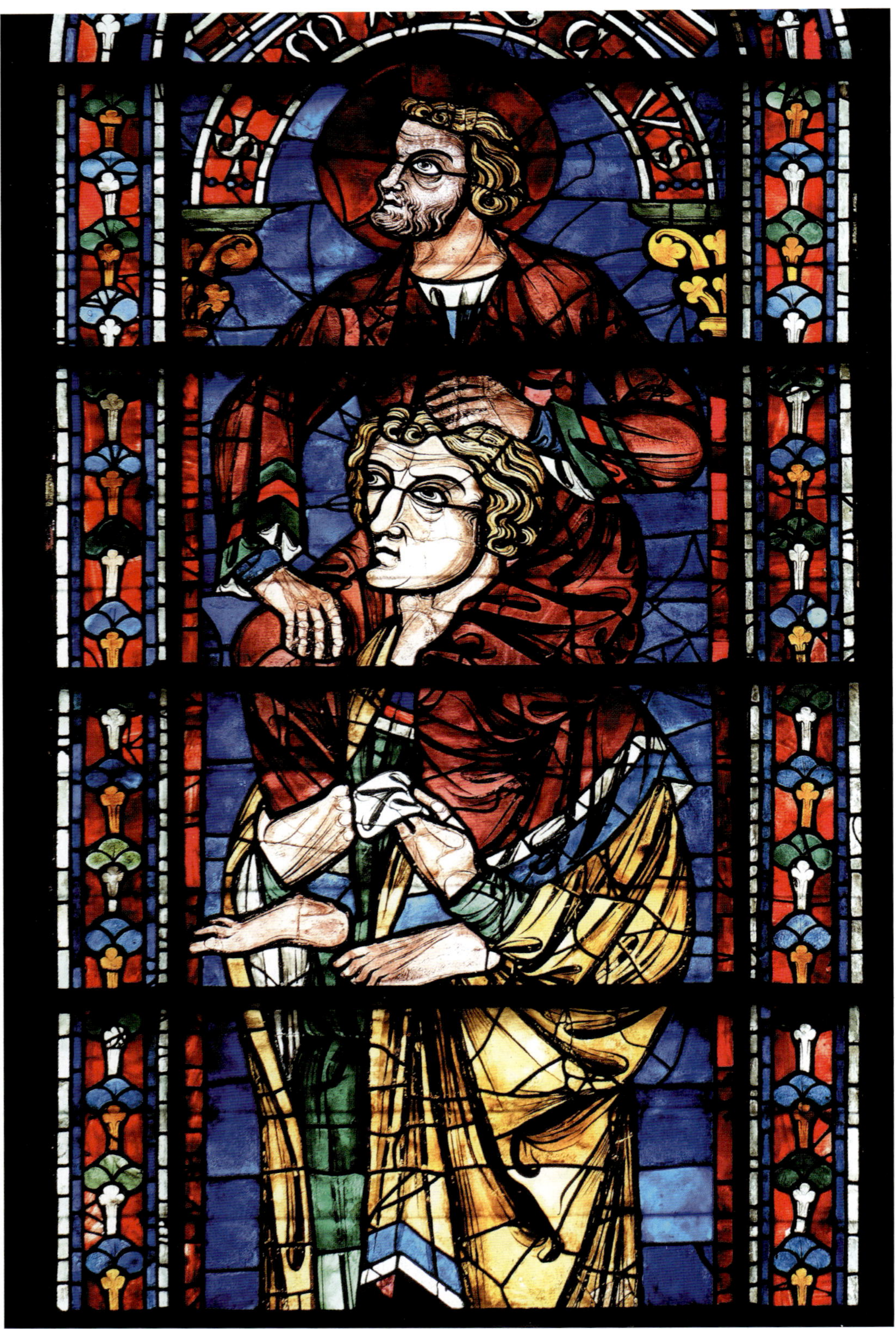

27 South transept lancet detail, Daniel carrying Mark, 1221–30.

Matthew, Ezekiel carrying John and Daniel carrying Mark (illus. 27). Celebrated as one of the most superbly designed compositions in stained glass, the window contrasts the circular pulsation in the rose against the vertical stability of the lancets. In the lancets, we find alternating swathes of blue and red behind the figures. In the rose, medallions all have blue grounds, except for that containing the central image of Christ. Here, variety is accomplished through the intermingling of whites, yellows, greens and reds in decorative borders. The draughtsmanship, visible in the lancets, is easily some of the most memorable in glass. The artist never lets direction become routine, aptly contriving a contrapuntal movement of interrelated curves. We admire a remarkable dynamism of line. A detail removed from its setting could easily find its place in an exhibition on twentieth-century Abstract Expressionism. Such intensity allows Daniel's youthful, heavy-jawed face to communicate a boldness of character, suitable to his renown as the young rescuer of the falsely accused Susanna (Daniel 13:45–62). His golden hair with its undulating curves is echoed by the deep scoop folds and cascading lines of his cloak. Warmer colours, the prophet's yellow cloak and the saint's russet robe, are balanced by the cooler green of Daniel's tunic.

We recognize the familiar theme of the continuity of the Old and New Testaments. This specific imagery, however, is unusual and was possibly inspired by a previous chancellor of the Cathedral Chapter, Bernard of Chartres. The renowned scholar compared his generation to dwarfs seated on the shoulders of giants. He observed that we could see more and further than previous generations, not because we have sharper vision or greater height, but because we are lifted up and held aloft thanks to their gigantic stature (recorded by John of Salisbury, *Metalogicon*, 1159). The very pairing prompts meditation. Jeremiah's Lamentations, especially Chapter Five, speaks of the sorrow of women, perhaps a reason for his association with Luke, the writer who recorded in most detail the Infancy of Christ. Isaiah (7:14) prophesied that a Virgin would give birth to a son who would be called Immanuel (meaning 'God with us'). The quote was repeated by Matthew (1:23–4) in his description of the angel reassuring Joseph of Christ's divine origins. Ezekiel's prophecies include a vision of God (Ezekiel 43:1–12), parallel to John's vision of the Apocalypse (Revelation 21). Daniel was cast into a den of lions (Daniel 6:10–23) and the evangelist Mark is symbolized by a lion based on his description of John the Baptist, 'the voice of one crying in the wilderness' (Mark 1:3).

Throughout the window, we find the arms of Pierre Mauclerc of the house of Dreux-Bretagne: a yellow and blue chequerboard with an ermine square at the upper left. Four representatives of the house are shown in attitudes of prayer

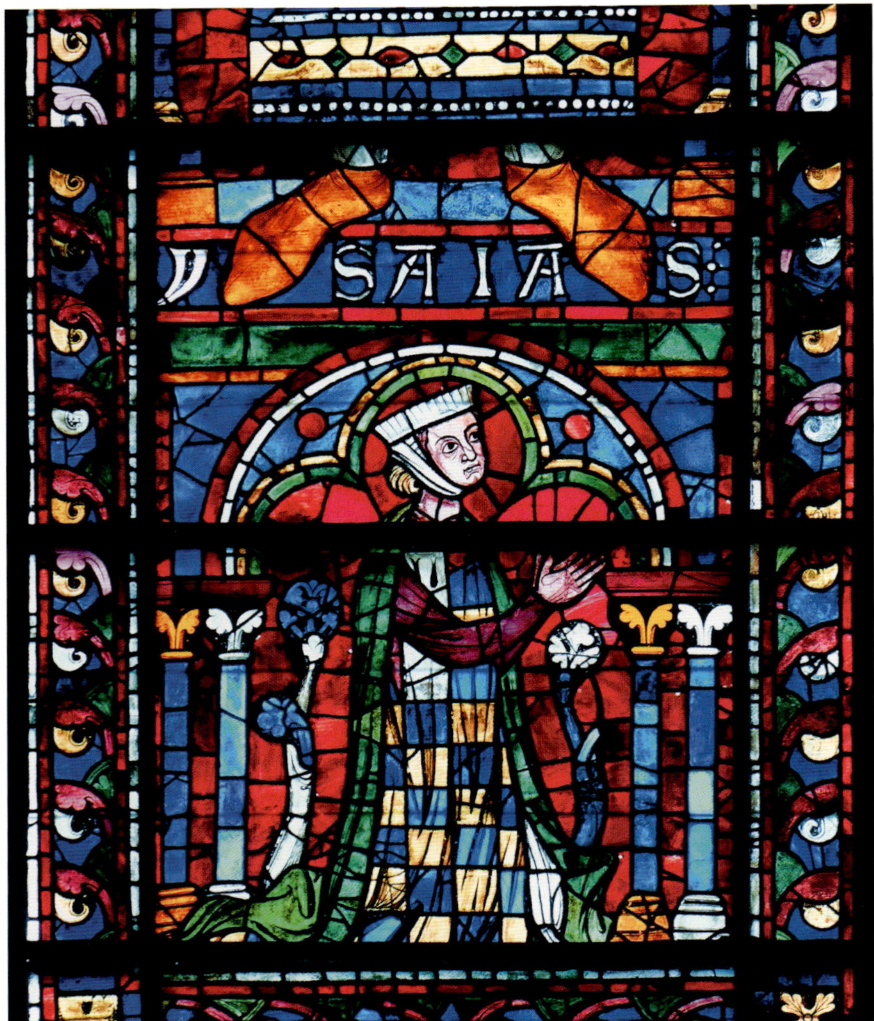

28 South transept lancet detail, under Isaiah, Alix of Thouars, donor, 1221–30.

below the prophets. Like the illumination of Louis and Blanche in the moralized Bible (see illus. 24), the figures kneel under trefoil arches supported by foliate capitals. Alix of Thouars (1200–1221) and Pierre Mauclerc (1187–1250) flank the coat of arms below the Virgin and Child. They are distinguished by the green accents that contrast with dominant red/blue harmonies. Both wear green clothes and a green moulding frames the arch, as it does the arch surmounting the evangelist and prophet above them. Their children, Yolande of Brittany (1218–1272) and John Le Roux (1217–1286), are at their sides. When the window was begun, Alix (illus. 28) was already deceased. As the daughter of Constance, Duchess of Brittany, and Guy of Thouars (d. 1213), in 1203, at the age of three, Alix had been recognized by the Breton barons as the legal inheritor of the Duchy of Brittany. Philip II was keenly interested in maintaining his influence over Brittany as it guarded the vital sea lane between France's southwestern region and England. He intervened to arrange her marriage at the age of twelve to his cousin, Pierre of Dreux, who became known as Pierre Mauclerc. Pierre ruled Brittany *jure uxoris* (by right of his wife) from 1213 to 1221, and afterwards as regent for their son John I until 1237. The relationship between the French Capetian monarchy and the house of Dreux was deeply intertwined at the time of the glazing of Chartres' transepts. The family took their title from their château in Dreux, a town in the Eure-et-Loir, about 40 kilometres (25 mi.) north of Chartres. The counts, however, are buried in one of the most spectacular, but underappreciated, churches of France, St-Yved of Braine.

The transepts proclaim dynastic relations, divine-right royals and the priesthood. With privilege, however, went the expectation of generosity to the arts and social welfare summed up as *noblesse oblige* (privilege has obligations). Did the clergy select the iconography to flatter the donor, or as demonstration to others of their powerful connections, regardless of monetary investment in a project? As a precedent, the apse mosaics of the basilica of San Vitale, Ravenna, dated to 547, depict the Byzantine rulers Justinian and Theodora with their courtiers. Neither of them ever visited Ravenna. Two bishops, first Ecclesius, then Maximian, depicted in the entourage around Justinian, are considered the patrons of the enterprise.

Narrative Windows

The lower level of Chartres brings us back to the representation of other 'parts' (illus. 29) that include workers in skilled trades, the lesser nobility and clerics. A total of 48 windows are designed in different patterns, each with between 18 and 30 narrative scenes. This vast array of saints' lives and gospel narratives makes Chartres one of the most memorable of medieval sites. The brilliance of the ensemble is associated by many with the apogee of the High Gothic style, in architecture and in image. Glass makers and window designers had developed a productive synergy. Sheets of glass could be produced in brilliant colours with many subtle variations. Designers understood how to vary the intensity of colour with surface paint that modulated the light as well as defining the image. The full windows demonstrate a variety of patterns. That of the Good Samaritan shows three quatrefoils alternating with circles and trilobes; that of Mary Magdalene (illus. 30) three circles alternating with canted squares and half

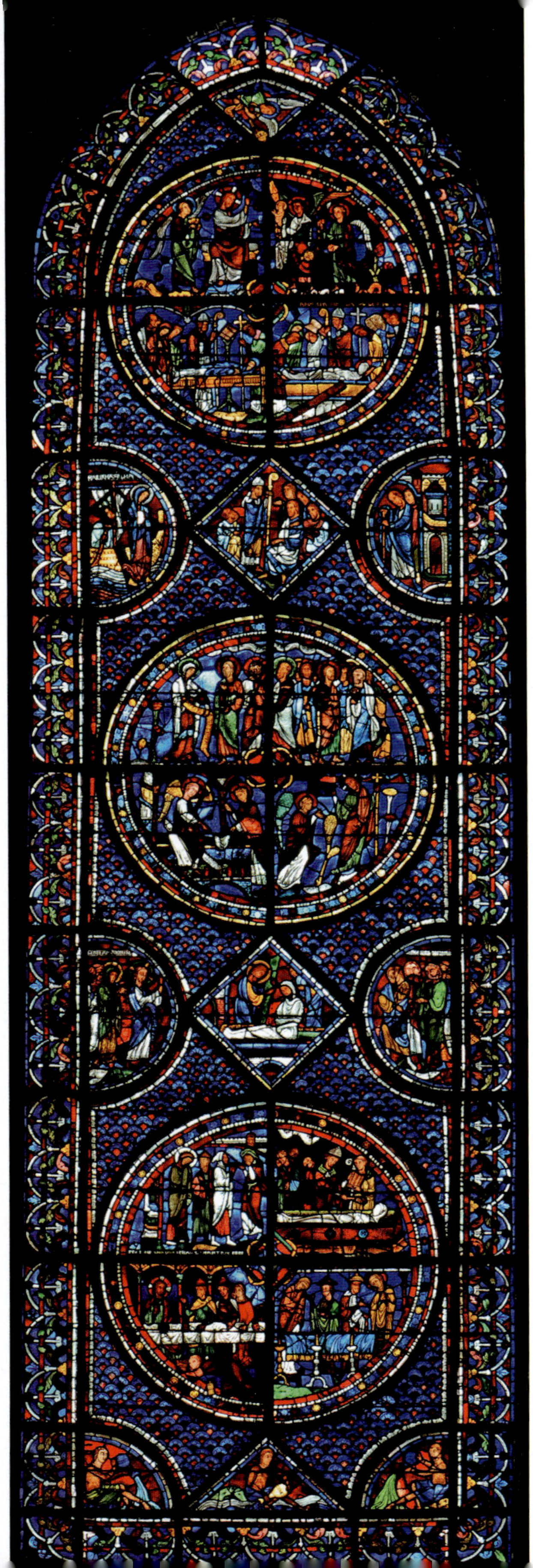

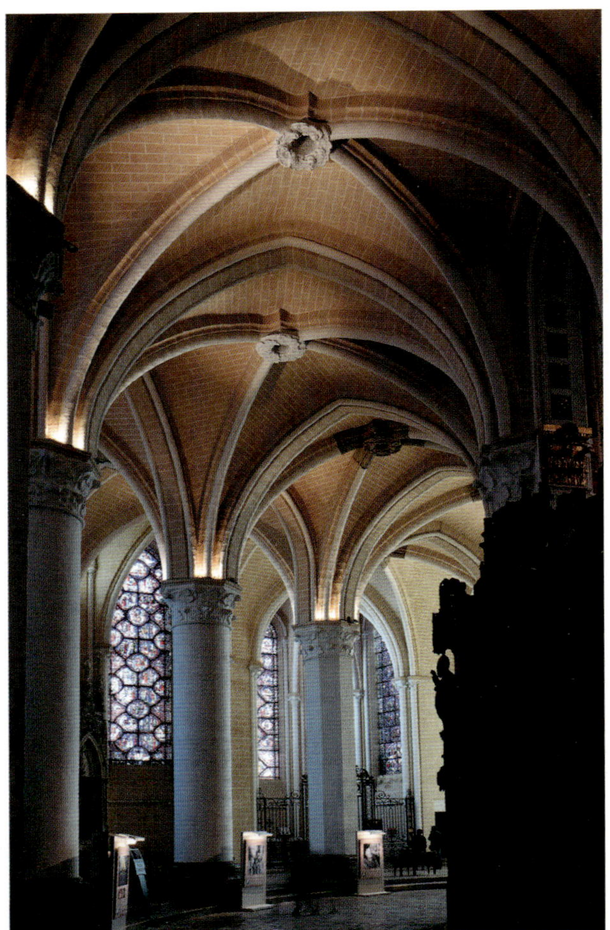

29 South ambulatory, showing
restoration of original wall colour.

30 St Mary Magdalene (46),
watercarriers, 1205–15.

circles. Dense patterns of tiles in curving or rectilinear shapes act as foils for the figural medallions. Abstracted delineations of form transcend any contemporary concept of verisimilitude. Symbolic representations conveyed a locale: a single tree, a forest; a crenelated wall, a fortress; an arch, the building of a cathedral; or a canopy, a royal throne room. These transformations of natural form were seen as serving the theological importance of the image. Peter Brieger thus explained the similarities between Gothic manuscripts and windows as

> not simply because they [illuminators] followed the example of the window designers, but because the geometric order establishing sequences and relations was the natural and logical as well as aesthetically appropriate one to be used by artists who were taught to visualise human and divine relations in terms of eternal validity, satisfying reason and faith and independent of change in place and time.[3]

A large majority of windows show images at the bottom that have long been identified as donors. Some are traditional clerics or nobles, such as the canon Henri Noblet, shown twice, praying before a statue of the Virgin and Child and before Christ blessing, in the window of Simon and Jude. A double lancet window shows members of the same family. Under the Life of St Nicolas, Jeffrey Chardonnel, Chancellor of Notre-Dame Cathedral, Paris, prays before a statue of the Virgin Mary and Etienne Chardonnel, a member of Chartres' Cathedral Chapter, assumes a similar pose under the story of St Germain of Auxerre.

Representations of the Trades

Other windows show workers at their trades. The organization of guilds and confraternities who contracted chantry chapels in churches and guild halls was a phenomenon of the later Middle Ages. Such wealth enabled merchants to claim privileges. For examples we can observe the private chapels of the families of John Clopton and Lawrence Martyn, prosperous wool merchants of the fifteenth century, which engulf the original chancel of Holy Trinity Church, Long Melford, Suffolk, England. However, like medieval York, we do not find guilds sponsoring stained-glass windows. They may have endowed chapels and given candles or statues to embellish the space, but there is no record of a specific guild-sponsored window. As at All Saints, North Street, York (see Chapter Five), despite the well-documented activities of the city's guilds and their sponsorship of liturgical drama, the recorded donors of the windows were individual families.

Chartres does show the trades at work, however. The window of Noah depicts wheelwrights, carpenters and coopers, that of Joseph, money changers and Nicolas, haberdashers, spice sellers, wood carriers and apothecaries. The Typological Redemption window shows blacksmiths and that of St Julian the Hospitaller shows carpenters, wheelwrights and coopers (illus. 31). The window of St Savinien and St Poténtian shows masons working on a church, and the following, dedicated to St Chéron, masons and sculptors (illus. 32). St Stephen's window shows shoemakers, the window of Charlemagne, an image of a furrier and that of St James, which follows, furriers and drapers. Under the window of the Apostles, in the centre of the axial chapel, three scenes show bakers making and selling bread. Continuing on the south, the heavily restored window of St Sylvester shows masons and tools. Then follows the windows of Thomas Becket with tanners and St Martin with leatherworkers and shoemakers. Two double lancet windows follow: under the signs of the Zodiac are vintners, and under the Life of the Virgin vintners as well as the count, Thibault of Chartres. After the lancet containing the repositioned twelfth-century Notre-Dame de la Belle Verrière, we find the narrative of St Anthony and St Paul the Hermit

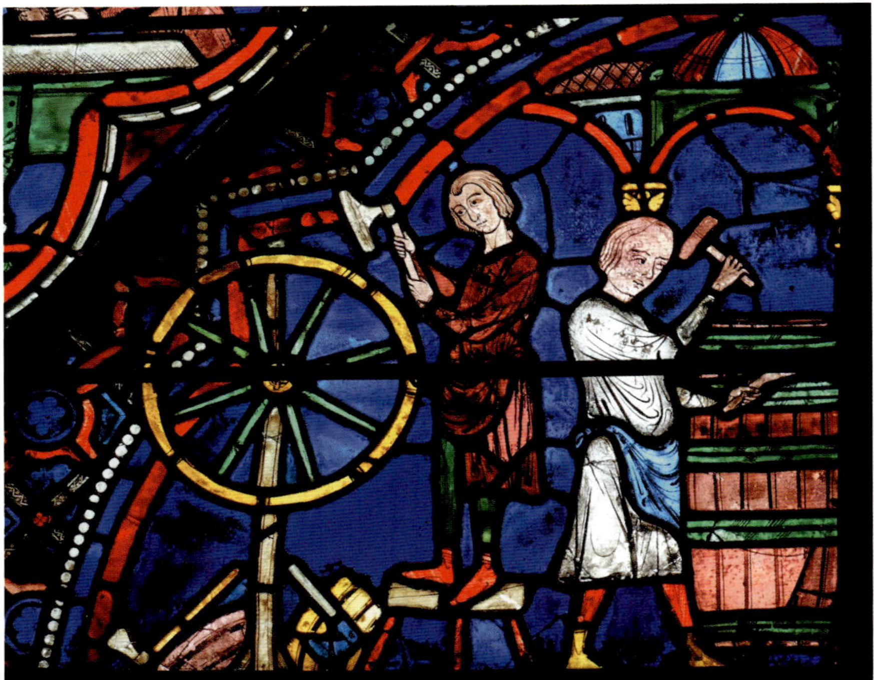

31 Legend of St Julien the Hospitaller (21), wheelwrights and coopers, 1215–25.

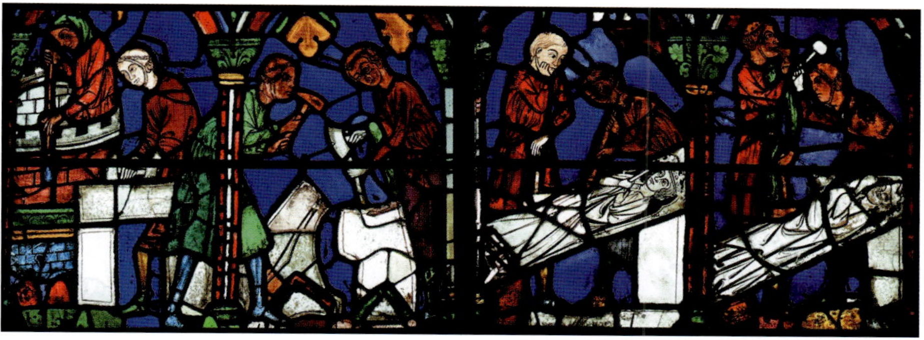

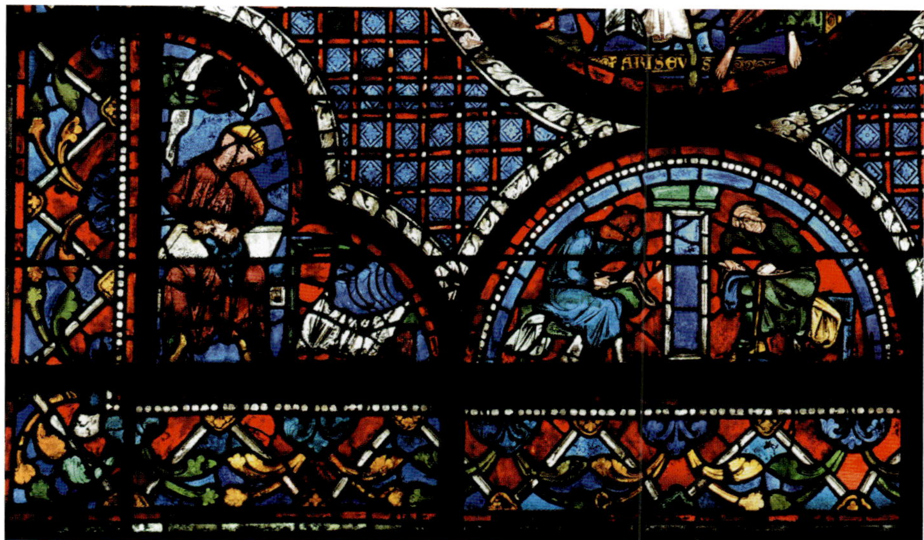

32 Legend of St Chéron (15), masons and sculptors, 1220–25.
33 Good Samaritan (44), shoemakers, 1205–15.

with fishmongers below. St Blaise shows moneychangers, and the Miracles of Notre-Dame shows butchers. Both the Death and Assumption of the Virgin Mary and the following Good Samaritan (illus. 33) show shoemakers. The window of Mary Magdalene shows three water carriers (see illus. 30), and the window of St John, close to the entrance, shows armourers. Unlike the clerical or noble patrons, none of the trade representations show anyone in the act of prayer, but several do include groups offering the representation of a window, such as the panel to the extreme lower right in the Life of St Stephen.

The trades also appear under the figures of saints and prophets on the upper level. Bakers, butchers and moneychangers are found in the windows of the choir. Bakers take pride of place under the axial window of the Virgin, directly above the bakers in the axial window of the choir. The adjacent window to the south also depicts bakers. Moneychangers appear in two windows. The remaining nine display the high nobility, including Louis IX and the king of Castile. The upper transept windows north and south prioritize priests and a few nobles. The nave, however, depicts what appear to be common citizens and some identifiable trades.

Trades in Bourges Cathedral

We can compare this distribution with windows in the cathedral at Bourges, built about the same time as Chartres. Bourges retains a significant amount of its windows from the early thirteenth century. Nine show images of the trades: the patriarch Joseph, wheelwrights and coopers (illus. 34); John the Evangelist, bakers; St Thomas, masons; the Passion window, five images of furriers; Prodigal Son, three images of tanners; and the New Covenant window, three images of butchers. The series continues with the Good Samaritan with weavers, the Relics of St Stephen with watercarriers (illus. 35), and Lazarus and Dives with three representations of masons. In the cathedral at Rouen, of the early thirteenth-century windows surviving, three offer images of noble donors, and three of the trades: St Julian the Hospitaller shows fishmongers, the story of Joseph drapers, and the Typological Passion window, masons. Although these windows repeat saints' lives portrayed at Chartres, they offer different trades as presumed donors. The similarity of the depictions of the wheelwrights and

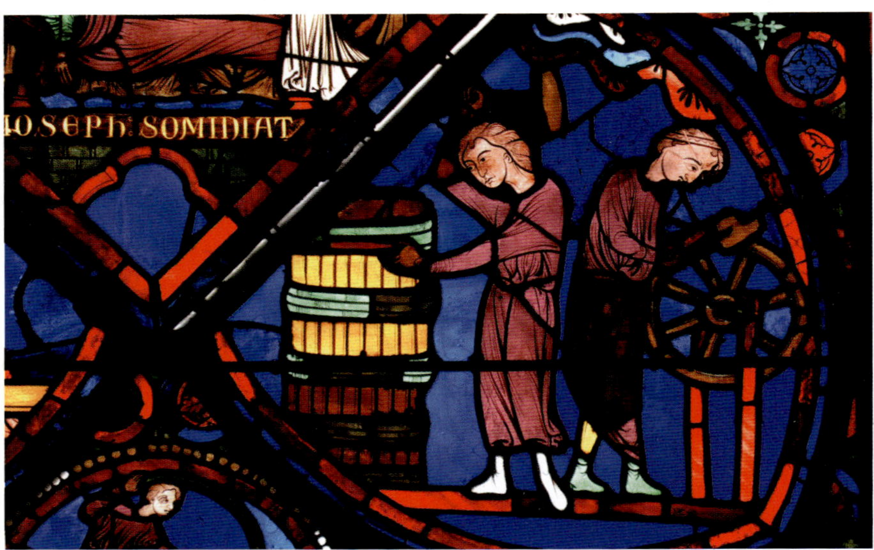

34 Bourges Cathedral (24), the patriarch Joseph, wheelwrights and coopers, 1210–15.

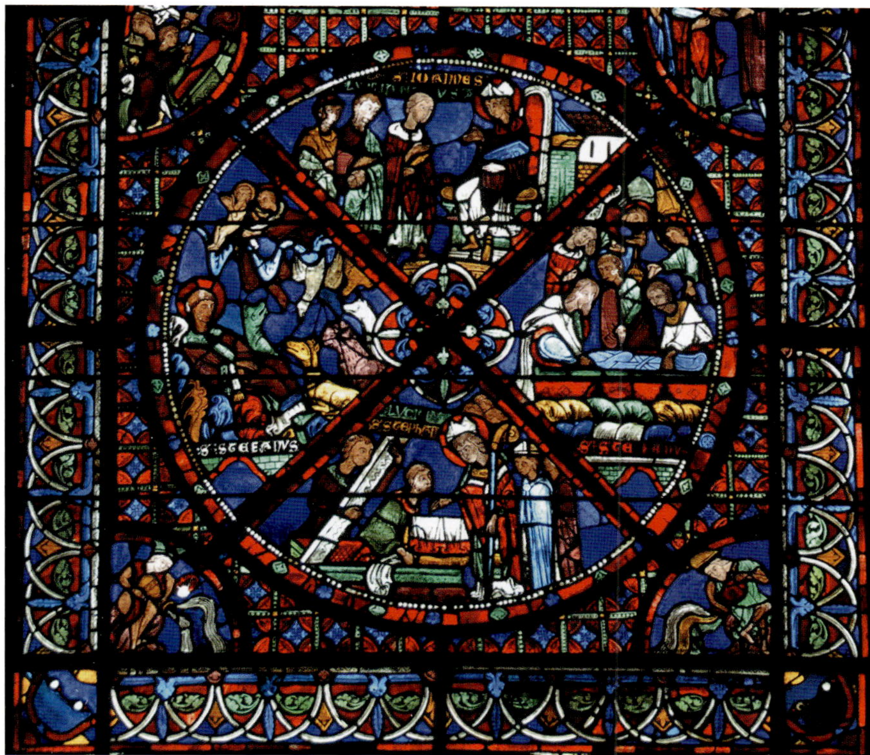

35 Bourges Cathedral (15), Relics of St Stephen,
Stephen's body discovered, watercarriers, 1210–15.

coopers at both Bourges and Chartres (see illus. 31 and 34), however, suggests
that the artists shared common sources. Even if the trades might have helped
finance the windows, these disparities give evidence that there was certainly
no agreed-upon patron saint, something that was routine for the nobility and
institutions. The papacy claimed St Peter, and the French monarchy St Michael.
Guilds of the later Middle Ages all had explicit patron saints. For example, St
Luke, who was reputed to have painted a portrait of the Virgin, was chosen by
painters throughout Europe. Antwerp's guild of St Luke, first recorded in 1382,
received privileges from the city in 1442.

Reflection on Fact and Custom

Some early documents concerning social and economic interactions at Chartres
remain but are still difficult to interpret. We discover that, on 26 May 1224, the
Chartres' Cathedral Chapter decreed that the moneychangers who normally
set their stalls in front of the church, on the porch, were obligated to relocate

them to the cloister, 'so that the moneychangers themselves might belong to the Chapter . . . that whoever might be elected to the deanship may not make claim to them'.[4] The document shows that it was the Cathedral Chapter that had unlimited power to regulate a trade, although it also attests that trades, apparently, enjoyed some organization with elected officials. As with Alix of Thouars, married at the age of twelve in deference to the king of France, and dead before her window was made, exactly what options were open to any individual in so controlled and stratified a society?

We must remember that in the Middle Ages prayer was a commodity, and the clergy 'banked' on the belief that their focused lives of prayer made their petitions particularly efficacious. Perhaps we can read the placement of bakers below the Virgin in Chartres' axial window in this light. But are we to believe that, amidst two kings and seven nobles, bakers were able to claim the most prestigious place in the upper choir? Rather, might this representation relate more closely to the clergy of Chartres claiming a responsibility for honouring the Virgin and thus bringing prosperity to the Beauce, so that it had become France's breadbasket? The busy bakers here could easily be seen as the evidence of the Chapter's efficacy in prayer.

The Donor in Charge

We may find a useful comparison by turning to Renaissance stained glass, which often articulated the individuality of the donors and their priorities. Nowhere is this more vividly demonstrated than in the cantons of Switzerland which celebrate their independence dating from 1291 (more explanation of Swiss glass follows in Chapter Seven). The average citizen played an extraordinary part in the prosperity and governance of his territory; local representation was integral to the social fabric. Civic organizations such as guilds, city councils and law courts invested in depicting their members. Husband and wife appeared in commemorative glass panels that were set within domestic and public architectural settings. A panel of 1612 from the canton of Fribourg (illus. 36) names three male donors, Théodule Michel, Jean du Villard and Pierre Walleian (also spelled Vallélian). Although we do not know the original destination of the panel, the donors are identified by their coats of arms and inscriptions at the bottom. Heraldic badges for individuals were not restricted to the nobility. Indeed, when called to civic duty, Swiss citizens were obligated to use their family shields, or construct one for themselves. This small panel could have been made for a church or confraternity hall, as well as a civic establishment.

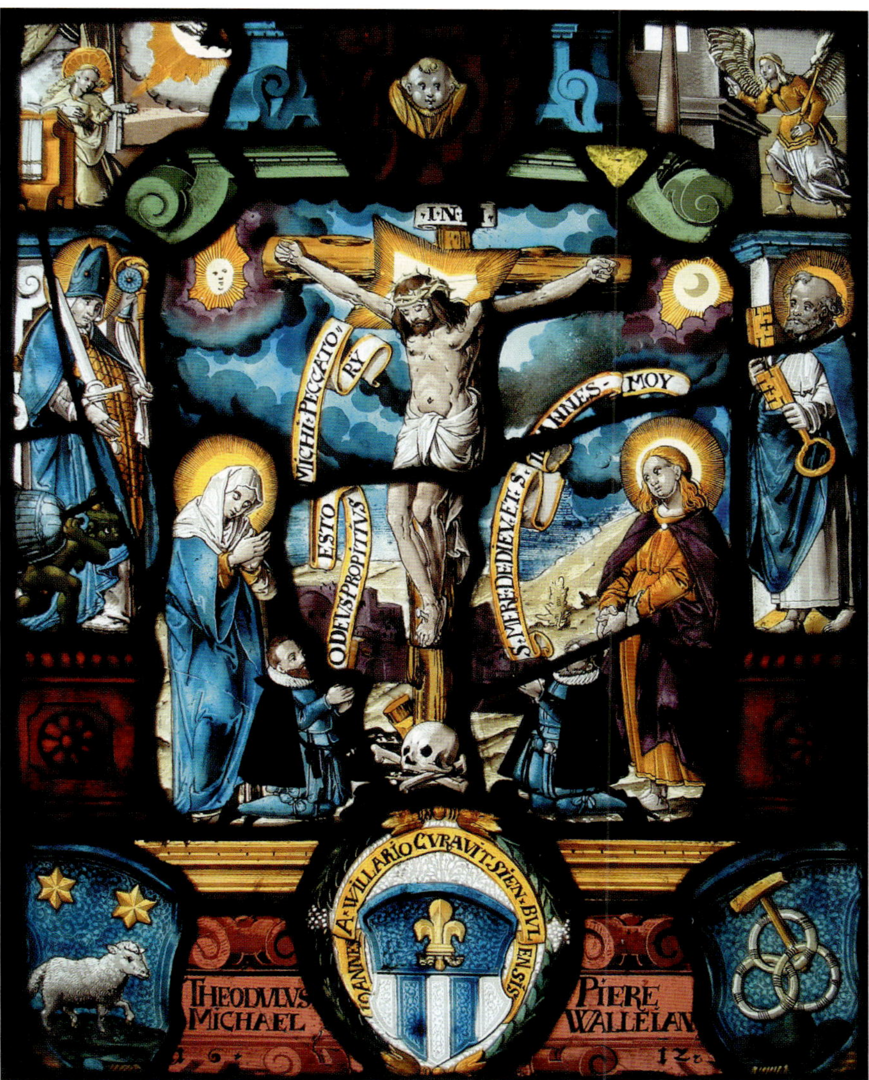

36 Crucifixion with arms of Michel, Vallélian and Villard, 1612, Switzerland, canton of Fribourg, now at the Los Angeles County Museum of Art.

We observe a confessional statement by two of the men kneeling at the foot of the cross. Each addresses the image of Christ, the Virgin Mary and St John that they see in their mind's eye. The Crucifixion is portrayed vividly, set against a cloudy landscape of blue, purple and yellow. At the base of the cross is a skull, a double reference to Golgotha meaning 'The Place of the Skull' (Mark 15:22) and to the belief that this was the site of Adam's tomb. Adam's burial directly below the Crucifixion associates Adam, whose actions caused harm to human-kind, with Christ, the new Adam (1 Corinthians 15), who brought eternal life.

To the left stands the Virgin Mary, dressed in a white wimple and blue mantle. Her head is bowed, and her hands are folded in prayer. On the right is St John the Evangelist in a purple mantle and gold robe. Both are traditional figures at the foot of the cross. At the top is the Annunciation; the Virgin kneeling at a prie-dieu on the left and on the right the angel Gabriel.

The status of the canton and city of Fribourg provides the background for the message and structure of this panel. At one time under the influence of Savoy, it gained independence as a Free Imperial City in 1478. In 1481, Fribourg joined the Swiss Confederation. The canton is on the edge of the divide between Catholic and Protestant Switzerland and its citizens clearly felt a strong need to define their allegiances. During the Middle Ages, the influence of the Church had been strong, with powerful abbeys founded by the Cistercians, Augustinians and Franciscans. It became a centre of Counter-Reformation activity and, in 1580, aware of the Protestant schools founded at Basel, Lausanne and Geneva, the government invited the celebrated Jesuit Peter Canisius to establish the College of St Michel to educate the youth. Canisius died in Fribourg on 21 November 1597. Thus, in 1612, we see the context for so articulate a manifestation of Catholic piety and the social and religious ties among men promoted by Jesuit education.

The donors' prayers, made explicit by the inscriptions below, are uttered both in Latin, the official language of the Catholic Church, and in the French vernacular. On the left, Théodule Michel petitions in French: *S. Mere de Diev et S. I[.]annes – moÿ* (Holy Mother of God and St John [remember] me); on the right, Pierre Walleian (Vallélian) utters a similar prayer in Latin: *O Deus propitivs esto michi peccatorÿ* (O God be well disposed to me concerning my sins); Jean du Villard's name is inscribed around the arms in the centre. The employment of Latin by the laity, here, stands as a critique of the rejection by both Martin Luther from Germany and Ulrich Zwingli from Switzerland of Latin as a language of prayer.

Théodule and Pierre Honour Their Patrons

Swiss archives record that Théodule Michel was a citizen of Bulle, the major city of the district of Gruyère, 20 kilometres (12 mi.) south of the city of Fribourg. He had exercised the profession of notary since 1612 and served as secretary of the bailiff tribunal (*curial*) of Bulle in 1641 and 1643. He also held the post of *banneret* in 1661. He was the father of Georges Michel (1620–after 1677), who was a doctor of theology and priest in Bulle from 1646 to 1677. Pierre Walleian

(Vallélian) is not identified, but the family name is local. He may have been of the same family as Loys Vallélian, a painter, coming from Gruyère. Jean du Villard is unverified in archival searches and thus his profession is unknown. He was, however, from the same city; *Bvlensis* in the inscription clearly refers to Bulle.

The donors clearly wanted to testify to their belief in the intercession of saints, a practice rejected by the Lutheran and Zwinglian reformers. Their patron saints watch from pedestals. On the left is St Théodule, Théodule Michel's patron, dressed as a bishop with a blue cope and mitre and a yellow chasuble. In one hand he holds a crosier, with a sudarium (veil) hanging from the top, and in the other he carries a sword with the blade resting on his shoulder. Théodule's diocese was the oldest in Switzerland and the image shows the power of his successors as secular lords as well as spiritual leaders. Théodule was particularly honoured in the area in the southwestern part of Switzerland, especially the cantons of Fribourg and Valais, which had remained Catholic. The region's conservative position can be associated with its unusual fusion of temporal and ecclesiastic. Valais, for example, was ruled by the prince-bishops of Sion, who traced their origins to St Théodule. At the saint's feet, a green demon equipped with yellow testicles struggles to carry a blue bell, referring to the legend that the bishop forced a demon to carry the papal gift of a bell across the presently named Theodul Pass.

Pierre Walleian's patron, St Peter, stands on the right. He wears a blue mantle and white robe and carries his traditional attribute, the keys. His keys are a reference to Christ's words to Peter, 'And I will give to thee the keys of the kingdom of heaven' (Matthew 16:19), which Catholics saw as establishing the primacy of the bishop of Rome, the pope. The Reformation was very much about a desire to distance congregations from the authority of Rome. Reformers argued that the papacy's secular power and system of clerical hierarchy had deformed the Church by suppressing the laity's direct contact with Christ. In this panel, the donors contradict that accusation by showing a moment of affective piety; a heartfelt meditation on Christ's redemptive sacrifice and association with saintly patrons who stand by to help.

Ultimately, whatever their mysteries, we are drawn to these works that exemplify such a high level of artistic and social forces. They speak in complex, possibly conflicting, voices. We see hardworking masons lifting stone, bakers kneading bread, devoted Swiss Catholics at prayer, and the beauty of the young Alix of Thouars. Whatever her short life, she reigns supreme in Chartres for the ages.

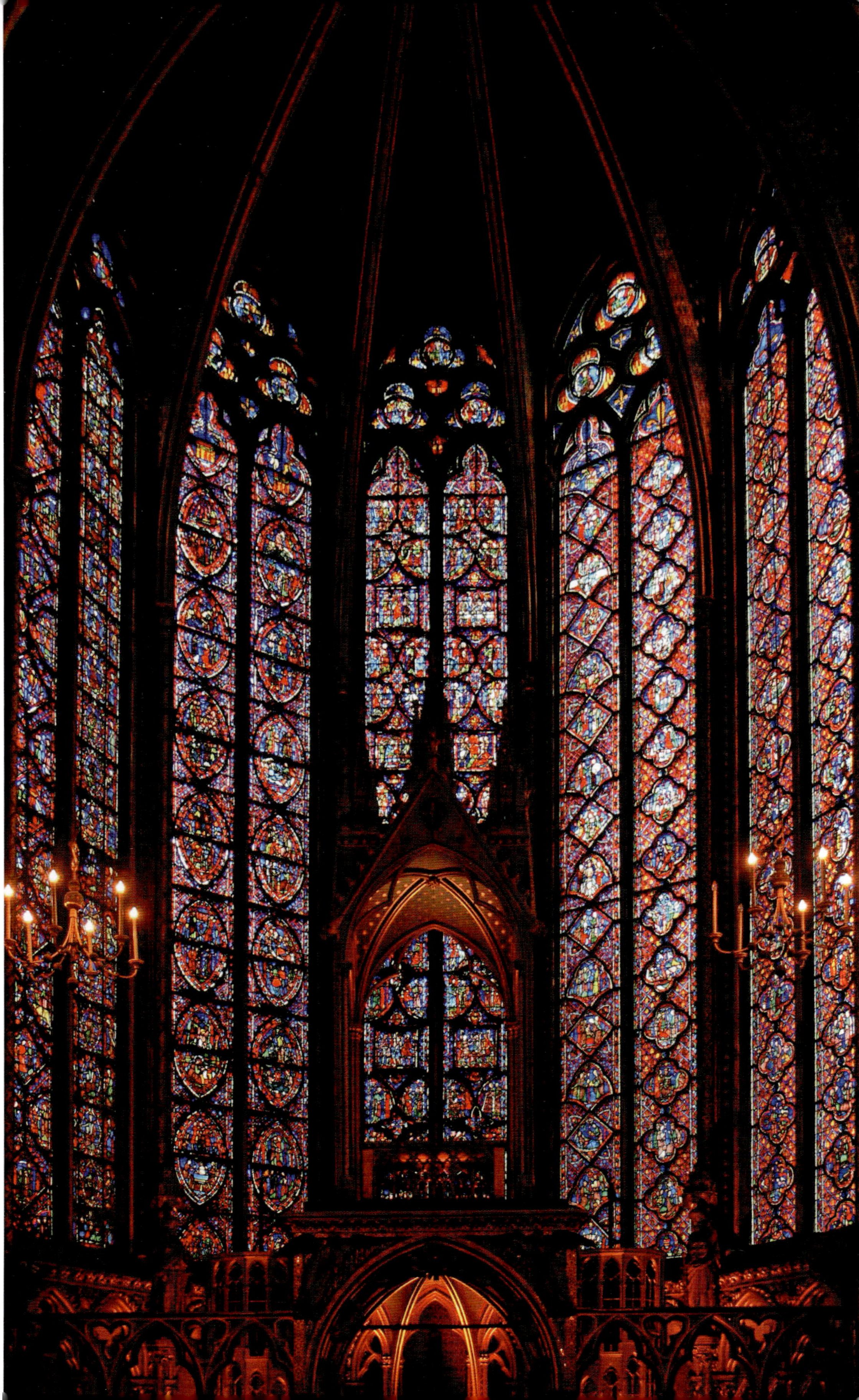

3

Sainte-Chapelle, Paris: Propaganda for the Monarch

—

Of extraordinary unity, the Sainte-Chapelle was completed in six years, from 1243 to 1248. Attached to the palace, as was typical of chapels associated with rulers, the edifice developed singular importance through its display of the relic of the Crown of Thorns as well as a fragment of the True Cross. Louis IX received the relics in 1239 from the emperor Baldwin II of Constantinople in gratitude for French assistance against Muslim invaders. Appearing as a cage of glass, the upper chapel has fifteen multi-lancet windows almost 15 metres (49 ft) high (illus. 37). An extremely rich decorative programme includes variegated foliage, censing angels (illus. 38), enamel quatrefoils of saints' lives and a series of statues of the Apostles (illus. 39). The windows show a coherent theme in the continuity of kingship: the Old Testament patriarchs, reign of Christ and of the Capetian kings of France. The glass is stylistically homologous, although different 'hands' or types of execution can be distinguished. Frequently royal insignia appear, the fleur-de-lis for France or the castles for Castile, the Spanish principality, the heritage of the king's influential mother Blanche of Castile.

A Great Relic and the Monarchy

Heralded from the beginning, two major texts record Sainte-Chapelle's founding. In the *History of the Reception of the Crown of Thorns*, the Archbishop of Sens, Gauthier Cornut (d. 1241), wrote that the Lord had selected France 'for the more devout veneration of this Passion'.[1] Innocent IV issued a papal bull in

37 Sainte-Chapelle, Paris, interior, apse, 1243–8.

63

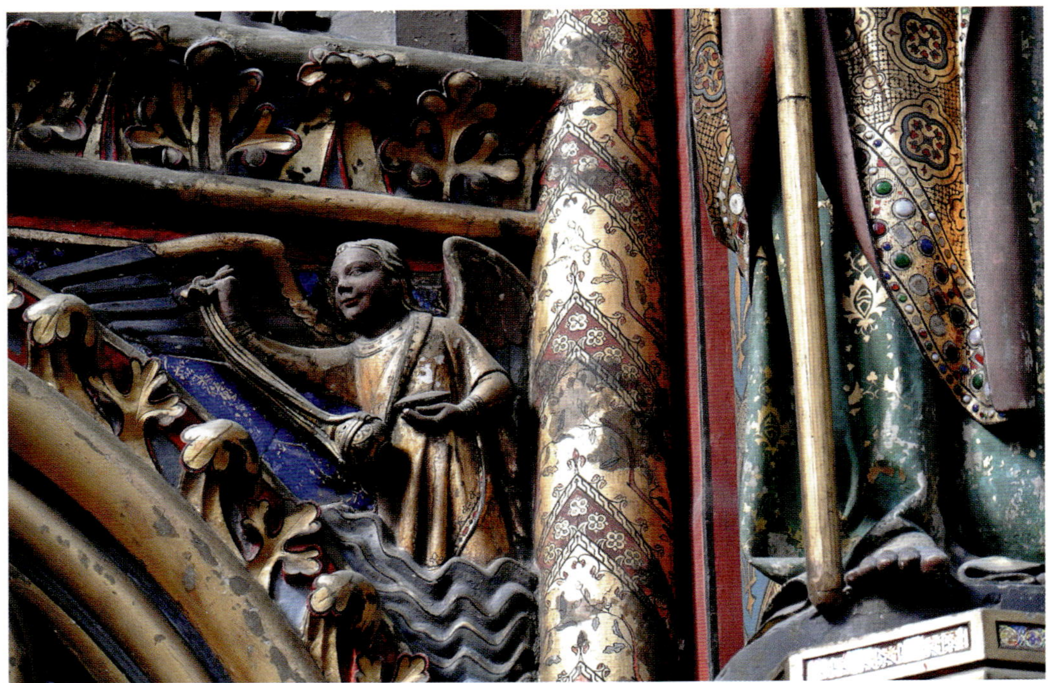

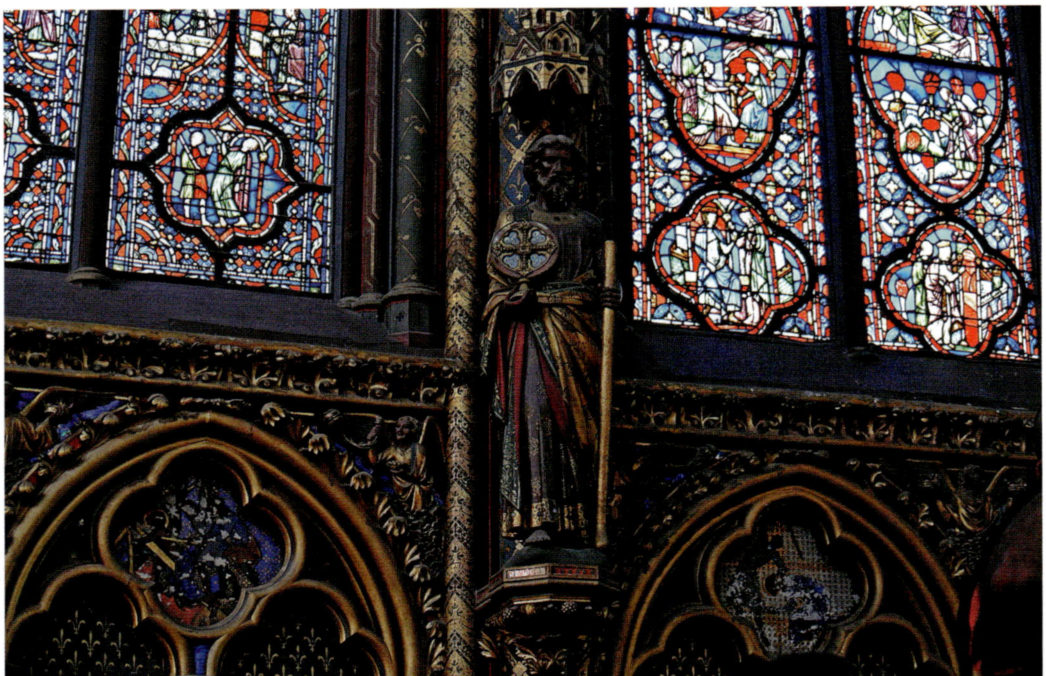

38 Sainte-Chapelle, interior, detail of censing angel in spandrel.

39 Sainte-Chapelle, interior, detail of south wall, Apostle statue
and lower segments of window restorations of 1845–55.

1244 declaring that Christ had crowned the French king with his own crown. John of Garland, who was born in England but spent most of his life teaching in France, was in Paris in 1245. In his *De triumphis ecclesiae* (On the Triumphs of the Church) dated 1245–52, he remarked that Louis had built the chapel to house the precious relics in order that they would be available to the nation. The poor as well as the rich would benefit from this act on the part of their pious monarch. Innocent IV used descriptions common for aesthetic praise of the time. Chief is the phrase that 'the workmanship surpassed the material' (*Materiam superbat opus*), taken from the Latin author Ovid's praise of the metal doors created by the god Vulcan for the palace of Apollo. Suger had used the term a century earlier when describing the 'golden panels' of metalwork that he commissioned for the high altar of Saint-Denis (*De Administratione* XXXIII). By Innocent IV using the phrase for a building destined to house relics, however, we are led to believe that he was comparing the building to metalwork associated with altars and reliquaries. The ensemble does suggest a reliquary turned outside in, the lower chapel a wide base and the upper chapel aglow with colours from reflecting and translucent materials.

There is no question that the building embodies secular as well as religious purpose. By the mid-thirteenth century Louis had succeeded in popularizing the French king as pre-eminent among the European monarchs. Louis ruled over what is almost the territory of modern-day France, the result of his grandfather Philip Augustus' victory over the English in 1214. We need to remind ourselves of the political status of Europe in the thirteenth century. Germany was then a collection of small principalities that would coalesce only after nineteenth-century struggles that led to the 1871 declaration of the Prussian-dominated German Empire. Italy was divided into many separate kingdoms until unified by the Risorgimento and the ultimate designation of Rome as its capital in 1871. Southern Spain still lay largely under Muslim control. France, indeed, was the most significant political and cultural force in Europe. Louis strategized ways to promulgate the concept. During his reign there were three revisions of the *Ordo* (ceremony of consecration), stressing that the oil with which the king was anointed had been miraculously delivered by God at the consecration of King Clovis in 508 after his conversion to Christianity. In addition, Louis' new coinage of 1260 bore his shield and the inscription *Christus vincit Christus regnat Christus imperat* (Christ conquers, Christ reigns, Christ commands).

Loss and Restoration

Today, barely half of the panels in the chapel's windows date from the time of Louis. Early interventions, such as the late thirteenth-century panel of *Four Men* in the Cluny Museum, removed from the building in 1850, can be determined by stylistic examination. Written texts appear in the later Middle Ages. In 1483 Charles VIII provided money for restorations. In 1485 documents record the ongoing restoration when the original west rose of the Apocalypse was presumably replaced with its present Renaissance glass. Additional documents of 1485 concerning a restoration campaign can be associated with further panels at Cluny, including *Joseph Sold by His Brothers*. The eighteenth century saw extensive interventions. Many panels surviving in fragmentary condition were then augmented with modern glass, altering the original subject-matter. Their sequence, in addition, has been rearranged several times, clearly compromising the original narrative. The interior decoration is no less altered. Of the Apostle statues (see illus. 39), six of the twelve are completely new and two heavily restored. The four intact originals are found at the fourth and fifth columns.

In 1837, a decision to restore the edifice was made, and a preliminary campaign focused on stabilizing the building, carried out by the renowned architect, restorer and writer on the Gothic, Eugène-Emmanuel Viollet-le-Duc (1814–1879). The architect lavished praise on the building: its fine stone, construction with iron clips and precision of superimposed layers composed and cut with extraordinary care. Such enthusiasm swayed the National Assembly, whose support of the restoration in 1845 made it a rallying cry for the rebirth of the Gothic. Practitioners saw the style continuing into an enlightened modern age. In many ways Gustave Eiffel's 1889 design of the 'Eiffel' tower shows a continuation of the lacy intricacies and towering heights of the Gothic.

Restorers contended with a seriously altered building. The French Revolution of 1789 had secularized the government and suppressed the religious authority that supported the Old Regime. In 1803, the administration of Paris installed the judicial archives in the chapel. The cabinets housing documents extended beyond the windows. Ferdinand de Guilhermy, archaeologist and art historian, mentions that 2 metres/6½ ft (actually 2.5 metres/8 ft) of the windows were obscured. An 1839 lithograph, *La Ste. Chapelle, Paris*, by Thomas Shotter Boys (online collection of the Los Angeles County Museum of Art), shows the lower portions of the windows boarded up. Although the armature was unchanged, it is assumed that many panels of glass were removed at this time, including the three from the story of Judith that are now in the Philadelphia Museum of Art.

Restoration of the windows began in 1845, guided by Guilhermy. He states that he was charged with replacing panels that had been removed, reconstituting their original order, and suggesting ways to complete the missing narratives in these series.[2] In 1847, the commission overseeing the windows directed that 'the new work must meld into the old in order to generate a perfect illusion.'[3] Some 22 studios submitted bids and 11 entered a practicum stage of actually making a copy of a panel. The final ranking placed the well-known Gothic-revival artist Henri Gérente of Paris first. He began the work in 1848 but with his premature death the following year, the commission passed to Antoine Lusson of Le Mans. The restoration was divided between Lusson for the fabrication and Louis Steinheil (1814–1885) for the panels' designs. By 1855, the fifteen windows of the nave were completed. At the time, authorities were convinced that contemporary glass painters could absorb the principles of their medieval predecessors and recreate the stylistic continuum of the thirteenth century. The architect Jean-Baptiste Lassus (1807–1857), for example, had described the 1839 Passion window at St-Germain-l'Auxerrois, Paris, designed by Steinheil, not as new work but 'the renewal of the example of ancient glass.'[4] Christopher Whall, however, in his *Stained Glass Work* of 1905, commented that the very quality of the restoration, which matched so closely the original, called into question the deeply felt need for meticulous retention of the authentic. The recent restoration of the nave, between 2008 and 2014, focused only on cleaning and the addition of protective glazing.

The themes stress the interchangeability of Christ, Louis and Old Testament rulers in an eternal present of shared power and responsibility. The chronology begins on the left (north side) with an almost entirely modern window of the Creation of the World from the book of Genesis, followed by a window of Exodus with God leading his people out of Egyptian captivity. The next three windows reference the books of Numbers, Leviticus, Deuteronomy, Joshua and Judges. The apse transitions into the story of the Life of Christ through the window of Isaiah, and his prophesy that Christ will be born from the stem of Jesse. This is followed by the story of the Infancy of Christ and John the Evangelist. In the centre is the window of the Passion, and to the right, John the Baptist and the prophet Daniel. The circuit continues with the prophet Ezekiel and scenes from Jeremiah, below the story of Tobit and his son, Tobias. Judith and Job feature in the next window, while Esther's story commands a full window to itself, as does the story of David from the Book of Kings. Finally, the cycle ends in the present with the story of the acquisition of the Crown of Thorns.

Empathy and Innovations in Piety

The central position of the Passion broke with the tradition of representations of Christ triumphant for the hemicycles of churches. Clearly, the theme draws attention to the presence of the Relics of the Passion; Christ's triumph achieved only through his sacrificial death. The episodes, often spread over several medallions, include Christ judged before Pilate, his Flagellation, Crowning of Thorns, Christ carrying his Cross, Burial, Crucifixion (modern), Descent from the Cross (original in a parish church in Twycross, Leicestershire, England), Christ resurrected, Christ appearing to his Apostles at Emmaus and the Apostles looking upward, interpreted as the Ascension and the Descent of the Holy Spirit. Of particular significance is the almost completely intact panel (illus. 40) of the Crowning of Thorns. In the same placement as it was before 1845, the scene is easily seen from the floor. Christ is not visibly suffering; rather, he blesses with his right hand. The gestures of the three men on either side could be interpreted

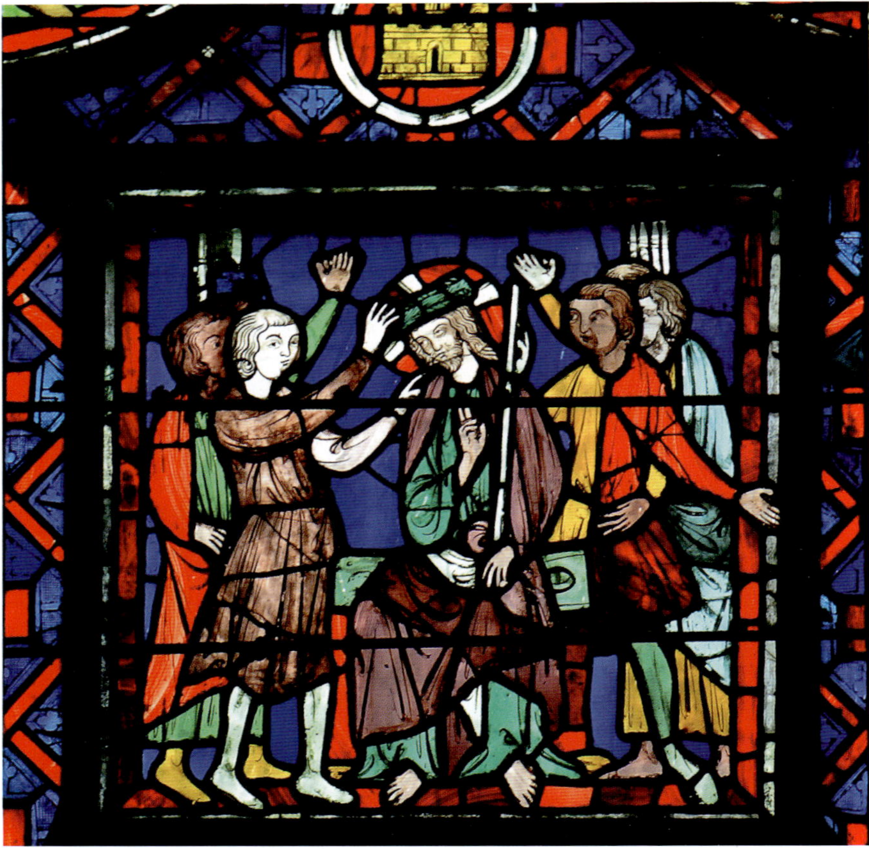

40 Sainte-Chapelle, Christ Crowned with Thorns, axial window (H-81).

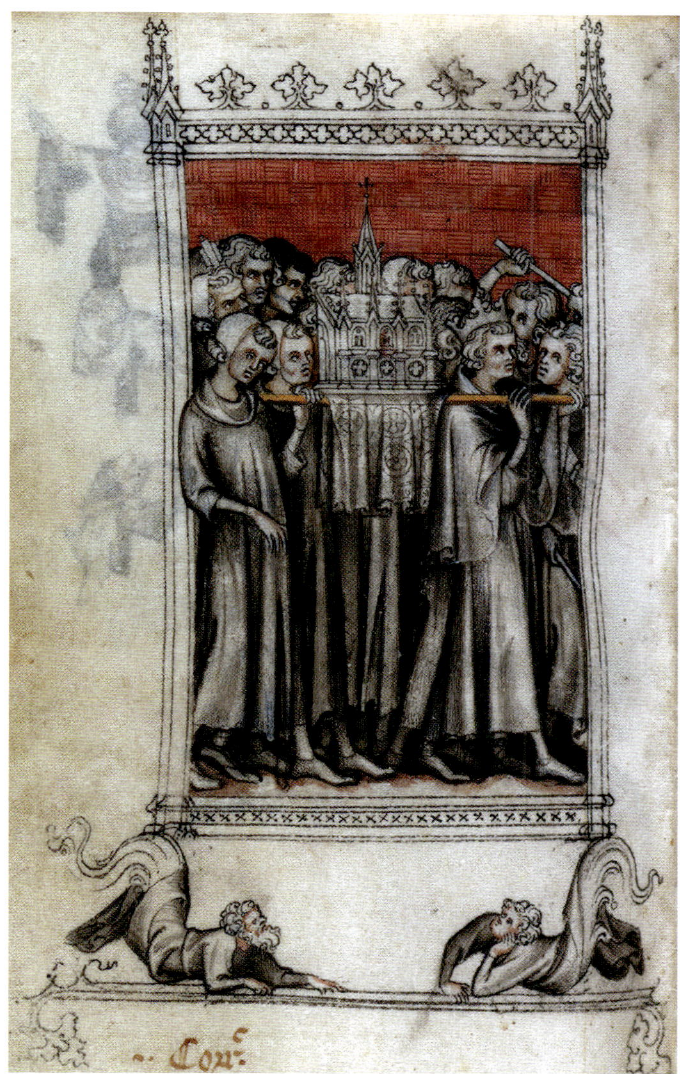

41 Jean Pucelle, *Philip* IV *carrying the Relics of St Louis,*
Hours of Jeanne d'Evreux, c. 1324–8, now at the Metropolitan
Museum of Art, Cloisters Collection.

as acclamations just as easily as insults. One cannot help but recall the mid-
fourth-century sarcophagus narrating the Passion, probably from the Catacomb
of Domitilla, Rome (Museo Pio Cristiano, Vatican, Rome). The carvings associate the Crown of Thorns with the laurel wreaths of victorious athletes, and
Christ stands erect as a soldier places the crown/wreath on his head.

This shift in emphasis towards Christ's Passion was influenced by the model
of Francis of Assisi (1181–1226), bonding so intensely with the suffering Christ

that he bore the Saviour's wounds in his own body. Louis was well known for his piety in supporting the evangelizing efforts of both the Dominicans and the Franciscans. Both orders are named as his confessors. At the Sainte-Chapelle, of the three annual services to commemorate the relics, one was conducted by the Franciscans and another by the Dominicans. The renowned Tuscan Franciscan, Bonaventure (1221–1274), who wrote the authorized biography of Francis (*Legenda Major*), came to Paris as a student and became a university lecturer. He is recorded as having preached frequently for the king. Louis was the only French monarch to be canonized, a process by which Rome recognized that an individual has entered the realm of the blessed to live eternally with Christ (illus. 41). In 1297, Pope Boniface VIII issued the proclamation from the papal palace in Orvieto.

Jean de Joinville (1224–1317), seigneur of Joinville, a lordship in Champagne, was a close associate of the king. He accompanied Louis on the Crusade leaving from Marseille in 1248, which returned only in 1254. Although he disagreed with the need and strategies for Louis' subsequent Crusade in 1267, during which the king died of dysentery in Tunis, he was interviewed at length during the process of Louis' canonization. Around 1298, he wrote a biography at the bequest of Jeanne de Navarre, Philippe le Bel's queen, reflecting her predecessor's 'holy words and edifying deeds' (I). Rich in detail, Joinville's text describes Louis' simple dress and his frugal meals, his bedtime chats to instruct his many children in their responsibilities and multiple examples of his generosity to the poor and to the Church.

Window Design and Narrative Purpose

The chapel's programme is reinforced by the formulas used to create the windows. Their simplified design depends on bold silhouettes with few figures per scene. The medallion format of the window consists of many small units where scenes, such as a messenger bringing news or someone issuing an order, are spread out over several medallions, often appearing to be interchangeable. The old parallels the new, showing royalty honoured, a festive dinner, administration of justice, birth of a child or military conflict in easily recognizable formats. They are meant to be the same so that they are interchangeable mentally. We may therefore reflect that the problematic question of the original sequence of scenes may be less destructive than imagined.

Granted, there are moments when highly familiar iconography is immediately recognizable, such as the appearance of God speaking to Moses from

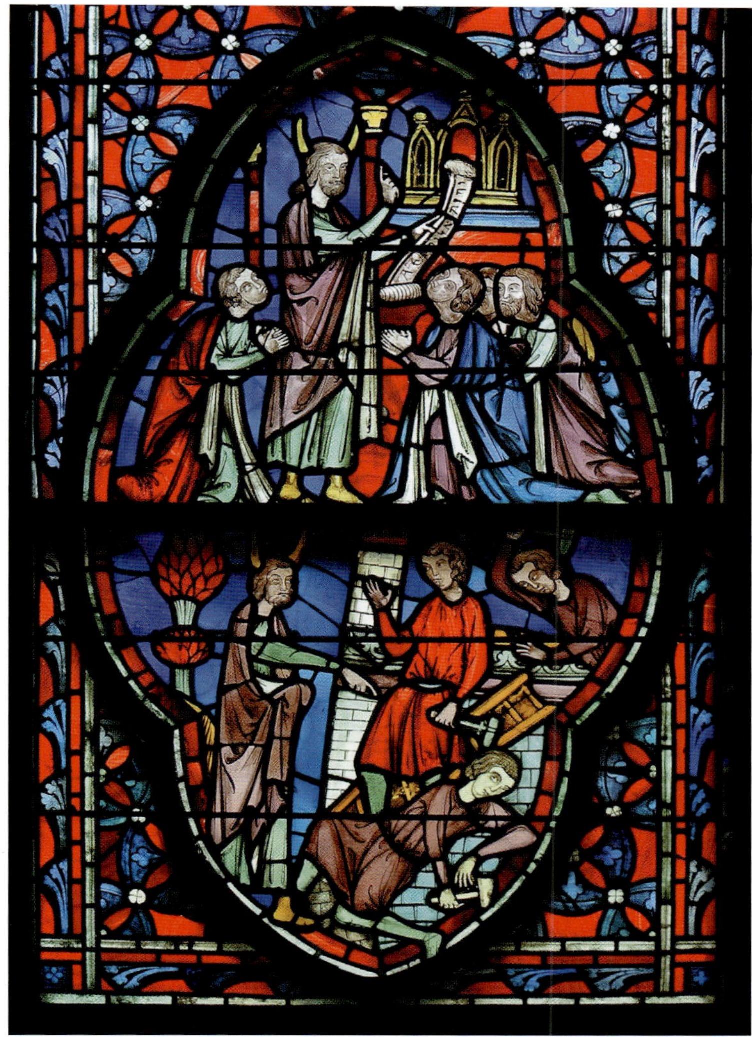

42 Sainte-Chapelle, Deuteronomy, Moses places the Books of the Law in the Ark (L-154) and Moses directs the construction of cities of refuge (L-158).

the burning bush or Aaron's staff turning into a serpent. Later, when God gives the commandments, Moses is clearly identified by his horns, the rays of light emanating from his head. Yet when these biblical images are examined more closely, contemporary references dominate. The scene of Moses commanding that the books of the law be transferred to the Ark of the Covenant (Deuteronomy 31:24–6) is not frequently depicted. The Ark's form of three Gothic arches, in addition, is suggestive of reliquaries, such as the one with Louis' own relics depicted in the *Hours of Jeanne d'Evreux* (see illus. 41). Below, Moses is shown constructing cities of refuge (Deuteronomy 4:41–3) for those

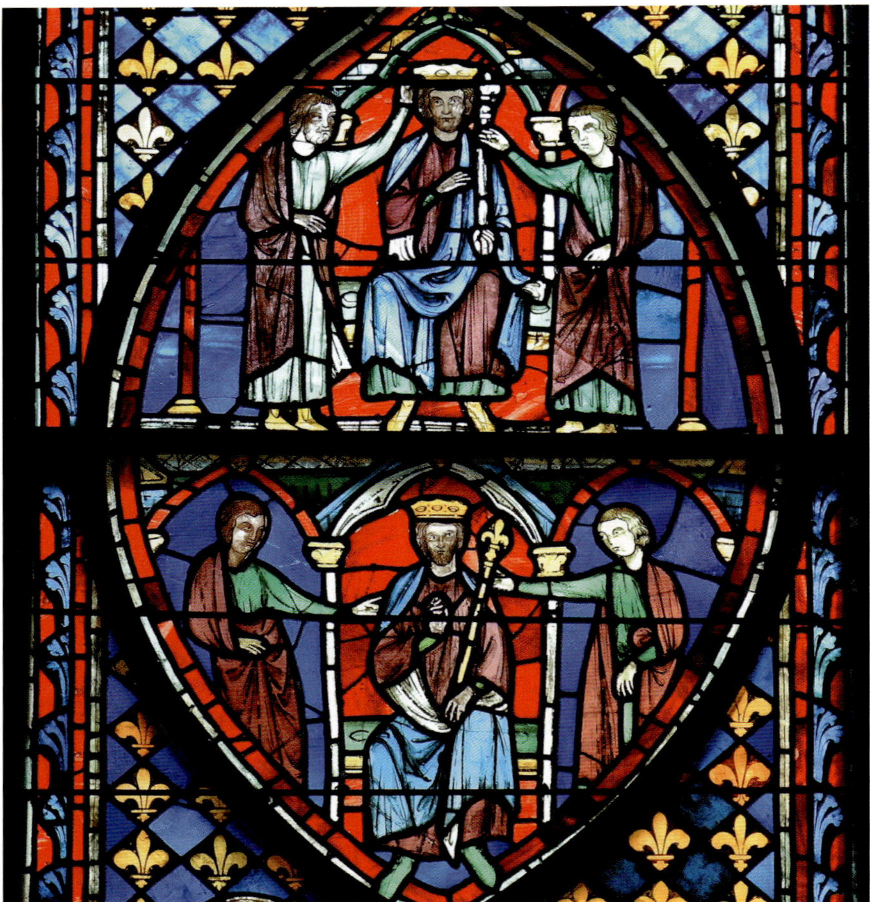

43 Sainte-Chapelle, Numbers: Coronations (M-163 and 167).

who may have unintentionally taken a life. The text in no way speaks of the construction of a city, simply that Moses 'set apart on the east side of the Jordan three cities'. The scene, however, is highly detailed (illus. 42). Moses directs workers with a vivid gesture, apparently addressing the man in red. Above and below him, men are labouring on a building that looks already well advanced. It is hard not to think that these two scenes relate as much to Louis' construction of the Sainte-Chapelle with its relics on an elevated altar, as they do to the book of Deuteronomy.

Long recognized by the casual visitor as well as the scholar, eight medallions in the window of Numbers show a series of coronations (illus. 43). These well-preserved scenes in the lower level of the window show a uniform series of frontally seated kings, each flanked by individuals extending their arms to him. In gestures of affirmation, they touch the central figure's shoulders, crown or sceptre. The Book of Numbers does address the delegation of authority within Jewish customs. However, there are no such references to this kind of ceremony. Clearly, the reference is to Louis' coronation and the sacred trust he had been given with the relic of the Crown of Thorns.

As much as the programme focuses on the king, the queen mother, Blanche of Castile, also looms large. Two of the windows address the stories of Judith and of Esther. In addition, references to parentage are common. In the story of Tobit and Tobias (illus. 44), preceding Judith, we see on the lower level a woman in bed, receiving her newborn child. The image has been identified as the Birth of Tobias (Tobit 1:9–10). Its proximity to the story of Judith, who is not recorded as a mother, suggests a conflation of images in praise of women. Additional imagery in the window shows several signature episodes as well as the continuation of the generic. Tobias, guided by the angel Raphael, pulls a fish from the water, an image unique to this story. Above, however, scenes of Sara accompanied by her parents and the wedding banquet of Tobias and Sara could apply equally to many of the narratives within the chapel.

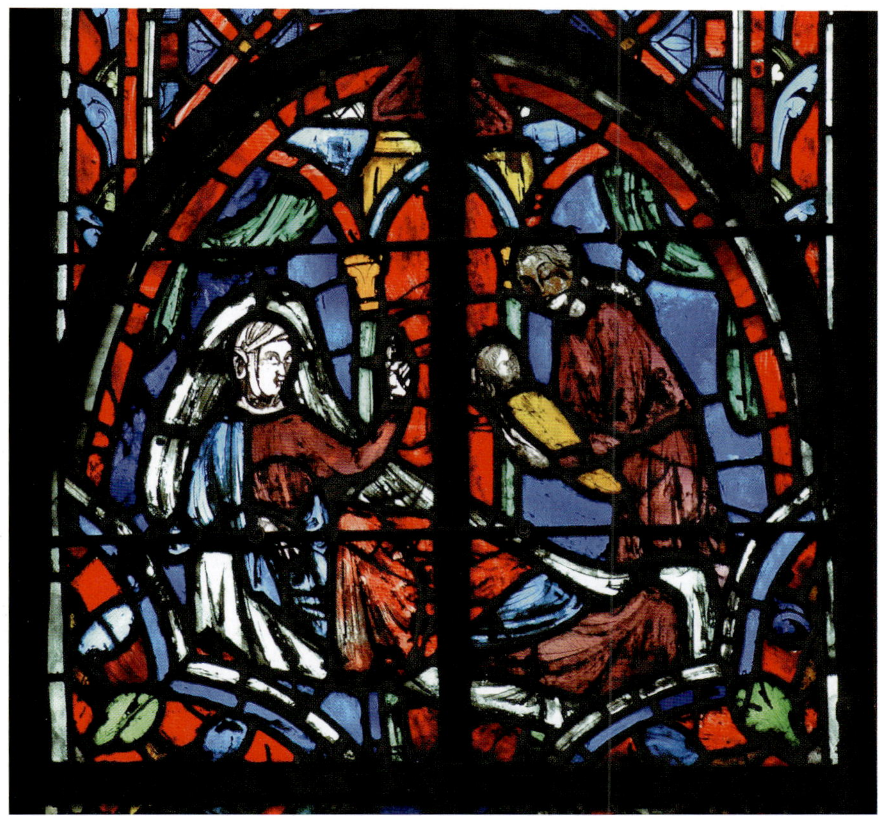

44 Sainte-Chapelle, Tobit, Birth of Tobias (E-89 and 90).

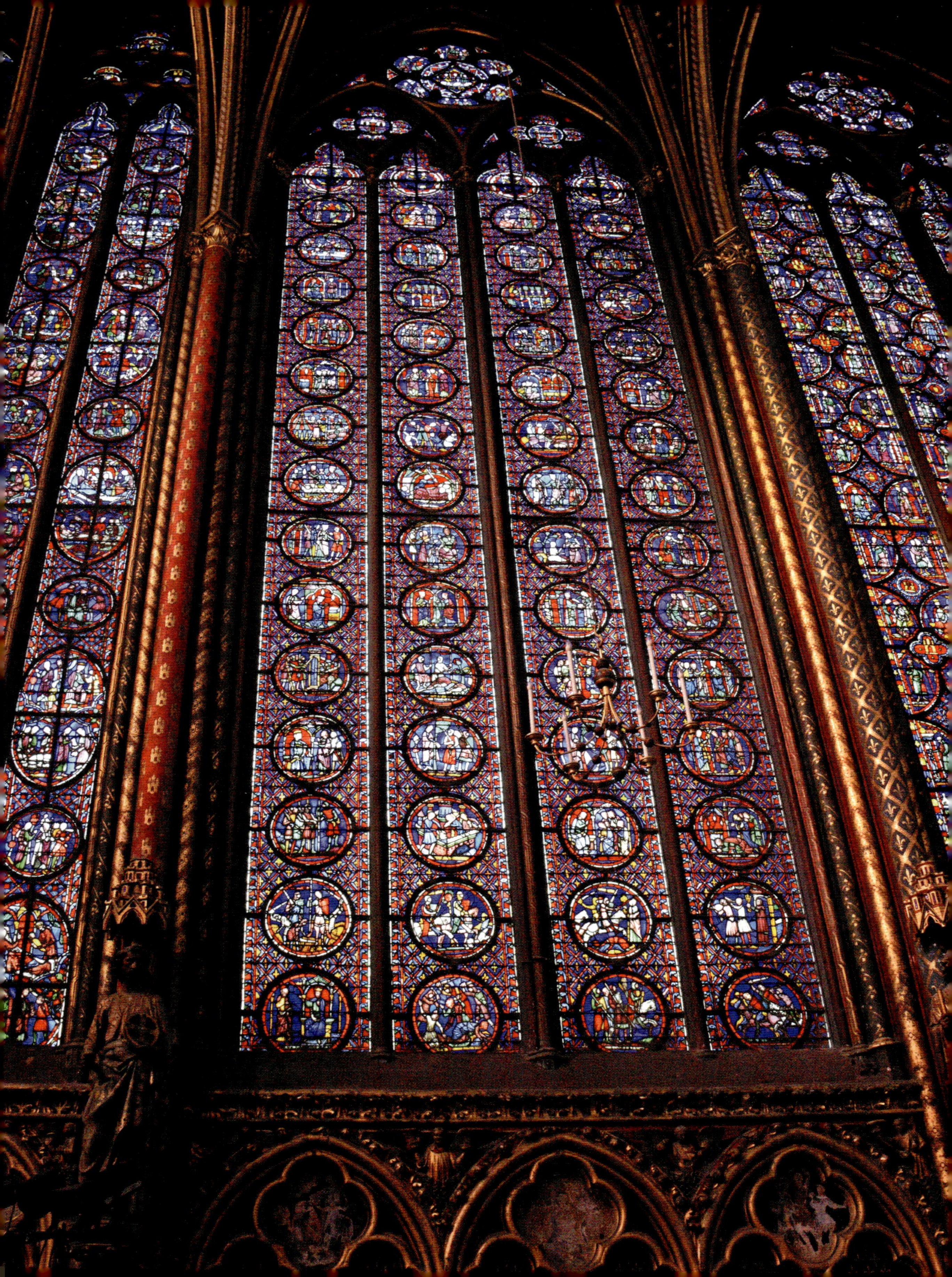

An Honourable Woman: Judith

The Book of Judith (illus. 45) is told with unusual verve, presenting a story of great courage. King Nebuchadnezzar had ordered the conquest of Israel, placing Holofernes at the head of the Assyrian army. The invading force 'covered the whole face of the earth to the west with their chariots and cavalry and picked foot soldiers' (Judith 2:19). 'He demolished all their shrines down their sacred groves' (Judith 3:7–8). The invaders are thus described not only as rapacious but sacrilegious. The text includes a review of Jewish history stating that 'as long as they did not sin against their God they prospered, for the God who hates iniquity is with them' (Judith 5:17). Judith was a widow, prudent in managing her estate and also beautiful. After speaking with the elders of the city of Bethulia, she prostrated herself with ashes on her head and begged God for strength. She then bathed, perfumed her body and arrayed herself in her best clothing and jewellery. With her female servant, she left the city. Meeting with an Assyrian patrol, she explained that she was seeking Holofernes to inform him of a way to capture the city without loss of any of his men. Judith said that the besieged Jews were about to kill their livestock and eat what God had forbidden them, thus incurring his displeasure. She would stay in the Assyrian camp, eating the food that she had brought and praying to God, who would reveal to her when the Jews had sinned. On the fourth day, Holofernes arranged a banquet and commanded Judith to attend. After consuming much wine, Holofernes was left alone in the tent with Judith but fell asleep in a drunken stupor. Judith then beheaded him with his own sword, giving the head to her maid, who concealed it in their food bag. Both women left the camp as if they were withdrawing for their nightly prayers but, instead, they returned to Bethulia. The city's elders met them with great joy and displayed Holofernes' head on the ramparts. With the morning and the discovery of Holofernes' death, the Assyrians fled in panic. The text continues with a joyous celebration and a long song of thanksgiving by Judith. Finally, we learn that Judith lived, honoured by her people, until the age of 105. For the modern reader, we may also ponder that Judith set her maid free, evidence of the widespread practice of slavery as well as manumission.

The window in the Sainte-Chapelle begins with the invasion of the armies of Holofernes. A panel shows the army passing over the Euphrates river (illus. 46). It must have occupied one of the lowest levels, beginning the narrative. The army cuts down the fields and runs off the flocks. The Jews come forward playing

45 Sainte-Chapelle, Tobit (E), Judith (D) and Esther (C).

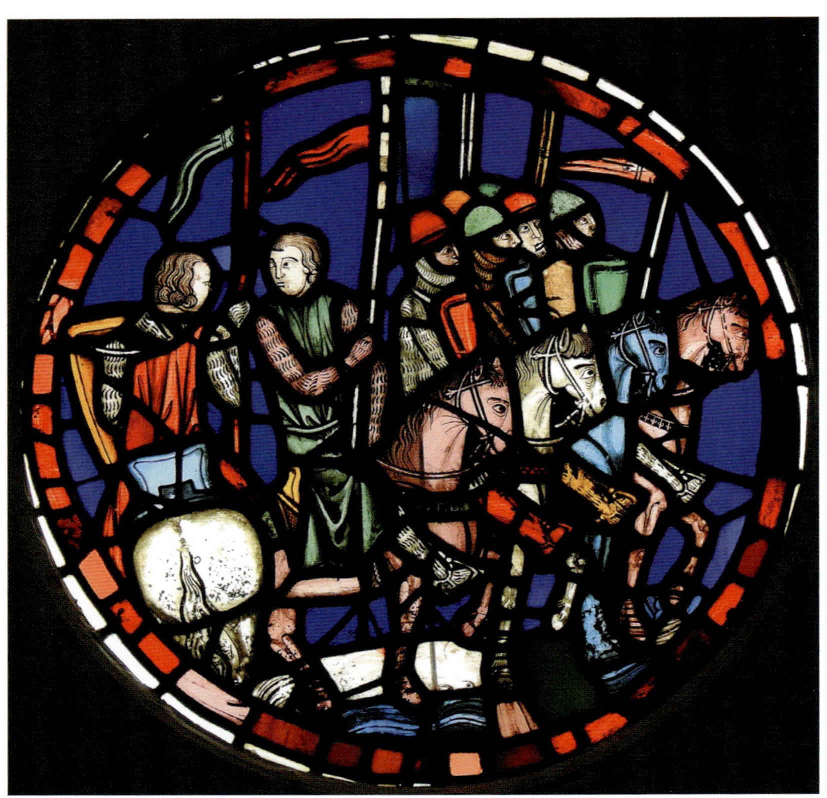

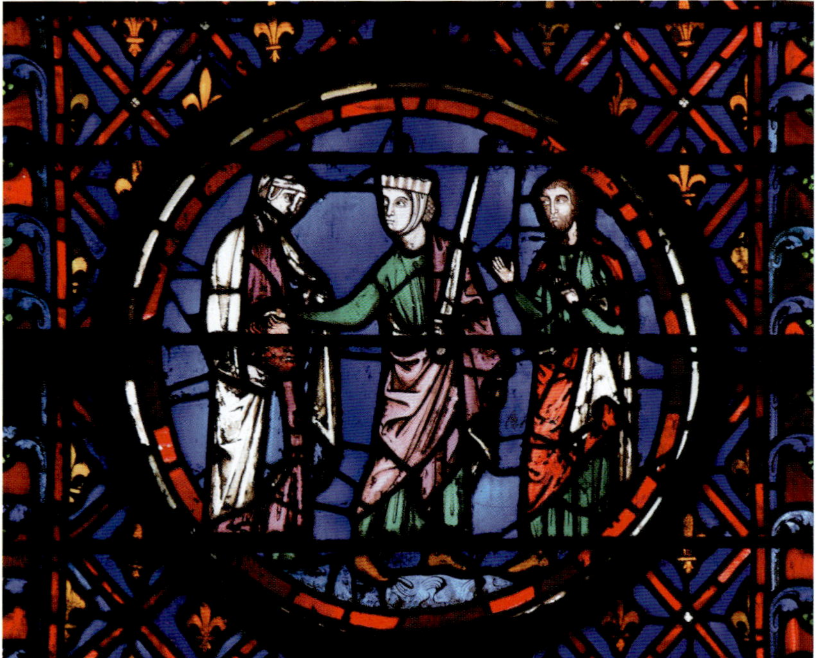

46 Sainte-Chapelle, Judith, Holofernes' army crosses
the Euphrates, now at the Philadelphia Museum of Art.

47 Sainte-Chapelle, Judith reveals the severed head of Holofernes (D-114).

music and offering gifts in a vain effort to appease the invader. Judith speaks to the elders and asks to intervene. On the sixth level, she prays to God for the power to conquer Holofernes. This panel keeps its French inscription: *ci prie ivdid dev qve le puist eninier* (Here Judith prays to God so that she can overcome). Judith then bathes and dresses elegantly. Out of place in the window is Judith meeting Holofernes with its inscription: *Ci est venve ivdid a oloferne ei si saciunte a li* (Here Judith comes to Holofernes and greets him). Judith then kills Holofernes in his bed. The following panel shows Judith taking the head from her maid to show it to her people (illus. 47). On the tenth level, Judith is honoured and at her death the people mourn, explained by the inscription *ci plevre la mort* (Here they mourn her death).

The well-preserved Philadelphia panel, removed from the chapel before 1803 and thus sheltered from urban pollution and misguided cleaning, enables us to see the glass painting in its pristine condition (see illus. 46). The subtle gradation of shading in the folds of the garments, bodies of the horses and faces evokes three-dimensionality. Volumetric depiction is reinforced by the dynamics of the composition. A phalange of men surges to the right. On the left, a man approaches, seen from behind, and one of the soldiers turns to address him. The calvary is depicted by just four horses, seen in repetitive profile. Only forelegs are visible, except for the horse ridden by the rider on the left, who holds a red banner.

An Honourable Woman: Esther

The appeal of the story of Esther extended across time, as demonstrated by the sixteenth-century Low Country prints and stained glass on the theme discussed in Chapter Eight. Queen Vashti had been deposed because she refused King Ahasuerus' request to appear before his courtiers at a banquet. Searching for a new queen, Ahasuerus selects Esther, a Jewish orphan raised by her cousin Mordechai. Esther does not reveal that she is Jewish but remains in close contact with her cousin. Mordechai overhears a plot by the courtiers Bigthan and Teresh to assassinate the king. Esther conveys this information to Ahasuerus; the plot is foiled and the conspirators hanged. Ahasuerus soon elevates the courtier Haman to the highest position and Haman demands that all bow down to him. Mordechai, as a devout Jew, refuses, inspiring Haman to plan the extermination of all Jews in the kingdom (Esther 3). Mordechai intercedes with Esther, who counsels that the Jews should pray and fast for three days. On the third day, she dares to enter the presence of the king unbidden, an offence

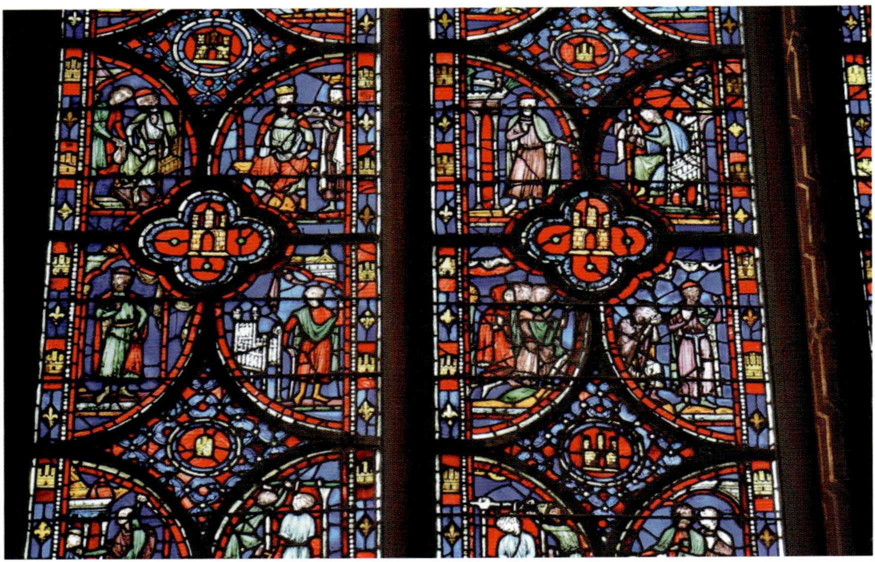

48 Sainte-Chapelle, Esther: Punishment of Conspirators and elevation of Haman to authority (D-168-171; D-156-159; D-144-147).

punishable by death. Ahasuerus, however, reaches out and touches her with his sceptre, indicating that she is exempt. She then requests that he and Haman come to a banquet that she will host. In the meantime, Haman had prepared gallows to hang Mordechai. That evening the king could not sleep and ordered that the records of his kingdom be read to him, a process that revealed how Mordechai had thwarted the plot to assassinate the king, but no reward had been extended to him. At the same time, Haman was in the courtyard and Ahasuerus asked him what should be done to a man that the king wished to honour. Haman assumed that the king was speaking about him and replied that the man should be clothed in royal robes, mounted on a horse that the king had ridden and led through the city. Ahasuerus then ordered that this be done for Mordechai. Haman and Ahasuerus then both attend the banquet prepared by Esther, where she reveals that she is Jewish, and that she knows that Haman is plotting her death and that of all her people. Enraged, and shocked by Haman's effort to petition Esther, Ahasuerus orders that he be hanged on the gallows he had prepared for Mordechai. The enemies of the Jews that Haman had united become subject to the king's wrath and are destroyed.

A well-preserved section of the window, the fourth through to the sixth levels to the left, allows us to understand its narrative strategies (illus. 48). On the lowest level we see the conspirators Bigthan and Teresh cast into prison. On the right, the two facing medallions show them hanged on gallows. These two medallions used the same cartoon (underlying drawing) but one is reversed. To the extreme right we see two officials watching the hanging. To the left a (modern) medallion shows Haman standing and looking across to his throne, which is guarded by a servant. The two following medallions form a single episode, Haman, on the far right, being honoured by a crowd of kneeling men. The reason for Mordechai's refusal to kneel becomes obvious. Above, facing a modern panel on the left, we see Ahasuerus giving his signet ring to Haman. To the right we see another classic depiction of authority. Haman stands beside the architecture of what might be the entrance to a palace while, on the right, a seated scribe writes down his orders. These kinds of scenes are then repeated in the upper parts of the window. The hanging of the two conspirators thus finds its parallel in the execution of Haman.

Crown of Thorns: Local Headlines

The final window honours the relics of the Crown of Thorns and its presence in the chapel. Although the major part of the window is modern, enough scenes remain of a distinctive iconography to identify the subject. One shows a prelate, presumably Gauthier Cornut, Archbishop of Sens, standing behind a balustrade and holding the relic, clearly distinguishable as a green circle. He is flanked by Louis and Blanche. Additional scenes show the transportation of relics, like the image of Philip IV carrying the Relics of St Louis from the *Hours of Jeanne d'Evreux* (see illus. 41).

Typical for the programme, references to the past accompany these scenes from contemporary history. The story of the Passion relics, in particular that of the True Cross, was elaborated by Louis' time; its codification, however, came as part of Jacobus de Voragine's *Golden Legend*, compiled around 1259–66. The emperor Constantine built the Church of the Holy Sepulchre in Jerusalem about 326. Tradition ascribes the discovery of the True Cross to the emperor's mother Helena. Medieval writers believed that Helena had divided the wood of the True Cross, leaving the largest portion in the Church of the Holy Sepulchre in Jerusalem, but distributing small sections to Rome and Constantinople. Accounts by Egeria, an Iberian pilgrim visiting Jerusalem between 381 and 384, describe the display and veneration of the Cross. In 614 the Persian emperor Chosroes captured Jerusalem and carried off the Cross and other relics. The Byzantine emperor Heraclius subsequently defeated the Persians and returned the relic to Jerusalem in 630. With the Muslim conquest of Jerusalem in 637, the Cross was transferred to Constantinople. In a lower level of the window, we see

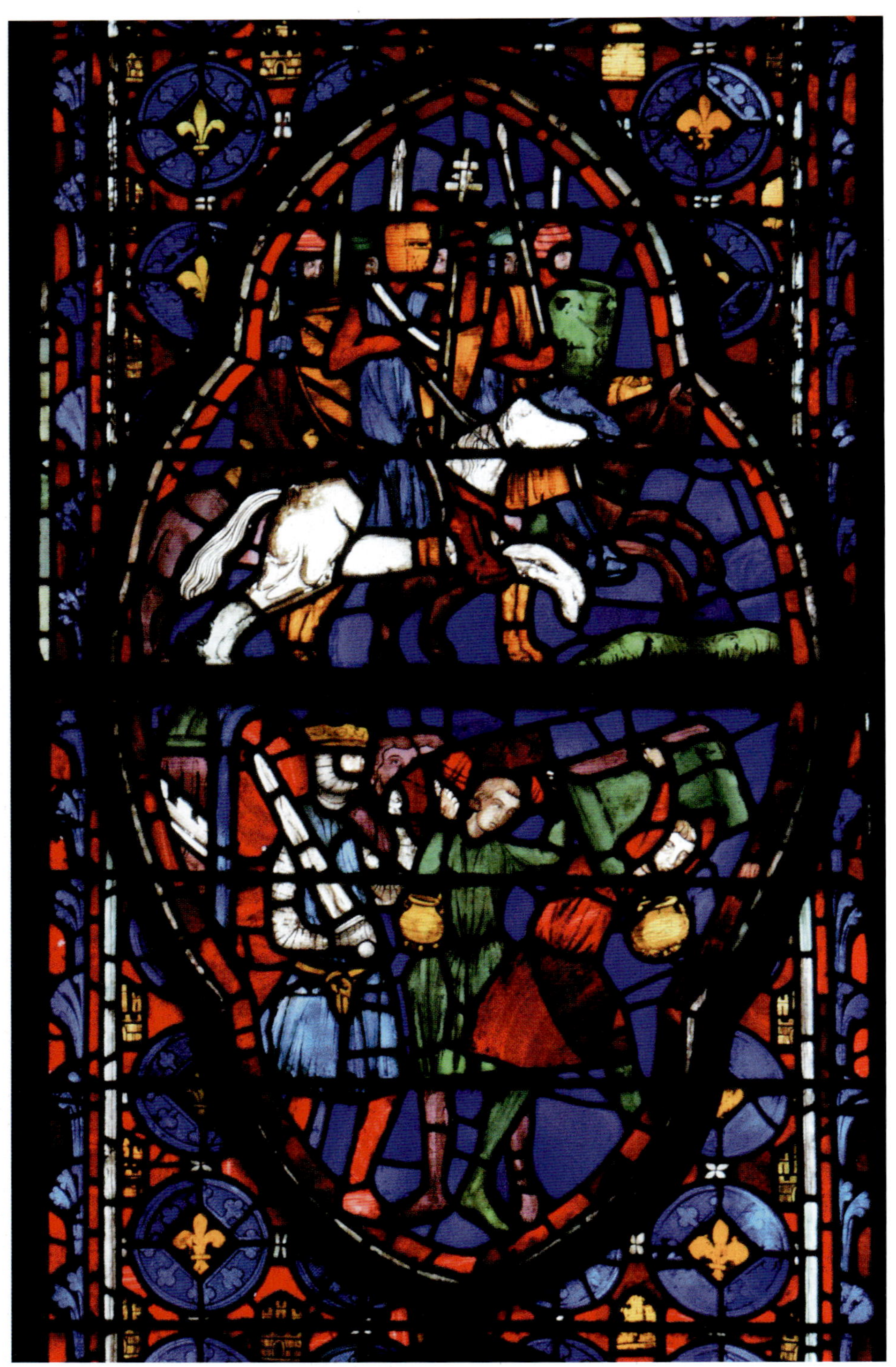

49 Sainte-Chapelle, relics: above, mounted warriors (A-125)
upper half restored, and below, booty carried off (A-129).

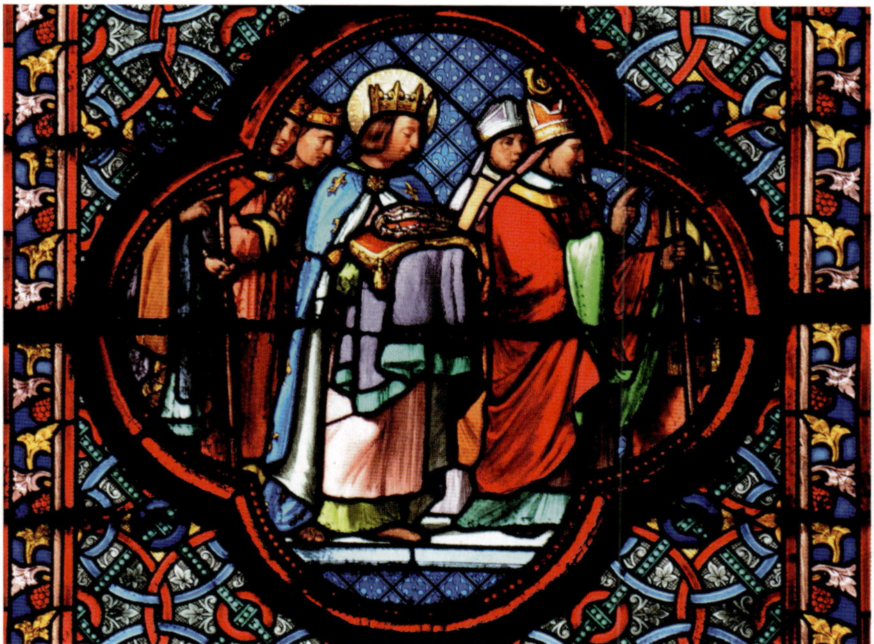

50 Sainte-Clotilde, Paris, apsidal chapel of St Louis, St Louis carries the Crown of Thorns, 1860s, Nicolas-Auguste Hesse, designer; Laurent and Gsell, fabricators.

scenes of conflict consonant with illustrations of both Chosroes' invasion and Heraclius' rescue. One scene shows booty; a warrior directs servants who carry trunks on their backs and golden vessels in their hands (illus. 49).

Indeed, it was this manifestation of St Louis, the means though which the relic of the Crown of Thorns reached France, that became the most identifiable image for the king. His iconography invariably included a blue robe strewn with yellow fleur-de-lis and the Crown of Thorns in his hands. The portrait was replicated in manuscript, wall painting and stained glass. Sainte-Clotilde's construction from 1846 to 1857, the first Parisian church built entirely in the neo-Gothic style, paralleled the restoration of the Sainte-Chapelle. One of its apsidal chapels was dedicated to St Louis; a quatrefoil medallion in its cycle of imagery shows the king carrying the Crown of Thorns on a cushion (illus. 50).

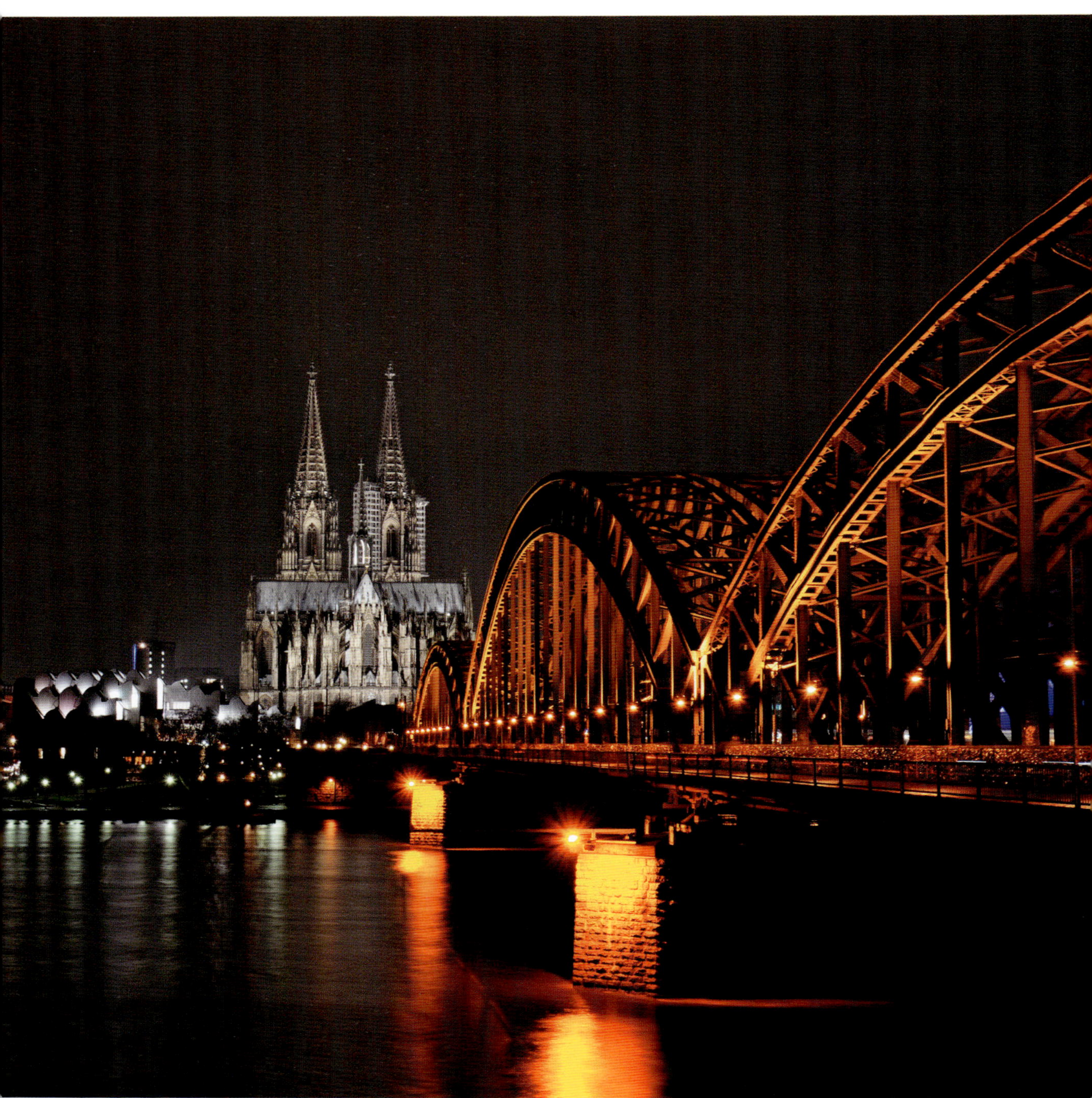

51 Cologne Cathedral seen at night from the Hohenzollern Bridge, 2012.

4

Cologne Cathedral:
A Building over Time

—

Cologne is one of Europe's great cities, in 1996 designated a World Heritage site, in recognition of a complex history reaching back more than 2,000 years (illus. 51 and 52). Strategically located on the Rhine, it was a vital point for Germanic tribes, conquering Romans, medieval emperors, Renaissance merchants and the German unification movement of the nineteenth century. The city was founded in 38 BCE by a Germanic tribe named the Ubi. By 50 CE the Roman Empire had reached the north and the city was known as Colonia Agrippina. In 310, the emperor Constantine built a bridge over the Rhine at Cologne, the first of many subsequent constructions, and by the mid-fourth century Christian buildings are documented. Considerable Roman vestiges remain in the city. The cathedral as it stands today is a Gothic edifice begun in 1248 as a replacement for Cologne's ninth-century version. Its windows can be dated to four great campaigns: medieval, Renaissance, historical revival (*Historismus*) and contemporary. Renaissance painters who created great altar-pieces in Cologne's churches also designed windows in the cathedral. At each point in its history, the cathedral engaged leading artists of international renown.

Medieval Cologne

By the end of the thirteenth century, the Archbishop of Cologne had become one of the seven electors of the Holy Roman Emperor. Cologne's great reliquary of the Three Magi stands as an exemplar of the relationship between cathedral, city and empire. After the defeat of Milan by the Holy Roman emperor Frederick Barbarossa, the relics of the Magi were transferred from Milan to Cologne by

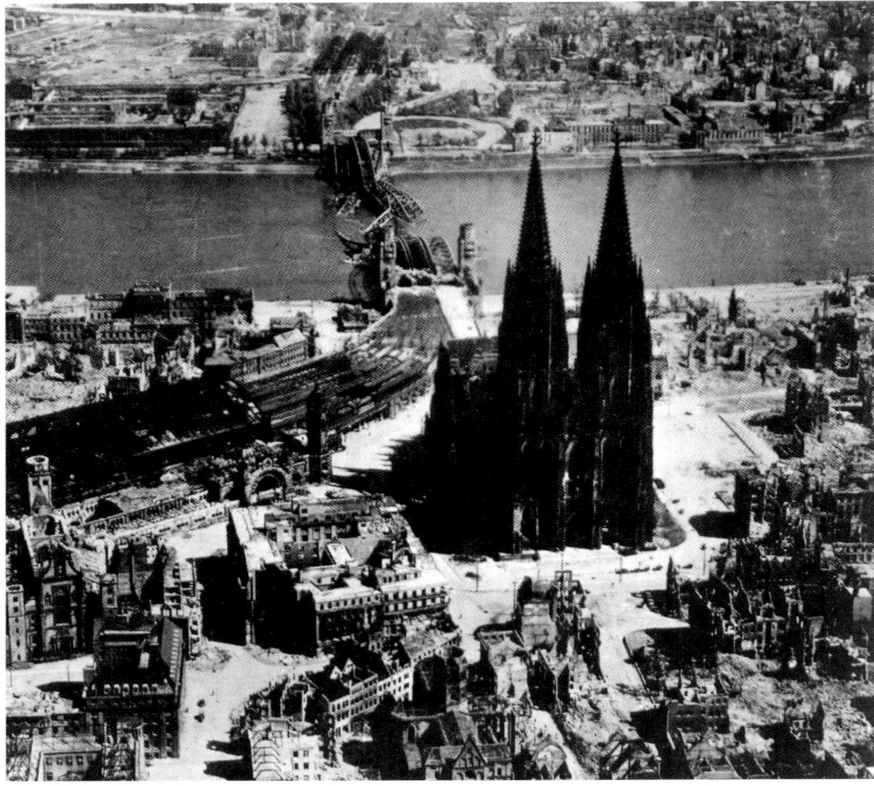

52 Bomb damage to Cologne, 14 March 1945.

Archbishop Reinhold von Dassel in 1164. The coat of arms of Cologne displays three crowns in honour of the relics. A shrine was commissioned in 1181 from the most distinguished metalworker of his time, Nicholas of Verdun, who had just completed the renowned pulpit (now altar) for the monastery of Klosterneuburg outside Vienna. The largest and most luxurious of surviving medieval reliquaries, the shrine is revered today. Set amid the towering majesty of the cathedral, the golden construction radiates a sense of power. The often-cited medieval principle of the relationship between microcosm and macrocosm is revealed as the immense building with its soaring vaulting and glittering windows weighs against the small house with its gables and arches of enamel, gold and precious stones. Both structures are populated with imagery. The kings parade in long rows in the window openings that encircle the choir. Apostles, kings and prophets appear beneath the curved arches that surround the sides of the shrine. In the Middle Ages, the small-scale object could be as significant as the monumental work; unlike our modern era, there was then no qualitative division among categories of painting, book illustration or the decorative arts.

A cathedral is the seat of a bishop, the central authority for all churches within his diocese. The clergy who inhabited the cathedral were not monks. Rather, they were connected only to their own establishment and, although celibate, had a high degree of interaction with their communities. Frequently from powerful families of the region, these clerics were highly educated and keenly aware of issues of art and architecture. They built in the new Gothic style, tapping into the economic development of the thirteenth century. The only completely new style since antiquity, the Gothic developed with stained glass as a necessary construction element. The high visibility attracted distinguished donors, as at Chartres, who are identified by their heraldic shields. Although the clergy still claimed its own space in cathedral choirs, the church building was a corporate structure, with a diverse population, and highly public. The cathedral's glazing responds to two equally important criteria, to bring the maximum amount of light into the interior and to elaborate a programme of imagery connected to ideals of its heritage, protecting saints and its power. The developing trend in glazing practices in England and France as well as Germany towards a combination of grisaille and figural glass was ideally suited to these needs.

Choir Windows, 1260–1320

We know that the original architect of the cathedral, referred to as master Gerhard, who probably died around 1260, was followed by master Arnold. The axial chapel was assuredly completed by 1260 with a figural window on a typological theme in the centre flanked by non-figural grisaille. We have already noted the deep interest in typology in Canterbury's glass, setting images of the Gospel story against prototypes from the Old Testament. The original grisaille windows have been lost in renovations over time, but the typological window remains in place (illus. 53). The upper levels followed almost half a century later with a series of 48 figures of kings under grisaille strapwork. They hold court in a soaring space under vaulting reaching 43.4 metres (142 ft). The axial window displays the *Adoration of the Three Kings* below a tall lancet populated with bust-length figures of kings and prophets reminiscent of a Tree of Jesse. To either side, the kings proceed in a dignified row, alternating youthful and mature figures and red and blue backgrounds. Above the kings, pot-metal banding enhances the design of the grisaille, which is carried through leadline alone. Below their feet are the shields of the donors, whose coats of arms identify them as from noble families from the Rhineland and from families of Cologne patricians.

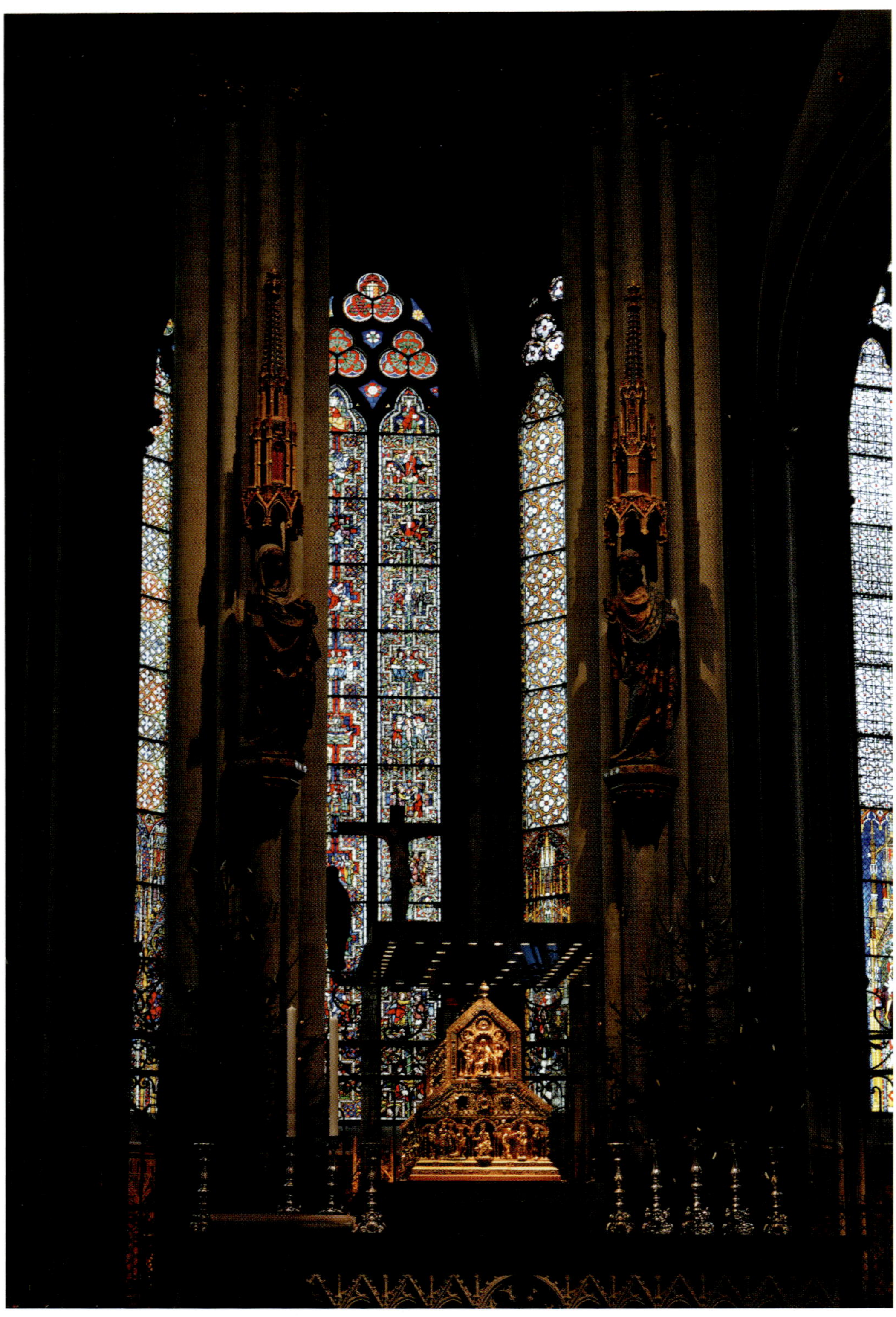

53 Cologne axial chapel and typological window, 1260,
with the shrine of the Three Magi, 1180–1225.

Most of the glass in the surrounding chapels was completed as the campaign was ending for the upper choir. New figural glass honouring saints with special ties to the archdiocese was substituted for the grisaille in the lower windows. The figures occupy the lowest two levels, their architectural canopies the next two and grisailles the remaining space. Dense pot-metal colours, such as red-and-green chequerboard backgrounds, intensify the visual dynamic. Two sainted bishops, St Severin and St Anno (illus. 54), in the St Agnes Chapel immediately to the south of the axial chapel stand as exemplars. Severin was revered as the third bishop of Cologne and was believed to have founded the city's church now known as St Severin. Anno was a prominent player in imperial and papal politics in the eleventh century. The window's background is a dense vertical and horizontal pattern of blue and red. The vestments of both bishops are similarly two-dimensional, Severin in a green, yellow and red grill pattern and Anno in alternating quatrefoils of gold and blue. They are both framed by brilliantly designed architectural niches inspired by the Gothic stonework of the time. Undulating leaves march in procession along the pointed arch and

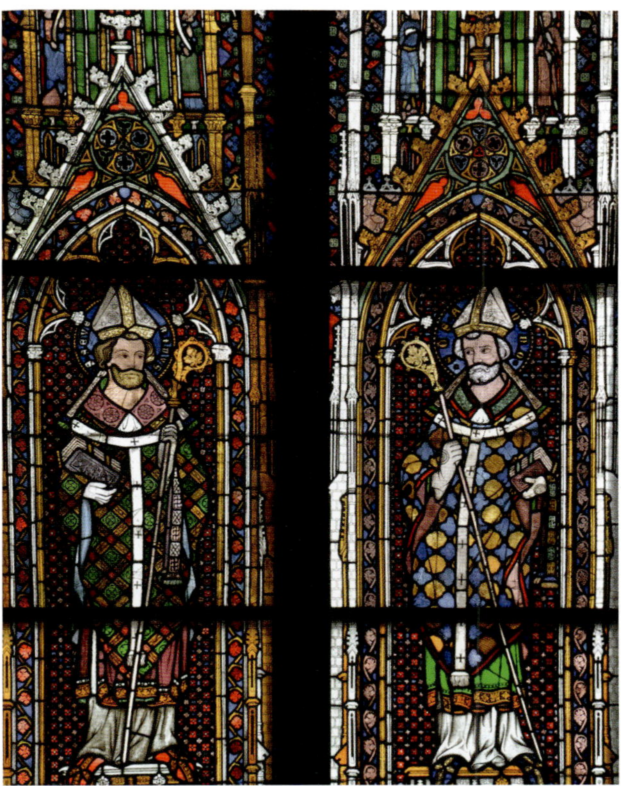

54 Sainted bishops of Cologne: *Severin and Anno*,
1315–20, Chapel of St Agnes, s.iv.

frame a rose window of six openings. Slender columns at the side continue above with a burst of additional tall narrow shafts.

Comprising 104 seats, the cathedral's choir stalls were installed at the time that the glazing was completed. Only slightly later, between 1332 and 1340, the choir screens to the north and south were adorned with a cycle of pictures. On the north we find stories of St Peter, Pope Sylvester and the emperor Constantine. On the south, are the Life of the Virgin, the story of the Three Magi and the legends of saints Felix and Nabor, whose relics were also preserved in the Shrine of the Magi. In a gesture like that of the glazing programme above, the lower level adds a row of archbishops of Cologne on the north who face on the south a complementary row of Roman and German emperors. As in the Sainte-Chapelle in Paris, a century earlier, the cathedral visualizes its fusion of both the secular and the sacred. The archbishops of Cologne, who served as electors of the Holy Roman emperors, were deeply involved in questions of state as well as religion. Taken as a whole, the choir's ensemble of sculpture, seating, wall painting and glass is among the most intact in Europe.

Renaissance Windows of the North Nave

The subsequent glazing campaign dates to the early sixteenth century when the north nave aisle of the cathedral was given windows associated with two important panel painters known as the Master of the Holy Kinship and the Master of St Severin (illus. 55). Highly prized for their brilliance, the five windows were described a century later by a chronicler of Cologne, Aegidius Gelenius, as 'greatly celebrated marvels'. The windows demonstrate the commitment of Cologne's archbishops to the building campaigns and their understanding of quality workmanship. Philipp von Daun, archbishop in 1508, appears twice, first, in the *Passion* window, attired as deacon and in the *Life of St Peter/Tree of Jesse* window as archbishop being presented by St Peter, who wears the papal tiara (illus. 56). St Sebastian, depicted as a handsome young man with flowing locks and dressed in Renaissance armour, appears on the right. Sixteen donor coats of arms surround the figures in a lively display of shields and crests consisting of helms surrounded by foliate design called 'mantling' in colours that match the shields. Above, we see, on the left, a series of episodes from the life of Peter, the first pope, culminating with his crucifixion upside down on the lower tier. The right side presents a single scene, the recumbent patriarch Jesse with a vine sprouting from his body. Bust-length figures of prophets and kings appear in the branches.

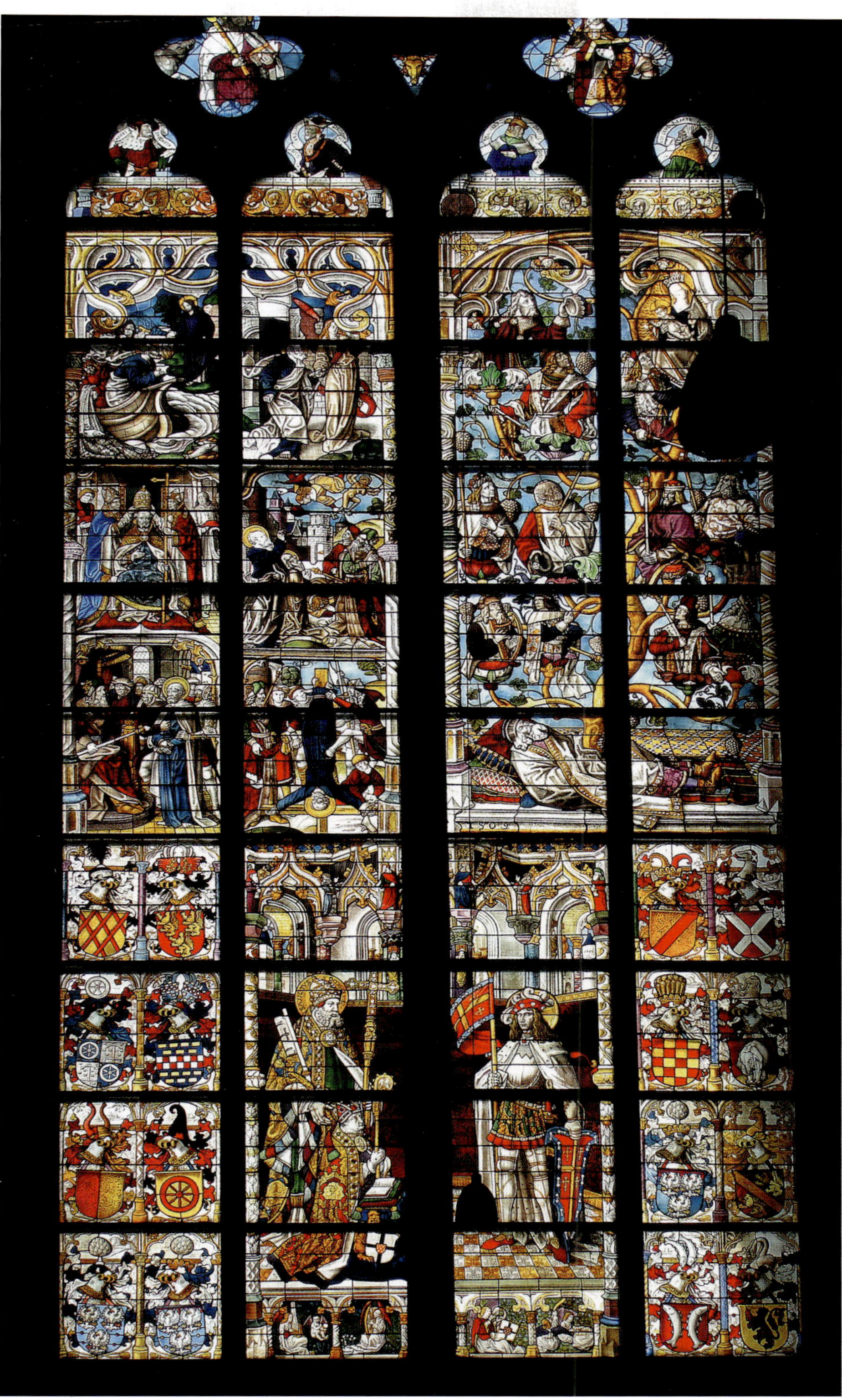

55 Master of St Severin and Hermann Pentelynck (?),
Life of St Peter and Tree of Jesse, 1509, inscribed on window, n.XXII.

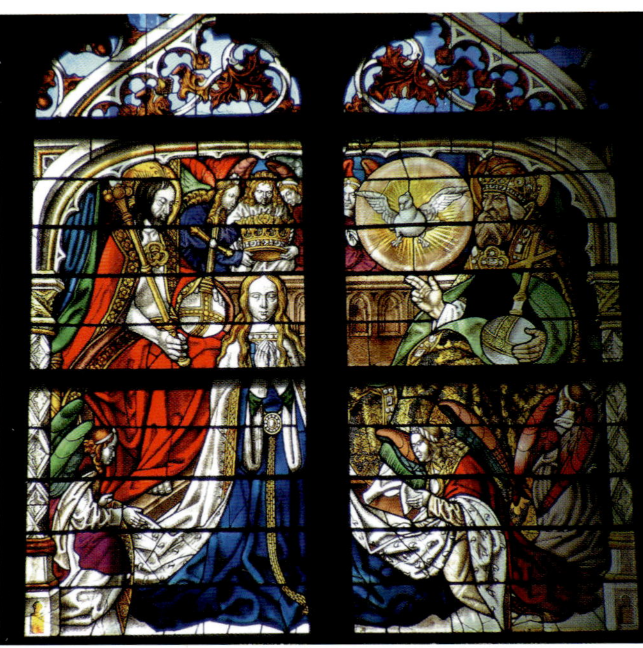

56 Master of St Severin and Hermann Pentelynck (?),
Coronation of the Virgin, 1509, n.xxv.

The later Middle Ages and Renaissance saw a resurgence of interest in twelfth-century themes such as typology and the lineage of Christ through the Tree of Jesse that are discussed in the chapters on Canterbury Cathedral and Fairford's parish church, the latter dating to the same era as Cologne's north aisle. In the *Three Kings* window, the Adoration of the Magi is preceded by the visit of the Queen of Sheba to Solomon. Cologne's *Typological/Nativity* window juxtaposes Moses and the Burning Bush with the Adoration of the Shepherds at the Birth of Christ. The theme honours the miraculous virginity of Mary, which burned, as did the bush from which God spoke to Moses, but was not consumed. Martial saints associated with the cathedral appear in the level below, just above the donors' arms. St George has his slain dragon at his feet. The other three were part of the renowned Theban Legion assembled by the emperor Maximian. Gregorius Maurus and Gereon served under its commander, Maurice. The legion subsequently converted to Christianity and refused to worship Rome's gods. They were massacred in Switzerland at a site now called St Maurice. At the time, Maurice and Gregorius Maurus were often shown as African to identify their origins in Egypt, but here all four saints are given long, fair hair. Gereon shares with St Ursula patronage of the city, seen in Stefan Lochner's great altarpiece painted for the cathedral in the 1440s.

The Master of the Holy Kinship, whose name piece, the *Holy Kinship*, dated about 1500–1503, is housed in Cologne's Wallraf-Richartz-Museum, designed the *Typological/Nativity* window and the *Three Kings* window. The Master of St Severin designed the *Passion*, the *Life of St Peter/Tree of Jesse*, and the *Coronation of the Virgin* (see illus. 55). This artist takes his name from the cycle of twenty pictures showing the legend of St Severin in the Basilica of St Severin in Cologne. The paintings depict episodes in the bishop's life, such as his preaching to a crowd, seated at an elaborate dinner or on his deathbed surrounded by the praying clergy, all with meticulous depiction of landscape and architectural setting that also characterize the stained glass from the monastery of Altenberg, long attributed to the Master's influence. Dated 1505–20, Altenberg's windows are now dispersed at sites that include the Victoria and Albert Museum, London, the Schnütgen Museum, Cologne, and the church of St Mary the Virgin, Shropshire. The Master's painting of the *Adoration of the Magi* (illus. 57) enables us to appreciate his linking of monumental three-dimensionality in the figures with the rich colour and surface embellishment of medieval painting. The eldest Magus, kneeling before the Christ child, wears

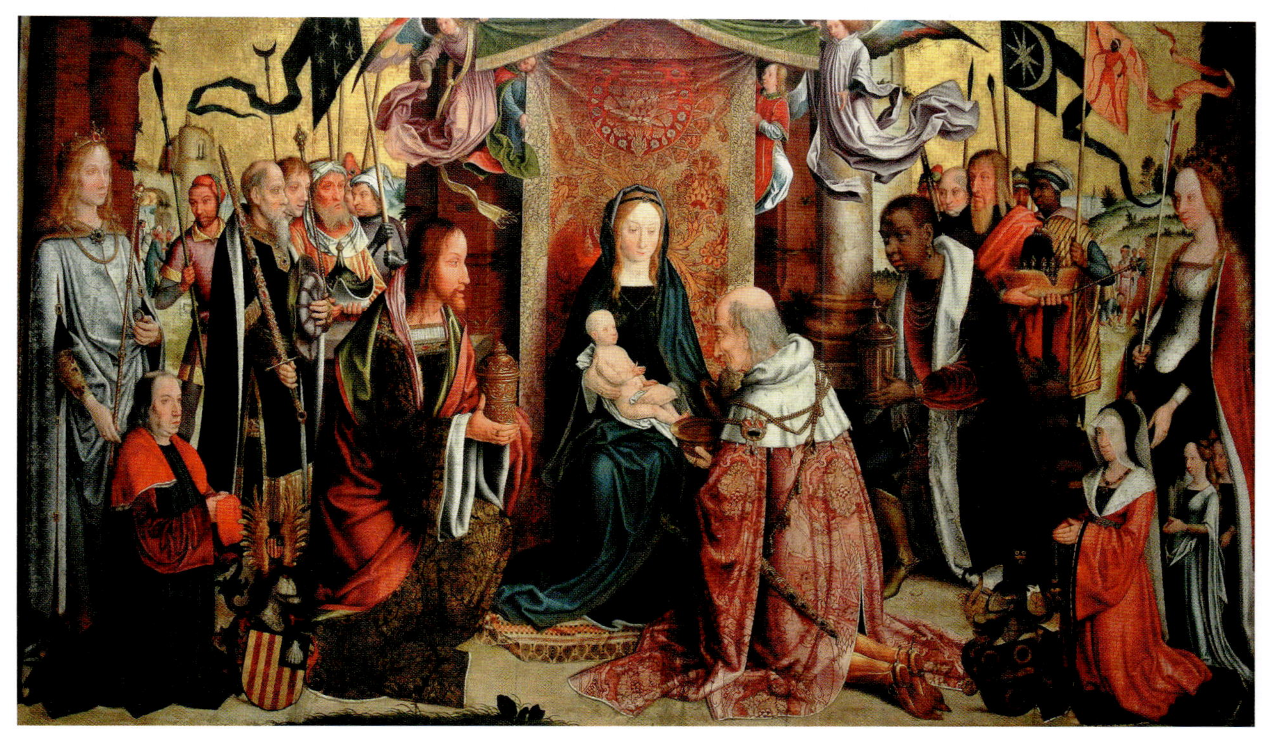

57 Master of St Severin, *Adoration of the Magi*, c. 1505, now at the Wallraf-Richartz-Museum, Cologne.

a rose mantle with a decoration of exuberant foliage and flowers. The cloth of honour behind the Virgin and other textiles show a similar richness and may be compared to the cope worn by Archbishop Philipp von Daun being presented by St Peter (illus. 58) from the *Life of St Peter/Tree of Jesse* window and the robes of God the Father in the *Coronation of the Virgin*. The altarpiece shows the same ability to incorporate donors, their arms and their patron saints as seen throughout the Cologne windows. It is highly probably that we can identify the name of the glass painter who executed the five windows on the north side aisle, Hermann Pentelynck. He preserved the architectural motifs that allow the windows to be integrated within the three-dimensional architecture

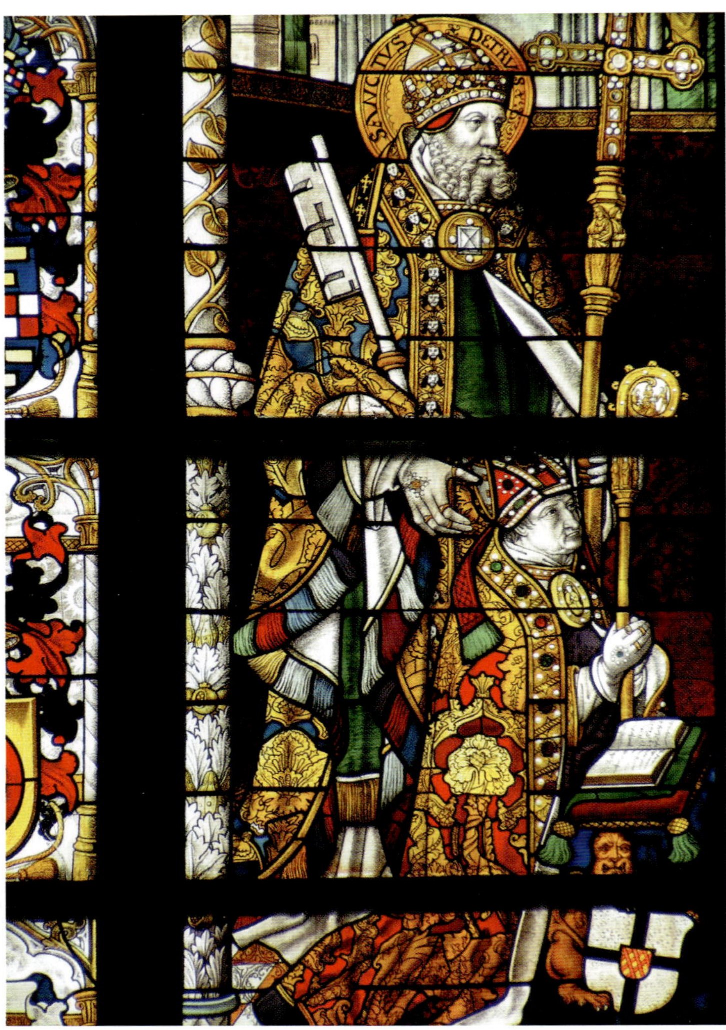

58 Master of St Severin and Hermann Pentelynck (?), *Archbishop Philipp von Daun Presented by St Peter*, 1509, n.xxii.

of the building. The painter preferred a granular, rather than a smooth, wash to define features. Silver stain, as well as yellow glass, plays an important part in the golden tonality of the windows.

Before we turn to the glass of the nineteenth and twenty-first centuries, we should take a moment to recognize the importance of this monument for its capacity to incorporate windows from now disused places. The challenge of preserving, and exhibiting, works of art from the past is formidable. We are grateful that the cathedral has been able to display glass that was transferred due to the secularization of monastic property between 1795 and 1814. In a significant restructuring of society, almost all the monasteries were closed and their lands redistributed. A Christological cycle dating to the 1470s from the female convent of St Cecilia in Cologne was installed in the Sacraments Chapel of the cathedral. The workshop responsible for these panels achieved the distinction of being named the St Cecilia workshop. These beautifully executed works, almost more like drawings, emphasize the subtle draughtsmanship of the era. Duplicates and triplicates of St Cecilia's cloister panels have migrated to British and American collections. Windows from Cistercian foundations, such as the monastery of St Apern's life of Bernard, are installed in the north transept.

Nineteenth-Century Revival of the Past

The cathedral's glazing continued in the nineteenth century when the nave and facade were finally completed. Although the choir had been finished in 1322 and the north nave in 1510, the facade was a truncated stump and the south nave, transept, towers and chapels had been left unfinished. Rebuilding began in 1823 and the cathedral's dedication took place in 1880. Governmental policy supported both the Church and the arts it employed, notably stained glass. Bavaria played a leading role as King Ludwig I (1786–1868) encouraged a revival of crafts, including mural painting and glass painting. He commissioned artists and funded research into glazing techniques. We must recognize that, as in England, the interest in the revival of stained glass had been awakened by collectors interested in old windows. Sulpiz Boisserée (1783–1854) and his brother Melchior (1786–1851) were major influences in the German Romantic movement, combining a love of beautiful objects with a deep Catholic faith and a conviction that great art would transform its beholder for the better. Visiting Paris in 1803, they were mesmerized by the collections amassed by Napoleon from conquered territories. They then began to form their own collection of medieval works, which they published with lithograph illustrations in 1823. Edmund Lévy, a Belgian historian and critic, comments that artists were invited to come to the Boisserée gallery to study the works. Study, in nineteenth-century terms, invariably involved the copying of a work. For example, the central part of Boisserée's *St Columba Altar* of 1455, by Rogier van der Weyden (Alte Pinakothek, Munich), showing the *Annunciation, Adoration of the Three Kings* and *Presentation in the Temple*, was reproduced in stained glass. In 1827 the Boisserée collection of more than two hundred paintings by German and Low Countries artists was sold to King Ludwig to form the core of his museum in Munich, opened in 1836 and later known as the Alte Pinakothek. This determination to honour the Germanic past supported the effort to complete the cathedral, championed most prominently by the Boisserée brothers, the scholar/journalist Joseph Görres (1776–1848) and the lawyer/politician August Reichensperger (1808–1895).

The development of the Bavarian/Rhenish style of glass painting was a part of contemporaneous trends in painting, expressive of new ideas of religious purpose and nationalism. The Romantic movement of the early years of the nineteenth century was deeply motivated by a renewed sense of the greatness of Germany historically and a sense of collective purpose. Johann Wolfgang Goethe's 1772 essay *Von deutscher Baukunst* (On German Architecture) was an early manifestation of a desire to see a national ethnic character in 'Germanic' art of the medieval world. In Nuremberg, in 1828, the ceremony for the laying of the founding stone celebrating the 300th anniversary of the death of Albrecht Dürer (1471–1528), attended by representatives from all German-speaking territories, took on the character of a national revival. As enunciated in Goethe's essay, art of the fourteenth to the early sixteenth century was seen as medieval. Therefore, Dürer and his contemporaries were characterized as the last great flowering of the Middle Ages. Ludwig of Bavaria's vigorous championing of the liturgical arts supported the designation of the Middle Ages as the high point of German artistic, religious and political power.

Nazarene Movement in Art

This view of the importance of art of the fifteenth and sixteenth centuries animated the Nazarene school of painting, without question the most significant influence for German nineteenth-century glass. Johann Friedrich Overbeck (1789–1869) set the movement's initial philosophy by founding the Brotherhood of St Luke and moving with followers into a secularized monastery on the outskirts of Rome in 1810. The Nazarenes produced images melding Catholic

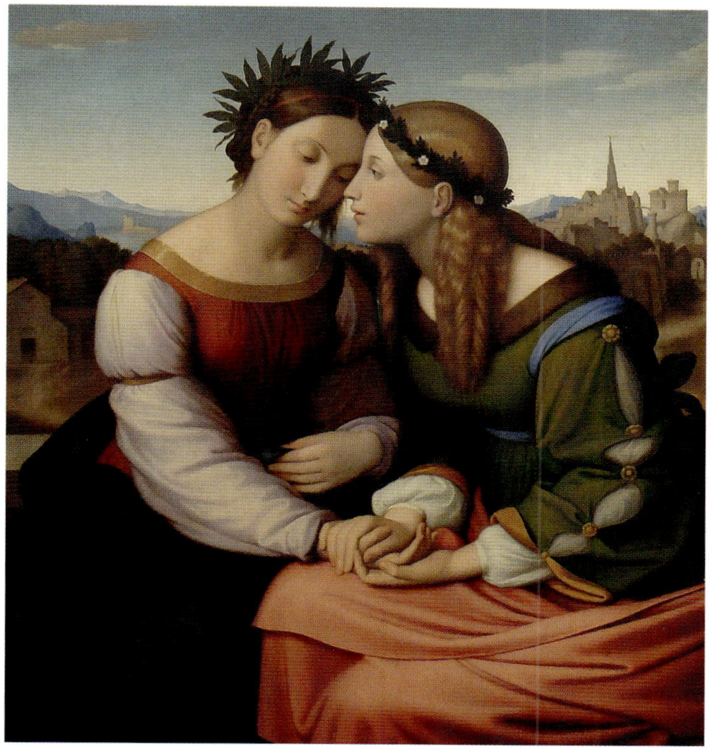

59 Johann Friedrich Overbeck, *Italia et Germania*, 1828, Neue Pinakothek, Munich.

religious sentiment with a Raphaelesque air of idealism and sweetness; they favoured glowing colours, Renaissance figural types and smoothly polished surfaces. The images thus fused the deeply felt religious sentiment of the north with the idealized Renaissance forms of the south. These qualities are vividly displayed in Overbeck's *Italia et Germania* of 1828 (illus. 59). Above all, the Nazarenes were imbued with the concept of moral teaching as the essential purpose of art. Heinrich Hess (1789–1863), who would later become prominent in the design of frescos and glass painting, was part of the first generation of artists grouped around Overbeck. Hess became the artistic manager of the Königliche Glasmalereianstalt (Royal Bavarian Manufactory) founded by Ludwig in Munich in 1827, the same year that he purchased the Boisserées' collection.

That the Nazarene painting style was able to be translated onto glass was facilitated by the technical experiments of Michael Sigmund Frank (1770–1847). In 1818, as a young prince, Ludwig secured Frank's appointment as painter for the royal porcelain establishments in Munich. Experiments were also carried out by the well-established Nymphenburger Porzellanmanufaktur in the north of the city. A generation later, a window such as the *Martyrdom of Stephen* (illus. 60)

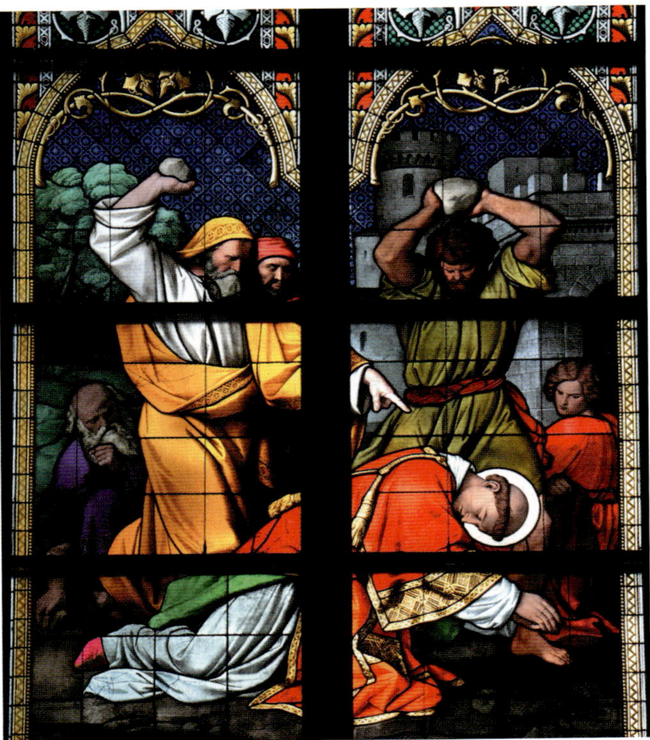

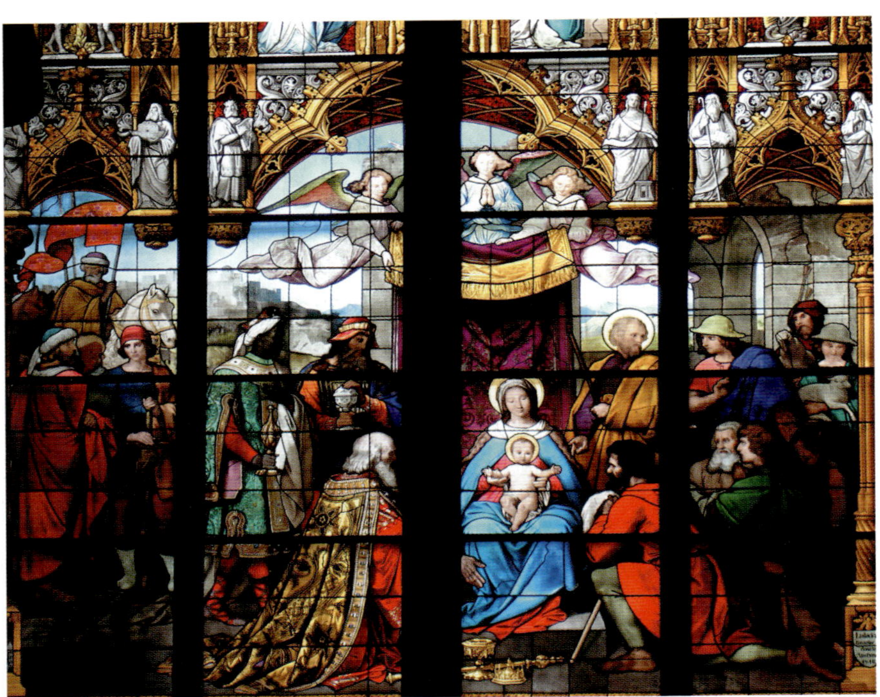

60 Königliche Glasmalereianstalt, Munich,
Martyrdom of St Stephen, 1844–8, south aisle.

61 Königliche Glasmalereianstalt, Munich,
Adoration of the Magi, 1844–8, south aisle.

could demonstrate the same fluidity of idealized forms, jewel-like colours and monumental narrative as Overbeck's oil paintings. Clearly challenged by the early sixteenth-century windows in the north aisle of the nave, the windows on the south installed by the Königliche Glasmalereianstalt, from 1844 to 1848, strove for impressive quality. The compositions of the south aisle windows followed sixteenth-century formats where a single scene could stretch across the mullion divisions of a window. As testimonials of Bavarian royal largesse, the windows exemplify the early brilliance of what later became known as the 'Munich' style in glass. The *Adoration of the Magi* (illus. 61) reiterates the cathedral's theme of patronage. Like its companion the *Pentecost* window, it displays a complex figural composition stretching over all four lancets of the window. A lavish, three-dimensional canopy above supports images of Mary and Gabriel from the Annunciation. In the base, the four great prophets, Isaiah, Jeremiah, Ezekiel and Daniel (the same group found in the south transept of Chartres), are framed as if they are statues in shallow niches. The silhouetting of the figure against damascene ground and the subtle balance of colour increases the visibility of the volumetric painting.

Defenders of the Faith, Past and Present

One of the most cherished windows, set in the south transept in 1856, honours Joseph Görres with an inscription naming him 'noble defender of the Catholic faith in Germany'. Görres developed an influential career as a teacher, historian and journalist. Profound changes had accompanied Napoleon's invasion of Germany, abruptly severing support for religious foundations after what had been a general decline in the viability of monasteries. Church was separated from state and many religious establishments, without sources of income, were abandoned. In 1814, after the defeat of Napoleon, Görres championed national independence for Germany, and founded the newspaper *Der rheinische Merkur* with a strong advocacy for Catholic renewal. The two-lancet window shows Görres in typical medieval format, kneeling before the Virgin and Child while St Joseph, his patron saint, stands behind him (illus. 62). The composition repeats that of many of the earlier windows, in particular Philipp von Daun presented by St Peter in the north nave.

Below Görres are the great medieval defenders of the faith, St Boniface and the emperor Charlemagne, whose Latin inscriptions name them: Apostle of the Germans and Emperor of the Germans (illus. 63). St Boniface, an English monk, had founded schools and monasteries and was named Archbishop of Mainz

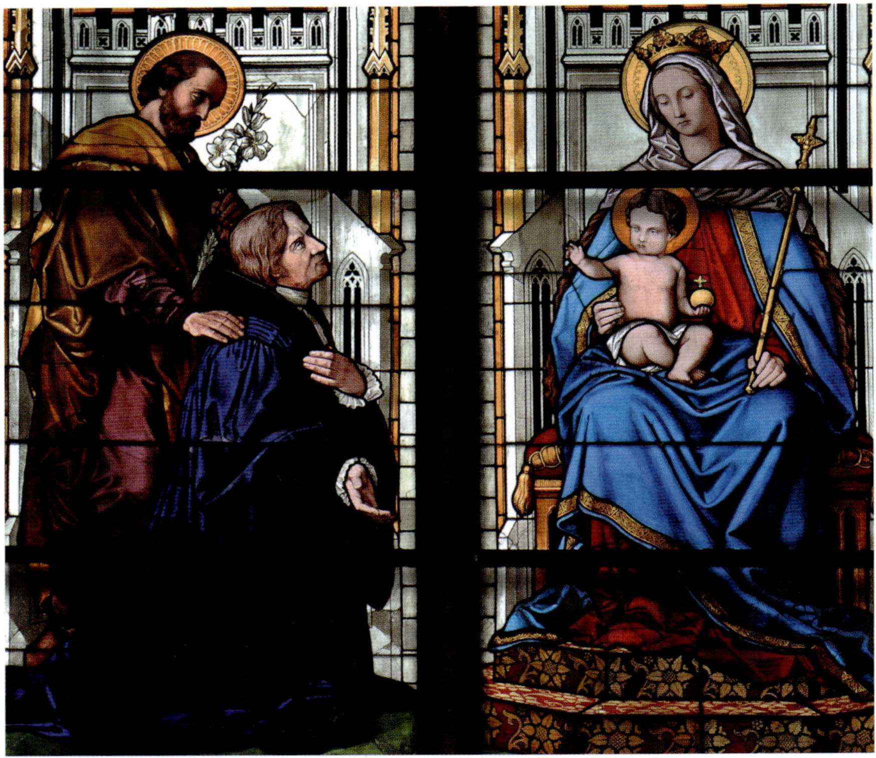

62 Königliche Glasmalereianstalt, Munich, *Joseph Görres Presented to the Virgin and Child by St Joseph*, 1856, south transept.

in 745(?). He is often shown with a fallen oak tree, a reference to his encounter with Druids and confutation of pagan beliefs. The emperor Charlemagne is 'famous in legend and song'. After the long instability following the collapse of the Roman Empire, Charlemagne managed to unify a territory that encompassed roughly what is now France, Belgium, the Netherlands, Germany, Switzerland and northern Italy. On Christmas day, in the year 800, he was crowned Holy Roman Emperor by Pope Leo III in Rome. Although this territory was subsequently divided among descendants, his rule established the tradition of a Germanic Empire. Aachen, Charlemagne's administrative centre, lies only 80 kilometres (50 mi.) west of Cologne. A comparison with the choir chapel image of the bishops St Severin and St Anno reveals the different strategies of the nineteenth-century painters. They were deeply attracted to the colour-drenched brilliance of the Middle Ages and yet were living in a modern era, when Renaissance perspective and three-dimensional modelling in space held sway. The newer windows did attempt to echo the dense colour grids that silhouette the figures. Architectural forms are abstracted and flattened even if a

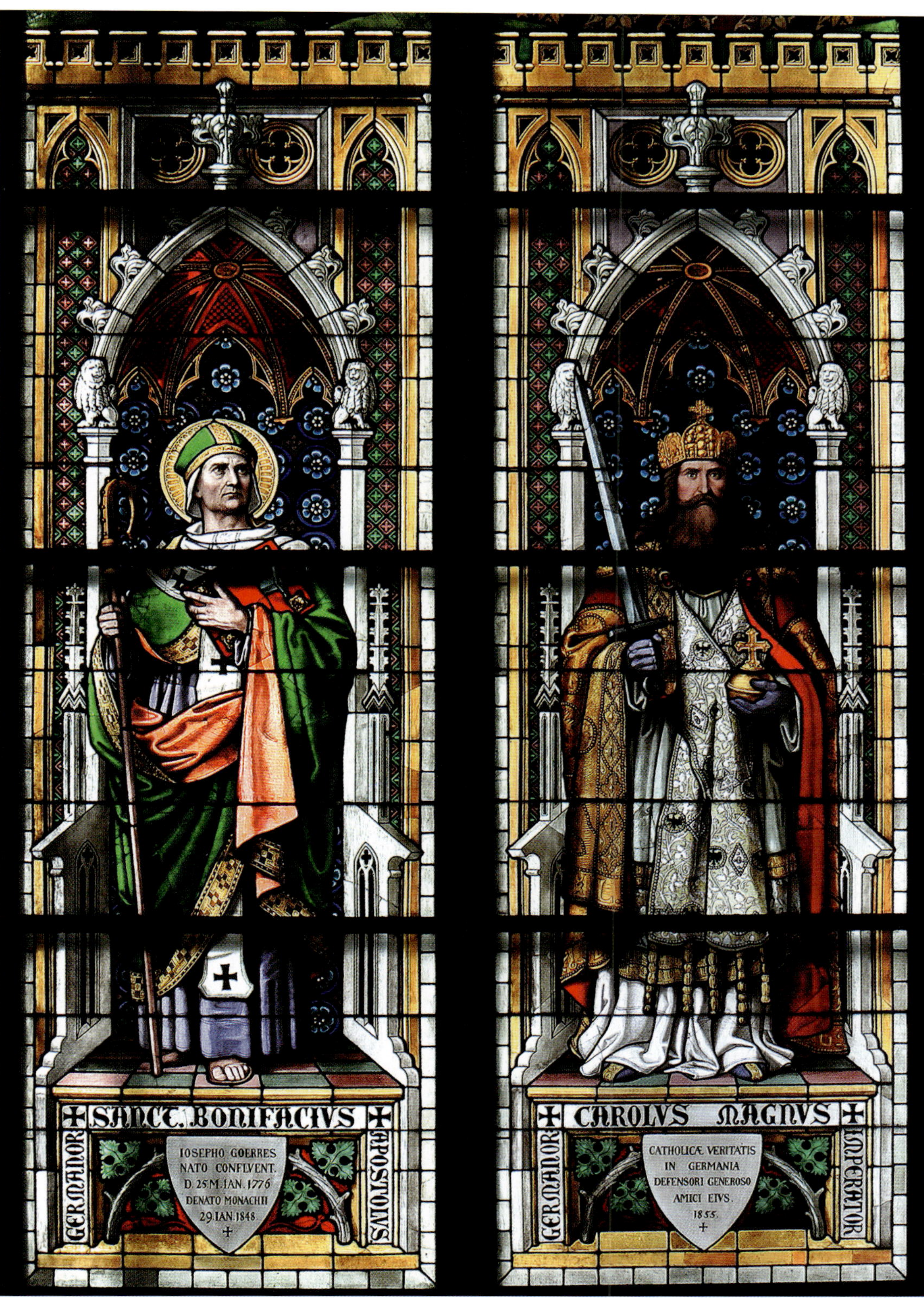

63 Königliche Glasmalereianstalt, Munich, Görres window,
St Boniface and *Charlemagne*, 1856, south transept.

ribbed vault is set over the figures. The bodies, however, are majestically three-dimensional and swathed in voluminous draperies. Charlemagne's image, with orb, sword and Imperial Crown, is taken from Albrecht Dürer's famed painting of the emperor, dated about 1512, in the German National Museum, Nuremberg.

These windows display brilliant handling of paint, meticulous attention to detail and harmonic contrasts of often acid colours. The style met with great success abroad, especially in the United States. The first bishop of the 'frontier' diocese of Buffalo, New York, John Timon, visited the deposed King Ludwig in 1854/5. He was able to petition for the support of the king's Ludwig-Missionsverein (St Louis Missionary Society), founded in 1838 to support Catholic efforts in Asia and North America. Ludwig gifted Timon with the three chancel windows of the *Nativity, Crucifixion* and *Resurrection*. Josef Scherer, their creator, who began his studies in Munich in 1832, was a prolific designer of glass and closely allied with the artistic philosophy of the Boisserée brothers. He also painted copies after old and new masters for the Boisserées. The Buffalo windows replicate the style of the 'Bavarians' of the south aisle of the cathedral by the Königliche Glasmalereianstalt, showing the same organization of a single dominant figural scene across all lancet subdivisions. The same colour harmonies of ochre, royal blue, lavender, emerald green and burgundy dominate the image and pulsate against the white and gold architectural surround. Ultimately the stained-glass studios of Munich and Innsbruck, Austria, who carried on the tradition of the Cologne windows into the end of the century, came to dominate American markets for Catholic patrons.

Windows of the Twenty-First Century

Because of its strategic placement, Cologne was one of the most heavily bombed cities in Germany during the Second World War (see illus. 52). Hitler had clearly foreseen the destruction to come. As early as 1938, at the time of the annexation of Czechoslovakia's Sudetenland, he ordered the cathedral's windows to be removed for protection. The Hohenzollern Bridge, which saw hundreds of trains, was destroyed in 1945 and subsequently reconstructed. The cathedral was only spared because of its role in providing pilots with compass directions. After the war, the shrine of the Three Magi was carried in procession through Cologne as the cathedral hovered over the devastated city like a protective angel.

Major artists in Germany, and in many other sites, are now producing in the medium of stained glass. Recent installations speak to the medium's contemporary ability to invest space with a timeless and immaterial presence. In

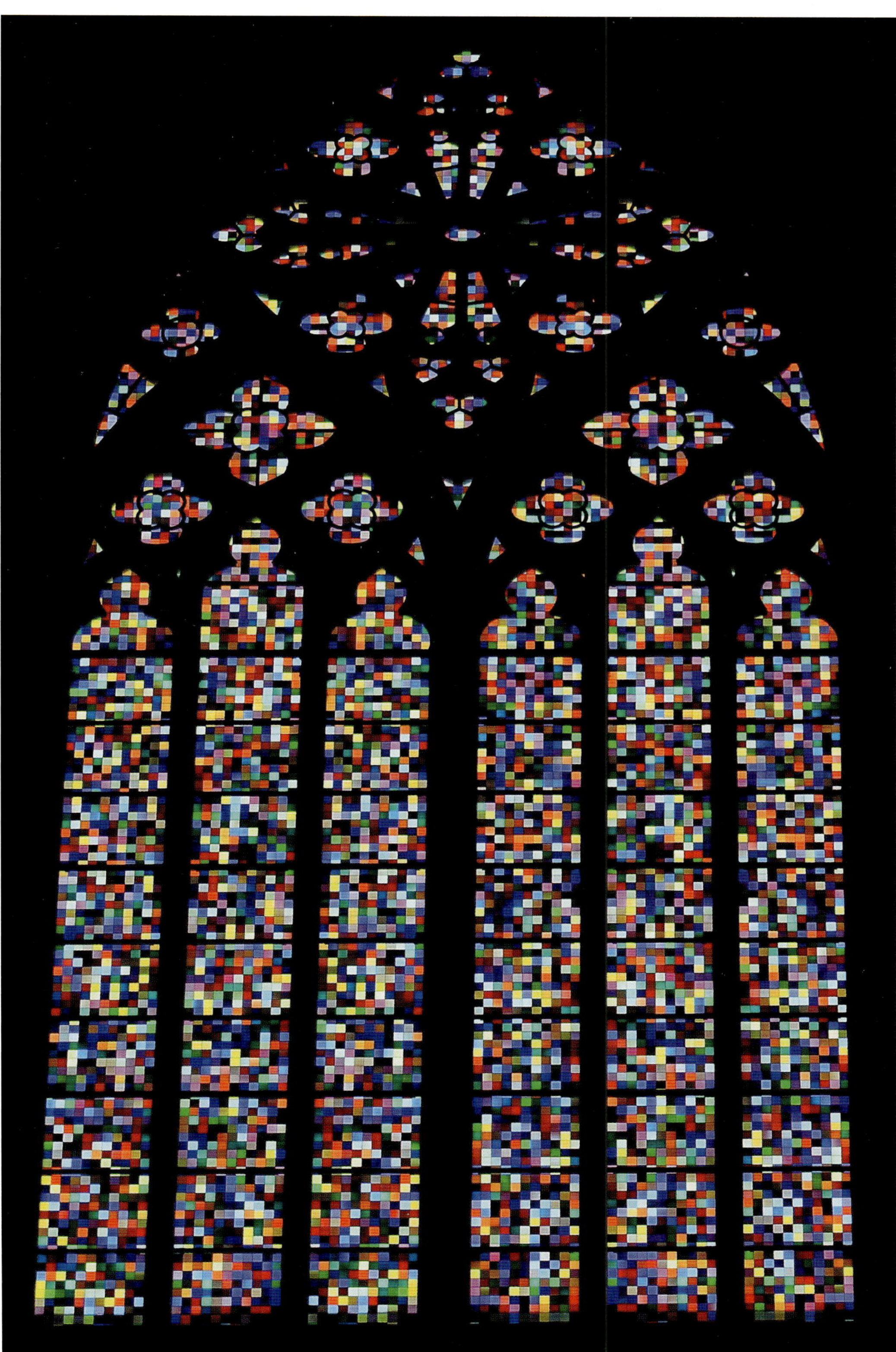

64 Gerhard Richter, south transept, installed 2007.

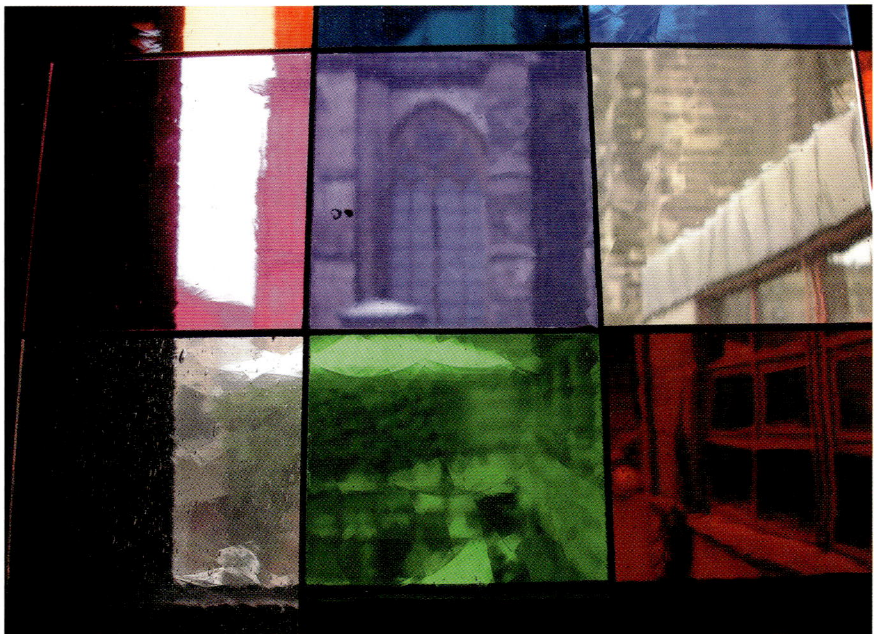

65 Gerhard Richter, glass panels set against a clear glass
window in Cologne cathedral's workshop, 2006.

2002, at the time of Gerhard Richter's major retrospective in the Museum of
Modern Art in New York, the cathedral commissioned him to provide glass for
the south transept (illus. 64). Richter (1932–) is one of the most multifaceted
artists of this era. His youth was spent in the troubled times of the rise of the
National Socialist state. Two of his mother's brothers, one named Rudolf, died
as soldiers, and their mentally ill sister Marianne was euthanized. In 1965 the
artist painted large, haunting images that looked like blurred photographs entitled *Aunt Marianne* and *Uncle Rudi*. As a young man, in 1951, Richter entered the
Dresden Academy of Fine Arts. Ten years later, he fled to West Germany shortly
before the Berlin Wall was erected. While studying at the Kunstakademie
Düsseldorf he was exposed to a dynamically varied artistic milieu. His own
work remained consistently independent, however, even if in communion with
international trends such as Pop art or Abstract Expressionism. Equally at home
in the abstract or realistic, the artist's moral depth is revealed in his monochro-
matic photo paintings of prominent individuals, as in the two portraits of his
deceased relatives, heads of state or seemingly innocent families. In 1983, Richter
resettled in Cologne. His fifteen works in monotone of 1988, entitled *October
18, 1977*, use imagery derived from newspaper, police and television images of
the radical Baader–Meinhof political movement.

Many assumed that the cathedral, so rich in storied windows, would be a place where Richter would explore this direction of his art. The artist, however, eventually came to believe in the power of the abstract to evoke transfigured space. Richter's success as an artist allowed him to forego any commission. In 1966, he had begun painting simple, uniform grids of coloured rectangles or squares on a white background. At first, Richter used commercial paint chips but later developed complex mathematical systems of colour interaction. It was this thinking that inspired his use of 11,500 small squares of glass in 72 different colours. The material is mouth-blown glass laminated to safety glass manufactured by Glashütte Lamberts, Waldsassen, using blowpipes and production techniques that have been passed down since glass making began. In the cathedral workshop (illus. 65), before installation, the distinctions of the segments seemed more precise and sequential. It was a rare moment to see through the colours, and to view the external architecture of the cathedral. The glass is unmodulated in colour, but with varying density so that light is variegated even as it penetrates. When in place, however, the colours are liberated, demolishing any sense of their distance and forming a pulsating, organic whole. The window seems a living entity suspending colour above space.

Neo-Expressionist Markus Lüpertz, for over twenty years the leader of the prestigious Kunstakademie Düsseldorf, also designed windows for the city. Equally admired for his work in sculpture and painting, Lüpertz executed twelve windows between 2005 and 2010 for the Dominican church of St Andreas, in Cologne. The theme of the south transept is taken from the presence of the shrine of the relics of the Maccabees, seven Jewish brothers and their mother who had refused to dishonour God's laws and were then one by one tortured and dismembered (2 Maccabees 7:1–41). The relics had come to Cologne in 1164 with the relics of the Three Kings in the cathedral. In typological fashion, the design juxtaposes the narrative of the Maccabees at the bottom and Christ's death on the Cross at the top. Lüpertz's design confronts us with abstracted piles of bodies whose wounds appear like roses, powerfully evoking memories of the Holocaust.

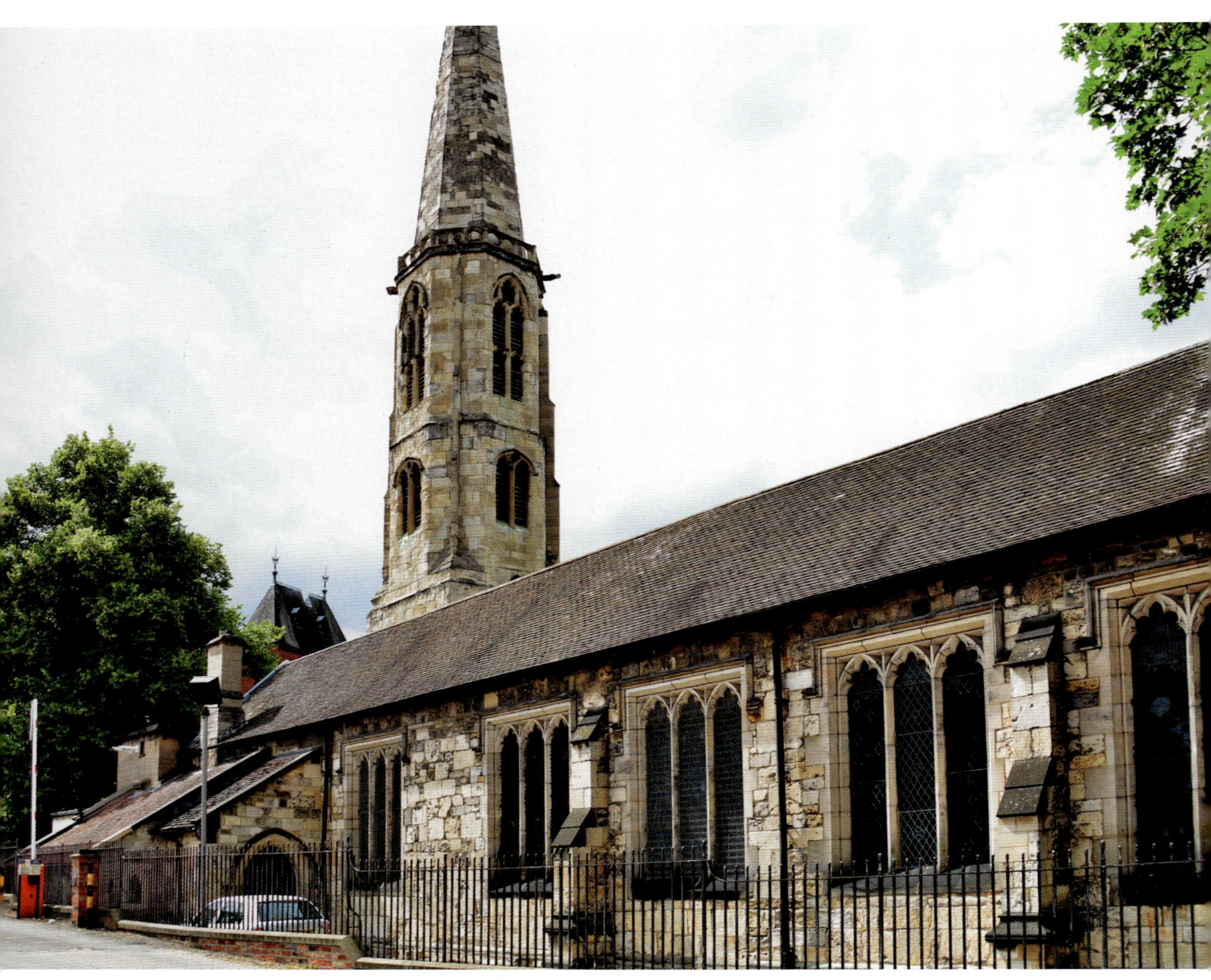

66 All Saints, North Street, York, exterior, *c.* 1400.

5

All Saints, North Street, York: Instructing a Parish

—

The parish church was the most important communal building of its time, the site of legal, social and artistic as well as religious activities. We see this even in great cities. York had been founded by the Romans in 71 CE. By the early fifteenth century, it had become a major wool-trading centre and was the capital of England's northern ecclesiastical province. Its guilds were powerful organizations, able to support the great *Corpus Christi* plays. Even in such cities, boasting a cathedral and several churches built by the religious Orders, parish churches abounded. All Saints, North Street, was one of around 45 medieval parish churches in York; happily, 15 remain substantially intact. Distinct from the cathedral, which was the site of great ecclesiastical power, these churches served ordinary lay folk, especially craftspeople and merchants, and depended on them for their support. Each parish was a place of intense social interaction as well as religious ritual and frequently significant works of art were funded by its members. A century later, St Mary's at Fairford would also serve a similar parish, but in a building financed almost exclusively by a single family. Unlike the artistically and thematically uniform programme at St Mary's, All Saints' windows testify to a variety of donors, who each show different priorities and made varied artistic choices. Exploration of the windows, spared from the destruction of reformer and of developer, reveals late-medieval changes in social status, piety, gender roles and also rising literacy, especially in the vernacular.

Although founded in the eleventh century, All Saints was almost completely rebuilt in the fourteenth and early fifteenth centuries and stands as a model for its era (illus. 66). We recognize similar features: a western entrance porch usually surmounted by a tower, a tall timber-roofed nave, windows in the aisles

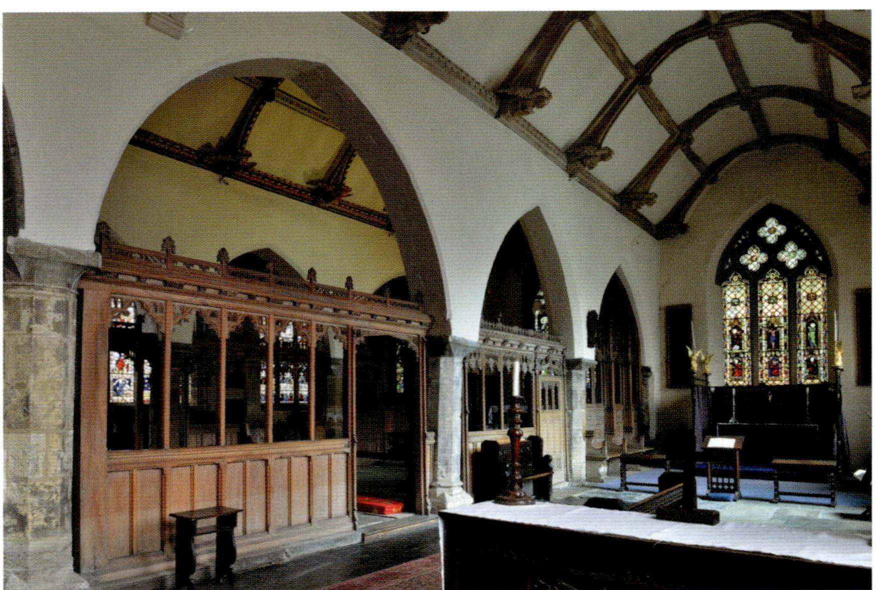

67 All Saints, interior, south aisle, looking east.

and a chancel on the east. The chancel, often of lower elevation and differently roofed, was marked off by a screen crowned by a freestanding cross (called a rood screen). Additional interior divisions appear as chapels, sometimes to the left and right of the chancel, and sometimes set in the aisles (illus. 67). Stained glass adorns many windows, most often portraying standing figures or scenes framed by light-coloured borders drawn to look like architecture, allowing considerable light into the interior space. Between about 1400 and 1530, seating arrangements in the churches transitioned to the use of pews, as at All Saints. At the beginning it was usual to construct benches only for the centre of the nave, leaving considerable space in front of the rood screen for the nave altars, the pulpit and performance of morality and mystery plays.

Eamon Duffy has done much to explain the busy and communal nature of worship of the time. The Church was the centre of social as well as religious life, verified by the many laws instituted by Henry VIII to control its authority. Parishioners routinely celebrated community bonds by gathering outside for Sunday masses and processing into the building to take their places either standing or in pews. This type of religious communal ritual was explicitly forbidden by Henry's Injunctions of 1547. What a modern person now labels the secular and the spiritual spheres of life were invariably fused. Trade unions, for example, can be traced to medieval guilds, which adopted special feast days for their patron saints. Henry's very prohibitions can be arguments for how universal such practices were, particularly those that banned 'keeping of private holy days, as bakers, brewers, smiths and shoemakers, and such others do'.[1] A study of these churches reveals the statues, paintings and stained glass directly tied to these pious practices.

Contemporary Memoirs

We are fortunate to have the memoirs of a contemporary layperson to help us understand the usage of the church spaces. *The Book of Margery Kempe* was transcribed shortly before 1440, and records life in England at the time that All Saints was designed. Although the original manuscript has been lost, a scribe now identified as Richard Salthouse, a monk at Norwich's cathedral priory, had made a copy in the same century. That manuscript was preserved by recusant Catholics, descending to the ownership of Colonel W. Butler-Bowdon and discovered in a Derbyshire country house in 1934. It has often been termed the first autobiography in the English language and chronicles a self-styled mystic and pilgrim, keenly interested in visiting churches at home and abroad. Margery Kempe was a middle-class woman who, after giving birth to fourteen children, took a vow of chastity which enabled her to travel in England and to make pilgrimages to Europe and the Holy Land. Her details of her travels, although

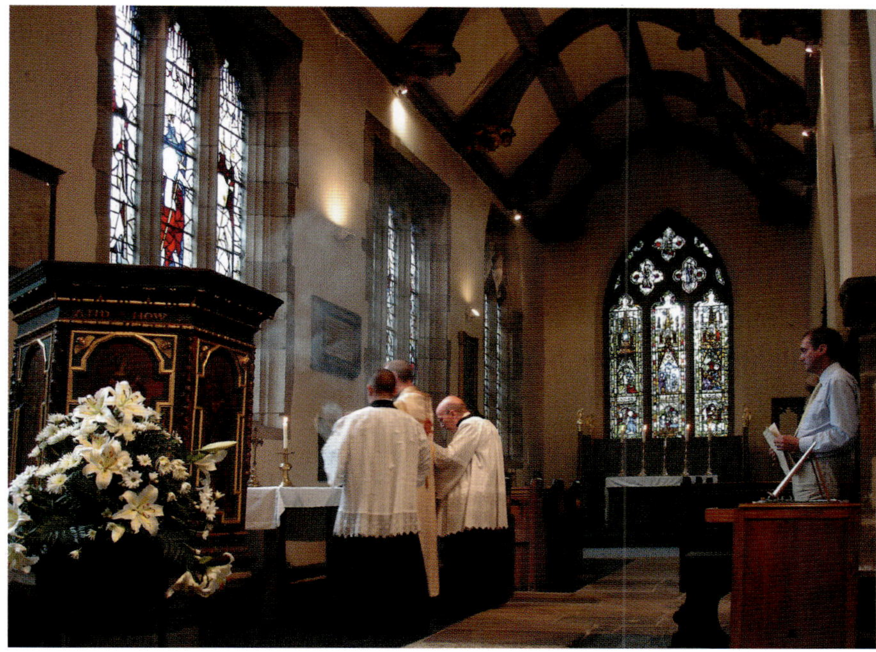

68 All Saints, interior, north aisle, censing a side altar, 2007.

ordered in an associative rather than systematic narrative, identify dozens of churches by name. Always attentive to the implications of locations, Kempe frequently mentions the precise part of a church in which an experience took place, such as the chancel, a particular chapel, the high altar or other locations.

Literacy was a flexible concept. Margery Kempe could neither read nor write, but she had run a brewing business, often the province of females in England. She was also up to date on trends in spirituality, such as the writings of St Bridget of Sweden (1303–1373), like Margery, married and a mother, who then became a 'bride of Christ'.[2] Bridget's accounts of her travels to holy sites in Italy and in Jerusalem were models for Kempe's journeys, where Kempe claimed that she had similar spiritual revelations. We infer that familiarity with Bridget was communicated orally.

Kempe describes divisions and interior furnishings such as the rood screen, tombs, baptismal font and altars that demarked spaces for different purposes (illus. 68 and see illus. 67). Chancel or choir screens had become standard church furniture since the early thirteenth century and by the fifteenth there was no church without a division between the space of the laity and the space of clerical performance. In England the screen was referred to as the rood, because of the freestanding cross above it. These crosses were particularly subject to reformist zeal during England's Reformation, and almost all have perished in the seventeenth-century purging of church imagery. At the time of the reconstruction of All Saints, it was normal to have rows of pews set horizontally (north to south) to enable the laity to view the high altar. In the chancel, however, seating was arranged east to west along each side of the wall, so that the clergy and acolytes would face each other for the antiphonal performance of the office.

Windows of All Saints

The placement of windows followed the importance of the site and the piety of the donors. No matter how complex a programme might be in its full elaboration, the artists consistently touched the hearts and minds of the unsophisticated viewer with images that elicited empathy. All Saints has preserved several remarkable windows. In the chancel, an early fifteenth-century three-light window shows *St John the Baptist, St Anne Teaching the Virgin Mary* and *St Christopher*, flanked by earlier, mid-fourteenth-century windows: on the

69 All Saints, central window east, *St John the Baptist, St Anne Teaching the Virgin Mary* and *St Christopher*, early 15th century.

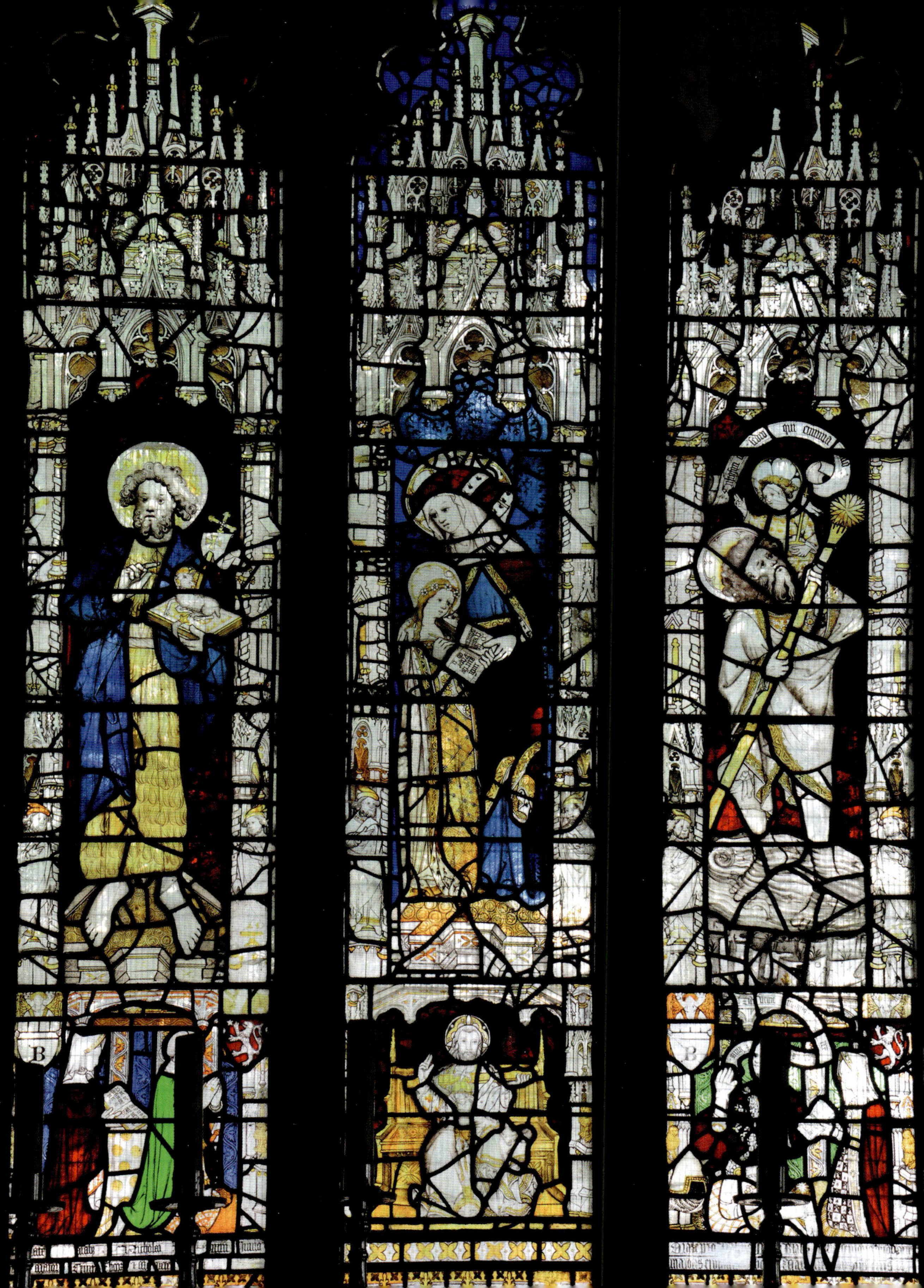

south the *Crucifixion with the Virgin and St John* and, on the north, the *Joys of the Virgin*. The *Joys of the Virgin*, dated about 1330, is the earliest in the church, and was originally above the high altar. Continuing on the north, we find the two windows for which the site is most renowned, the *Pricke of Conscience* and *Corporal Works of Mercy*. Other windows from the early fifteenth century include one containing *St Thomas, Resurrected Christ and an Archbishop*, possibly Thomas Becket, another of *St James, the Virgin and Child and Christ appearing to St Gregory during Mass*, and a third depicting the *Nine Choirs of Angels*. Additional windows include one dating to the mid-fifteenth century of St Michael and St John, another showing heraldic badges and another with reset fragments against grisaille glass.

The window of the high altar (illus. 69) was given by the Blackburn family and shows, at the bottom, Nicholas Sr and his wife Margaret on the right and Nicholas Jr and wife, also named Margaret, on the left. They face, in the centre, the Throne of Mercy, God the Father holding the crucified Christ between his knees with the Dove of the Holy Spirit between them. Such a representation suggests that the Trinity can also be thought of as a family. The central figure, St Anne, had achieved elevated status as she represented extended family relationships, the bonds that functioned for entrepreneurial enterprises of the time. Anne was believed to have married two additional husbands who gave her daughters. They became the mothers of John, James the Greater, James the Less, Simon and Jude, who became Christ's disciples, as recounted in the late thirteenth-century *Golden Legend*. This tradition came to be called the Holy Kinship, widely represented in art of the late Middle Ages, but suppressed after the sixteenth century. John the Baptist, on the left, is mentioned in the Gospels as the son of Mary's cousin, Elizabeth (Luke 1:39–80). Thus he is also the cousin of Christ. Over centuries, many paintings of the Virgin and Child and of St Anne with the Virgin and Child also include the infant John the Baptist. John holds a book and an image of a lamb with the banner of the Resurrection, a reference to his words: 'Behold the Lamb of God who takes away the sins of the world' (John 1:29).

St Christopher, with several levels of associations, appears on the right. He was one of the most frequently depicted saints of the later Middle Ages, as he was credited with protection of travellers. Thus the merchant classes, dependent on the movement of goods, would feel a particular devotion. In many parish churches, a wall painting of the saint was placed close to the door, as an association with coming and going. Christopher appears as a large man, wading through water. This refers to his vocation of carrying travellers across a dangerous river. Due to his massive stature, he was able to perform the service as an act of charity. One day a small child appeared on the riverbank and asked for his help. As Christopher waded through the water, he felt the child become heavier and heavier. Almost at the end of his strength, he reached the opposite bank and placed the child on firm ground, only to hear the child inform him that he had carried Christ, who bears the weight of the world. His name refers to this action, *Christophoros*, from the Greek meaning 'bearing', thus the carrier of Christ. The value of honest labour is explicit in this story. Christopher performs a task and viewers are prompted to reflect on those longed-for words, 'Well done, good and faithful servant!' (Matthew 25:21) and hope that their labour will also be accepted by their God.

Female Literacy and Piety

Perhaps most striking to the modern viewer is the clear evidence of female literacy. At the time that this window was installed a considerable number of the laity were literate. Female members of the family were often expected to achieve high literacy through their use of reading Books of Hours. These books contained daily prayers for various hours of the day, a practice taken from the texts used by monks and the clergy in their breviaries. They were a mark of status, and with the advent of the printing press became one of the first categories of texts to reach a broad public. Margaret, wife of Nicholas Jr on the left, is reading *Domine, ne in furore tuo arguas me, neque in ira tua* (Psalm 6:2; O Lord, rebuke me not in thy indignation, nor chastise me in thy wrath), and Margaret, wife of Nicholas Sr, reads *Domine, labia mea aperies, et os meum annuntiabit laudem tuam* (Psalm 50:17; O Lord, thou wilt open my lips: and my mouth shall declare thy praise). In the centre of the window St Anne holds an open book while the Virgin Mary reads (illus. 70). The young girl is clearly in the process of learning as she holds a pointer in her hand to indicate the letters. Anne is shown as a distinguished matron through the richness of her clothes, including ermine trim on her headdress, and the Virgin Mary follows suit in an elaborately embroidered dress. She reads *Domine exaudi orationem meam auribus percipe obsecrationem meam* (Psalm 142:1; Hear, O Lord, my prayer: give ear to my supplication). Chaucer's *Canterbury Tales*, written shortly before the window was made, includes a description of such childhood learning in *The Prioress's Tale* (lines 516–17). The Prioress recounts a story of a child filled with great devotion to the Virgin Mary and explains his dutiful lessons: *This litel child, his litel book lernynge,/ As he sat in the scole at his prymer* (This little

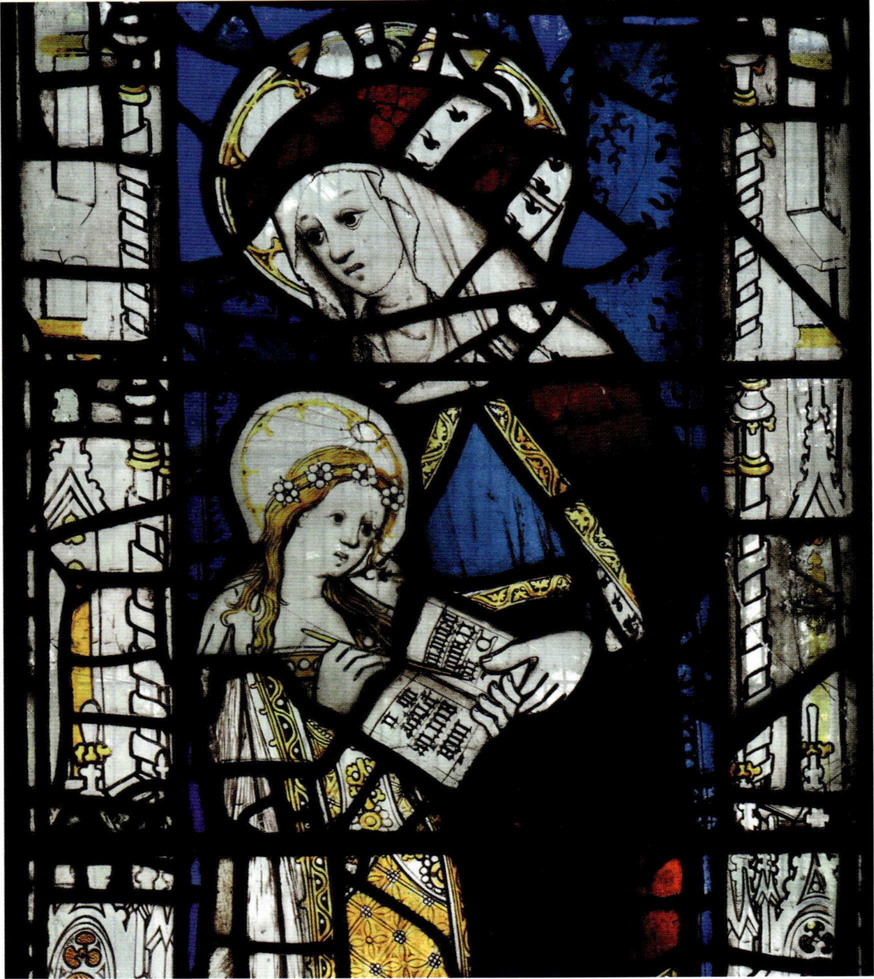

70 All Saints, central window, detail, *St Anne Teaching the Virgin Mary.*

child, learning his little book, as he sat in the school at his primer). Primer was another term for a Book of Hours.

Popular piety also animates the selection of the themes in many other windows. The laity wished to experience a personal connection to the sacred. This desire surfaces in Margery Kempe's narrations of Christ's communications to her while she meditated in sacred spaces. Early in her memoir she speaks of hearing Mass, most probably in her local church of St Margaret's, King's Lynn, saying that she experienced a vision of the Eucharist fluttering above the chalice, that not even St Brigid had seen. Her account is most probably associated with the then common practice of placing the reserved Eucharistic host in a statue of a dove that was suspended by chains over the altar. Kempe's devotion to the

Eucharist is reiterated at All Saints in a window of St Gregory saying Mass. Pope Gregory (540–604) was believed to have been given a vision of Christ in the Eucharist, a confirmation to onlookers of the Real Presence. Another window presents the doubting Thomas, a theme which also speaks to personal interaction. Thomas was absent when Christ first appeared to the Apostles, and refused to believe their account. Christ appeared again and asked Thomas to put his finger into his side, a verification that Christ's physical body had risen from the dead and was not an apparition (John 20:24–9). All Saints' selection of these themes allows us to understand that intimacy with Christ was prized.

The draughting style of these windows is exquisite. By the early fifteenth century, the symbolic representation of the High Gothic through bold colours, flat backgrounds and abstracted forms gave way to more realistic spatial conventions. These English windows used a considerable amount of uncoloured glass, relegating darker colours to backgrounds or selected accents in clothing or landscape. Thus their ability to support intricate painting was considerably enhanced. Delicate lines follow the contour of St Anne's veil, supported by more gradual modulations that suggest folds. The architectural framing, however, is executed with uniform trace lines that differ only in thickness. Silver stain is a constant feature that enlivens decorative elements such as architecture, halos, hair and banding on robes as well as creating swathes of cloth, as in the young Virgin's dress. Facial expression may be one of the most attractive elements of English art of this era. Female faces are oval with rounded eyes framed by double lines for the upper and lower lids. Delicate brows are set amid a high forehead. Below the long nose, a tiny, bud-like mouth is accented by a small indentation below the lower lip. Male physiognomy is less graceful, but shows individual character, invariably with abundant curly hair for both face and head, as exemplified by John the Baptist.

The convention of single figures in lancets was but one of the artist's choices. Narrative windows, so prominent in Gothic programmes, still retained the system of separate scenes to tell a story. Three windows at All Saints, *Pricke of Conscience*, *Works of Mercy* and *Nine Choirs of Angels*, employ bands of small rectangular panels, unlike the complex systems of interlocking medallions at Canterbury or at Chartres. We are easily prompted to associate the system with comic books or, as better termed by their Belgian innovators, drawn bands (*bande dessinées* or *stripverhalen*). The story unfolds from either the bottom (*Pricke of Conscience*) or the top (*Works of Mercy*) and moves from left to right, engaging viewers as if they were reading a book.

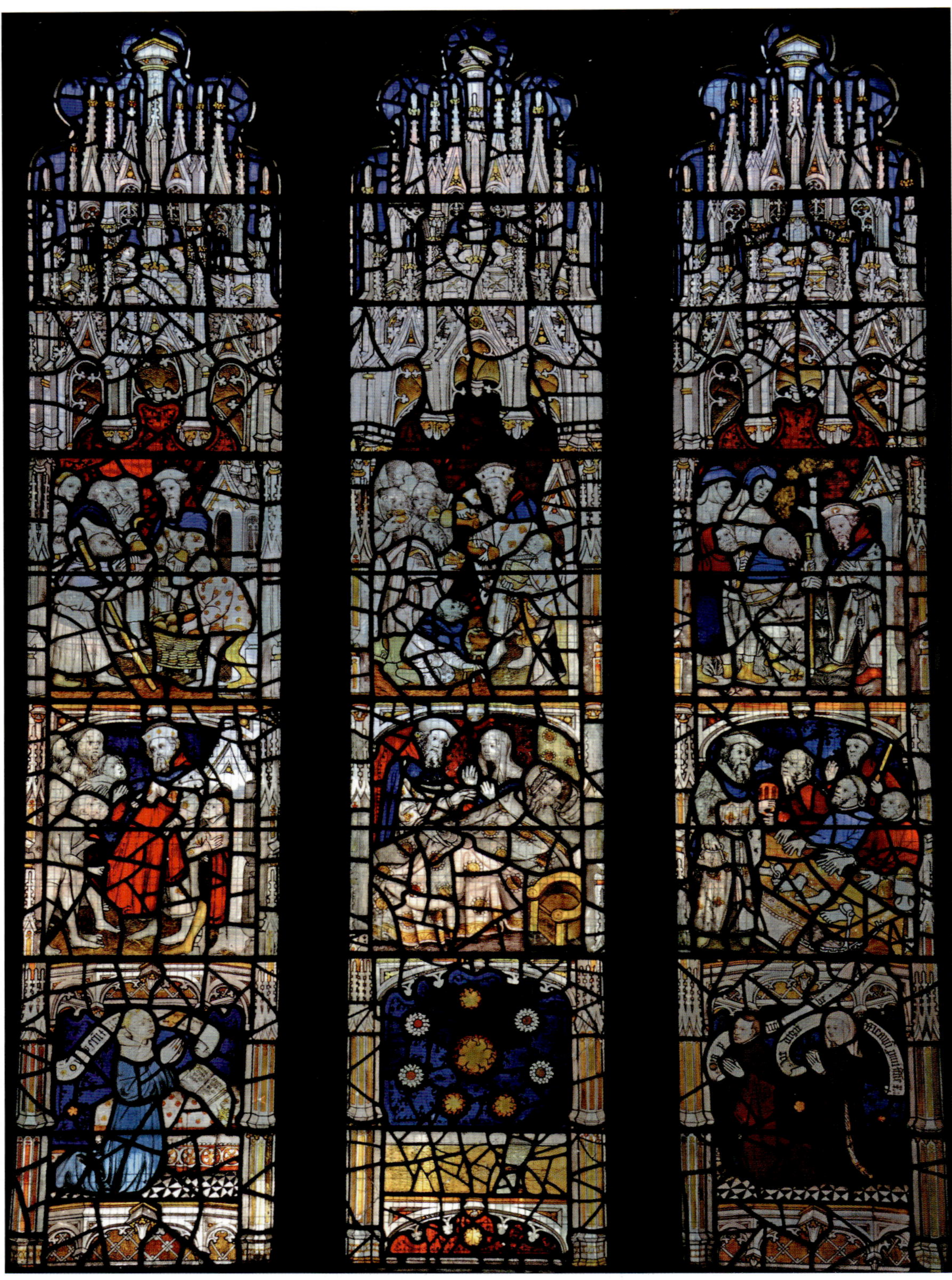

71 All Saints, north aisle window (n.4),
Corporal Works of Mercy, early 15th century.

Works of Mercy Window

One of the most frequently cited windows, for its theme as well as its artistry, is that of the *Corporal Works of Mercy* (illus. 71). The list corresponded to systems designed to teach. Effective means of reaching the faithful were essential, and a popular strategy was the construction of lists, seven being a common series number. A meditative series, such as the Seven Sorrows and the Seven Joys of the Virgin Mary, helped listeners and viewers to focus empathetically on events in the Life of Christ. All Saints' original chancel window showed this theme, and the large east window of the church of St Peter and Paul, East Harling, dated 1463 to 1480, is a brilliant example of the sequence. For centuries, the pastoral efforts of the Church grouped seven specific good works as 'corporal works of mercy'.

In 1281, under John Peckham, Archbishop of Canterbury, lay instruction was included in the Lambeth Constitutions. Lambeth Palace was the official London residence of the archbishop. Section nine of the constitutions included 'instruction to be given by the clergy to their flocks, and directs them to explain four times a year, in the vulgar [English] tongue, the creed, the ten commandments, the two evangelical precepts, the seven works of mercy, the seven mortal sins, the seven cardinal virtues, and the seven sacraments'.[3] *The Lay Folks' Catechism*, issued in both Latin and English versions by William Thoresby, archbishop of York in 1357, continued to emphasize the importance of humanitarian actions. The text, in use until the Reformation, stated that the seven works of mercy will be 'rehearsed' by God from each Christian soul on the day of doom. The *Catechism* gives the list for which the first six are represented in the window. All Saints shows the scenes listed in order, starting at the top, which shows a man distributing bread from a basket.

> *Of whilk the first is to fede tham that er hungry.*
> *That other, for to gif tham drynk that er thirsty.*
> *The third, for to clethe tham that er clatheless*
> *The ferthe is to herber tham that er houseless.*
> *The fifte, for visite tham that ligges in sekenesse.*
> *The sext, is to help tham that in prisoner.*
> *The sevent, to bery dede man that has mister.*

Of which the first is to feed those that are hungry.
The next, to give drink to those who are thirsty.

The third, to clothe those who are without clothes.

The fourth is to shelter those who are homeless.

The fifth is to visit those who lay in sickness.

The sixth is to help those in prison.

The seventh is to bury the dead who are churched.

Representations of this theme were plentiful, in wall painting, manuscript illumination and stained glass. One of the most complete secular installations of the Works of Mercy was in the ground-floor windows of 18 Highcross Street, Leicester (now the Jewry Wall Museum), containing 29 roundels dated to 1500. All Saints, however, contains one of the most celebrated. Each scene is envisioned with a practical model. Giving shelter to the homeless is shown as welcoming pilgrims, easily a scene that could illustrate Chaucer's *Canterbury Tales*. Indeed, the image of the host recalls Chaucer's description of the Merchant from the Prologue *with a forked berd,/ In mottelee . . ./ Upon his heed a Flaundryssh bever hat* (with forked beard and motley gown upon his head a Flemish beaver hat (ll. 270–72). The scenes exemplify the new attraction of more realistic depiction,

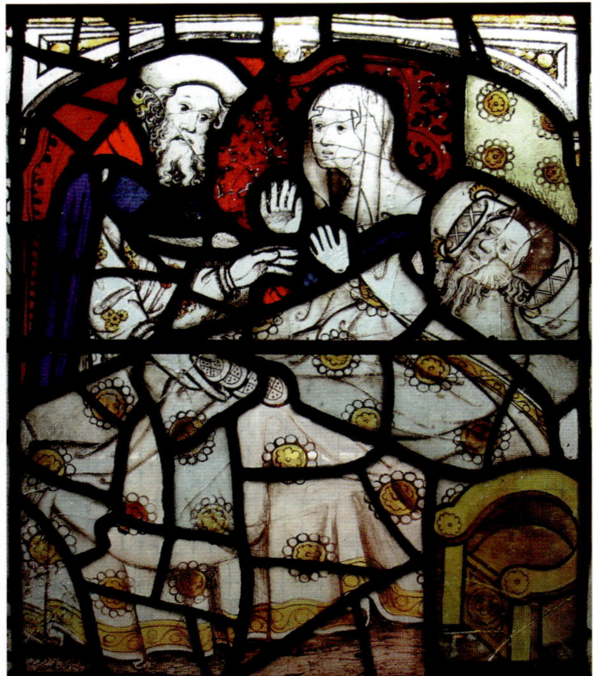

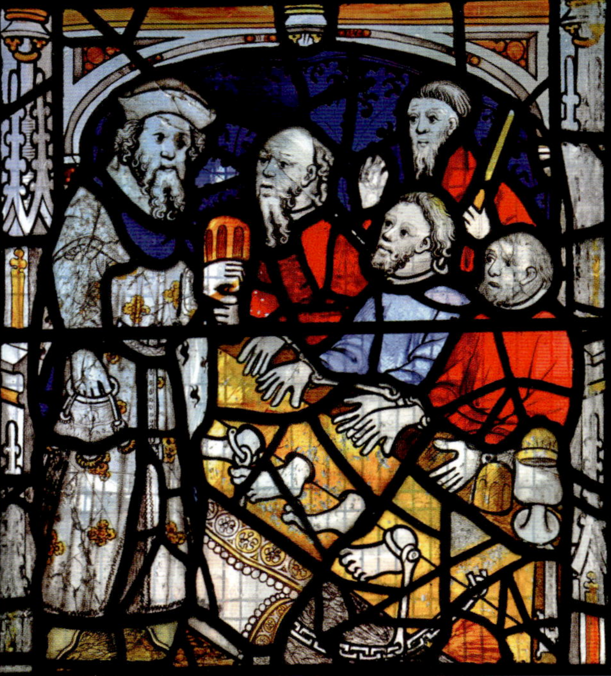

72 All Saints, Corporal Works of Mercy, detail: Visiting the Sick.

73 All Saints, Corporal Works of Mercy, detail: Visiting the Imprisoned.

although not yet the three-dimensional landscape that would be introduced with the windows of St Mary's at Fairford.

All Saints' depictions of visiting the sick and the imprisoned are particularly vivid. The first (illus. 72) shows a scene dominated by a bed where a man rests his head against a delicate pillow over a bolster. He wears a cap to keep warm. A well-dressed man, in cloak and hat, stands at the bedside. He lays coins on the bedspread, received with a happy gesture by the ailing man's wife. The bed and headboard are covered in a rich fabric; a carved stool is at the side. Surely this is not a home of the poor. Rather, the image encourages the viewer to consider the frequent reversals of fortune even among the virtuous. The visitor, arguably of the same class, might imagine himself in such a position. In the following scene (illus. 73) three imprisoned men sit bound in stocks, manacled hand and foot, with the jailor behind them. The silver-stain yellow of the wooden stock catches our eye and we are convinced of a realistic recession in space. The scenes seem to play as if we were watching actors on a small stage.

Street Theatre by Trade Guilds

Such representational strategies may have found support in the experiences of staging and viewing what is known as the York Corpus Christi Plays. A performance of the Crucifixion of Christ, staged in July 2007 (illus. 74), incorporated a similar density of figural grouping as the window. These dramatic enactments were experienced in the streets. York sponsored mobile theatre that presented the entire Christian story from Creation to the Last Judgement in 48 pageants. The plays were organized, financed and performed by the craft guilds of the city from the mid-fourteenth century until their suppression in 1569, traditionally presented on the feast day of Corpus Christi, celebrated between late May and late June. The modern era has seen revivals in York since the 1950s. A performance documented in 1376 makes it clear that, by that time, pageant wagons were already in use. These were paraded through the streets, stopping at twelve playing stations for maximum audience engagement.

In the Crucifixion of Christ, sponsored by the nailers and painters, an intense exchange occurs among the four soldiers. They complain at length about having to wait to get their jobs done while others relax in town. The soldiers pull violently on ropes to stretch Christ's limbs, one commenting on having thrown his shoulder out of joint, another needing to drive in a nail 'so that no faute be foune' (so that no fault is found), and reporting back to their masters about their excellent work. For parishioners at All Saints, its Crucifixion window in

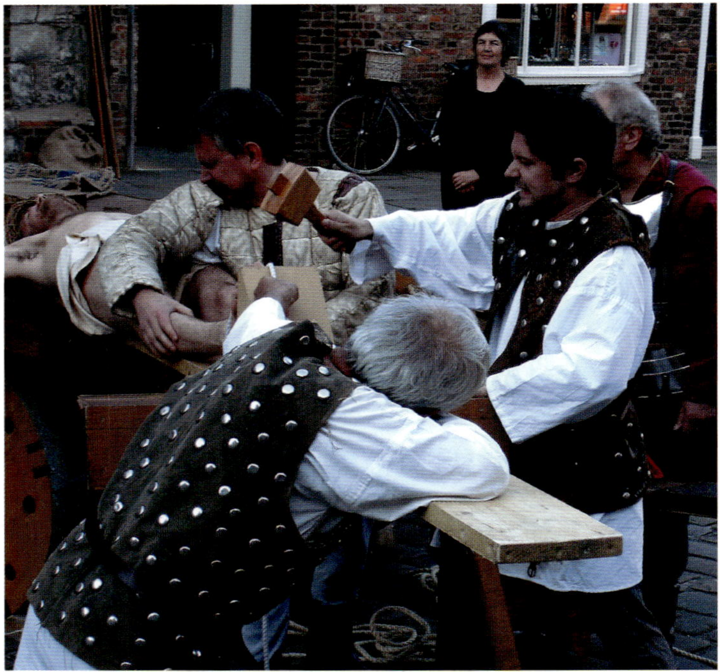

74 Corpus Christi Play, Pinners and Painters Guild,
nailing Christ to the Cross, July 2007.

the south aisle was brought to life in this vivid performance by local trade guilds.
Christ speaks but a short passage that includes: 'Forgiffis thes men that dois me
pyne' (Forgive these men who hurt me). The ending is magisterial as the drama
unfolds about Christ's garments. The Gospel narrative of the soldiers casting
lots for Christ's robe was well known through sermon and through image:
'And they crucified him, and parted his garments, casting lots: that it might be
fulfilled which was spoken by the prophet: "They parted my garments among
them, and upon my vesture did they cast lots"' (Matthew 27:35). The moment
is also recorded in the Gospels of Mark, Luke and John. The action in the play,
however, responds to another truth, one of lived experience; in a group of soldiers, there is a commander. The play's action demonstrates that the first soldier
has seniority and can demand obedience.

> First Soldier: *For certis us nedis anodir note.*
> Here is another matter.
> *This kirtill wolde I of you crave.*
> Grant that I take his robe.
> Second Soldier: *Nay, nay, sir, we will loke be lotte*

No, no, sir, we'll draw lots.
Whilke of us foure fallis it to have.
And see which of us four is lucky.

There then follows discussion among the four soldiers but the first is adamant:

First Soldier: *Felowes, ye thar noght flyte,*
Comrades, there is no need to argue,
For this mantell is myne.
Because the robe is mine.

The play ends with the second soldier admitting that they should leave, as discussion is a waste of time. Scripturally inaccurate but practically true, the scene convinces the spectator of being an actual eyewitness at the sacred scene.

Pricke of Conscience Window

A companion window in three panels of six tiers (illus. 75) is based on a poem called the *Pricke of Conscience*. The text narrates the final fifteen days of the world; each panel illustrates a day with an image and a paraphrase of the poem. Once attributed to Richard Rolle, it is now ascribed to an anonymous fourteenth-century author. In the early fifteenth century, copies of the poem were known to have been in the possession of important members of the Yorkshire laity, including Alice Bolton, who gave windows to All Saints. It is likely, however, that the Henryson and Hessle families paid for the window. The two families were related by marriage and noted as among the urban elite of York. Before discussing the window in detail, we can look again at the tradition of the York Corpus Christi plays. Vivid imagery as narrative backdrop was a part of many of the pageant carts, imagery that may very well have inspired the depictions of landscape in the window.

Most plays demanded few trained actors. However, there were no professional actors in the fifteenth century. In York, at least 22 men played the part of Christ. *The Creation through the Fifth Day*, the second play, sponsored by the plasterers, for example, is simply the recitation by God the Father. The pageant wagon was certainly equipped with stage scenery. As descriptions of the firmament, then earth, and then the animals of the land, sky and sea were declaimed, painted images were very likely to have been revealed on the wagon. Like the rest of the plays, the language is descriptive and engaging. God speaks:

> *Now sene the erthe thus ordand es*
> Now see the earth thus ordained
> *Mesurid and made by myn assent,*
> measured and made by my own design,
> *Grathely for to growe with gres*
> truly to be overgrown with grass
> *And wedis that sone away bese went*
> and plants that attract the bees[4]

The lines suggest that God was imagined as a craftsman. Scholars believe that the actor may have been dressed as one, carrying a large set of masons' compasses. Such imagery is well known from Creation narratives in manuscripts. Local stained glass also shows precedents. York Minster's east window, executed between 1405 and 1408, is the largest expanse of medieval stained glass in England. The upper level shows a series of nine panels recounting the story of Creation through to Adam and Eve's first sin. Several of the panels could easily serve as visual backdrops to the story, especially the creation of fish and birds in the centre. The play's lines are equally vivid:

> *The see now will I set within*
> You see how I set within
> *Whallis whikly for to dewell,*
> Whales who actively dwell there,
> *And othir fysch to flet with fyne,*
> With other fishes who move with fins,
> *Sum with skale and sum with skell*
> Some with scales and some with shells[5]

The *Pricke of Conscience* expounds a penitential programme reinforced by a vision of the end of the world. In seven sections, the poem first addresses the wretchedness of humankind and its flaunting of God's laws and moves to discourses on death and purgatory. At the end, we read of the pains of hell and the joys of heaven. In between, in part five, we find the Anti-Christ and the fifteen 'tokens' of Doomsday (Book v, ll. 729–800): 1) the seas rise; 2) they fall; 3) they return to their former level; 4) fishes and monsters rise; 5) the sea catches fire; 6) bloody dew falls; 7) earthquakes come and buildings fall; 8) rocks crash together and the earth swallows them; 9) people try to escape by hiding in holes; 10) nothing remains but a flat earth; 11) people come out of their holes

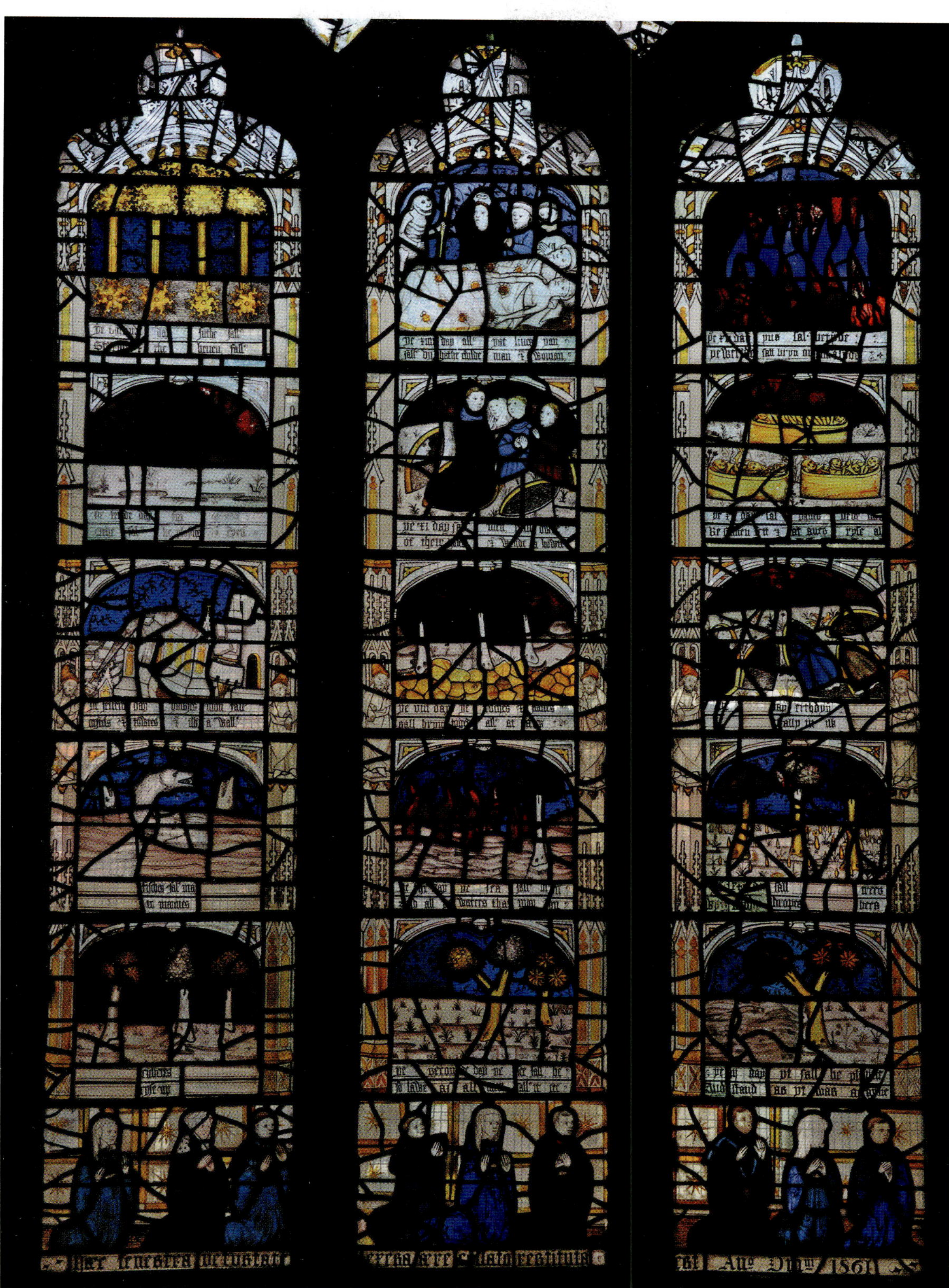

75 All Saints, north aisle window (n.3), *Pricke of Conscience*, early 15th century.

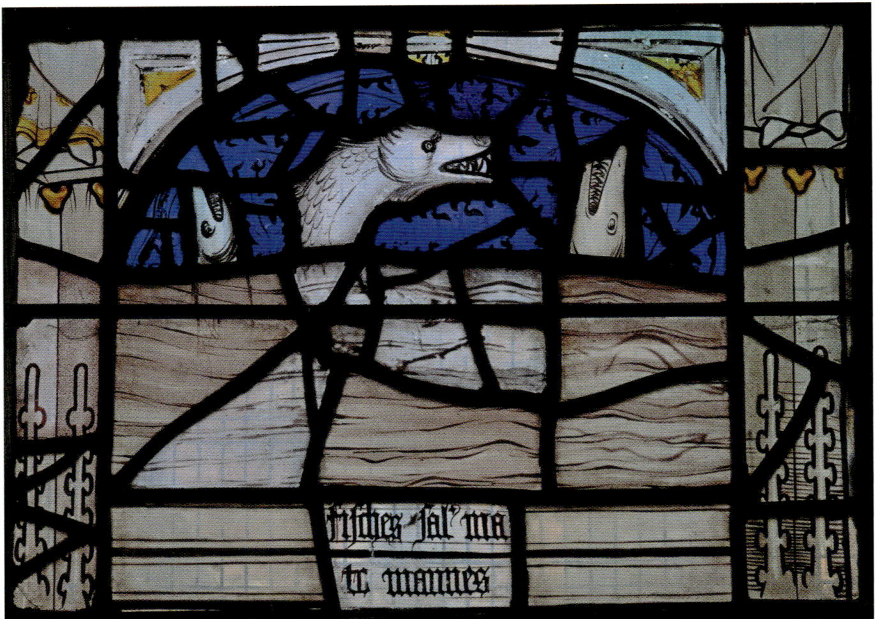

76 All Saints, *Pricke of Conscience*, detail: Day Four,
the Fishes Rise from the Sea.

to pray; 12) the stars and other signs fall from the heavens; 13) the bones of the dead arise from their coffins (days 12 and 13 are exchanged in the window); 14) death comes to all; 15) fire consumes the world.

In energetic detail, the viewers see each event portrayed. One of the most engaging is the fourth day (illus. 76), when sea monsters rise up and invade the earth, their fishy heads sticking out of the waves:

The fierth day, sal swilk a wonder be
The fourth day, there shall be such a wonder
The mast wondreful fisshes of the se
The most marvellous fishes of the sea
Sal com to-gyder and mak swilk roryng
Shall come together and make such a roaring
That it sal be hydus til mans heryng
That it will be hideous to hear
Bot what that roryng sal signify,
But what that roaring shall signify,
Na man whit, bot God almyghty.
No man knows but God Almighty.[6]

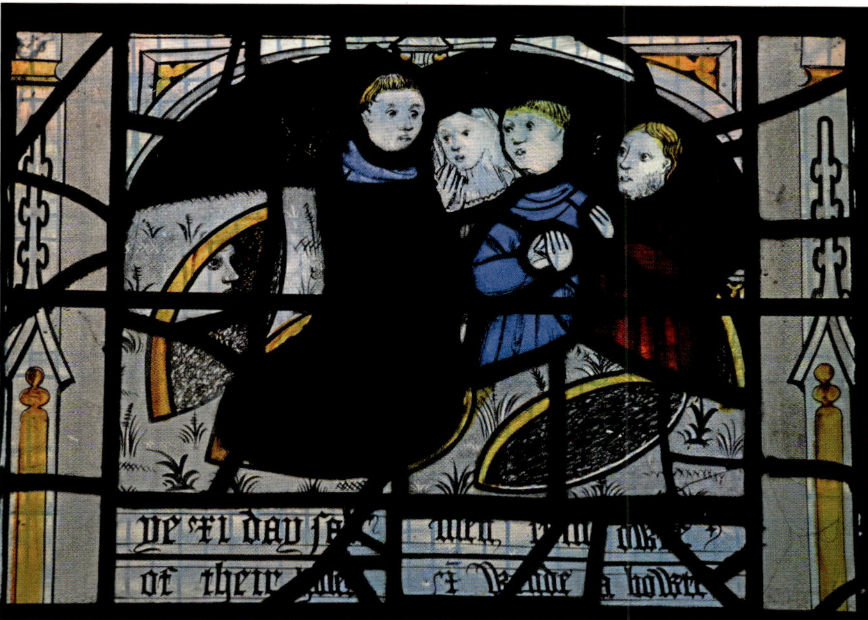

77 All Saints, *Pricke of Conscience*, detail: Day Eleven,
People Come Out of Their Holes to Pray.

Similarly effective visual language allows us to recognize the ellipses signifying
holes in the earth where humans had sheltered on the eleventh day (illus. 77).
Three men and a woman kneel praying while the face of a fifth person is glimpsed
in profile, still hiding.

> *The ellevend day men sal com out*
> The eleventh day man shall come out
> *Of caves, and holes and wend about,*
> Of caves and holes and move about,
> *Als wode men that na witt can;*
> As if they had lost their minds;
> *And nane sal spek til other than*
> And none of them will speak to each other[7]

Conservation and Reconstruction

All Saints also preserves a window that in fragmentary state had long puzzled
researchers (illus. 78). Its subject of the *Nine Choirs of Angels* was revealed
through the discovery of a 1670 drawing (Bodleian Library, Oxford) made

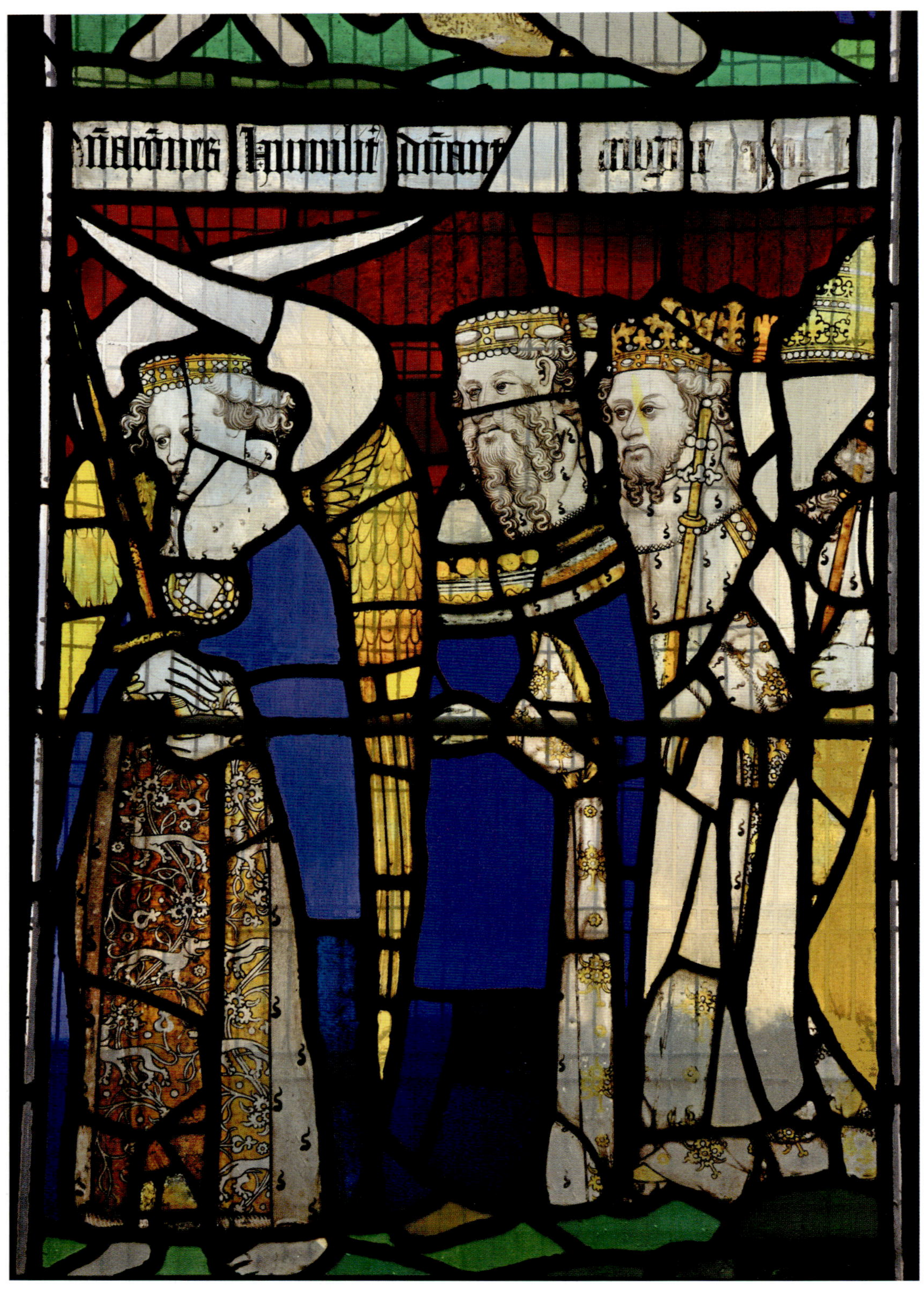

78 All Saints, *Nine Choirs of Angels* (s.5),
detail of Dominations, early 15th century.

by the antiquarian Henry Johnston. The ordering of angelic beings into hierarchies was the subject of an influential book by a fifth-century writer later known as Pseudo-Dionysius. He placed them in three hierarchies. The first three, Seraphim, Cherubim and Thrones, contemplate God; the Dominations, Principalities and Powers hold sway over God's plan for the universe; and the last three, Virtues, Archangels and Angels, watch over human affairs. The popularity of the theme speaks to our understanding of medieval York still embracing social hierarchies. There were appointed roles, and individuals were expected to exercise them to the best of their abilities. Despite the loss of much of the glass, the sensitive restoration allows us to appreciate the dignified composition, as each angel leads a group of individuals in procession. The angel representing the Dominations carries a sword and wears a gem-studded crown. Its ermine-lined cloak opens to reveal an exquisite silver-stained tunic embroidered with foliage and hunting dogs. The window's refined draughtsmanship, expressed in delicate line detailing contours of the face and hair, makes it clear that the small parish could easily support craftsmanship equal to that found in the great Minster. The pride we saw in the craft guilds who sponsored the plays can be found equally in the heart of the glass painter.

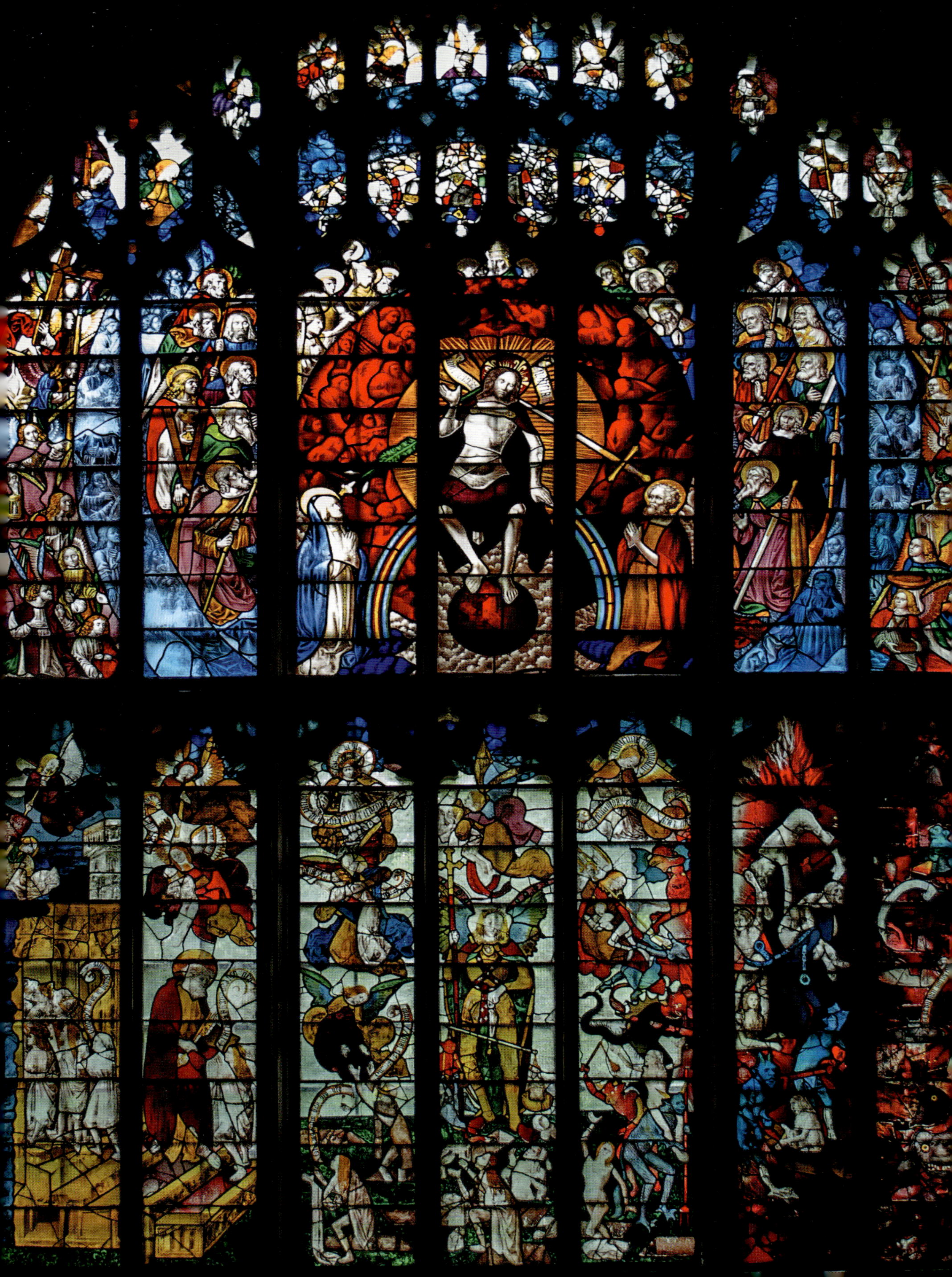

6

St Mary's Parish Church, Fairford, Gloucestershire: Surviving Iconoclasm

—

The work of Low Countries glaziers, Fairford's 28 windows display a remarkably detailed presentation of biblical subjects focused on the Life of Christ. The imagery parallels meditative literature, in particular, Nicholas Love's early fifteenth-century *The Mirror of the Blessed Life of Jesus Christ*, a translation of the Latin *Meditationes vitae Christi* of Franciscan tradition. A great deal has changed in the almost three centuries since the glazing of Chartres. First, this is a parish church, which supported both the religious and the social needs of the locality. As mentioned in the discussion of All Saints in Chapter Five, citizens were born, married and interred within the church's authority, whose obligation was to record these vital statistics. New religious Orders, such as the Franciscans, had been founded to engage directly in preaching to a lay, rather than clerical, population. Literacy had greatly increased, demonstrated by the popularity of Love's work. Prosperous merchants had climbed to the top of the patronage order, rivalling the landed nobility. Like the nobility, the merchant maintained status through largesse distributed in the community. Records of acts of personal piety are known to us through wills from this era. They attest to the veneration of statues and the embellishing of church ritual through expensive vestments and candles. Both the wealthy and the ordinary could empathize with these stories portrayed with three-dimensional realism.

79 St Mary's Parish Church, Last Judgment w.i., 1513–18.

Prosperity and the Wool Trade

The history of the town of Fairford in the Cotswolds parallels that of many other prosperous English towns of the late Middle Ages. Located at a river crossing and amid an area renowned for its woollen cloth, it thrived as a market town from the end of the twelfth century. However, England's wars with France (sporadically from 1337 to 1453) and frequent outbursts of plague and famine diminished its prosperity. In the late 1490s, around the time when the church (illus. 80) was built, its construction depended almost entirely on the patronage of a single-family donor, John Tame and his heirs. Born around 1431, Tame was apparently a self-made man, who seized opportunities that opened up after the conclusion of the civil unrest marked by the Wars of the Roses (1455–87). He came from a family dealing in woollen cloth in Cirencester, about 11 kilometres (7 mi.) away. At the age of thirty he married Alice Twyniho, also from a prosperous mercantile family. She died ten years later, after giving birth to their children, William, Edmund, Thomas and Eleanor. At a time when Fairford's property values were depressed, Tame took the initiative to acquire large tracts of land for raising sheep as well as harnessing waterpower provided by the Coln river. He subsequently transferred his residence and business, becoming one of the era's best-known clothing merchants as well as being appointed Justice of the Peace for the County of Gloucester in 1496. He probably began the reconstruction of the church in the late 1490s, replacing all the fabric except the central tower. John's tomb chest with its monumental brass relief is on the north side of the chancel, a location traditionally occupied by a principal patron.

After his death in 1500, his son Edmund (1471–1534) was responsible for the installation of the glass (illus. 79). Some scholars have suggested that Henry VIII (r. 1509–47) may have financially supported some of the windows. He knighted Edmund Tame in 1516. In the south aisle, three windows show the elements of the creed presented by the Twelve Apostles. The tracery lights contain ostrich feathers and the inscription *Ich dene* (I serve), the motto of the Prince of Wales. Other scholars remind us that such associations can serve as a donor's 'name dropping', listing important associations that they enjoyed. Certainly, they were displayed with pride for Henry's royal visit to Fairford in 1520.

Although all scholars agree that Fairford's windows were produced by artists who had trained in the Lowlands, the date as well as the artists' identities has been debated. Barnard Flower, who executed the glass at King's College Chapel, Cambridge, for two years preceding his death in 1517, has often been named. Keith Barley has raised the fascinating suggestion that Michel Sittow

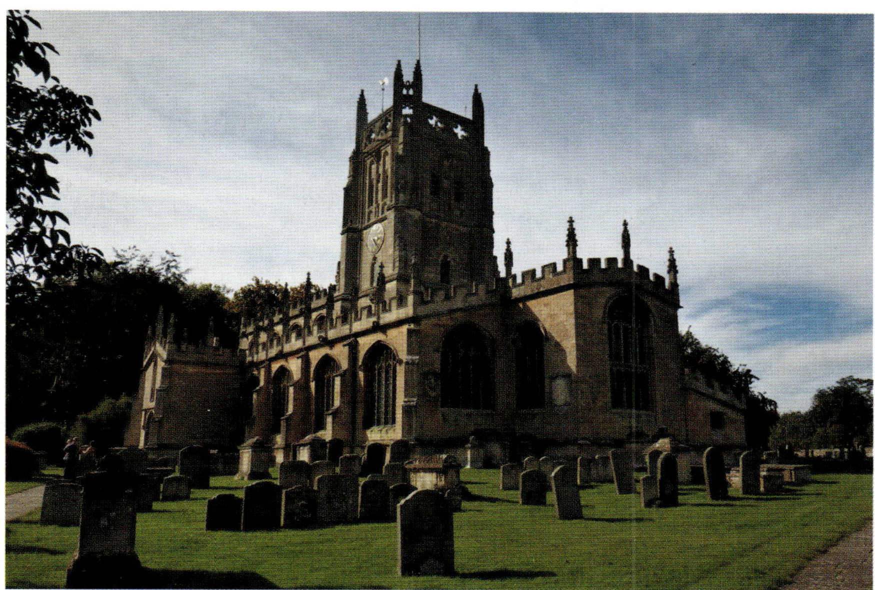

80 Fairford Parish Church, Fairford, Gloucestershire, exterior, *c.* 1490–1500.

(1469–1525) may have designed the glass around 1503–5 for other artists to paint. Sittow had studied with Hans Memling of Bruges. Memling's work, especially his *Last Judgement* triptych (1467–71, National Museum, Gdańsk, Poland), shows striking similarities with Fairford's west window.

Survival through the Reformation

The windows' survival stands in marked contrast to the loss of the vast majority of England's medieval church decoration, statuary, service vestments and liturgical furniture. Henry VIII broke with the papacy but still supported traditional ritual. Under his son, Edward VI (r. 1547–53), however, court-sanctioned iconoclasm became normative. Royal injunctions mandated reformers to 'destroy all shrines … pictures, paintings and all other monuments of feigned miracles … so that there remain no memory of the same in walls, glass-windows, or elsewhere within their church or houses' (Injunction 28). Under Elizabeth, destruction lessened, but normative procedure was to replace, not repair, historic church furnishings. A second wave of iconoclasm came during the Civil Wars of 1642–51 and the influence of the Puritan leader (Lord Protector), Oliver Cromwell, until his death in 1658.

Although parclose screens and misericords are preserved, the rest of Fairford's Pre-Reformation liturgical furniture is gone. The church boasts commemorative monuments such as the monumental brasses of John Tame and his wife and several descendants, and later stone effigies of Roger Lygon and his wife Katherine, widow of the grandson of John Tame. We find elegant carved wooden screens from about 1520 and a 1626 altar, moved from the chancel to the south chapel in 1920. A 'mazer' or drinking bowl from about 1484 remains with the church, but all the liturgical vessels, such as the 1576 chalice and paten, are post-Reform. The windows may have been whitewashed to obscure images at some time. If they were, by the 1630s the whitewash clearly had been removed, as two visitors commented on the windows in verse, both poems entitled *Upon Fairford Windows*. Richard Corbet (1582–1635) was bishop of Oxford and then Norwich. William Strode (1602–1645) was Public Orator of Christ Church College, Oxford.

North: Life of Mary and Infancy of Christ

On entering the church, a parishioner would have been confronted by the two huge windows that anchor the longitudinal axis (see illus. 79 and 85). At the front (east) the Death of Christ, and at the back (west) the Last Judgement. These themes dominated Christian thinking. The faithful believed that the sacrificial death of Christ enabled those who followed him to live forever. However, at the Last Judgement, humanity's Doom, Christ would judge the living and the dead, separating the faithful from the faithless. The complex revelation of this story is played out in the windows set in the aisles. Those flanking the Death of Christ, four on the north and four on the south, present an accessible narrative of the history of salvation. To medieval Christians, many Christian events were foretold in the Hebrew Scriptures. The sequence began with a four-light window (illus. 81) showing the Serpent tempting Eve to eat the forbidden fruit (Genesis 3:1–6), God appearing to Moses in the Burning Bush (Exodus 3:1–6), Joshua as the successor of Moses, kneeling close to Gideon's fleece (Joshua 1:1–9; Judges 6:36–40) and the Queen of Sheba coming to hear the wisdom of King Solomon (1 Kings 10:1–13). All four of these themes are found in the *Biblia Pauperum* (illus. 82), a pictorial commentary showing correspondences between the Old and New Testaments that gained wide popularity in block-book form during the fifteenth century.

81 Fairford Parish Church, Temptation of Eve, Burning Bush,
Joshua with Gideon's Fleece and Queen of Sheba, n.v.

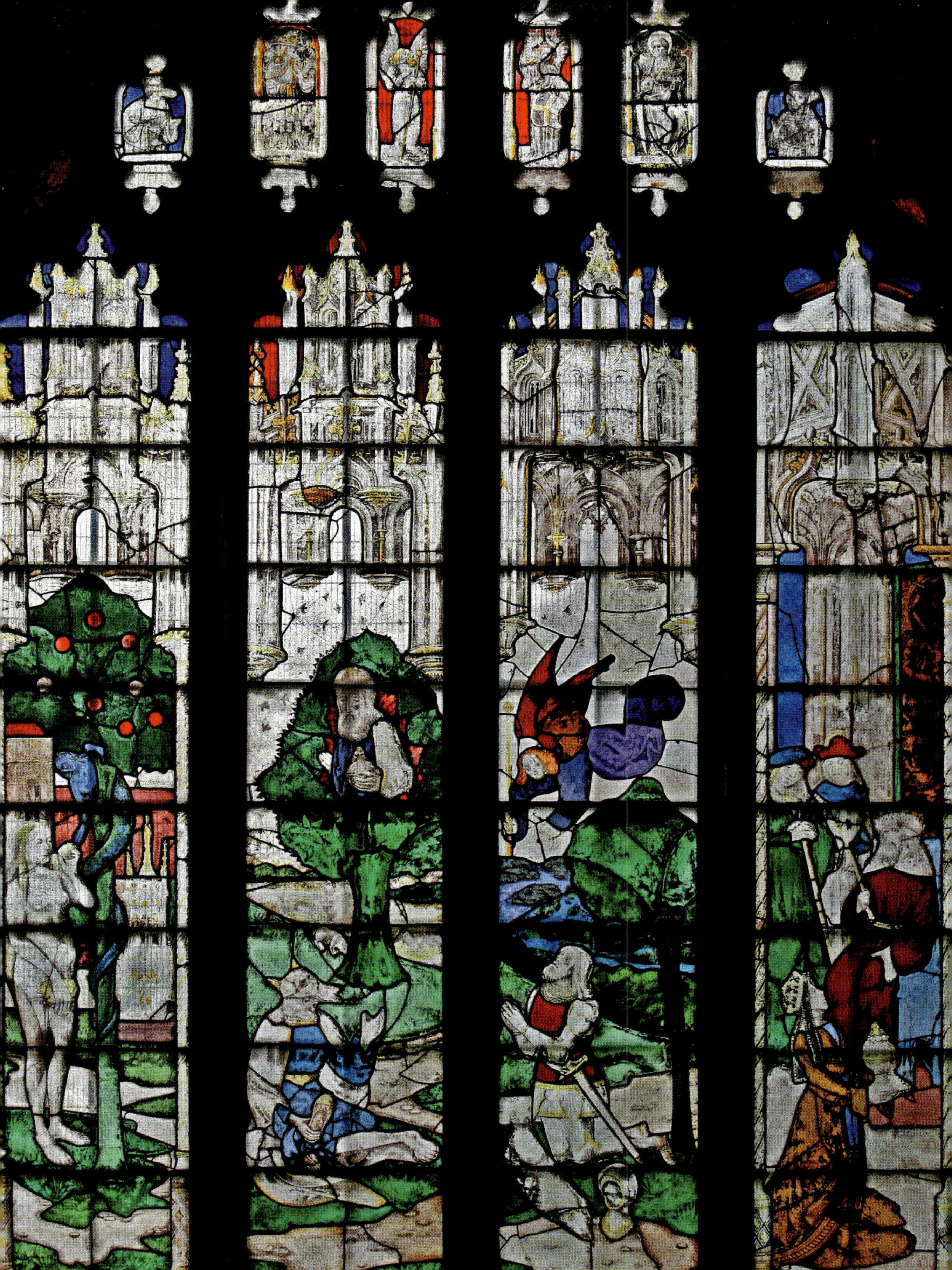

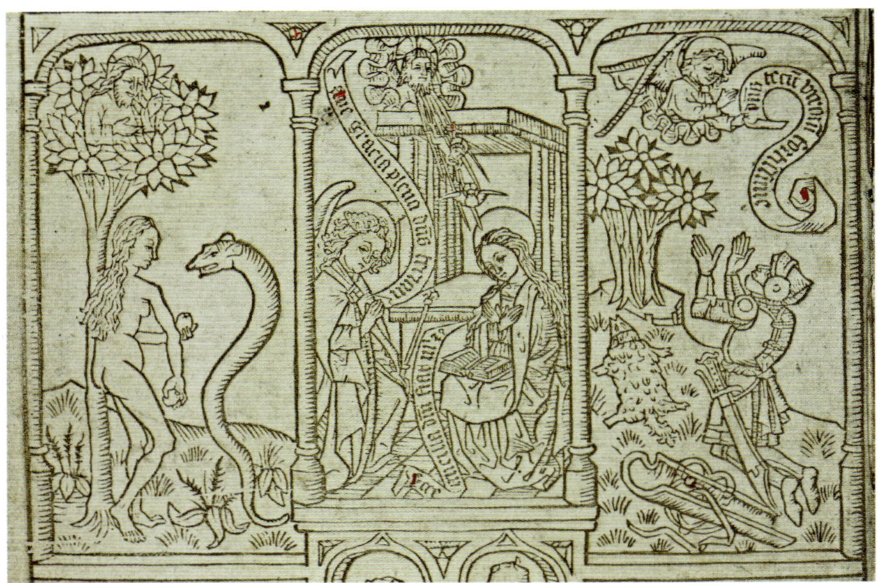

82 *Biblia Pauperum*, folio a, Temptation of Eve, Annunciation and Gideon's Fleece, Netherlands or Germany, *c.* 1470.

Building on this precedent, events surrounding the life of the Virgin Mary follow. Sadly, although there is very little glass that is not original, this window has lost much painted detail. Mary's parents, Anna and Joachim, greet each other at the Golden Gate of Jerusalem. Anna, long barren, has been told by an angel that she has conceived. Joachim, rejected because of his inability to sire a child, has returned to the city. In the next frame, Anna gives birth to Mary and in the following, Mary, as a child, is presented to the Temple. The last scene is the betrothal of Joseph and Mary blessed by the High Priest. These episodes are not described in any of the four Gospels. They come from the Protoevangelium of James, written in the second century, probably in Syria, that describes the life of the Virgin Mary and the infancy of Christ. More accessible to a local audience, however, was Nicholas Love's *The Mirror of the Blessed Life of Jesus Christ*. Love was a Carthusian monk at Mount Grace Priory, North Yorkshire, now an English Heritage Site. The Franciscan Latin text probably dates from the early fourteenth century and Love's version, arranged into meditations for each day of the week, to 1410. The Monday Mediation includes the text: 'as it is written in the Life of Our Lady Saint Mary, when she was three years old, she was offered in the Temple by her father and mother and there she abode and dwelled until her fourteenth year.' These details were important to the citizens of the time. As medieval society became more like the modern world, ordinary

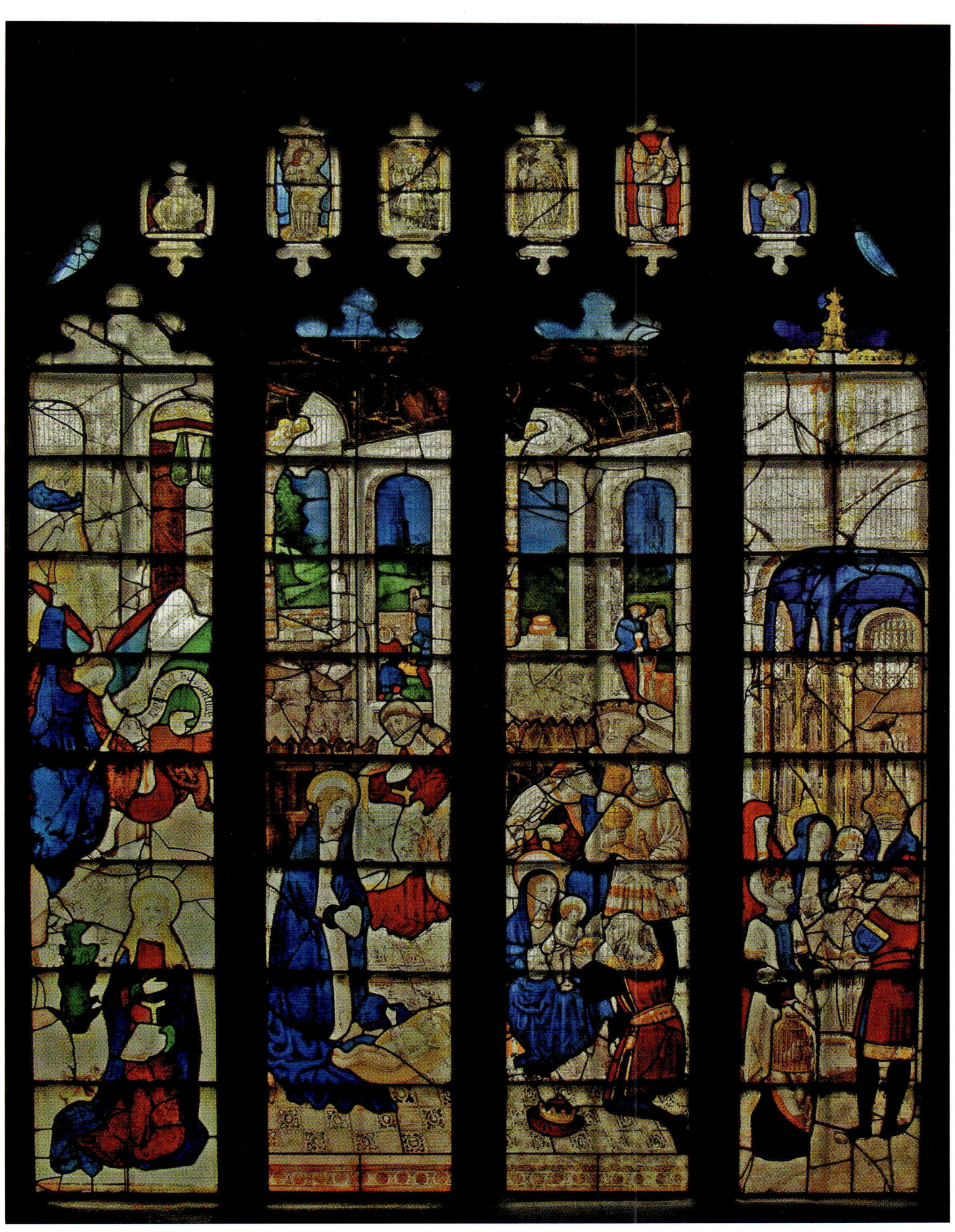

83 Fairford Parish Church, Annunciation, Nativity, Adoration of the Magi, Presentation of the Infant in the Temple, n.III.

citizens, not monks, exerted considerable influence on the building and decoration of churches. Their lives were dominated by family relations, the negotiations of marriage and the joys and dangers of giving birth. They supported imagery that spoke to their world.

The third window (illus. 83) of the Annunciation, Nativity, Adoration of the Magi and Presentation in the Temple is solidly within scriptural tradition, but for the parishioner of the era, there was little difference between canonical text and received practice. Although a growing number were literate, scripture was largely confined to Latin. The late fourteenth-century so-called Wycliffe Bible, associated with the Lollard movement, was available, but could be seen as tainted. The parish was primarily instructed in the faith through sermon and image. Gabriel appears to the Virgin asking that she consent to become the mother of the Saviour (Luke 1:26–38). The *Biblia Pauperum* places the image of Eve tempted next to the Annunciation. Love's text (Monday) presents a rhymed couplet: 'Also this day the first woman, Eve, through pride, assenting to the serpent, the devil of hell, was the cause of man's damnation. And this day the blessed maiden Marie through meekness, believing in the angel Gabriel, was the cause of man's salvation.' Then follows Christ's birth (Luke 2:5–20). Mary kneels, adoring the naked child, and Joseph is behind her. Through a window at the back of the stable the shepherds are seen approaching. In the next lancet is the Adoration of the Magi (Matthew 2:1–12): the oldest king takes off his hat to kneel before Mary holding her child. Finally, the Presentation of the Infant in the Temple (Luke 2:21–38) includes a cage with two doves, as required for Mary's Purification (Luke 2:24). This ancient ritual of blessing women after childbirth was in active practice at the time of Fairford's windows. It was a standard part of parish life. After birth, a woman remained at home, cared for by her relatives until presented in a ceremony called 'churching', most often at the southern porch of these churches.

The following window sets the Assumption of the Virgin Mary in the centre. She is lifted into heaven and crowned by two angels; God the Father is above. To the left is the Rest on the Flight to Egypt (Matthew 2:13–18) (illus. 84) and to the right the Finding of the Boy Jesus in the Temple (Luke 2:41–51). Both episodes are dramatic, reaching out with stories of parental concern. The Holy Family have fled to Egypt to protect their child from Herod's command to slay infant boys. Mary sits on the ground holding her child while the hard-working donkey grazes. Behind her, Joseph reaches up to gather dates from a tree. We see on the left an angel bending its branches, a detail derived from the Gospel of Pseudo-Matthew. The apocryphal text narrates that the Christ-Child heard

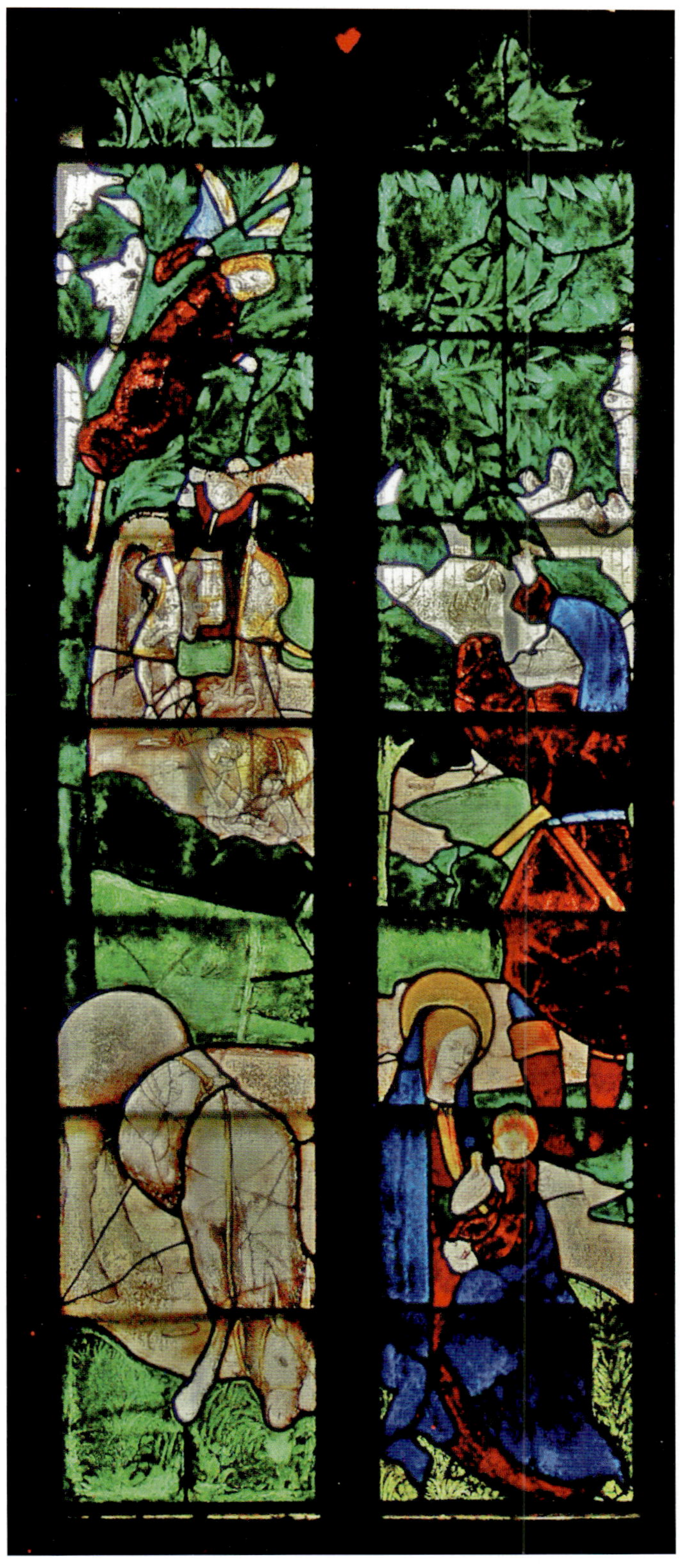

84 Fairford Parish Church, Flight into Egypt, n.11.

his mother long for the dates and commanded: 'O tree, bend thy branches, and refresh my mother with thy fruit' (Pseudo Matthew 20). Terror, however, lurks behind them. In the distance Herod's soldiers murder three children, while a mother, dressed in red, lifts her arms in lament.

Chancel: Christ Suffering and Death

The large window in the chancel narrates the Passion of Christ (illus. 85). On the left, the lower level begins with Christ seated on a donkey about to enter the gates of Jerusalem (Luke 19:20–40). This moment includes the earlier episode of Christ meeting Zacchaeus (Luke 19:1–10). Short of stature, the wealthy tax-collector had climbed a tree to get a better look at Christ passing. Jesus called him down and announced that he would stay with him that night. Zacchaeus' neighbours grumbled that he was corrupt, an accusation that must have resonated with the businessman Edmund Tame, who funded the window. Zacchaeus replied 'Look, half of my possessions, Lord, I will give to the poor; and if I have defrauded anyone of anything, I will pay back four times as much' (Luke 19:8).

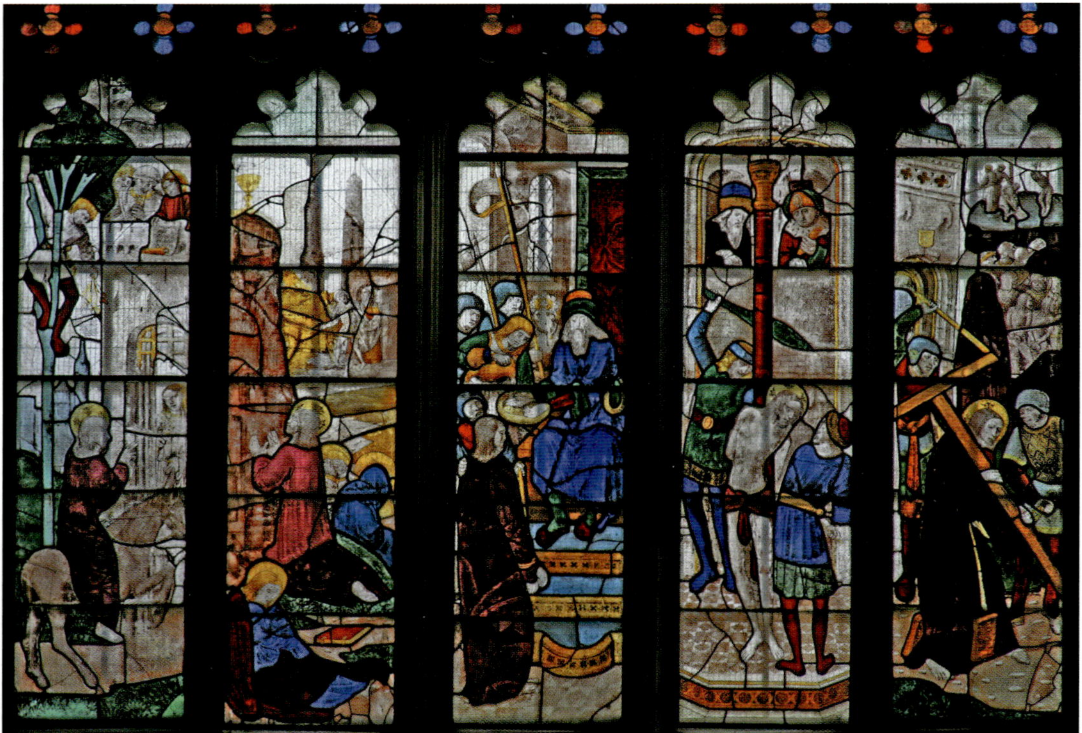

85 Fairford Parish Church, Passion: Entry into Jerusalem, Agony in the Garden, Christ before Pilate, Flagellation, Christ Carries His Cross, n.1.

The series continues with Christ praying in the Garden of Gethsemane before his death, then Christ brought before the Roman governor Pilate, who washes his hands after condemning him. The central position of the judgement, with the enthroned Pilate in blue before a red damasked cloth, clearly related to Edmund Tame's position as high sheriff of Gloucestershire. Christ is then beaten and, finally, he carries his cross on the way to Golgotha, exiting the gate he entered in the first scene. Above, at either end of a long horizonal scene, mounted spectators appear to debate the meaning of what they see. Christ, in the centre, is on the cross; angels hover in the air on either side, while Longinus pierces Christ's side with his lance. Flanking him are the two thieves also crucified. To the left (on Christ's right) the Good Thief looks down on John comforting the Virgin Mary, who swoons in his arms.

South: Christ's Resurrection and Triumph over Death

The window to the south (illus. 86) shows three events immediately following. Christ is taken down from the cross and then he is buried (Luke 23:50–53; Matthew 27:57–60; John 19:38–42). William Strode, the poet mentioned above, was particularly moved by Christ's pale and lifeless body as it is lowered from the cross:

> See where he suffers for thee: see
> His body taken from the Tree:
> Had ever death such life before?
> The limber corps, besullyd ore
> With meager palenesse, doth display
> A middle state twixt Flesh and Clay:
> His armes and leggs, his head and crowne,
> Like a true Lambskinne dangling downe.[1]

The tall, narrow lancet intensifies the relationship between the figures. Joseph of Arimathea and Nicodemus can probably be identified as the two figures actively engaged. One holds the limp body in his arms; the other waits below with outstretched arms, surely a gesture recognized by a parishioner as the desire to embrace the body of a beloved companion. The form of Christ's body may very well have been inspired by the emblem of the Order of the Golden Fleece (a reference to the Greek story of Jason and the Argonauts). Established in 1430 by Philip the Good, Duke of Burgundy, it was the most distinguished chivalric

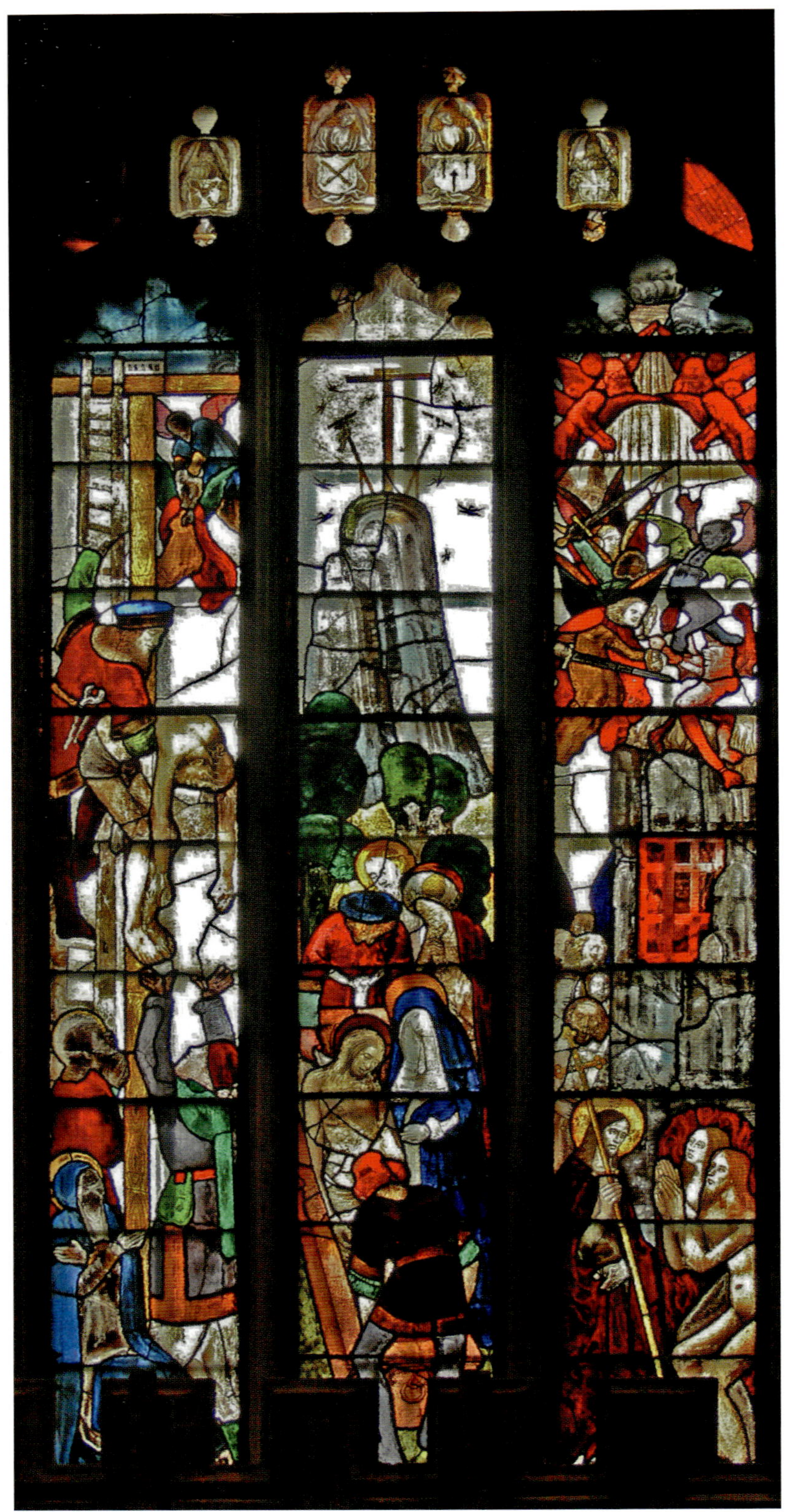

86 Fairford Parish Church, Deposition, Burial, Harrowing of Hell, s.II.

order of its time and certainly familiar to a Lowlands artist. The badge of the Golden Fleece displays a dangling lambskin, curving like Christ's body, with the head midway. The scene of the burial repeats some of the same protagonists: the man in red with the blue hat reappears to lay Christ's body in the grave and Mary, again in blue, stands next to her son, as if she must take one last look. Above them towers Golgotha, with Christ's empty cross in the centre, the two thieves still attached to theirs, while carrion fill the air.

Christ then descends to purgatory, where the souls of the just await liberation. This event is not textualized in the Gospels but is implicit. The scene of the Harrowing of Hell was a standard illustration in English manuscripts, at least from the eleventh century, exemplified by the Tiberius Psalter (British Library, Cotton MS Tiberius C.VI). Inspiring many subsequent illustrations, the composition shows Christ approaching a dragon's open maw, symbolic of the jaws of hell, and pulling out the liberated souls. At the bottom of the window, Christ confronts Adam and Eve framed in a red mandorla. The gates of hell glow a fiery red and angels fight with demons. Nicholas Love sets forth a Sunday meditation:

Afterwards, the Prince and the mightiest conqueror, Jesus, through his bitter passion and hardest death, thus cancelled and utterly overcame the sovereign tyrant, and man's enemy and his adversary, Satan, with all his wicked hosts. As soon as the soul was departed from the body, he went to that tyrant's prison of hell . . . By his sovereign might and righteousness he broke the gates of that prison and entered with unspeakable joy and bliss to the chosen people there that has been in distress from many thousand years before. And then that prison turned into a blissful paradise through his presence. And all that blessed fellowship with mirth and joy, that may not be spoken or thought of, honoured and worshipped and thanked sovereignly their Lord that had so graciously delivered them. So, in hymns and joyful songs, the prophecy fulfilled first Adam and his progeny, afterwards Noah and Abraham, Moses and David with all their holy fathers and prophets loving and thanking our Lord Jesus . . . And when it drew towards the third day from his Passion, our Lord spoke to them all and said in this manner of words: 'Now it is time that I release my body from death to life and therefore now I shall go and take my body again.'

Reassurance to the Living

Christ's Transfiguration (illus. 87) commands the centre of the next window, standing as a prefiguration of the Resurrection, which is not depicted at Fairford. After Christ revealed his divinity to Peter, James and John, he commanded them, 'Tell no one about the vision until after the Son of Man has been raised from the dead' (Matthew 17:9). On the left, that promise is fulfilled as the resurrected Christ appears to his mother. Love's text assures the reader of Christ's bond with her, coming to comfort her first. The passage begins by describing her sorrowful prayer:

> 'Almighty God the father, most merciful and most piteous,
> well you know that my dear son Jesus is dead and buried. For
> he was nailed to the cross and hung between two thieves. After
> he was dead, I helped to bury him with my own hands, he whom
> I conceived without corruption and bore without travail and
> sorrow. And he was all my good, all my desire, all the life, and the
> comfort of my soul. But at the last he passed away from me . . . all
> his enemies had risen against him and scorned him and damned
> him. And his own disciples forsake and fled from him and I,
> his sorrowful mother, could not help him' . . . As she was praying
> with sweet tears shedding, low, suddenly our Lord Jesus came
> and appeared to her. He was in all the whitest of clothes and with
> glad and loving demeanour greeted her with these words: *Salve*
> *sancta parens*, that is to say, hail, holy mother. And then, turning
> her head, she said, 'Art thou Jesus my blessed son?' And therewith,
> kneeling down, she honoured him. And he also was kneeling
> at her side: 'My dear mother I am he, I have risen, and low,
> I am with thee.'

On the right, Christ speaks with the three women who have come to anoint him in his tomb. Jesus had already mentioned them when speaking with his blessed mother. 'Among other loving communications, he told her of the great energies and the fervent search of Mary Magdalene and said that he would go and show himself bodily to comfort her. And our Lady gladdened and spoke thereof, "My blessed son, go in peace and comfort her for she loves full much and was fully sorrowful at your death."' Love then explains:

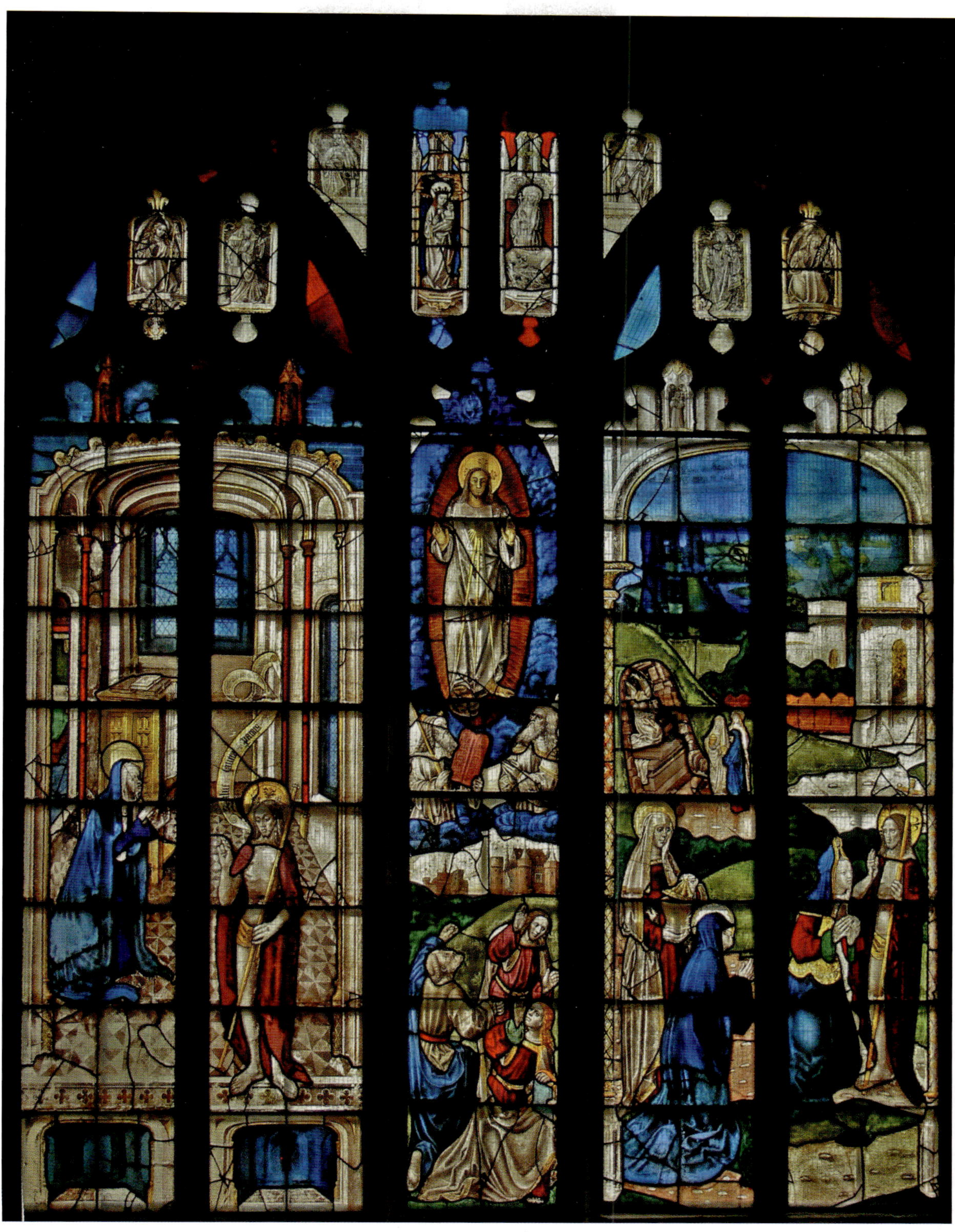

87 Fairford Parish Church, Christ Appears to His Mother, Transfiguration, Appearance of Christ to Three Marys, III.

And then he was in the garden where Magdalene was and
said to her, 'Woman whom do you seek and why do you weep?'
Nevertheless, she, not knowing him, both distracted and out of
herself, supposed that he had been a gardener. She said, 'Sir if you
have taken him away tell me where and what you have done to
him that I may bring him to me' . . . And then our Lord having compassion on such great sorrow and abundant weeping, called her
by her familiar name and said, 'Mary'. By these words suddenly
all sorrow was healed and she knew him. With unspeakable joy
she said, '*Raboni*' (meaning Master). 'Be you he that I have so long
sought and was so long hidden from me?'

The image in this window, however, does not concentrate on this singular
apparition of the risen Christ to Magdalene. The message is more communal,
stressing the collective work experienced by women of the time. In the background, the scene shows all three Marys greeted by the angel at the empty grave.
In the foreground, the three Marys confront the risen Christ as described in the
Gospel of Matthew (28:1–10). Love's text offers this meditation:

Furthermore, as these three Marys went towards the city, our cour-
teous Lord met with them along the way, meekly greeting them and
saying, hail to thee. And they were so joyful in his presence that it
may not be told. They fell down at his feet and held them and kissed
them with joyful tears. And they also spoke with him and he with
them with familiar words of spiritual comfort. They beheld his
glorious body with unspeakable joy; the same which they had
beheld three days before with such sovereign sorrow. And then
our Lord Jesus said to them that they should go and see to his
brethren in Galilee.

The next window is divided into two scenes that emphasize Christ's relationship with his male disciples. When several travel to Emmaus, they are joined
by a man who expounds on the necessity of Christ's sacrificial death, as foretold
by the prophets. At dinner, and the 'breaking of the bread', they recognize that
their companion is Christ (Luke 24:13–32). Christ also appeared to his disciples
who gathered in Jerusalem. At one moment he addresses Thomas, asking him to
verify the truth of the bodily resurrection by placing his finger into the wounds in
his side (John 20:23–9). The following window shows the Miraculous Draught

of Fishes (John 21:1–14), another instance when Christ was unrecognized by his disciples. They were fishing and he called to them from the shore. Then follows the Ascension (Luke 24:50–51) and the Descent of the Holy Spirit, or Pentecost (Acts 2:1–4). The Virgin Mary, as befits the dedication of the church, is most prominent, clad in blue and sitting in the centre of the Apostles.

Doctrine and Confrontation

Four windows that follow are more doctrinal than reflective. The first three present the Twelve Apostles, each with a verse from the Apostles Creed (illus. 88). A strong, if inaccurate, tradition associated the text with the Apostles themselves, as a collective proclamation:

> I believe in God, the Father almighty, Creator of heaven and earth, and in Jesus Christ, his only Son, our Lord, who was conceived by the Holy Spirit, born of the Virgin Mary, suffered under Pontius Pilate, was crucified, died and was buried; he descended into hell; on the third day he rose again from the dead; he ascended into heaven, and is seated at the right hand of God the Father almighty; from there he will come to judge the living and the dead. I believe in the Holy Spirit, the holy Catholic Church, the communion of saints, the forgiveness of sins, the resurrection of the body, and life everlasting.

The idea was widely illustrated, for example in a programme of about 1420–35, associated with Hereford Cathedral (illus. 89), and now in the Museum of Fine Arts, Boston. James the Less holds a banderole with the Latin text *ecclesiam catholicam, sanctorum communionem* (the holy Catholic Church, the communion of saints). Indeed, it is this creed that is played out through the entire iconographic programme of Fairford's windows. The Apostles are followed by a window of the four great Church Fathers, from left to right: Jerome (347–420), Gregory the Great (540–604), Ambrose (340–397) and Augustine (354–430). Directly across from them, on the north, are their counterparts: the Four Evangelists and then twelve prophets, each with lines from their prophecies.

The four upper windows of the church show a dramatic confrontation of persecutors and defenders of the faith. On the north the series begins with wicked priests: Annas offering money to Judas, Judas putting it into his bag and the High Priest Caiaphas, who condemned Christ (illus. 90). Generic images

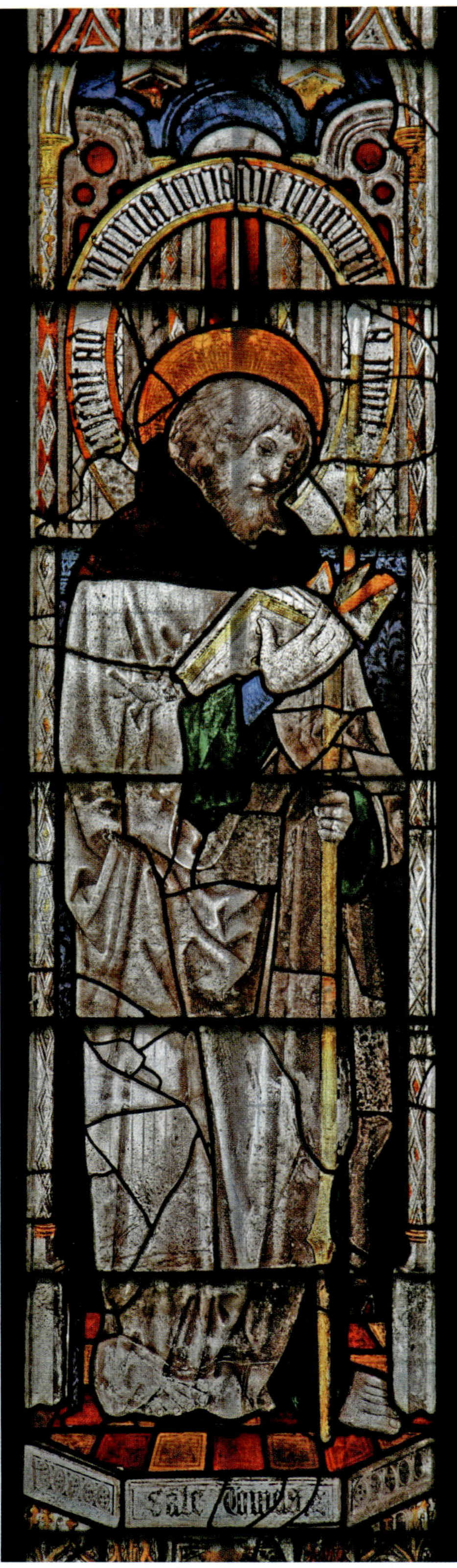

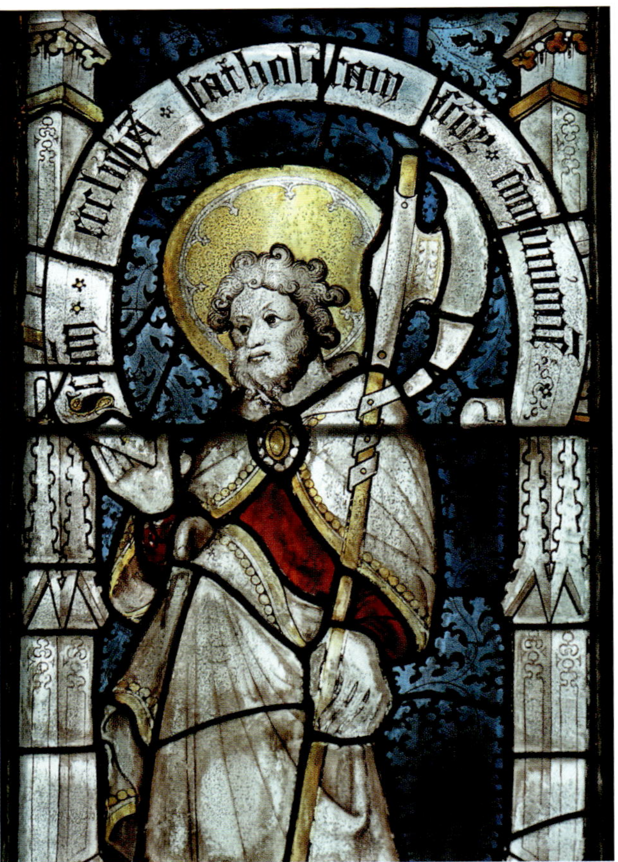

88 Fairford Parish Church, St Thomas
with lines of the Apostle Creed, s.VII.

89 James the Less with lines of the Apostle Creed,
1420–35, probably from Hereford Cathedral,
now at the Museum of Fine Arts, Boston.

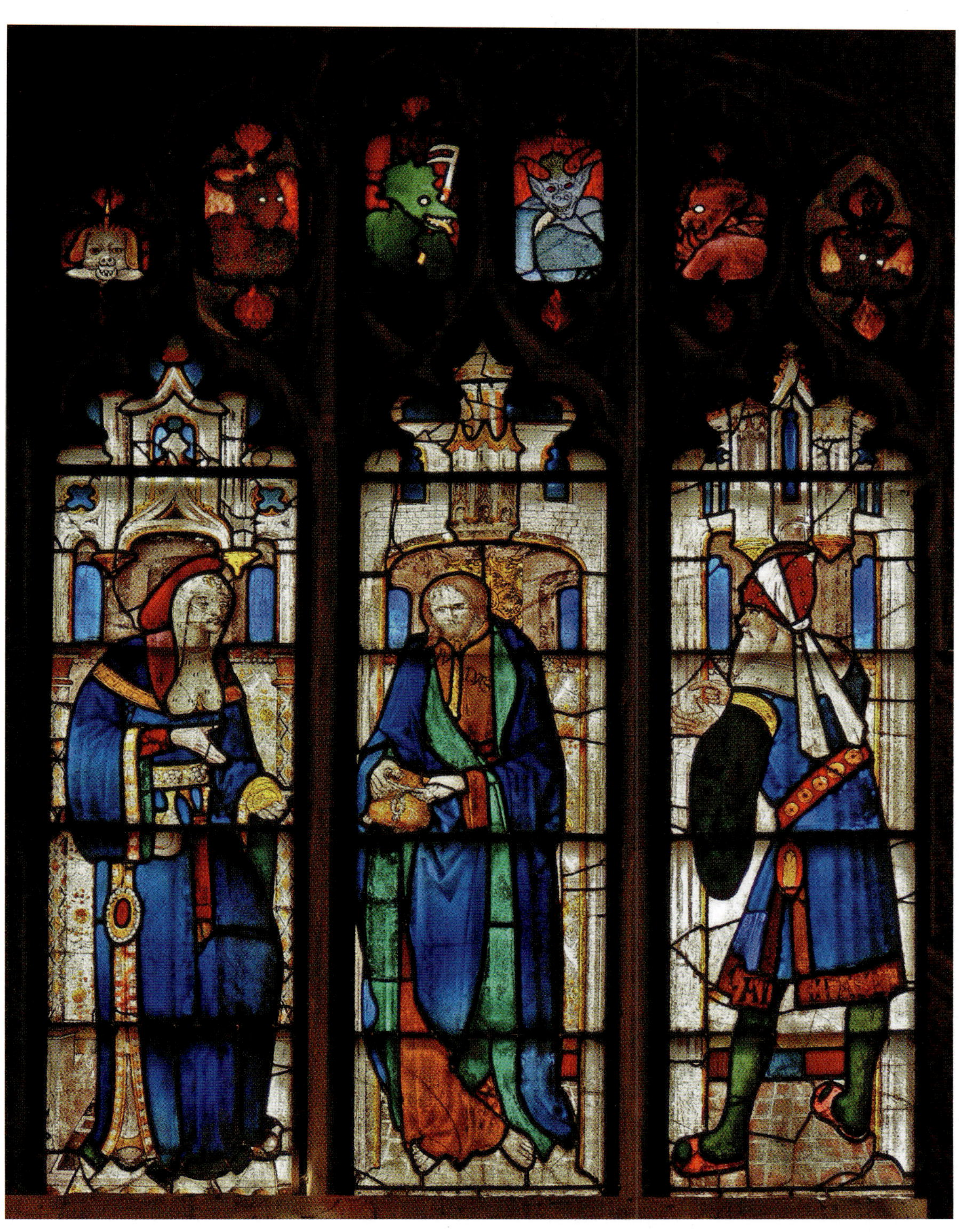

90 Fairford Parish Church, Wicked Priests: Annas offering money to Judas,
Judas putting it into his bag, and the High Priest Caiaphas, n.VII.

of soldiers follow, invariably carrying a severed head. Herod the Great can be identified holding a murdered Innocent, a reminder of the scene from the Flight into Egypt in the north aisle (see illus. 84), and the emperor Nero by an inscription. They are surmounted by tracery with vivid, colourful demons against a fiery background. On the south, surmounted by angels, are sixteen saints who confront the sinners on the north. Some are easily identifiable by their attributes, such as Margaret, patron of women in childbirth, with her dragon at her feet, or Sebastian, patron of those stricken with plague, riddled with arrows. Others are generic: a king, emperor, bishop or cardinal.

Last Judgement

The western windows were damaged in a storm of 1703. Christ is in Judgement (illus. 91, and see illus. 81); on his right hand (viewer's left) are the just, accepted into heaven. On his left, the damned are cast into the eternal fires of hell. The two lower windows at the sides were interchanged during a restoration. King David sits in Judgement against the Amalekite who falsely boasted that he had executed Saul. Saul, fearful of capture and humiliation, had fallen on his own sword (1 Samuel 31:4). The image should be under Christ's left, for it condemns an evil doer. The Judgement of Solomon, where he discerns the true mother of an infant by her compassion (1 Kings 3:16–28), a demonstration of the just judge, should be under Christ's right hand.

The Last Judgement's upper portions were severely damaged in the 1703 storm but conserved in their fragmentary state. The restoration, by the Chance Brothers of Birmingham, under the direction of Sebastian Evans, however, was disastrous. In 1860 the firm had restored the figures of the Apostles Thaddeus (Jude) and Matthias, making copies of many of the original pieces so that now only about 25 per cent of the original glass remains. Between 1863 and 1864, they worked on the Last Judgement, making copies of all the extant pieces; nothing of the original now appears in the upper half of the window. This time, the restoration provoked intense criticism. The Revd J. G. Joyce, who was then working on a scholarly study of the windows, led the effort to secure a historically sensitive restorer, Nathaniel H. J. Westlake, from the firm of Lavers, Barraud and Westlake, who would later author the monumental *History of Design in Stained Glass* (4 vols, London, 1891–4). In 2010, the Barley Studio, Dunnington, York, finished a twenty-year, widely praised, conservation of the windows.

Happily, lower sections of the window retain authentic glass. In the centre, the Archangel Michael weighs the souls. As in many Last Judgements, the

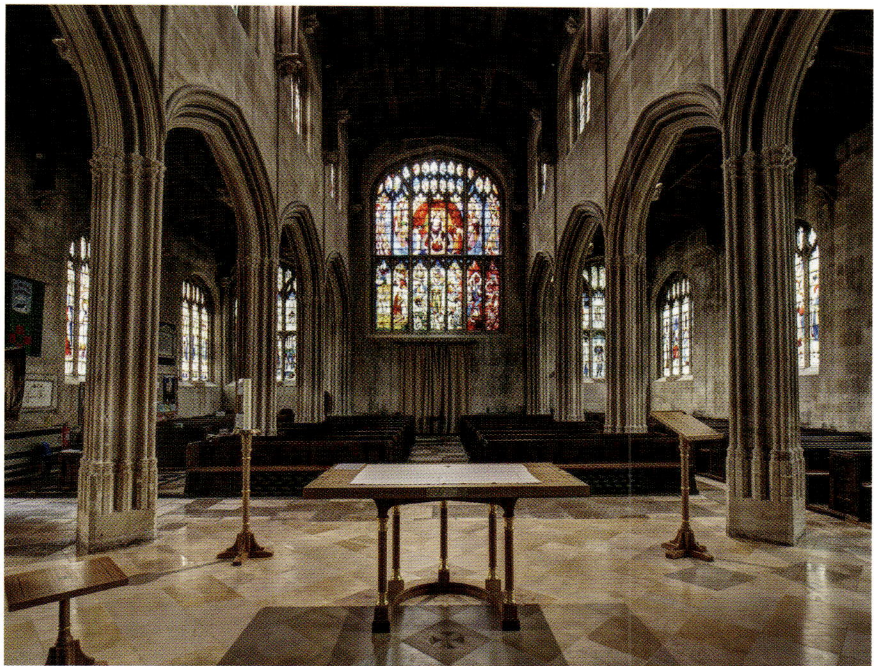

91 Fairford Parish Church, interior looking west, window, 1513–18.

tortures of the damned unleashed the inventiveness of artists. Since the goal of the narrative was to engage the viewer, the more variety, the better. Fairford's windows became renowned for their exotic depiction of the demonic. The church preserves a sheet of notes dated 1767 by a visitor from Cirencester named Samuel Rudder. He included sketches of horned demons: one attacks a man with a sword, another transports a woman in a wheelbarrow and another carries a woman on its shoulders.

The Lowlands Style and 'Alien' Glaziers

We reflect on Fairford's, and our, great fortune, 'Thy Church hath kept, what all have lost;/ And is preserved from the bane,/ Of either warr, or Puritane,' in the words of the bishop and poet Richard Corbet. Fairford's windows survive to testify to Great Britain's deeply international outlook at the time. They represent cutting-edge awareness of European changes in style. Naturally, small, portable works of art invariably led the way, such as Sir John Donne's *Enthroned Virgin and Child* (illus. 92), which he commissioned from the leading artist of Bruges, Hans Memling. Sir John was a member of Edward IV's inner circle and present in Bruges in 1468 for the wedding of Margaret of York, the king's

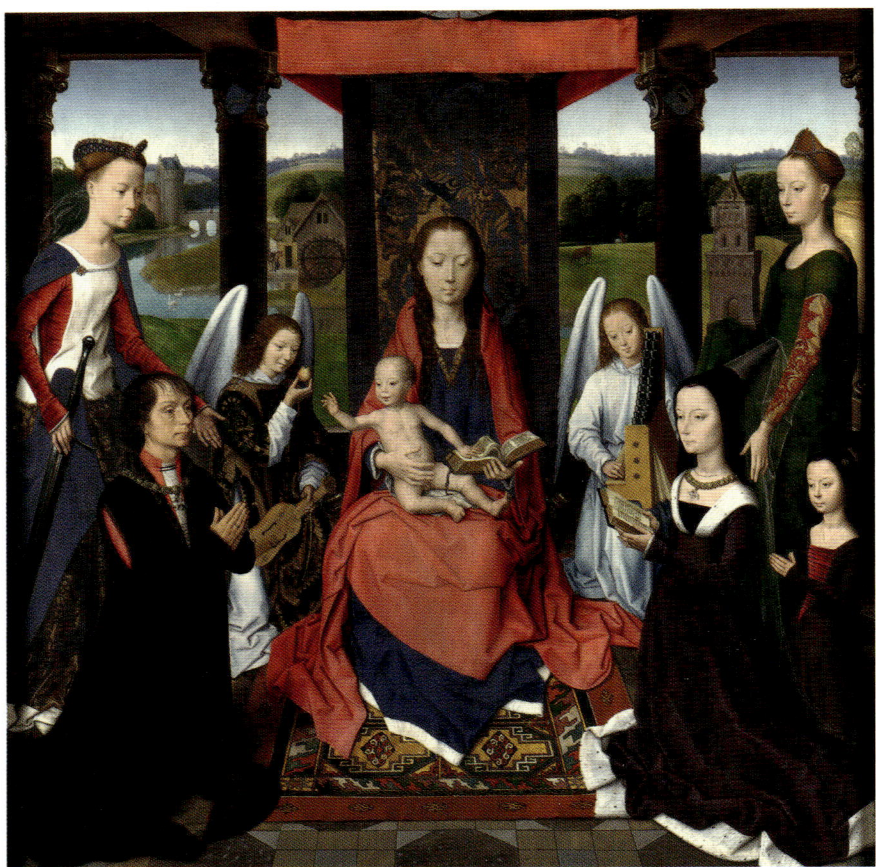

92 Hans Memling, *Enthroned Virgin and Child*, 1470s, commissioned by Sir John Donne, now at the National Gallery of Art, London.

sister, to Charles the Bold, Duke of Burgundy. Probably commissioned while he was on diplomatic mission in Bruges in 1477, the altarpiece shows Sir John, his wife Elizabeth Hastings and a daughter, as well as his two name-saints, John the Baptist and John the Evangelist, in the folding wings. The glass painters in Fairford favoured three-dimensional renderings of the figure, realistic architectural settings and distant landscape vistas. The artists employed gradual washes in a painterly, rather than 'graphic', mode, that is, following the model of oil painting in its gradual transition from light to dark. The graphic mode of the early fifteenth century is visible in the face of St Bartholomew from Hereford (see illus. 89).

By the late fifteenth century, immigrant artists in stained glass had begun to settle in England, causing the London Guild of Glaziers to protest in 1474 against more than 28 'alien glaziers' working in the city. Although much of the glass documented by these early Lowlands artists has been lost, it is certain that they were responsible for major commissions, including windows in Westminster Abbey, the Pilgrimage Chapel at Walsingham, St George's Chapel at Windsor and the east window and choir aisles of Winchester Cathedral. The huge series of windows for King's College Chapel of 1515–47 is a great example. There, native-born artists, recorded as Bond, Reve and Symondes, soon adopted the style of the foreign glaziers, their work becoming indistinguishable from that of Barnard Flower, Galyon Hone or Dirck Vellert. At King's, however, the dramatic figures seem much more self-sufficient and appear to dominate the architecture, rather than being subservient to realistic spaces of both landscape and interior, as in Fairford.

Early commentators have admired Fairford's windows' realism, a hallmark of the new trends in the Lowlands. The imagery in the windows multiplies instances of personalized human interest by giving attention to situations that resonate with everyday life. William Strode described Fairford's custom of explaining the windows to parishioners and visitors by pointing at specific details with a fishing rod. He wrote, 'When with a fishing rodde the Clarke/ Saint Peters draught of fish doth marke,/ Such is the scale, the eye, the finne,/ Youd thinke they strive and leape within.'[2] The window is the Miraculous Draught of Fishes from the south aisle with its meticulous depiction of fish in the net and on the shore. A pen-and-ink drawing of about 1840 actually shows an old clerk using a fishing rod. Strode suggested that the realism of the art dissuaded fanatics from intervention: 'The Puritans were sure deceivd,/ And thought those shadowes movde and heavde,/ So held from stoning Christ.'[3] Fairford's scriptural narrative dominates; a few images of saints appear in the upper windows but these are far from central. Imagery had begun to be tolerated, as exemplified by a stained-glass panel of Christ taken down from the cross made for Hampton Court in 1629 (Victoria and Albert Museum, London, c.62-1927). It is inscribed 'the truth hereof of historical devine, and not superstitious'. Whatever the contemporary viewer's persuasion, this rich programme now enables us to empathize with a parish, its wealthy patron and its ordinary citizens in ways that transcend time.

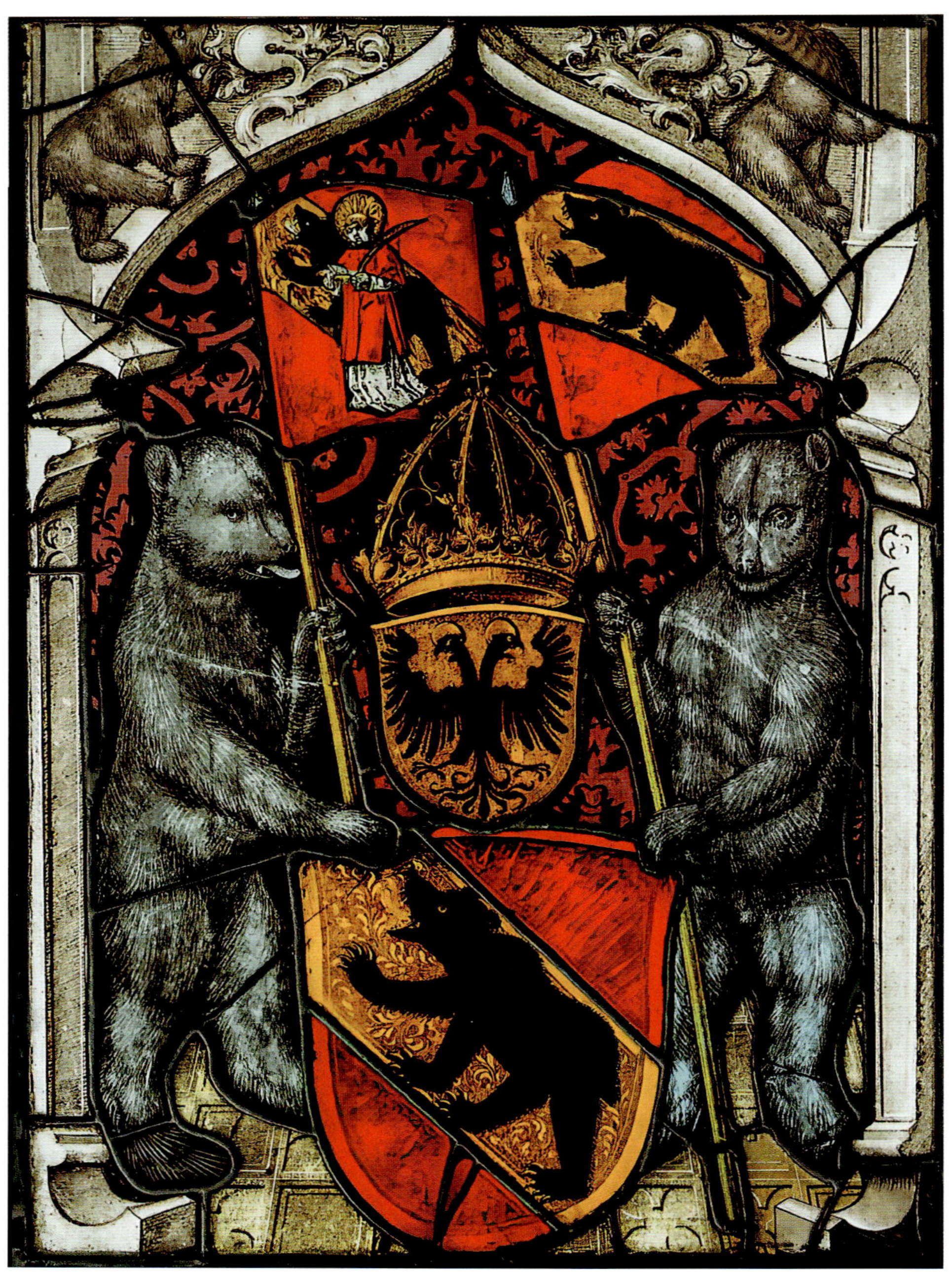

93 Lukas Zeiner, *Arms of the Canton or City of Bern*, 1500–1501, from the *Tagsatzungssaal*, Baden, Schwyz, now in a private collection.

7

Renaissance Donors in Switzerland: An Art of Exchange

—

In Switzerland, the medieval subject of stained glass was claimed by the Renaissance working class, whose labour had made it prosperous enough to donate small panels that graced the lattice windows of an inn, town hall, parlour or church. These people, for the most part, had not inherited their wealth, but were a part of the local citizenry who had prospered from changing political and social structures and were eager to demonstrate their loyalty to civic and religious organizations. Measuring about 35 × 25 centimetres (14 × 10 in.), and popular in Switzerland and southern Germany, the panels celebrated marriage alliances, trade guilds and professions. Switzerland's initiation of a democratic form of government was among the earliest in Europe. We can reflect on the country's independence, and its emphasis on local citizens. Voltaire praised the Swiss as pioneers of democracy in his essay 'Helvetia' in the *Dictionnaire philosophique* of 1764:

> Happy Helvetia! to what charter do you owe your liberty?
> to your courage, to your resolution, to your mountains.
> 'But I am your emperor.'
> 'But I do not want you any longer.'
> 'But your fathers were my father's slaves.'
> 'It is for that very reason that their children do not wish to serve you.'
> 'But I had the right belonging to my rank.'
> 'And we have the right of nature.'
> Why is liberty so rare?
> Because it is the chiefest good.[1]

Swiss Independence

The original Swiss Confederation comprised eight cantons, which gained their independence between 1291 and 1353. After the Swabian War of 1499, when the confederacy defeated the forces of the House of Habsburg, the nation was essentially sovereign. The need for self-sufficiency for a population spread across a mountainous landscape encouraged cooperative enterprises. In many smaller towns, the glass painter also worked at other occupations, such as innkeeper. Members of town councils and law courts exercised these positions periodically, most having other trades. The small panels were given as testimonials of solidarity and friendship and were produced in large numbers. A panel of the *Crucifixion* given by several individuals from the canton of Fribourg exercising the profession of lecturer has been discussed in Chapter Two.

The cantonal governments played a leading role in the development of the Swiss custom of giving windows. After their victory in the Burgundian Wars of 1474–7, the cantons expressed their enhanced status through the tradition of the *Standesscheiben* (panels showing arms of the canton). These panels, which the governments began to gift in large numbers to institutions and important people from the last quarter of the fifteenth century, contributed significantly to the custom of window donations. It became almost obligatory for cantons to exchange stained-glass panels containing their coats of arms for newly constructed town halls. The *Chronicle of Lucerne* (illus. 94) illustrates the vital role played by such windows.[2] Produced in 1513 by Diebold Schilling the Younger of Lucerne, the manuscript contains 443 illustrations within its 688 pages that record the history of the Swiss Confederation. An illustration at the beginning of the manuscript (page 13) shows the author presenting his chronicle in the Lucerne *Rathaus* (city hall). The bullseye windows depict arms of the early members of the Swiss Confederation. On the rear wall, from left to right, are the banners of Lucerne (blue and white), Uri (bull's head), Schwyz (red with small cross) and Solothurn (red and white). Lucerne's *Rathaus* appears several times (pages 245, 248, 530, 541, 619), each time showing windows depicting banners, but with slightly different sequences of cantons.

Arms of the Cantons

One of the most significant cycles of *Standesscheiben* was produced between 1500 and 1501 by Lukas Zeiner (1454–1513) for the *Tagsatzungssaal* in Baden, at the time functioning as Switzerland's parliament. Zeiner and other artists

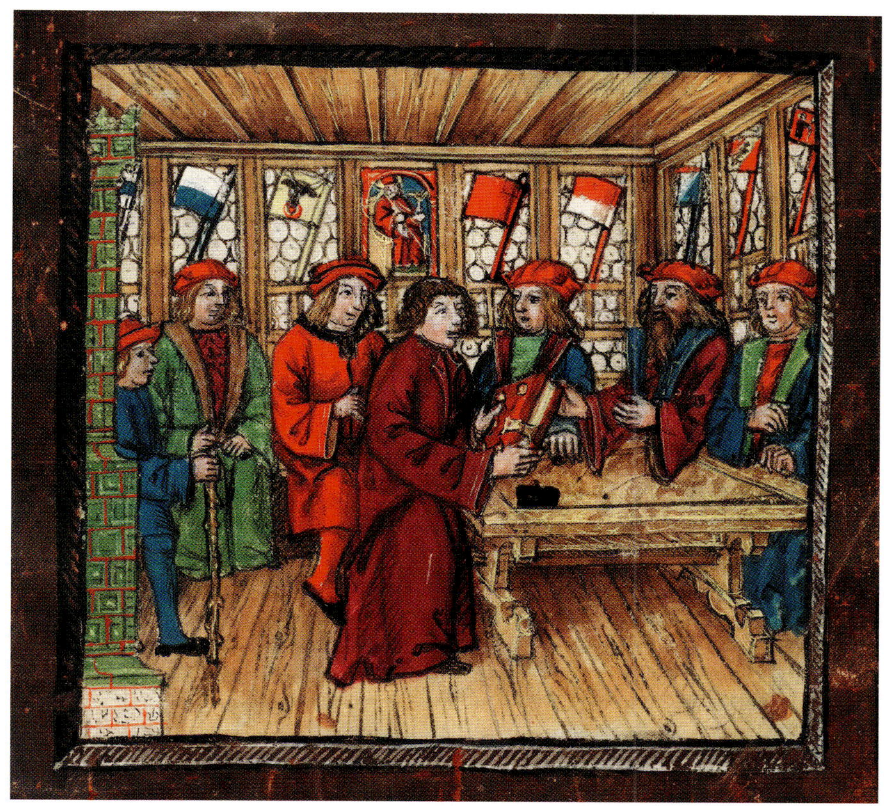

94 Diebold Schilling the Younger, *Presentation Ceremony*,
Chronicle of Lucerne, Lucerne, 1513.

repeated the model for many subsequent cycles, basically codifying the form.
The *Standesscheibe* of Bern (illus. 93) with canting arms, *Bär* (bear), exemplifies
the format. A centrally placed shield is surmounted by the arms of the Holy
Roman Empire, a double-headed black eagle on a gold ground. The arms are
flanked by two supporters who invariably carry the banners of the city or canton.
The use of a bear on the city's seal dates from the thirteenth century. By 1373
texts and images document the format of a red ground with a golden stripe, in
heraldic terms a 'bend', on which a black bear strides forward. Zeiner's panels are
enhanced by engaging figures in the border, often perched on top of the capitals
and moving out into space. This illusionistic effect imitates ornate, late Gothic
city-portal armorials with their symbolic guardians in the spandrels. Zeiner
offers great variety. The shield of Bern includes bears in the spandrels, that of
Schwyz, a hunter sounding his horn with a leaping stag, and for Glarus, two
men confronting each other with long spears. At this time, windows were constructed of traditional pot-metal glass of varied colours: rose in the damascene

background, light blue-grey for the bears, red in the flags and shields and yellow in the bends and Imperial shield and crown. Silver stain tints the gold staffs held by the bears. Zeiner is prone to embellish with surface ornament, such as damascene on the Imperial shield and the gold bend of the shield of Bern. His brushwork is precise, frequently using a continuous outline in trace or stick work to enclose a form, as seen in the spandrels, and attention to texture, as in the pelts of the bears.

Swiss History for a Bookseller

A window of 1601, given by the Zurich resident Hans Felix Haller, a bookseller, and his wife Elisabeth Vogler (illus. 95), illustrates episodes from Swiss history. Signed by the Zurich artist Josias Murer (1564–1631), who became the exclusive glass painter of the city's town hall in 1591, the subject enables us to understand the intensity of civic pride in Switzerland. Murer was a member of a distinguished family of artists, and he often worked with his father Jos Murer and his brother Christoph, the designer of the emblem book, XL *emblemata miscella nova* (see illus. 101). The panel shows the resistance of citizens to unjust overlords, illustrated by six episodes from the early fourteenth century. The upper left scene recounts the cruelty of the Vogt (governor) Landenberg, who ordered the confiscation of a yoke of oxen owned by Heinrich von Melchtal for late taxes. When the Vogt's men arrived, Heinrich and his son Arnold were ploughing their modest farm. Arnold protested, striking the men, and then was forced to flee to Uri and the protection of Walter Fürst. As punishment, Landenberg ordered that Heinrich be tortured and blinded – the scene in the window. On the right, Konrad Baumgarten of Altzellen kills the bailiff Wolfenschiessen in the bathtub for making advances towards his wife. Two episodes of William Tell are in the middle register. On the left, Tell shoots the apple off his son's head. Tell was renowned as a marksman but, to taunt him, the governor forced him to prove his accuracy at the risk of his son's life. On the right, Tell shoots the governor Gessler as he and his henchman ride through Hohle Gasse near Küssnacht, in central Switzerland. On the bottom left, peasants bring tithes to the bailiff of Landenberg, and on the right, the legendary founders of Switzerland take what has become known as the Rütli oath, after the mountain meadow near Lake Lucerne. Traditionally dated to 1307, the oath is here inscribed as 1308. It marks the foundation of the Old Swiss Confederacy by representatives of the three founding cantons, Werner Stauffacher of Schwyz, Walter Fürst of Uri and Arnold von Melchtal of Unterwalden.

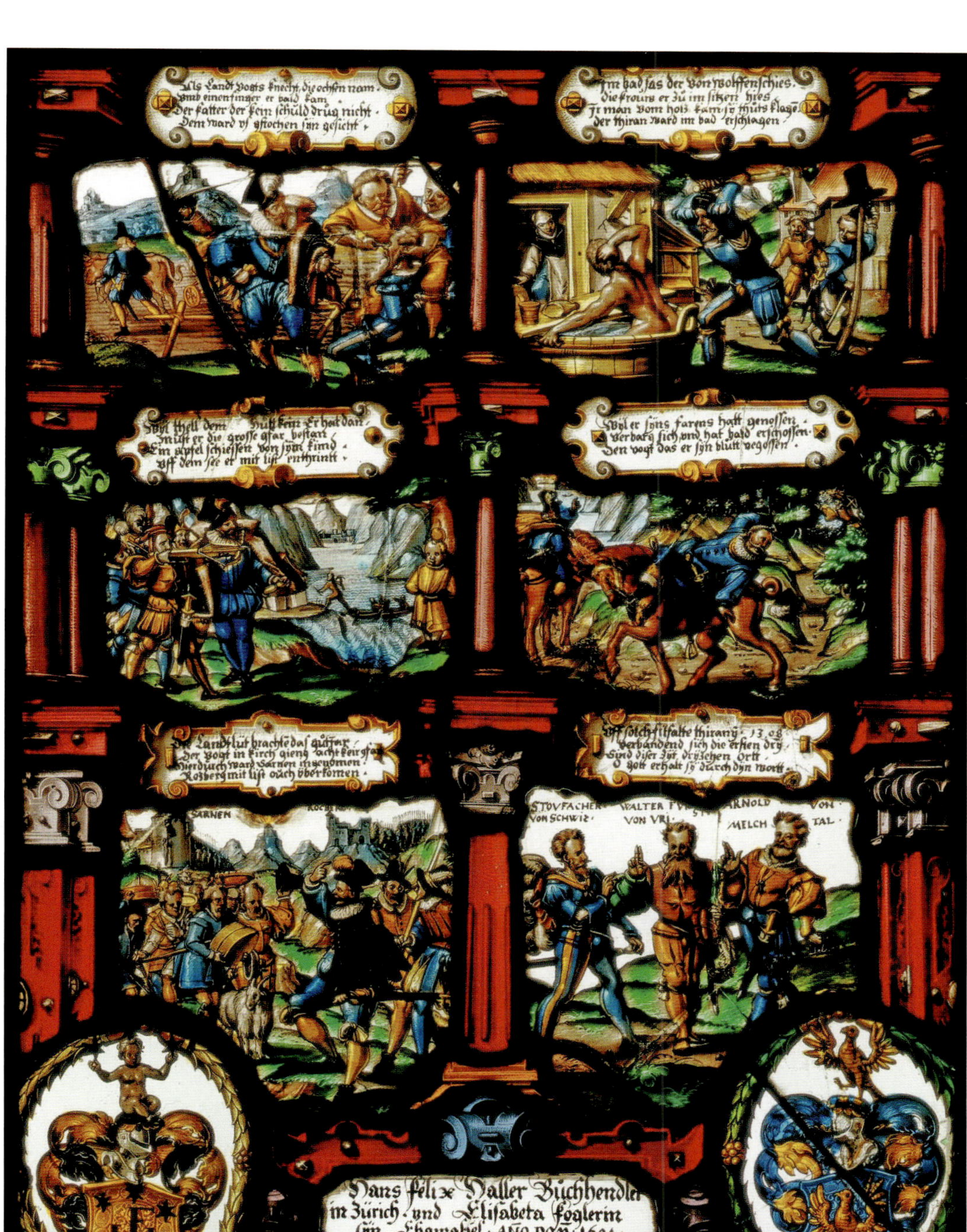

95 Josias Murer, *Episodes from Swiss History*, 1601, Vitromusée, Romont, Switzerland.

While in other areas a coat of arms was associated with nobility, Switzerland's political history allowed most citizens to have their own coat of arms regardless of class. Many of these 'badges' proclaimed the trade of the individual, a vintner's pruning knife, a tailor's pair of shears, a baker's pretzel or a farmer's ploughshare, such as that in the shield of Niklaus Holdermeyer, who gave the panel of the *Adoration of the Magi* to Rathausen (illus. 96). Quite frequently a housemark was chosen (*mark de maison, Hausmarke*). These were abstract signs, designed to be easily cut or engraved with a knife on livestock, property or buildings, and were used universally by farmers, tradesmen, merchants, artisans and other town burghers. In the panel discussed above, Hans Felix Haller's shield displays a housemark constructed from his initials F, H and H. His wife's shield refers to her family name 'Vogler' and shows a bird, in German *Vogel*, in heraldic display. Referred to as 'canting arms', this solution appears again in the shields of Bern and of Hans Jakob Bär (see illus. 93 and 102).

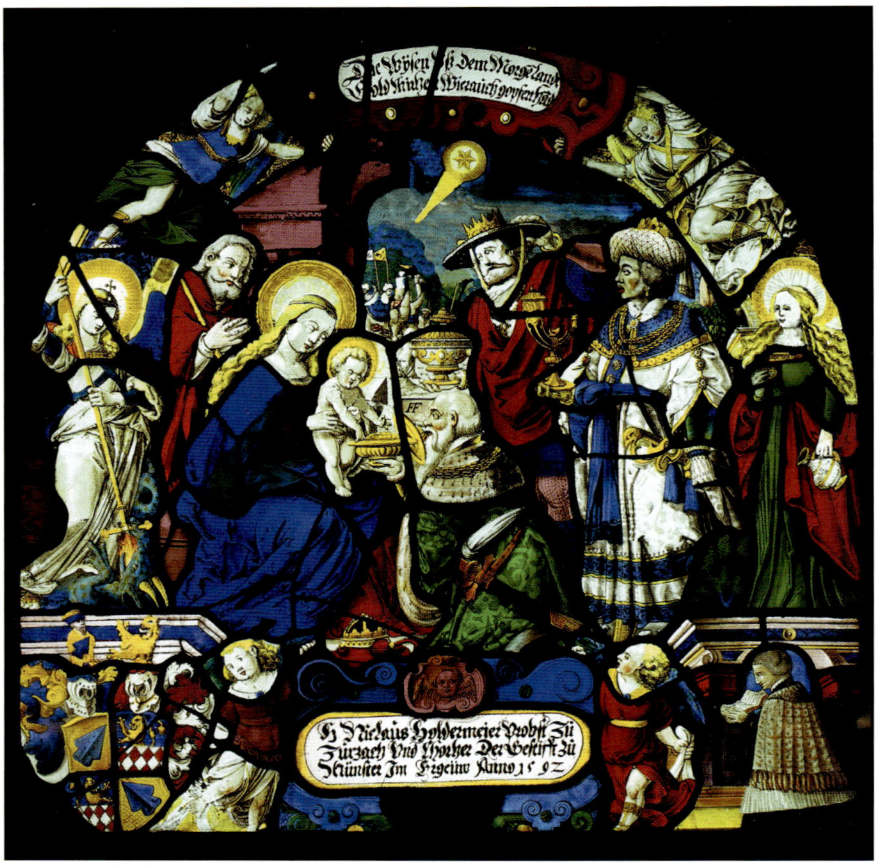

96 Franz Fallenter, *Adoration of the Magi*, 1592, from Rathausen, now at the Los Angeles County Museum of Art.

Donations to Monasteries and Convents

Donations to powerful religious institutions, as we have seen at Chartres, continued. The cloister of the Cistercian convent of Rathausen, 5 kilometres (3 mi.) north of the city of Lucerne, was completed in 1591. During the next 32 years, donors gradually filled the 67 openings with stained glass depicting a theologically articulate programme. Today 55 panels are now in public collections in Switzerland, Germany and the United States. A standard format consisting of a richly coloured and detailed narrative set within an architectural frame was followed throughout the programme. Patron saints stand at the side of the frame and the donor's family heraldry is at the bottom. The programme is an extensive reflection on the economy of salvation from the creation of the first man and woman to the Last Judgement. The east wing began with four panels of the Creation and Fall, a panel of Abraham and one of David. The remaining fourteen panels depicted the life of Christ from the Annunciation to the Transfiguration. The *Adoration of the Magi*, now in the Los Angeles County Museum of Art, marked the midpoint.

We are fortunate to have the letters of the abbesses from 1591 to 1623 seeking donations of windows from a wide variety of patrons, including governmental representatives from Spain, France and Savoy. They promised 'eternal and heavenly reward for the gifts'. A total of 21 of the panels were donated by religious institutions or officials of institutions, such as an abbess or abbot. For example, *The Transfiguration* in the Metropolitan Museum was given by the abbot of Muri (MMA 51.146.2) and, in Los Angeles, a panel of *Mary and Martha* was given by the abbot of Einsiedeln (Los Angeles County Museum of Art 45.21.38). Secular patrons, such as the cities of Sursee, Lucerne and Rottweil, were responsible for sixteen panels. Private citizens, identified in the inscriptions as majors, captains, ambassadors, governors and other officials, often with their spouses, gave the remaining thirty. Fortunately, two impressive monastic sites in the canton of Aargau preserve windows in situ. The Cistercian monastery of Wettingen, located about 24 kilometres (15 mi.) northwest of Zurich, houses the most comprehensive collection with 79 windows preserved at an original site. Although a few panels date to the late thirteenth century, most of the windows were installed from around 1517 to 1648. The Benedictine abbey of Muri, about 26 kilometres (16 mi.) southwest of Zurich, retains 57 windows, most dating from 1554 to 1564 (see illus. 1). Like the patronage of Rathausen, both sites show donations by the Swiss cantons and monasteries, noble families, burghers and secular and religious officials near and far. Unlike Rathausen's windows, however, the panels are in rectangular format and more frequently show heraldic as well as narrative schemas.

Franz Fallenter (1574–1612), who produced almost all Rathausen's windows, was considered the foremost glass painter of his generation in Lucerne. Executed during the second year of the project, the *Adoration of the Magi* (illus. 96) was among the earliest of the series. The monogram of FF appears prominently next to the face of the kneeling Magus. Above the scene we read *Die Wÿsen Vß Dem Morgēlandt/Gold Mirhen Wierauch gopfert hād* (The Wise Men from the East offered gold, myrrh and incense) and below is the donor's inscription, *H. Niclaūs Holdermeier Probst Zū/Zūrzach Vnd Chorher Der Gestifft Zū/Münster Jm Ergeüw Anno 1592* (Mr Niklaus Holdermeyer provost in Zurzach, and canon of the collegiate church of Beromünster in Aargau the year 1592). Beromünster, today in the canton of Lucerne, is about 24 kilometres (15 mi.) north of Rathausen. Holdermeyer was a member of the collegiate church of St Michael's, and recognized as the administrative head of the clergy in Zurzach, today Bad Zurzach, on the Swiss/German border. The panel is substantially intact except for the segment on the lower right showing the donor. Although dressed as a canon, the donor exhibits a physiognomy and style of painting of later date, probably around the mid-seventeenth century. The reverse side of the segment also shows an entirely different application of the blue enamel. There may have been damage or, for some reason, the donor or his inheritor desired a more up-to-date image. Physical examination of these 'relics' of our past reveals many fascinating, but often unexplained, anomalies.

The supporters, in typical male and female division, present the archangel Michael transfixing the dragon with a cruciform staff and St Verena, the patroness of Zurzach. Verena was associated with St Maurice of the Theban Legion, who frequently appears as a patron in Swiss corporate and personal histories. Legend asserted that families could travel with soldiers to administer to their needs; Verena was believed to have been engaged to St Victor, one of the soldiers under St Maurice. After the conversion of the legion *en masse* to Christianity in the year 286, the soldiers were martyred. Afterwards, Verena lived the life of a recluse, first in Solothurn, then in a cave near Zurich. Skilled in nursing from her experience as military support staff, she helped local families, especially young girls. She was renowned for caring for the poor and the sick, even the lepers, bringing them food and medicine, symbolized by the pitcher and comb in her hand.

Husband and Wife

Most Swiss panels, including those of Muri and Wettingen, are smaller, with proportionally more space given to the donor. Often the Swiss panels display the coats of arms of both husband and wife, with the traditional sinister/dexter hierarchy, male to the viewer's left and female to the viewer's right. The shields stand either between the couple or at their feet. Exemplifying this convention is a *Stained Glass Design for a Married Couple* (illus. 97). The inscription reads *Bicius Haller Vnd Barblÿ Fluomanin (Flühmann) Hußfrouw 1553* (Sulpitius Haller and his wife Barbara Flühmann). Haller (*c.* 1525–1564) was a statesman from Bern. The crested helms of the nobility are gone and in their place are beehives, symbols of domestic industry. The male supporter stares at the female, who

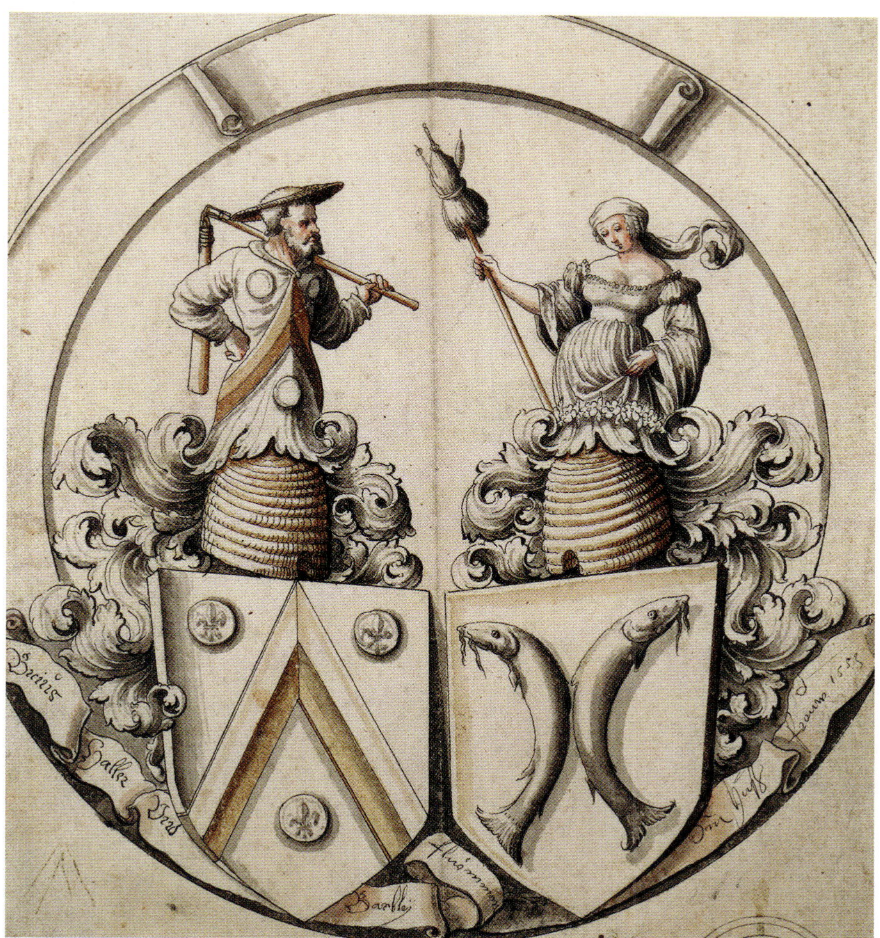

97 Unidentified Bern artist, *Stained Glass Design for a Married Couple*, from Bern, 1553, now at the J. Paul Getty Museum, Los Angeles.

demurely casts her eyes downward. He carries a flail used in threshing to separate grains from their husks. The female holds a distaff, wound with wool or flax for spinning. Both emblems were long associated with gendered divisions of labour, the male with the outdoor labour of farming and the female with the home-bound production of textiles.

Trade Guilds

The same themes of loyalty and codependence and hierarchy of gender and class are vividly demonstrated by imagery commissioned by trade guilds. In the sixteenth and seventeenth centuries, the guild panel (*Zunftscheibe*) had as much diversity in form as other association panels (*Gesellschaftsscheibe*),

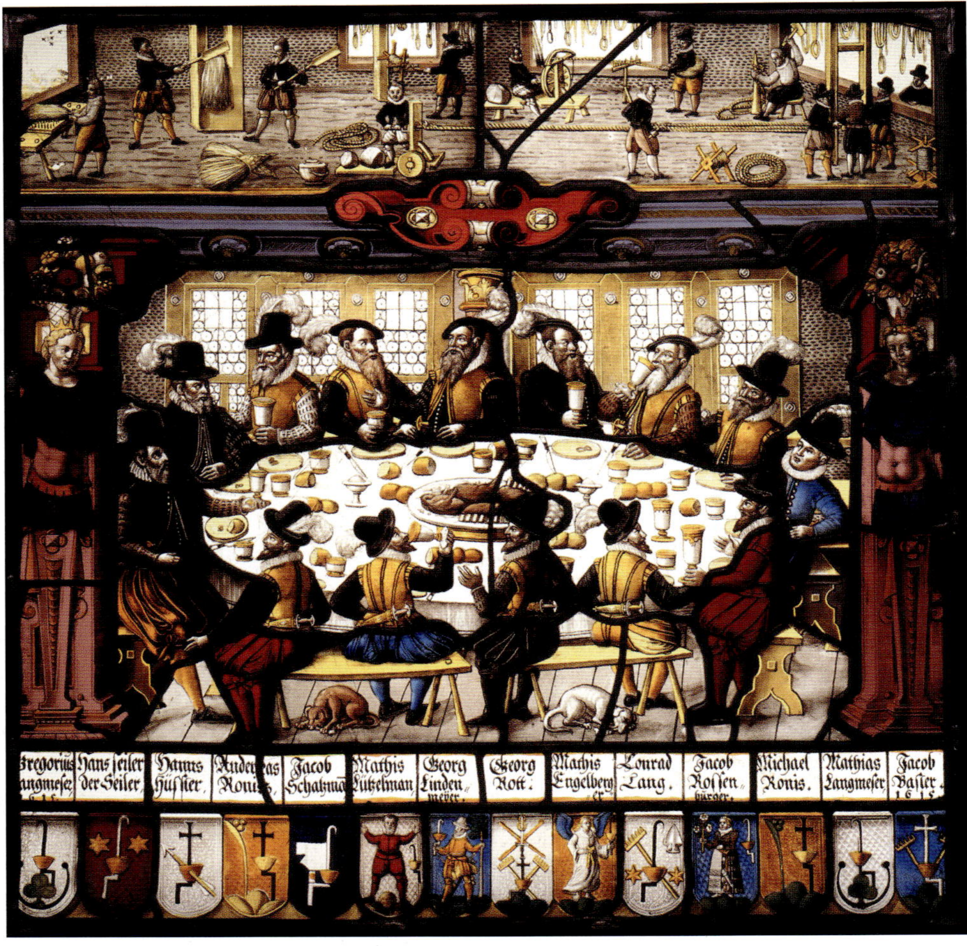

98 Hieronymus Vischer, *Banquet of the Basel Ropemakers Guild*, 1615, now at the Historisches Museum, Basel.

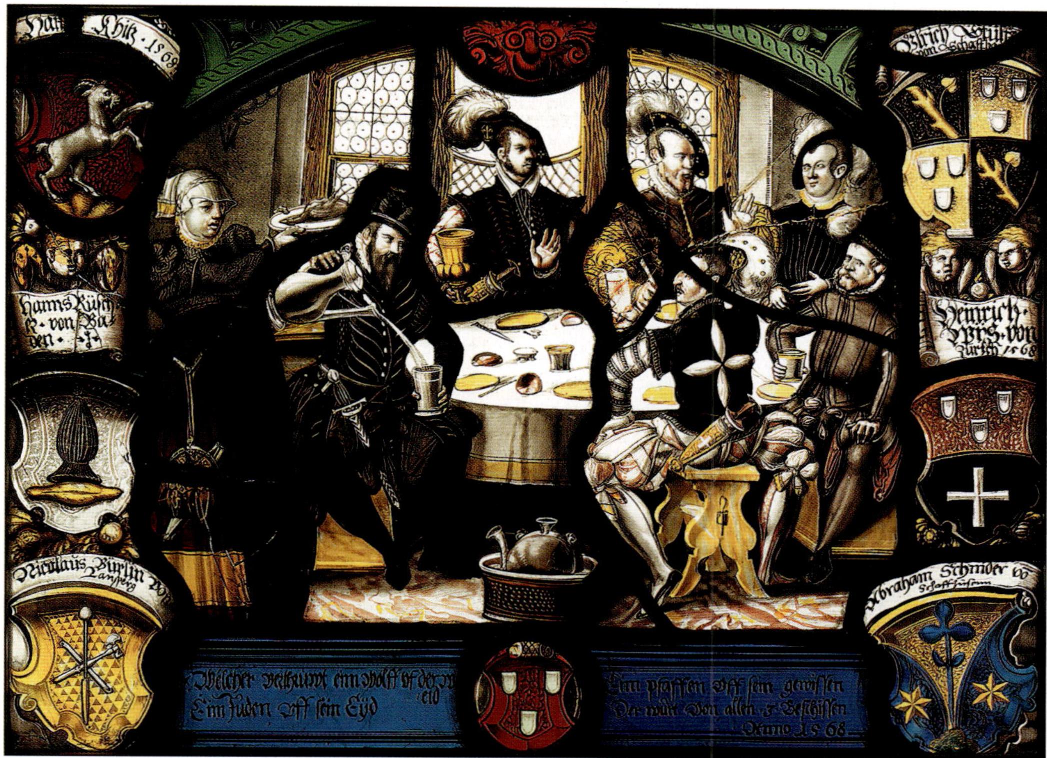

99 Felix Lindtmayer the Younger, attrib., *A Group of Workers in Glass*, 1568, now at the Museum zu Allerheiligen, Schaffhausen.

particularly in Basel, Zurich and Winterthur, where guilds were traditionally strong. In these representations, the members are recognized primarily by their inscribed names and arms, which usually surround the main scene and correspond in number to the figures assembled. One of the most famous examples is Hieronymus Vischer's *Banquet of the Basel Ropemakers Guild* of 1615 (illus. 98). Fourteen men sit at the table with their shields and names arranged on the lowest tier. We observe the exclusion of women from the trades, although represented in positions of service. The segment at the top of the panel shows the guild members producing rope, from the beating of the hemp to the twisting of the rope. The larger panel below shows the members enjoying the fruits of their labours and meeting for a festive banquet in a guild hall or inn. The banquet hall is characterized by rows of bull's-eye windows, which are regularly interrupted at the top by a small rectangular area in which colourful gift panels of the kind we are studying would have been inserted. At the side, the architectural frames are standard, Baroque ornaments, here showing caryatids with female heads supporting baskets of fruit, symbolic of prosperity.

A grouping of glass painters (illus. 99) seems at once more intimate and livelier. The names of the six donors are inscribed on their shields. All but two are documented in the city's archives as involved in the trade of making windows. Starting from the upper left we read: Hans Khitz, Hans Rüscher from Baden (glass painter) and Nikolaus Bürlin from Landsberg (glazier). On the right, we find Ulrich Stülz from Schaffhausen (glass painter), Heinrich Wis from Zurich (glass painter) and Abraham Schnyder from Schaffhausen. The shield of Nikolaus Bürlin, on the lower left, carries glazing tools: a glass cutter, a soldering iron to solder the lead cames at their joints and a mallet to hammer the nails that hold elements of the panel in place as it is being assembled. Measuring 29.2 × 39.3 centimetres (11½ × 15½ in.), the panel has a horizontal emphasis. The men, as in the guild panel of the ropemakers, are in their fanciest clothes and enjoying a convivial dinner at an inn. One of the participants pours wine into a beaker while on the floor another pitcher of wine sits cooling in a tub of water. The date of 1568 appears in both the lower inscription and after the name of Hans Khitz. The time fits well with the career of Felix Lindtmayer the Younger (*c.* 1524–1574), a prominent artist in Schaffhausen, a city that had sided with the Reformation since 1528. He was the son of the glass painter Felix Lindtmayer the Elder (d. 1543), whose father Sebastian Lindtmayer (d. 1519) had moved to Schaffhausen from southern Germany. Felix the Younger was also a member of the Schaffhausen municipal court and the Great Council. His son, Daniel Lindtmayer (1552–*c.* 1607), was a notable artist in his own right and the last of this influential dynasty of glass painters.

Honest Labour Ennobles

Donors frequently selected personalized narratives, exemplified by a panel of 1649 given by a blacksmith (illus. 100). Thomas Neyenmann (Neuenmann) and his wife Maria Speckhammer resided in the town of Trogen (canton of Appenzell) in northeastern Switzerland. The central image is based on a print and allows us to see the extensive interplay between the print and visual culture of the era. Literacy and the circulation of books were widespread. One of the most important examples of the intersection of image and text were 'emblem books', in wide usage since the sixteenth century. The genre most frequently juxtaposes an image, a motto and text explaining the connection between the image and motto. The text is frequently in verse to create more pleasurable reading and aid memory retention. These emblem books descended from medieval bestiaries based on proverbs and fables, including those from Greek and

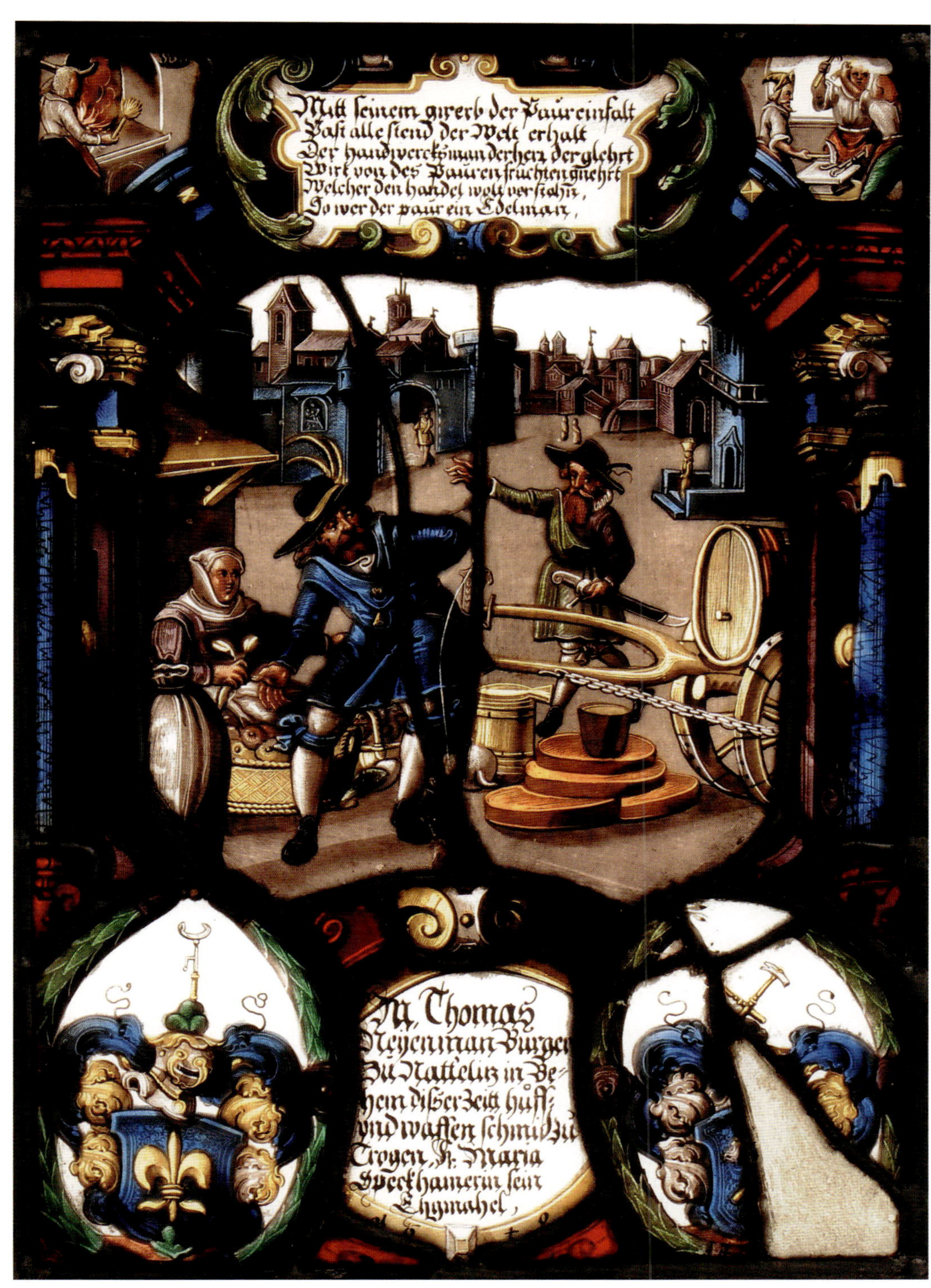

100 Heinrich Guldi of St Gallen, attrib.,
The Farmer, 1649, now in a private collection.

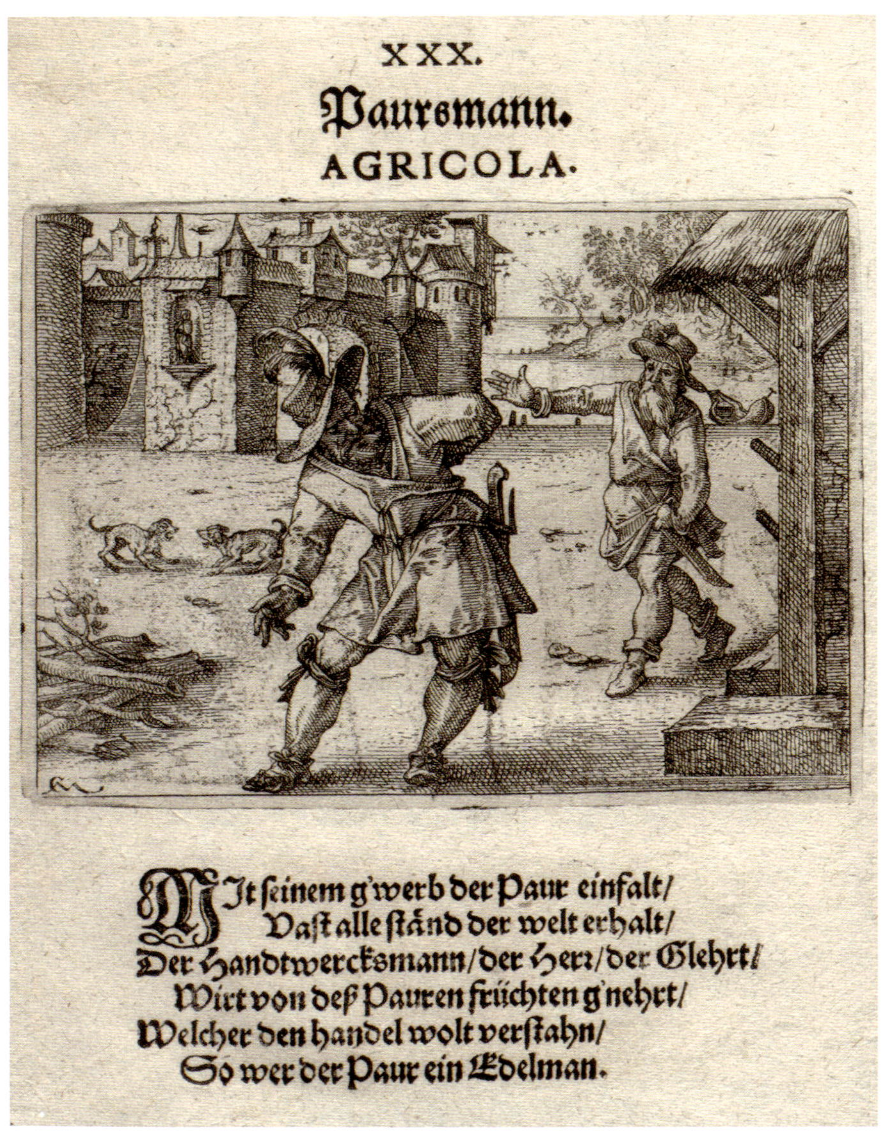

101 Christoph Murer, *The Farmer*,
from *XL emblemata miscella nova*, Zurich, 1622.

Roman sources such as Aesop's Fables and Plutarch's *Lives*. The Neuenmann/
Speckhammer panel is based on Christoph Murer's *XL emblemata miscella nova*
(illus. 101). Published in Zurich in 1622, the book contains forty full-page illustrations, each with a poem of three rhymed couplets on themes such as peace,
ingratitude, ambition or Aesop's Fables, such as the story of the mouse and
the frog. Neuenmann was clearly interested in honouring the value of work.
The text for the Farmer reads: *Paursmann* [Latin] *Agricola: Mit seinem g'werb*

der Paur einfalt/ Vast alle stand der welt erhalt/ Der Handtwercksmann, der Herr, der Glehrt/ Wirt von des Pauren früchten g'nehrt/ Welcher den handel wolt verstahn/ So wer der Paur ein Edelman (The Farmer: with his business, the farmer is the essential element in the world. The craftsman, the nobleman, the scholar is nourished from the farmer's products. As one who truly understands this trade, the farmer is a gentleman).

We can never really know what may have transpired between a patron and an artist, but here we might imagine a lively exchange. The glass painter was probably Heinrich Guldi (1606–*c*. 1650) of St Gallen. Neuenmann identifies his profession *Huf- und Waffenschmied* (farrier and weaponsmith) in the dedication inscription. At the top of the window his trade is illustrated, to the left a man tending a forge and, on the right, three men with hammers working on an anvil. The narrative scene, however, shows a farmer, but Murer's emblem-book image is significantly expanded. Additional civic buildings are added to the city wall in the background so that the farmer now stands within a town square, not outside the walls. What is arguably the farmer's wife is seated on the left, occupied with plucking fowl. Produce from the farm is clustered around the farmer: a wagon carrying a large barrel with a stopper, evidently an indication of wine, different kinds of cheeses next to what looks like a butter churn and fruits and vegetables piled in baskets. Thus the actual work of the farmer is made more visible to the viewer. The emblem book's three rhymed couplets can be read above the scene. Imagery of the produce of the land and the activities of the skilled trades within a prosperous city sends the message that all are equal in their labour. The inclusion of both the husband and the wife in the central image parallels their representation via their arms and the dedicatory inscription.

A Family of Bears

A panel dated 1657 shows a husband, wife and children in more symbolic form (illus. 102). The donors are Hans Jakob Bär from the Albis, a mountainous area just south of Zurich, and his wife Elisabeth Frickeni (Fricker). Bär notes that he is an officer and his arms appear in the centre, a bear rampant on a gold ground. The couple's eight children are included in the inscription: Heinrich, Jacob, Hans Jacob, Hans, Hans Heinrich, Ulrich, Rudolf and Adelheit (*die bëren al ire eliche Kinder*: all the bears' worthy children) and represented above as bears. They are variously dressed, all with belts with swords and/or daggers, the Swiss *Dolch*. Three are given mail collars and one holds an open book. The famed weaponry that made the Swiss so valuable as mercenaries appears, from left to right: the

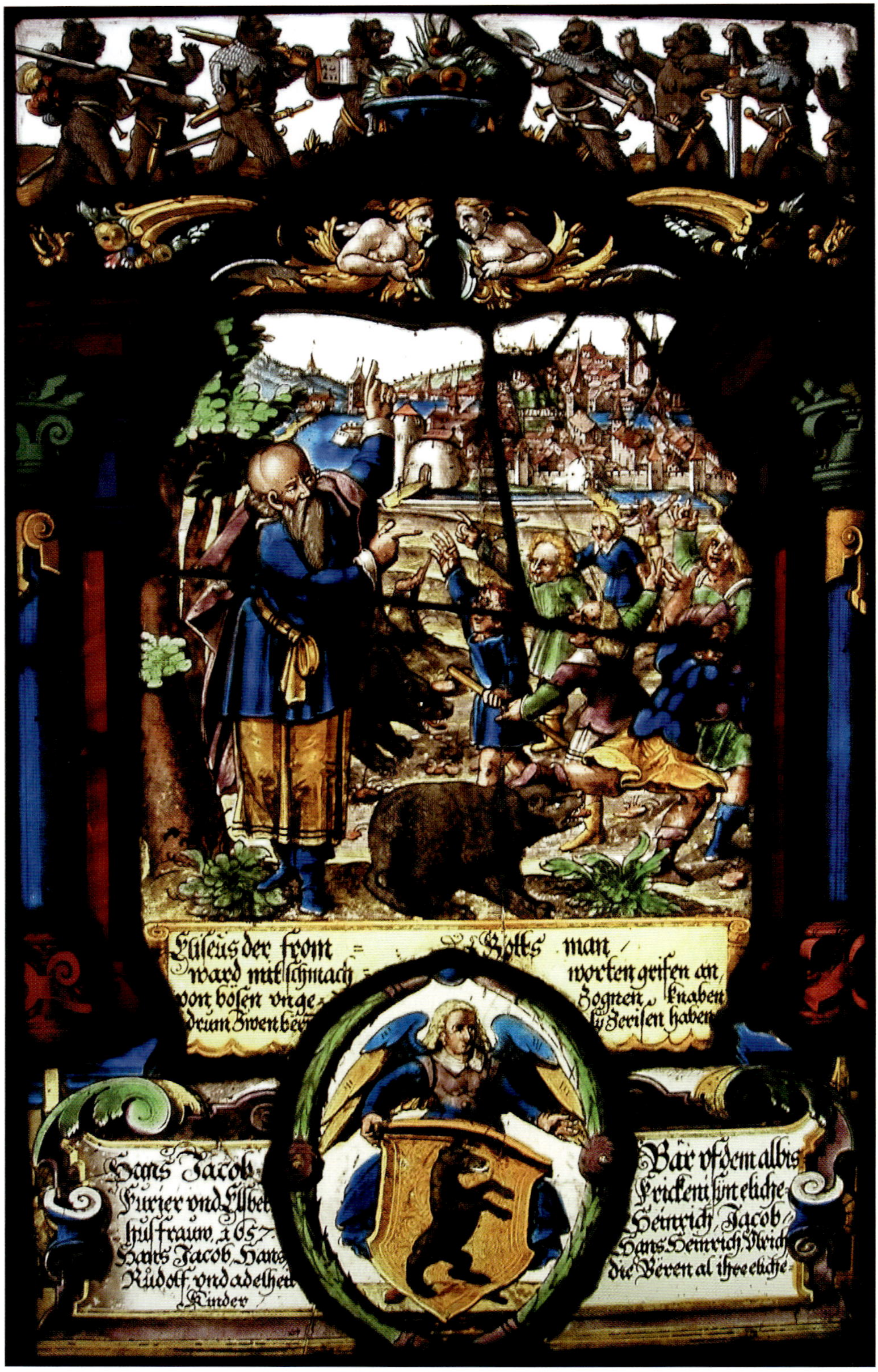

102 Workshop of Jakob Nüscheler the Younger, attrib.,
Elisha Taunted by Boys, 1657, now in a private collection.

musket, the halberd and the double-handed sword. The unusual central image is inscribed: *Eliseus der from Gotts man/ward mit schmach worten grifen an/von bösen vngezognen Knaben drum Zwen ber[en] sÿ Zerisen haben* (Elisha, who was from God, was attacked with abusive words; by bad naughty boys, thus they were torn [mauled] by two bears). This incident in the life of the prophet Elisha is found in the Bible:

> Then he went up from there to Bethel; and as he was going up the
> road, some youths came from the city and mocked him, and said
> to him, 'Go up, you baldhead! Go up, you baldhead!' So he turned
> around and looked at them, and pronounced a curse on them in the
> name of the Lord. And two female bears came out of the woods
> and mauled 42 of the youths
> (2 Kings 2:23–5).

Clearly this is an esoteric story, carefully selected for Bär's name, and his seven male children. Elisha is vividly bald, with a prominent forehead. He gestures up to heaven with his left hand while he points to the boys with his right. Two bears with open jaws move towards the seven unruly boys. In the background is a view of the city of Zurich. Precisely detailed, it shows the curving gate along the fortified wall on the southern side, and the twin towers of the cathedral on the north. The panel was probably made in the workshop of Hans Jakob Nüscheler the Younger (1614–1658); alongside Christoph and Josiah Murer, he and his father Hans Jakob the Elder were among the most important glass painters in Zurich.

A Schoolteacher and Spouse

Even when a scene is generic, Swiss Catholics could personalize it by including representations of their name saints. In Chapter Two we saw that the 1612 Fribourg panel took this path. Théodule Michel and Pierre Vallélian included their name saints Théodule of Sion and Peter. From the same era, dated 1605, a panel of the *Coronation of the Virgin Mary* (illus. 103) displays a core belief for Catholics, the bodily assumption of the Virgin Mary into heaven and her reception by the Trinity. We easily recognize God the Father on the right, the Son on the left and the Dove of the Holy Spirit above. The donors are listed as Jacob Rotmund, a teacher, identified as *Schuolmeister*, in Glarus, and his spouse, Margaretha Merz. They appear below, kneeling, praying with rosary beads, next to both their family arms. A Latin inscription around Jacob's head reads *Maria Mater dei, memento mei* (Mary, Mother of God, remember me). Jacob's name saint, James the Apostle, is above him, distinguished by his pilgrim's attire. The saint's hat and shoulders are adorned with pilgrims' badges as mentioned in Chapter One. Showing scallop shells and crossed staffs, they are souvenirs of the pilgrimage to James's shrine of Santiago de Compostela in northwestern Spain. It was one of the premier destinations throughout the Middle Ages and remained a cherished goal for the Swiss of the Early Modern era.

St Margaret appears over Margaretha Merz. Margaret was among the most important of late medieval saints throughout all of Western Europe. Along with Barbara and Catherine she formed a trio referred to as the 'three holy maidens'. The immediate identification of these saints with their symbols of dragon, tower and wheel is evidenced by the folk rhyme: *Sankt Margaretha mit dem Wurm, Sankt Barbara mit dem Turm, Sankt Katharina mit dem Radl, das sind die heiligen Madl* (St Margaret with the dragon, St Barbara with the tower, St Catherine with the wheel; these are the holy maidens). These three were the female representatives within the *Vierzehnheiligen* (the Fourteen Holy Helpers or Auxiliary Saints), an association that had begun in the fourteenth century in response to the plague. This popular devotion enabled the faithful to address each of the saints for the cure of specific diseases or the amelioration of bodily conditions. Margaret was invoked by women for help in pregnancy and childbirth. Jan van Eyck's *The Arnolfini Portrait* (1434), at London's National Gallery, shows a carving of Margaret with her dragon prominently displayed on the Arnolfini couple's bedpost.

Margaret was included in the late thirteenth-century *Golden Legend*. Her name is first associated with a precious jewel, a margarita, or pearl. She was born in Antioch from nobility but, influenced by her nurse, baptized a Christian. Olybrius, prefect of the region, caught a glimpse of Margaret and was inflamed with passion. He demanded her in marriage but she refused, declaring that she was the bride of Christ. While imprisoned, Margaret confronted her true enemy, Satan, in the guise of a dragon. The dragon swallowed her, 'but when he was trying to digest her, she shielded herself with the sign of the cross and by the power of the cross the dragon burst open and the virgin emerged unscathed.' A marvellously spotted dragon is at Margaret's feet. Although the *Golden Legend* adds that this story is apocryphal, it remained the standard legend associated with Margaret, and the origin of her symbol. The text, however, does state that before the saint died, she prayed that 'any woman that invoked her when faced with a difficult labour would give birth to a healthy child.'

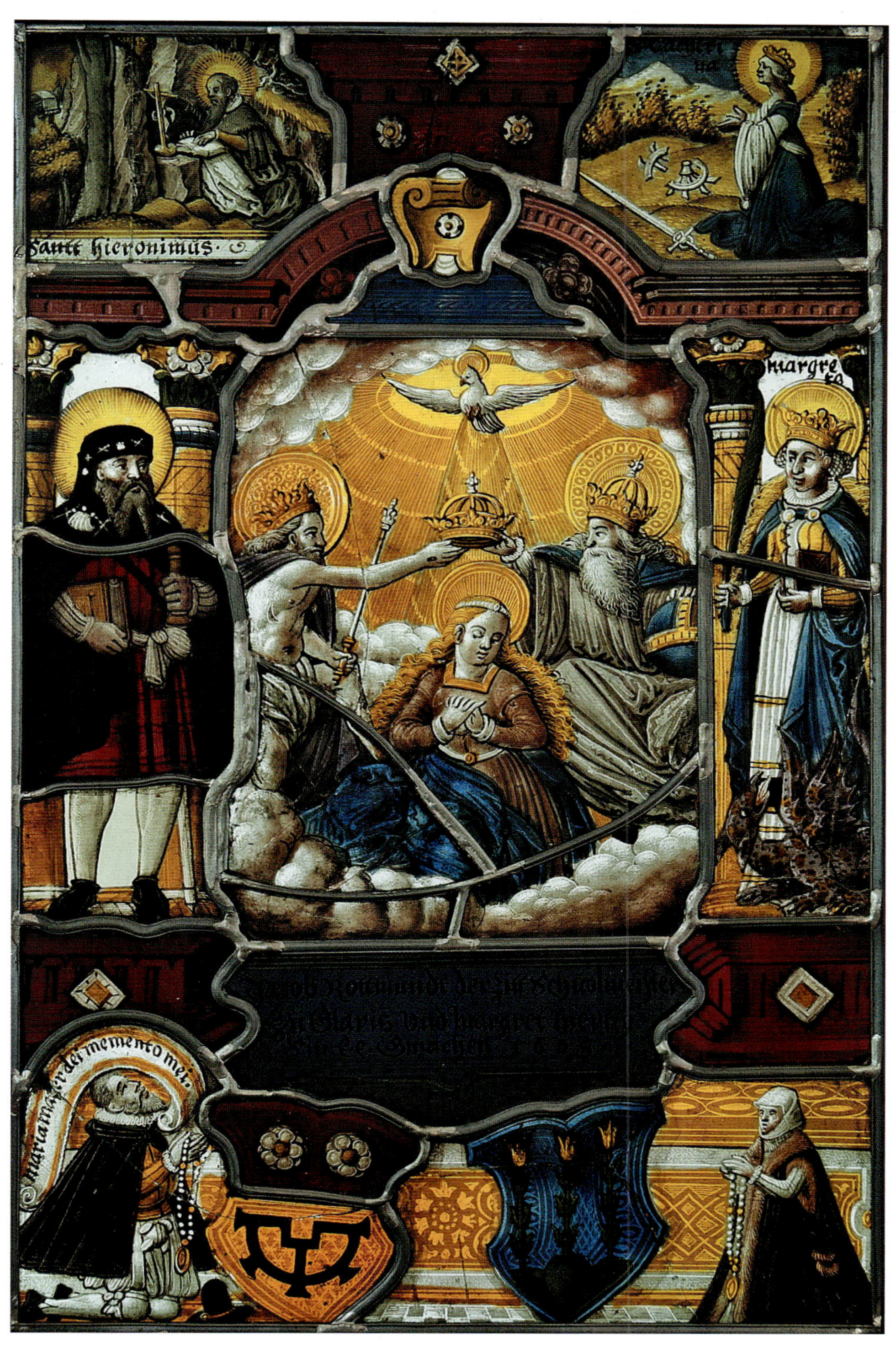

103 Unidentified artist, *Coronation of the Virgin Mary*,
1605, now in a private collection.

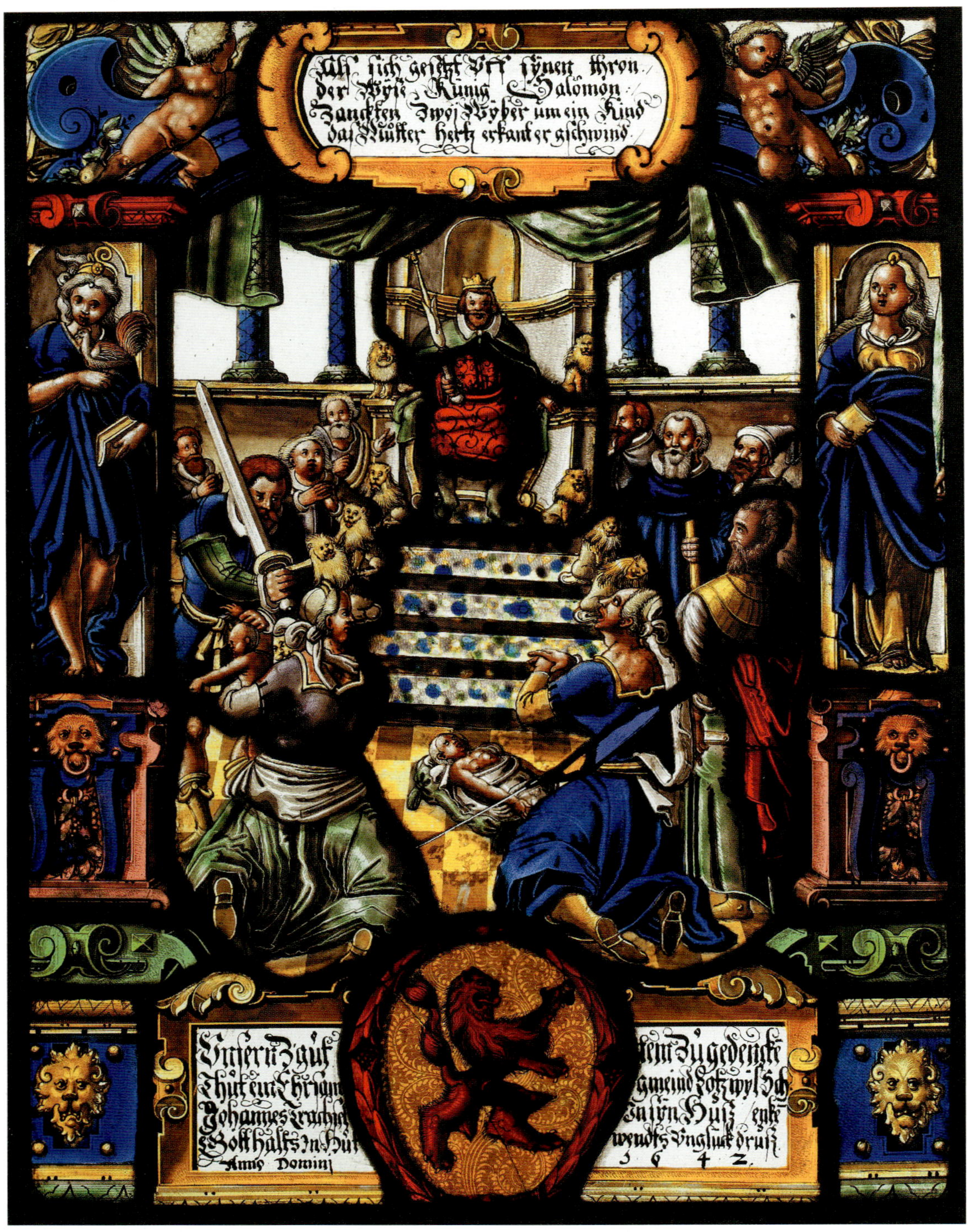

104 Christian Kupferschmied or his son Heinrich Kupferschmied
of Burgdorf, attrib., *Judgement of Solomon*, 1642, now in the
Royal Museums of Art and History, Brussels.

Above the image, two additional saints similarly reflect the priorities of husband and wife. Both are associated with learning. Jerome (*c.* 342–420), labelled *Hieronymus*, is recognized as a Doctor of the Church for his copious writings. Chief among them is the translation of the Bible to Latin, the *Vulgate*, which became the official scriptural text for the Christian Church. As a student in Rome, Jerome had converted to Christianity and withdrew for some time to northern Syria to live the life of a hermit. A traditional image is seen in the window, Jerome in the Syrian wilderness, praying before a crucifix. St Catherine was equally revered as an intellectual model, based on the legend that the emperor Maximian (r. 286–305 CE) assembled fifty pagan philosophers to convince her of the errors of Christianity. Catherine triumphed in the debate, inspiring many of the philosophers to convert. The philosophers were executed and Catherine condemned to death on a spiked wheel. She was spared when the wheel shattered, killing her torturers, but she was then beheaded. The shattered wheel and the sword appear in the picture. Widely depicted in art, she was seen as the patroness of female students and of lawyers.

Honouring a Judge with a Window for the Home

When searching for a way to understand the past, we are invariably confronted with the investment of institutions in the documentation of their histories. The private person rarely enjoys such corporate continuity. The original destinations for many Swiss stained-glass cycles are known due to dutiful record-keeping by municipalities. Some panels in a cycle may be still on site, allowing for comparative identification. Others in museums have preserved their lineage through the institutional donor. We have, however, thousands of single Swiss panels worldwide in museums or private collections of unknown origin. Scholars are certain that many of them were given as testimonies of gratitude and that they were displayed in private homes. We are fortunate to have a panel dated 1642 associated with a specific private destination (illus. 104). The inscription explains that the municipality of Lotzwil created the panel to honour the work of Johannes Trachsel, for him to display in his home. It ends with the wish, in rhymed couplet form, translated: 'God keep his house and keep misfortune from it. The year of Our Lord 1642.'

The narrative scene shows the Judgement of Solomon with a text above: 'When the wise king Solomon sat on the throne, two women quarrelled over a child, Solomon immediately recognized the [true] mother's heart.' The theme of Solomon (1 Kings 3:16–28) often appeared in art from the Middle Ages through the Renaissance as an emblem of wise rulership and inspired legal judgments. A Judgement of Solomon panel dating to 1660, now in the historic town hall of Bremgarten, about 20 kilometres (12 mi.) west of Zurich, attests to its broad and long-standing employment. The scene is surrounded by shields of ten individuals and the inscription reads: 'A wise judge and ruler makes decisions based on true principles, as did the wise Solomon. As his judgements were made then, so may they be made in this world.' In the Brussels panel, Solomon sits on top of a throne whose steps are guarded by lions. He clearly dominates the composition, looking down at two women and the dead child lying before them. The two mothers argue; they both have given birth but one had rolled over during her sleep, suffocating her child. She took the child of her companion, substituting the dead child in its stead. Upon awakening, the second woman found the dead child but recognized that it was not hers. The dispute was brought to King Solomon. He asked that a sword be brought, as we see on the left, and proposed to cut the living child in half so that each of the mothers would be satisfied. The mother whose child had died agreed, but the mother of the living child pleaded that the child be kept alive, even if it were to be given to another. Solomon then proclaimed her to be the true mother.

Lotzwil, which commissioned the panel, is a little village in the canton of Bern. It was the main settlement of the bailiwick (*Vogtei*) of Lotzwil, which was under the rule of the city of Burgdorf (1431–1798). Municipal records allow us to identify Johannes Trachsel, goldsmith and council member in the city of Burgdorf. He held the position of baili (*Vogt*) of Lotzwil from 1637 to 1642 and as such he presided over judicial functions. Lotzwil's councillors presented the panel to Trachsel at the end of his term as baili. It was designated for his house in Burgdorf, located in the Schmiedengasse (street of the blacksmiths). The image of Solomon honours Trachsel as having exercised wise judgements during his office. Its style associates it with Christian Kupferschmied (fl. 1607–52) or his son Heinrich Kupferschmied (1623–1689) who were both glass painters in Burgdorf. As was customary for the era, the panel is delineated mainly through enamel paint and silver stain. Pot-metal red glass is evident in Solomon's gown, the capitals supporting the architrave, the cloak of the man on the right, and Lotzwil's shield.

Swiss panels of the Early Modern era became objects of foreign collectors' interests. Produced in massive quantities, these small-scale works exemplify three hundred years of civic pride extending from the early fifteenth through to the early eighteenth century and represent a wide range of individuals of all social classes. Interest in collecting this material began at the end of the eighteenth century when historically inspired revival architecture looked for authentic decorative elements. In 1786, for example, Prince Franz von Sachsen-Anhalt installed his collection in his 'Gothic House' at Wörlitz, designated a World Heritage site in 2000. As part of the Grand Tour, the English collected stained-glass panels as souvenirs from Switzerland. These were installed in country houses and rural churches, notably St Michael and Our Lady Church in Wragby, West Yorkshire. The interest by foreign collectors was a catalyst for newly founded Swiss museums and patriotic sentiment enabled the institutions to buy back many of these historic works from the art market. Today, the great collections of the Swiss National Museum in Zurich, the Historisches Museum in Bern and the Badisches Landesmuseum in Karlsruhe, among others, facilitate our viewing of this impressive heritage.

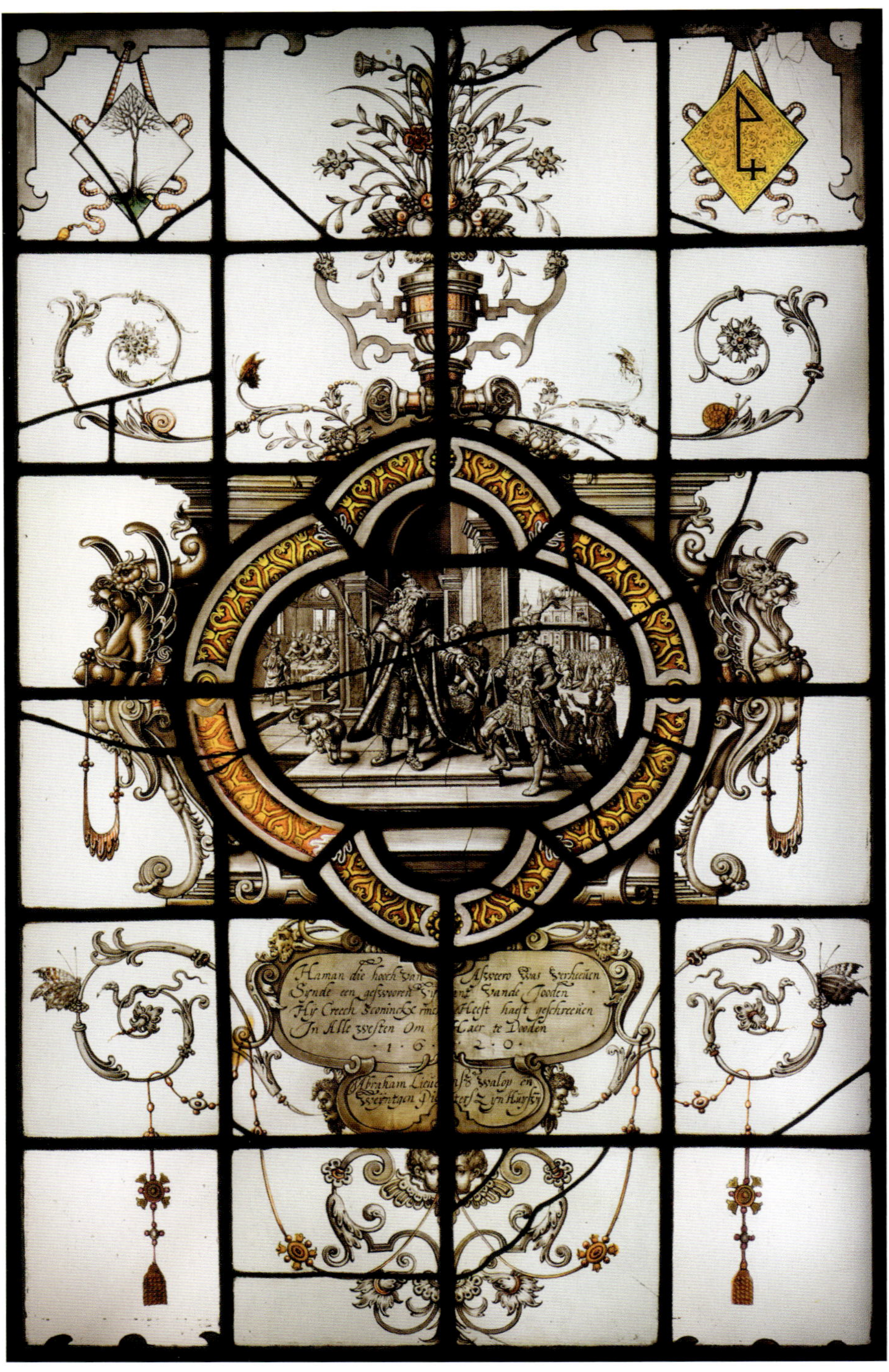

105 Northern Low Countries, Haarlem (?), *Ahasuerus Giving His Ring to Haman*, after Maarten van Heemskerck, 1620, now in the Los Angeles County Museum of Art.

8

Renaissance Roundels: The Transformation of European Image Making

—

Nothing transformed the production of images more than the invention of the printing press. It was a watershed in the history of both art and society. Johannes Gutenberg's moveable type appeared in 1450, but the use of the woodblock to print image and text had already gained great popularity by the 1430s. We begin to see the reiteration of widely disseminated texts and images often quite removed in time and in place from their original manifestation. Printing's influence on stained glass affected both the arrangement of the glass workshops and the expectations of the patron. Patrons often knew a set of images from prints and were eager to see these same forms in their commissions. Workshops, similarly, made sure that they had direct access, or access by drawings based on prints, to present to potential clients.

Designers of Windows

Throughout the Middle Ages, designers had been integrated within stained-glass workshops and took an active part in painting and in supervising the fabrication of windows. We recognize their individual work in the varied draughtsmanship and composition of these great ensembles. The artists, however, remain unnamed, typical of an era where paper had not yet been introduced and almost all documentation was written in Latin on expensive parchment. With the rise of a mercantile economy around 1400, which saw the development of printing, paper use and writing in the vernacular, designs for painting on glass were frequently produced by artists who also achieved prominence in other media. These artists were noted through their business activities, tax records and even contemporaneous biography.

By the early sixteenth century, dissemination of prints had become standard. The printmaker commissioned a series of drawings by an artist who anticipated their rendition as woodcuts or engravings or stained glass. We need to remind ourselves that before the nineteenth century the production of art was never an isolated occupation. Art was produced in workshops. Even in the smallest shop of a single painter, assistance was necessary to prepare the colours and the panel or canvas on which the artist would work. Raw materials for the pigments were purchased, usually in accordance with a commission paid in advance. They were then pulverized and mixed with various binders that ranged from egg white to oil. Panels needed to be constructed, bound, given a plaster coat and finally polished smooth. If the ground was canvas, the fabric needed to be attached to a wooden support, stretched and sized so that it would not absorb the paint. Much of this work was carried out by younger apprentices.

The production of prints, like windows, was even more complex and multi-staged. Whether the images originated from outside or within the workshop, individuals were needed who could transfer the desired image to either a wooden or a metal plate. A wooden plate was a part of 'relief' printing, meaning that the image receiving the ink was on the top of the plate. The carver cut into the plate to remove elements that would constitute the background. The resultant woodcut was a relatively inexpensive production. A printer simply inked the wood and placed a sheet of paper on top. Using a level of exertion roughly equal to that of a pastry rolling pin, the paper was pressed to the block and ink would adhere. Many images of this type were acquired by the average person. They were often sold at pilgrimage sites. A lovely example of a woodcut of St Christopher with additional colour is tacked up over the fireplace in the Master of Flemalle's *Annunciation* (1415–25) at the Royal Museums of Fine Arts, Brussels.

Intaglio printing, which developed about the same time, reversed the process. The image was incised onto a metal plate. This was a far more expensive process, due to the value of the metal, most often copper, and the labour entailed. It allowed much more complexity, however, easily seen in the banknote engraving of our contemporary currency. The artist used a sharp V-shaped tool called a burin to cut into the metal. The plate was subsequently smeared with ink and its surface wiped clean, leaving ink only in the incised lines. To achieve an impression, a dampened sheet of paper was laid onto the plate and soft fabric provided further cushioning. The plate was then sent through a hand-powered roller which created enough pressure to squeeze ink from the crevices in the plate onto the paper.

Roundels, a new type of stained glass, developed within this social and economic context. Small pieces of uncoloured glass, rectangular as well as round, were painted in a manner in keeping with prints and drawings. Decorated primarily with vitreous paint and silver stain, these works allowed the artist to manipulate light and shade as well as a bold or delicate graphic to embody the story. This innovation met the needs of a new wealthy mercantile class. Its intimate scale responded to the spaces of their urban town houses and halls. Imagery in glass had distinctive advantages. Unlike paper, glass is a durable medium, impervious to water, exposure to the sun, or superficial dirt. Prints can only be viewed in relatively private circumstances, alone or with one or two others. Stained glass is a far more public art, capable of embellishing architecture. These new works could intersect with the daily lives of all viewers, just as they had since the very origins of the medium.

Towards 1500, many artists in glass had achieved prominence in other media. They furnished the designs for both larger leaded panels and roundels, but the fabrication was carried out by specialists within glass workshops. In Germany, such designers included Albrecht Dürer, Hans Holbein the Younger, Hans Baldung Grien, Hans Süss von Kulmbach, H. L. Schäufelein, Albrecht Altdorfer and Sebald Beham. We know that the Hirsvogel family executed glass in Nuremberg for several of the city's artists. The contemporary reader needs to reassess the values of our current art market and those that supported the creation of art of the past. Today, value is often placed on the individuality of the artist, and terms such as innovation, personal expression, uniqueness or one-of-a-kind apparently augment the value of a work in a buyer's eye. Innovation, before the nineteenth century, was rarely invoked. Rather, the artist was seen as continuing a tradition, becoming distinguished by making it better. Artists were viewed as representatives who more eloquently voiced the values embraced by others. Therefore, the repetition of similar themes and even similar compositions was accepted, even prized.

Roundels in Their Architectural Settings

Several roundels still within their original windows allow us to see the function of these small drawings on glass. The Los Angeles County Museum of Art has two windows on the story of Esther, dated 1620 (see illus. 105 and 108). Their designs follow the prints of Maarten van Heemskerck (1498–1574), who

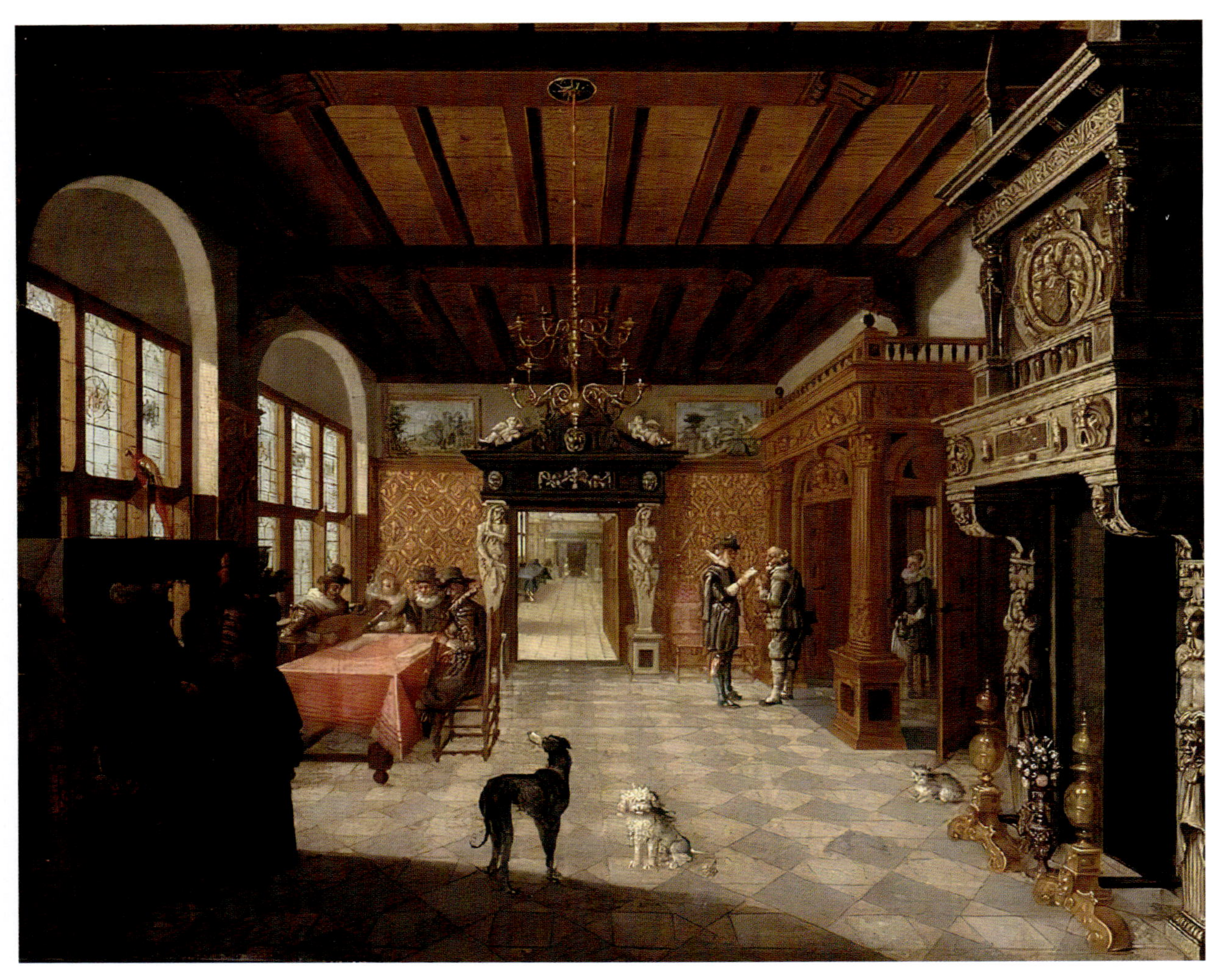

106 Nicolaes de Gyselaer, *Interior of a Hall*, 1621,
now in the Fitzwilliam Museum, Cambridge.

had learned his trade in the city of Harlem, working under the more senior artist Jan van Scorel. Like Scorel, Heemskerck saw the Italian Renaissance as an essential inspiration for subject-matter as well as artistic form. In 1532 he travelled to Rome, where he stayed for four years, absorbing the culture and producing numerous drawings and paintings. Many of those depict classical statuary, such as the Belvedere Torso in the Vatican Museum (drawing in the Gemäldegalerie, Berlin) or the head and limbs of the colossal statue of Constantine in the Capitoline Museum (drawing in the Staatliche Museen, Berlin). By such practices, the artist acquired a mastery of three dimensionality and classical depiction of the human form. Heemskerck is also credited with innovations in production by cooperating with printmakers such as Dirk Volkertsz. Coornhert (1522–1590) to make drawings that could be converted to prints. The drama in Ahasuerus giving his ring to Haman, with its portents of the extermination of a people, exemplifies the artist's narrative prowess.

The panels undoubtedly belonged to a larger series of windows of the story of Esther. The Hebrew Bible account of the Jewish Esther, who married Ahasuerus (Xerxes), king of Persia (Judith 8–13), was popular in Renaissance and Baroque art. Her heroism saved her people from destruction, a theme that has been summarized in Chapter Three. Heemskerck's print series contains eight episodes: 1) Esther crowned by Ahasuerus; 2) Mordecai overhearing the treason of Bigthan and Teresh; 3) Ahasuerus giving his ring of authority to Haman; 4) Esther preparing to intercede for the Jews; 5) Esther before Ahasuerus. A brilliantly executed panel of about 1580, after Heemskerck's engraving, is now in the Gotisches Haus Wörlitz, Germany; 6) Ahasuerus consulting the records and learning of Mordecai's service (this panel from the Los Angeles series is now in the Victoria and Albert Museum, London, 1257–1855); 7) Ahasuerus consulting with Haman; and 8) Esther accusing Haman at the banquet.

Esther's heroic actions, including the reversal of fortune that brought down the prosecutor and vindicated the unjustly accused, resonated with the images of judgement that were popular themes in the Lowlands. The story of Esther was the subject selected by the Rhetoricians Guild of Antwerp in 1554 for their annual play based on themes of the Old and New Testaments. The performance may have influenced Heemskerck's drawings of 1563. Among the prints by Heemskerck's own hand are an eight-image cycle of Judith and Holofernes and four prints of the story of Judah and Tamar (2 Kings 13), all displaying similar themes of threatened females and justice meted out to condemn the wicked and rescue the oppressed. Other print cycles after Heemskerck include the story of Susanna (Daniel 13), possibly one of the most popular morality tales of the time, Isaac and Rebecca (Genesis 24), the Parable of the Unmerciful Servant (Matthew 18:23–35), the Seven Works of Mercy and the Cycle of Change in Human Affairs. The works display the common theme of human actions and the need for prudent management and compassionate exercise of power, lest one be laid low by one's own submission to arrogance, lust, greed or other human folly. The development of a powerful mercantile economy in the Lowlands, coupled with a movement towards a reformed religion that stressed human responsibility over divine right to rule, undoubtedly encouraged the reiteration of such models as warnings to magistrates and other prominent citizens.

From Print to Glass

The glass painter of the Los Angeles series followed the model of the engravings closely (illus. 107 and 108). We observe the precise details of the clothing worn by Haman, such as the masks hanging from his elaborate belt and garter, the three levels of fringe decorating his sleeve, and the complex folds of his turban with its plume finial. Every curl in Ahasuerus' beard, the cabochon jewels studding his cloak, the fur trim of his mantle and even the precisely folded napkin on the table is reproduced. We observe the delicate mesh over Esther's arms and her long skirt. No detail is seen as trivial, even the placement of each flower strewn around the festive banquet table. The artist's use of a superbly blended mixture of vitreous paint enabled smooth application of washes. A highly controlled use of dark trace and the removal of paint with a needle or sharp stick develop the image.

Like its companion (see illus. 105), the roundel is set in a large window of uncoloured glass executed in silver stain, enamel and vitreous paint. In the upper left and right corners, shields containing heraldic devices hang from ribbons. Surrounding the quatrefoil is an architectural backdrop of entablatures and scroll work. To the left and right, sphinxes function as herms, taking the place of heraldic supporters. Topping the quatrefoil is an urn filled with fruit and flowers. Branches terminating in a flower and inhabited by snails and butterflies curve from the base. As a compositional pendant to the urn, a cartouche below contains the inscriptions. Curving from its sides are two branches like those above, except for snakes rather than snails. Below the inscription is a cupid's head surrounded by similar curving, floral motifs.

The end page of *The Triumph of Antwerp*, printed in 1550 by Pieter Coecke van Aelst, shows this popular scroll work with fruit, animals and figures. In the

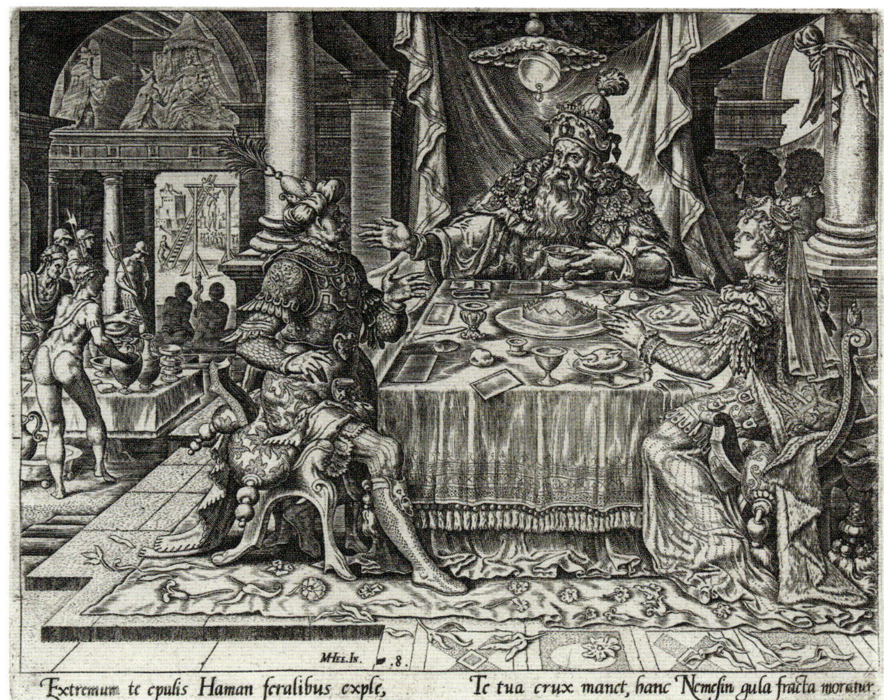

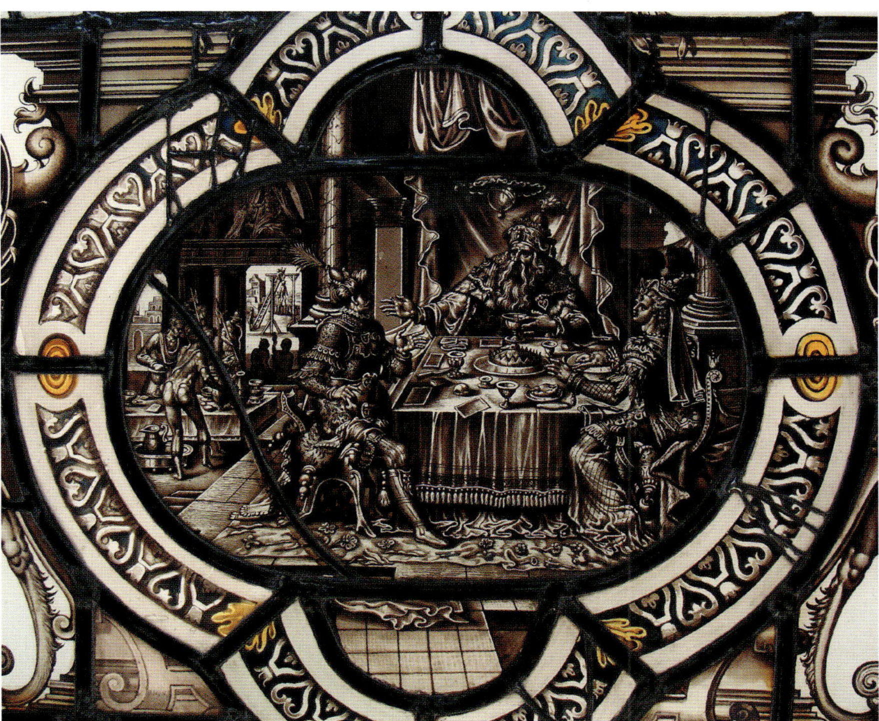

107 Philips Galle after Maarten van Heemskerck, *Esther Accusing Haman at Her Banquet*, 1563, now in the Rijksmuseum, Amsterdam.

108 North Lowlands, Haarlem (?), *Esther Accusing Haman at Her Banquet*, after Maarten van Heemskerck, 1620, now in the Los Angeles County Museum of Art.

seventeenth century, these new forms became a part of the everyday setting of rooms. Architects published books of furniture design to ensure stylistic unity in the interiors of their buildings. The craftspeople, who presumably included those in the workshops of stained glass, could have a ready reference of designs that could be applied to beds, tables, chests, mirror frames and windows.

The windows presumably were made to decorate a room for a wealthy Dutch citizen. A painting by Nicolaes de Gyselaer, *Interior of a Hall* (1621), records such a room (illus. 106). The scene shows similar circular images accenting the centre of two triple-light windows leaded in rectangular white quarries. Most telling in this interior is the profusion of sculptural decoration in herms supporting fireplaces and doorways, cartouches set within elaborate frames, swags, entablatures and grotesque masks. Repetition of the same decorative motifs in architecture, furniture and windows linked all elements of the Dutch house into an organic whole. In addition, given the moralizing and heraldic nature of Dutch glass after the Reformation, many similarities in content and form link domestic and public imagery.

Furniture Displaying Parallel Imagery

The prosperous Dutch commissioned elaborate furniture to testify to core beliefs as well as their commercial achievements. Often such furniture was a prized element of a young woman's dowry. A Dutch cupboard called a *beelenkast* (picture cupboard or wardrobe), dated around 1610–20 in Boston's Museum of Fine Arts (illus. 109), displays themes related to family and to virtuous, and therefore prosperous, living. The two narratives in square formats at the top of the cupboard recount the story of Joseph from the Hebrew Bible, a model for the self-made man who ultimately becomes the saviour of a family who initially rejected him. Both images are based on a series of etchings by Dirk Volkertsz. Coornhert, after designs by Maarten van Heemskerck.

On the upper level, the scene to the left depicts *Joseph and His Brothers Feasting at Joseph's House*. The print source is dated 1549–50. Jealous of their father's affection for their younger brother, Jacob's older sons sold him to Egyptian traders. Joseph, however, rose to prominence to become governor of Egypt. During a famine, for which Joseph had prudently prepared, his brothers travelled to Egypt to buy grain. Joseph recognized them and insisted that one of the brothers remain in Egypt until the youngest brother Benjamin was brought to him. After exhausting their purchase from Egypt, the brothers, with Benjamin, returned to Joseph. Joseph commanded a feast be prepared (Genesis

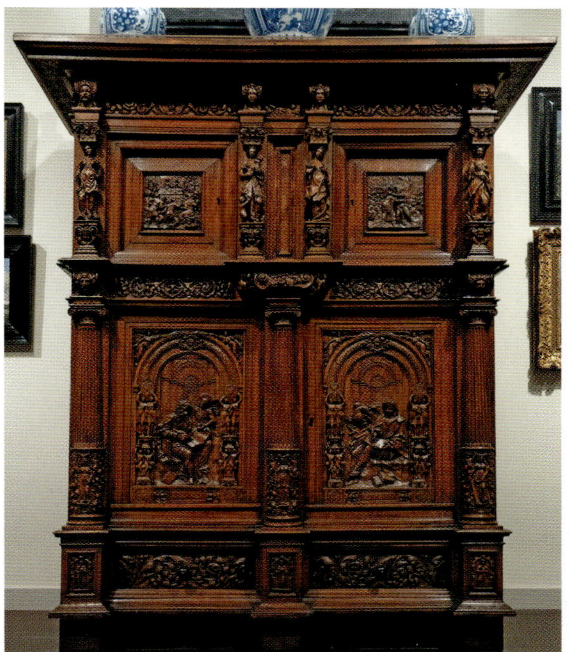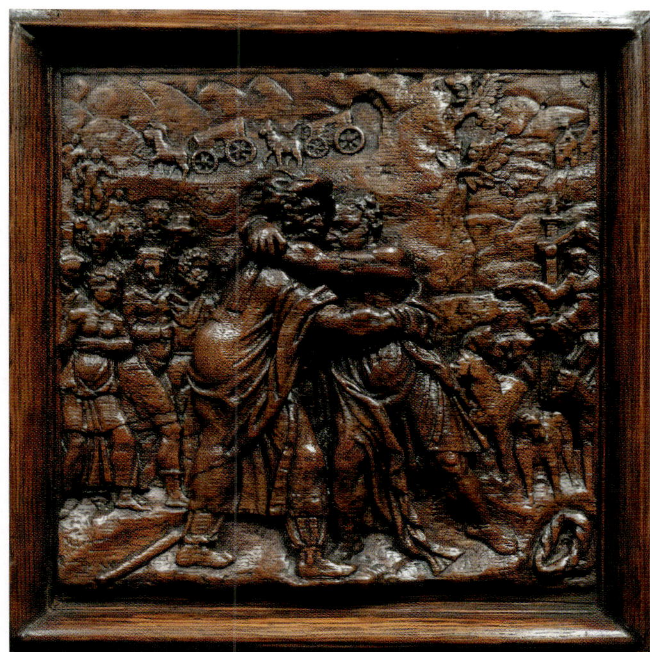

109 North Low Countries, cupboard (*beelenkast*), 1610–20,
now in the Museum of Fine Arts, Boston.

110 North Low Countries, cupboard, detail of the *Meeting of Jacob
and Joseph*, after a print by Maarten van Heemskerck.

43:16). Heemskerck depicts Joseph and Benjamin at the head of the table, and
the agitated brothers speaking with each other, not knowing why they were being
treated with such distinction. The panel on the right (illus. 110) shows the sequel
to the story. After Joseph revealed himself to his brothers he informed them that
the famine would endure for five years. To save his family, Joseph invited them
to live in Egypt. The brothers return to Canaan and Jacob accepts the invitation
(Genesis 46:29). The cupboard reproduces the print showing Jacob in transit
with his entire household. Joseph meets the caravan and clasps his father in
a heartfelt embrace. The widespread popularity of the series is demonstrated
by the print being used as the basis for a window dated about 1550–60 in the
Hospital of St Elizabeth in Lier, Belgium (illus. 111).

Prosperity and Family Ties

The cupboard's imagery, like many glazing programmes, is clearly focused on
'family values' enabling a prosperous life, articulated through biblical, allegorical

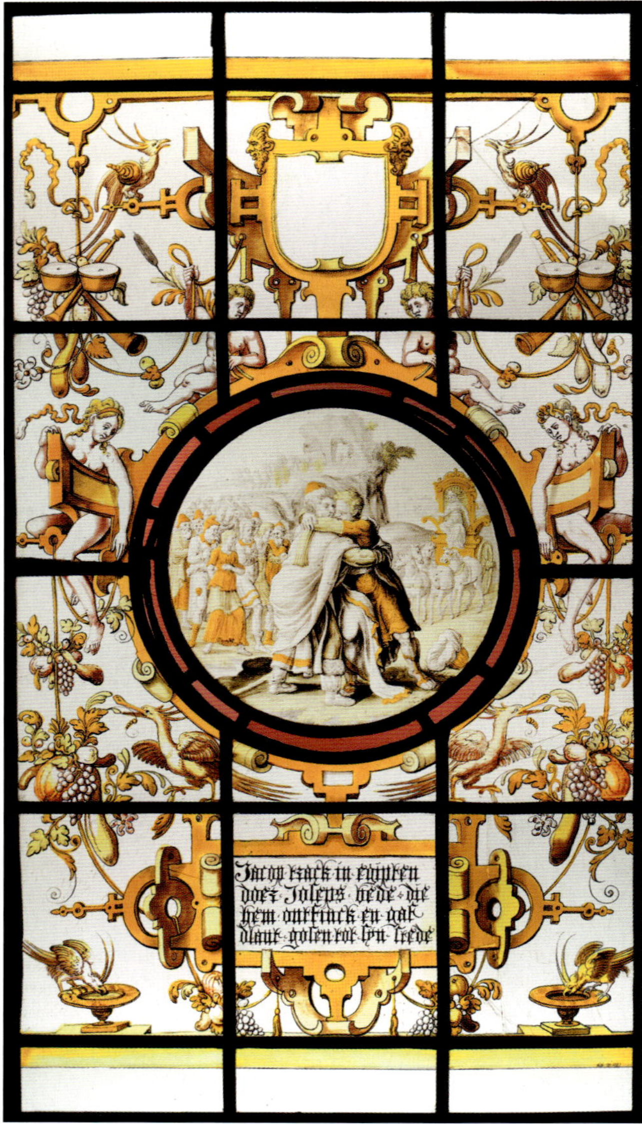

111 South Low Countries, window with scene of the *Meeting
of Jacob and Joseph*, after print by Maarten van Heemskerck,
1550–60, Hospital of St Elizabeth, Lier, Belgium.

and classical references. Two Evangelists' portraits, Matthew and John, dominate the lower level. The decorative framing around them is loosely based on
the 1583 print of *The Ten Commandments* by Hendrick Goltzius, Antwerp.
Three-dimensional figures of the Four Cardinal and Three Theological Virtues
populate multiple levels, very possibly inspired by Goltzius' designs for a series of
Virtues printed by Jacob Matham. Classical references, like those inspiring the

decorative surrounds of the stained glass, dominate the leafy bands. Heads, at the top and the sides, show heroic warriors and commanding goddesses. Within the classical meander of acanthus leaves and fruits are naked male children referred to as putti, some straddling wine barrels, a reference to Bacchus, the god of wine. A female figure holding a sickle and a sheath of wheat may allude to Ceres, the goddess of agriculture and grain crops. At the time, the educated classes were prone to referencing classical literature, such as Terrance's aphorism: *Sine Cerere et Baccho friget Venus* (Without Ceres and Bacchus, Venus freezes). We might rephrase this as 'Neither love nor the continuity of life is possible without the support of food and drink.' The theme inspired many artists, exemplified by Jan Pietersz. Saenredam's engraving after Abraham Bloemaert (about 1600) and paintings by Hendrick Goltzius (1600–1603) and Peter Paul Rubens (1615).

All the arts, literary and visual, including what we now call 'decorative arts', were interrelated. The window from the Hospital of St Elizabeth in Lier (illus. 111), like the Esther window, displays a central roundel as the only biblical subject. It anchors the window, however, profiling an image of a father and son embracing with an intensity that evokes reciprocal memories in the viewer of their encounters with loved ones. Composed of clear glass segments, except for the circular rose frame of the roundel, the window allows a maximum amount of light as well as providing an eye-catching image. The individuals responsible for the programme sought a universal message in the same way that the patron of the cupboard reflected on domestic values of family and virtuous behaviour. The classical motifs were also seen as universals. Nude female figures, modestly entwined in the architecture, are joined by putti. Symbols of prosperity, such as festoons of grapes, apples and gourds, anchor all four corners. Fanciful plumed birds reach out greedily to eat. Two flank the inscription plate and perch to drink on the rim of a shallow raised dish. Music appears in the horns and drums added to the two clusters of fruit at the top. Two shades of silver stain enliven the contrast of yellows while the precisely controlled painted outlines enhance the clarity of the forms. The narrative roundel was executed by another painter in the workshop, one who favoured more subtlety in the form and blending of shadows. The antique strapwork design that supports the roundel, inscription and upper cartouche was a popular device that embellished many title pages of books, as already mentioned. The seventeenth-century Lowlands saw itself reinvigorated by classical renewal, distinct from what it viewed as an unenlightened medieval past. Clearly this decorative framing was a statement of progressive thinking, not a superfluous embellishment.

Works of Mercy

Heemskerck also made a series of drawings for *The Last Judgement* and *Seven Works of Mercy* that were produced as prints by Dirck Volkertsz. Coornhert in 1552 (illus. 112). This was a time-honoured list of good works enjoined on the Christian: giving drink to the thirsty, giving food to the hungry, clothing the naked, giving shelter to the homeless, aiding the sick, visiting the imprisoned and burying the dead, a theme discussed in Chapter Five. A roundel of *Housing the Stranger* (illus. 113), now in the J. Paul Getty Museum, Los Angeles, dated about 1560–80, is a close adaptation of Heemskerck's design. A wealthy man clothed in a flowing robe over a fur-trimmed tunic stands on the threshold of a house. Behind him, the interior shows a man with a bare torso sitting on a bed. On the left, a visitor walks up the steps to clasp the host's outstretched right hand.

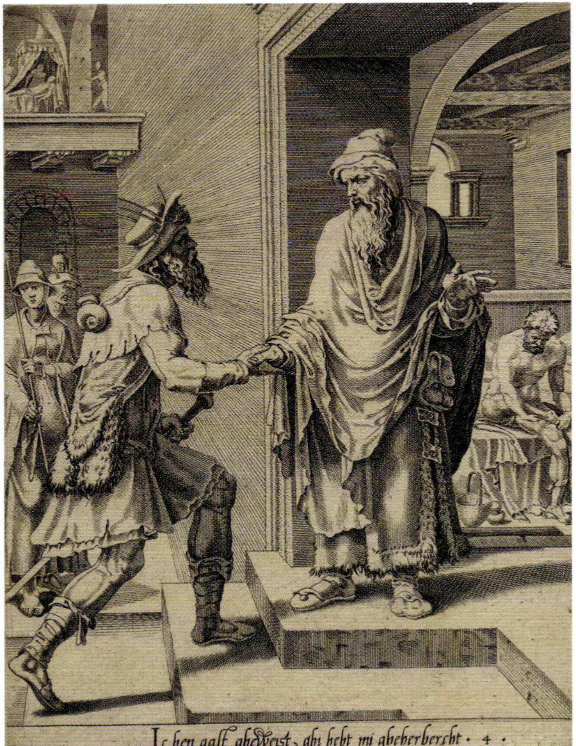
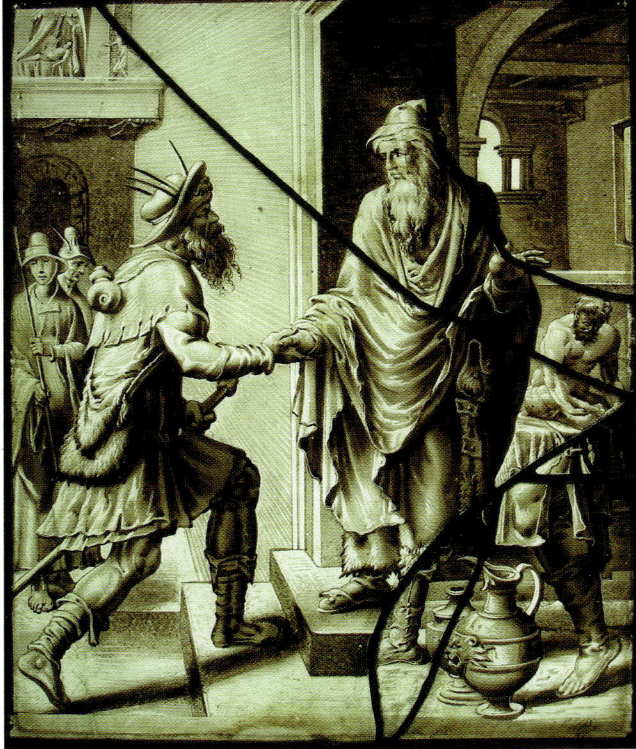

112 Dirk Volkertsz. Coornhert after designs by Maarten van Heemskerck, *Giving Shelter to the Homeless*, from *The Last Judgement and Six Works of Mercy*, 1552, now in the British Museum, London.

113 North Low Countries, after Maarten van Heemskerck, *c.* 1560–80, *Housing the Stranger*, from a series of the *Corporal Works of Mercy* now in the J. Paul Getty Museum, Los Angeles.

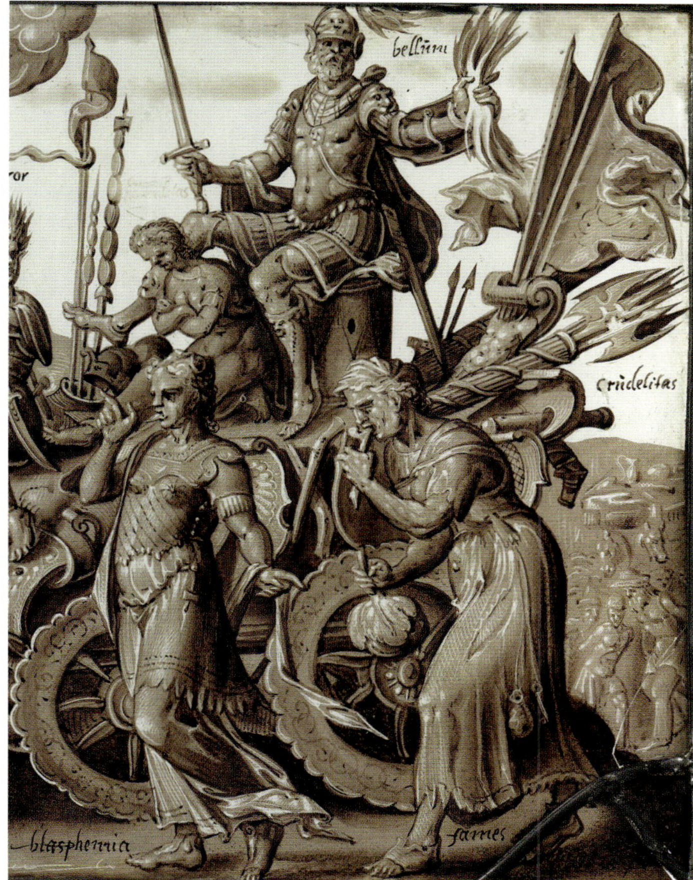

114 North Low Countries, *Triumph of War*, detail, after Maarten
van Heemskerck, *The Cycle of Vicissitudes of Human Affairs*,
1564–1600, now in the Rijksmuseum, Amsterdam.

He holds a walking stick and is clad in a knee-length skirt, leather pouch and
short cape. Behind the visitor, in the entrance way, two additional men approach,
one holding a walking stick. A stopgap at the lower right of the roundel contains
elements of another scene in the series, Giving Drink to the Thirsty.

The list reflects Christ's words to his followers: 'Amen I say to you, as long
as you did it not to one of these least, neither did you do it to me' (Matthew
25:45). In several prints, the visitor is represented as Christ. A German engraver,
Georg Pencz, produced a series around 1529–39 showing the stranger with an
aureole of light around his head (Art Institute of Chicago, 1919.2303-1919.2305).
In the Getty panel of *Housing the Stranger*, the petitioner appears as a pilgrim
with what seems to be a scallop shell on his hat. The image referenced the value
of pilgrimage at a moment when the time-honoured practice was under attack

by the Protestant Reformation. The Rijksmuseum houses other prints from the series: *Last Judgement*, *Feeding the Hungry* and *Giving Drink to the Thirsty*, all 1552, and *Clothing the Naked*, 1551. They were widely replicated. The survey by William Cole for English sites, for example, reveals a rich variety of execution among 69 roundels after designs by Heemskerck. *Housing the Stranger* is found at several sites, including the church of St Mary the Virgin, Addington, Buckinghamshire, the church of St Laurence, Church Stretton, Shropshire, and Oxburgh Hall, Norfolk.

The roundel in the J. Paul Getty Museum uses two shades of vitreous paint. Back-painting forms a solid wash across the entire exterior surface, creating an opaque mask that gives a uniform effect regardless of the angle of light. The artist shows a sophisticated mastery of three-dimensional representation using subtle washes and linear accents to bring the narrative into relief. The matt of the background gives the work a particularly rich texture, from the smooth uniformity of the wall to the 'juicy' darkness of the shadowed portal on the left and interior spaces on the right. The painter uses parallel lines brilliantly to accent the perspectival recession of the wall. Under close inspection, we observe extremely fine stickwork, accomplished with a needle, as on the shoulder of the visitor being welcomed. The artist is clearly able to exploit many varieties of painting on glass. Such skill is found in another series based on Heemskerck's work, *The Cycle of Vicissitudes of Human Affairs*, printed by Cornelius Court and published by Hieronymus Cock in 1564. Roundels from this series in the Rijksmuseum, Amsterdam, show smooth washes of grisaille that give weight to the composition. The female personifications of Blasphemy and Famine who walk beside War's chariot (illus. 114) show similar techniques to *Housing the Stranger*, which uses subtle gradations of wash to create depth. Most strikingly, the artists of both the Rijksmuseum panels and the Getty *Housing the Stranger* remove the wash with delicate strokes to accent contours and create texture.

Life of Christ: The Saviour's Passion

Imagery that narrated Christ's life remained a highly popular theme for Renaissance and Baroque building programmes. Jacob Cornelisz. van Oostsanen (*c.* 1472/77–1533) produced prints on the Passion of Christ that appeared in roundel cycles exemplified by the roundel *Christ Led to Jerusalem*, now in the J. Paul Getty Museum (illus. 115). Twelve prints encompass the events just before and after Christ's death: 1) Last Supper; 2) Agony in the Garden; 3) The Betrayal; 4) Christ Led to Jerusalem (illus. 116); 5) Mocking of Christ;

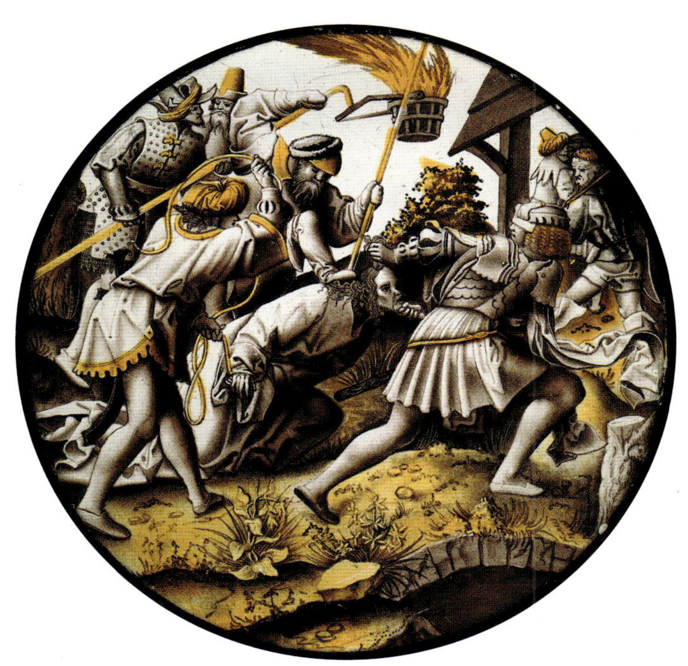

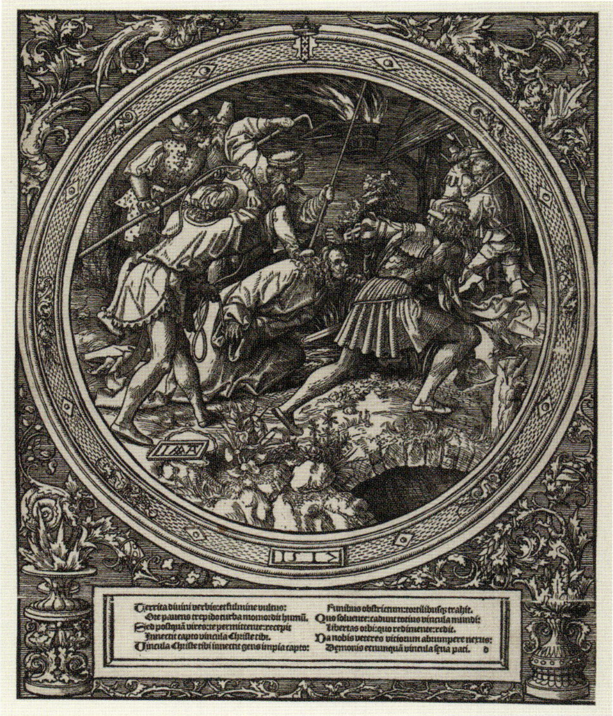

115 North Low Countries, *Christ Led to Jerusalem* or the *Captivity of Christ* after Jacob Cornelisz. van Oostsanen, 1515–20, now in the J. Paul Getty Museum, Los Angeles.

116 Jacob Cornelisz. van Oostsanen, *Christ Led to Jerusalem* or *Captivity of Christ*, 1517, no. 4 of the *Large Circular Passion*, now in the Rijksmuseum, Amsterdam.

6) Flagellation; 7) Crowning with Thorns; 8) Ecce Homo (Christ displayed to the Crowd); 9) Bearing of the Cross; 10) Crucifixion; 11) Entombment; and 12) Resurrection. The first impressions had no borders and were sold separately, as early proofs. Some are monogrammed and dated 1511–14, dates that were cut out of later reprinting. The monogram in the lower middle reads 'IMVA' (W upside down). The series was then published as a whole, in two versions with narrow, circular frames. In one series the border contains putti and instruments of the Passion, in the other, busts of Old and New Testament figures alternate with instruments of the Passion. In 1517, the publishers augmented the circular narratives by setting them into rectangular surrounds containing Latin meditative inscriptions. A third edition followed with new rectangular frames and the addition of small Old Testament scenes that prefigured the Passion scene above, in the tradition of the *Biblia Pauperum*. These latter prints were designed so that they could be exhibited together, constituting a continuous architectural display measuring 2 metres (6½ ft) wide. A fourth edition with square ornamental frames filled with fruit was published by Johannes Mommart, Brussels, in 1651, more than a century later. Such re-editions testify to the widespread popularity of the subject-matter and van Oostsanen's designs.

Van Oostsanen was a member of a family of painters and printmakers located primarily in Amsterdam. Scholars have identified about 200 woodcuts and 27 paintings in the artist's oeuvre; the clarity of his designs made translation into glass popular. Early depictions of these scenes incorporated many details, encouraging a discursive reading. In the *Large Circular Passion*, each image in the series focuses on a specific moment in time. Extraneous detail is minimized and almost all the figures are on the same plane. In the roundel of *Christ Led to Jerusalem*, the viewer is unavoidably confronted by the pathos of a docile Christ, pulled, beaten, whipped and kicked. The composition of the panel is enmeshed in the long and vigorous tradition of Passion representation in the Lowlands. Parallel conventions in prints and manuscripts are used to highlight the immediacy of the soldiers' brutality. The art historian James Marrow suggests that the image of Christ trodden underfoot can be traced to Old Testament prophesies such as Isaiah 51:23, 'thou hast laid thy body as the ground, and as a way to them that went over,' or Psalm 55:2–3, which begins 'Have mercy on me, O God, for man hath trodden me under foot.' Thus the individual kicking Christ is paralleled in several prints and manuscripts. Simon Bening's exquisite miniature of the Way to Calvary from the manuscript the *Prayer Book of Cardinal Albrecht of Brandenburg* (c. 1525–30) shows the convention of the soldier preceding Christ, who is seen from the back, and pivoting to strike him with a club.[1] In the roundel,

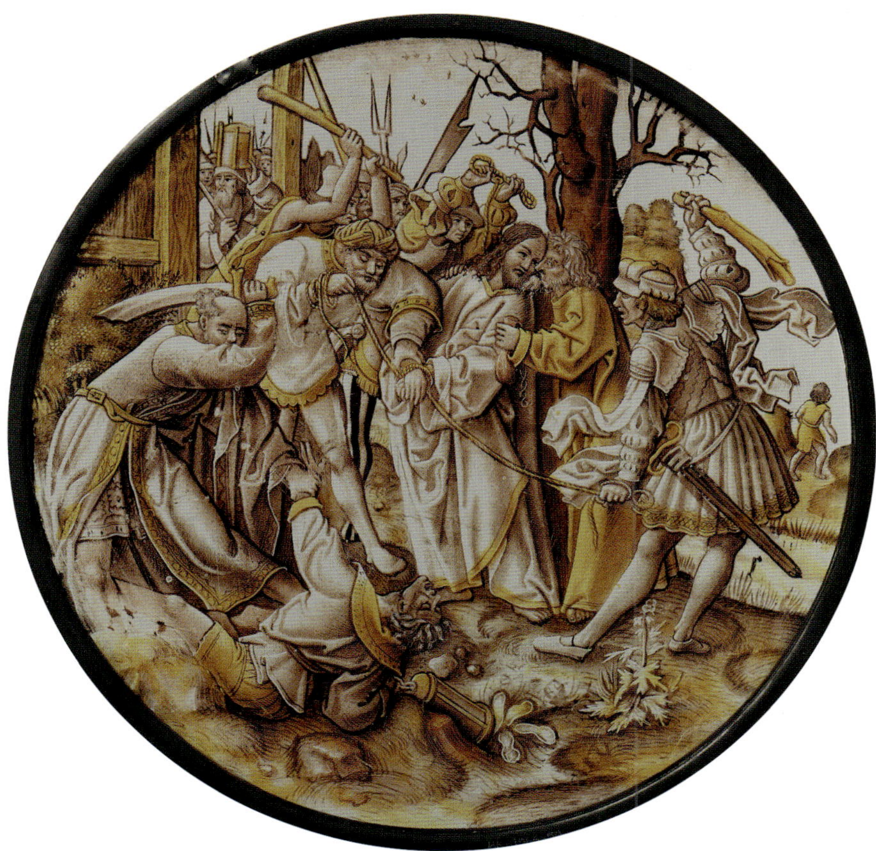

117 North Low Countries, after Jacob Cornelisz. van Oostsanen,
Betrayal, 1515–20, now in the Rijksmuseum, Amsterdam.

however, the soldier turns to pull Christ's beard. This is a reference to another
of Isaiah's prophecies (50:6): 'I gave my back to the smiters, and my cheeks to
them that plucked off the hair: I hid not my face from shame and spitting.'
The quotation was so well known that in 1742 it entered the lyrics of Handel's
iconic orchestral masterpiece, the *Messiah*.

The roundel is faithful to the print source, giving precise renditions of composition and details, except for the omission of the tree stump and monogram
on the left and the flattening of the large rock in the foreground. The identity
of the painter, or workshop, that created the glass, however, is more elusive.
Painting transforms the woodcut's dense parallel lines in the ground and sky
and the cross-hatch on the figures into stippled washes that form solid, tonal
areas. Stickwork, or paint removal, is deliberative, rather than gestural. The effect
is almost sculptural. We see the same control in the application of trace line to

delineate areas of Christ's hair, the elements of the soldiers' armour or even the plants at the bottom of the composition.

Silver stain unifies the panel, forming a coherent mass that silhouettes the figures against a yellow ground and adds a richness not seen in the print. A single shade of paint applied as a stippled wash is highlighted by restricted use of thin trace, exemplified in the figure of the soldier on the right. Using various levels of intensity in the washes and the removal of paint to create highlights, the image achieves a sense of volume. Such illusion of depth is further enhanced by the application of back-painting on the reverse of the glass in areas meant to be in shadow.

The variety as well as popularity of roundel series can be seen by comparison with a roundel in Amsterdam's Rijksmuseum from van Oostsanen's *Large Circular Passion*. It depicts the Betrayal, also known as the Kiss of Judas (illus. 117), when Judas enters the garden of Gethsemane where Christ has been praying and identifies him to the soldiers by a kiss. Like the roundel of Christ led to Jerusalem, and dated to the same era, it follows the print with great precision. Close examination, however, indicates that it was executed by another hand. The artist of the Betrayal shows much the same linear emphasis, defining the face and hair as in the Getty roundel. Both favour the technique of stippling to model contours to achieve three-dimensionality. The Rijksmuseum roundel, however, uses several different hues of vitreous paint, adds more delicate stickwork and introduces cross-hatching to shade in some areas. It is possible that within large workshops several different painters collaborated, even on a single series. Each retained some individual habits of execution, although the end results conveyed uniformity from a distance.

Choice and Artistic Integrity

Even if the full series of prints is known, a stained-glass commission may have limited the scenes because of the specific architectural context, for example, a series of four, or of six, window openings. The patron would then select the scenes from the print series most important to the narrative, for example, only a few images of Christ's Passion since they would have been sufficient to evoke the rest of the story. Even a single image, such as Christ being led to Jerusalem, allows the viewer to fully empathize with a saviour willingly accepting humiliation, pain and ultimately death for the sake of another. The series of the *Works of Mercy*, however, was invariably a fixed set, except for the final work of burying the dead, a responsibility associated with the clergy. The depictions emphasized the commonplace, showing individuals engaged in everyday tasks, such as opening a door to welcome a guest. Thus the imagery called upon all viewers to follow suit.

With this new resource of print models, the artist did not cede artistic control to the patron, despite what the modern reader might consider as a borrowed design. In a world before prints, patrons communicated their wishes through comparisons with other media. For the windows at Canterbury, we find strong affinities between manuscripts in Canterbury's scriptorium and the glass. We may only assume that the designers of works on parchment and in glass shared resources, most probably encouraged by their patrons. In large programmes, theological experts advised both patrons and artists. The complexity of the programmes and the rare evidence of literacy except among the clerical elite would argue that literate advisors were essential. Artists were never passive recipients; their very choices of modulating the tone of vitreous paint and silver stain always transformed the image, no matter how exact its replication of the print. The structure of windows invariably differed, for example a round format necessitating changes to the rectangular print design. Artists created new designs to frame the roundel, developing a myriad of inventive experiments with strapwork, foliage and animal and human forms.

These artists exercised vital roles in the promulgation of changing social paradigms. The story of Esther, for example, had been popular throughout the Middle Ages, and received prominence in the programme of Louis IX's Sainte-Chapelle in Paris. In the mid-thirteenth century, the theme was viewed as a demonstration of the wise judgement of a monarch and the heroic behaviour of his queen. The considerable narrative space given to women in the programme may have been in deference to the king's influential mother Blanche of Castile, still living four years after the consecration of the building. In the Renaissance, rather than a single heroic individual, however, Esther became an example of a well-run legal system. Her story stressed due process, verifying evidence and public cross-examination. Esther urges the king to consult his records, and to judge individuals on their own merit. We thus see these Lowlands roundels speaking of the importance of the individual, as opposed to the state or the Roman Church, to exercise justice in human society. It is in the public setting, and the art of the glass painter, that we see this most vividly.

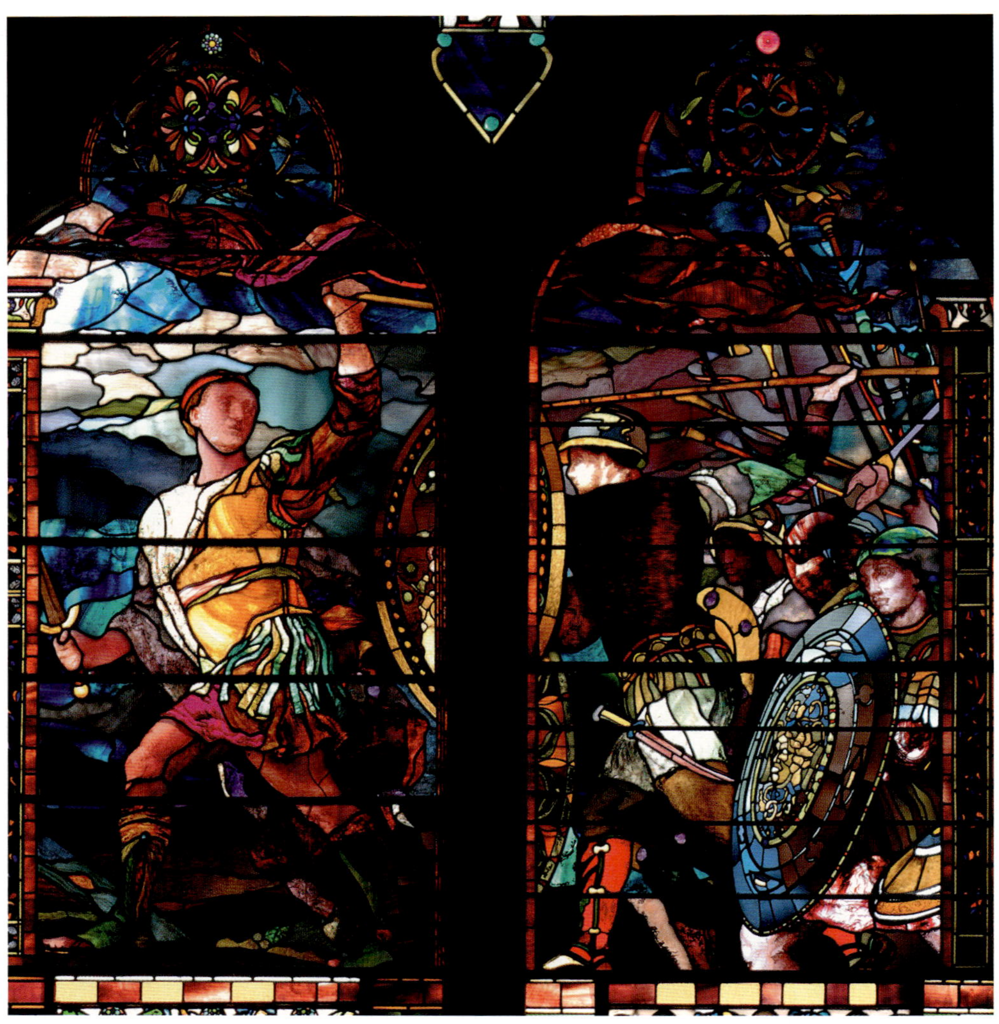

118 John La Farge, *Battle Window*, central scene, donor class of 1860, 1881.

9

Harvard University's Memorial Hall: Honouring the Dead, the Nation and Art

—

Designed by William Ware (Harvard class of 1852) and Henry Van Brunt (Harvard class of 1854), and completed between 1870 and 1876, Memorial Hall met three needs of the college. It provided a memorial to the fallen in the War Between the States in its central transept, a dining hall to the west and, to the east, the auditorium space of Sanders Theatre. At the time of its construction, the president and fellows characterized the hall as 'the most valuable gift which the University has ever received, in respect alike to cost, daily usefulness, and moral significance'. Built in a Victorian Gothic style, Memorial Hall is not only a monument to fallen classmates but the embodiment of the intellectual and artistic self-confidence of Boston in the late nineteenth century. Harvard was the mirror of Boston's elite, who looked with gratitude and pride on a university educational system that now challenged Europe's supremacy.[1]

The Building: Memorial and Proclamation

The hall also demonstrates the economic and political purposes that unified the nation after the Civil War of 1861–5. With the triumph of the industrialized North over the agrarian South, the nation felt confirmed in its capitalist expansion and its valuing of commerce. An inscription in the 'Brimmer' window of the transept addresses subsequent generations: 'Those institutions which they by dying preserved, you cultivate while you live so that men among us may be more free, happy, united'. One-sixth of the Harvard volunteers died in the war. Although the hall was built to commemorate the sacrifices made by these young men, with the end of the Reconstruction era in 1877, African Americans in the

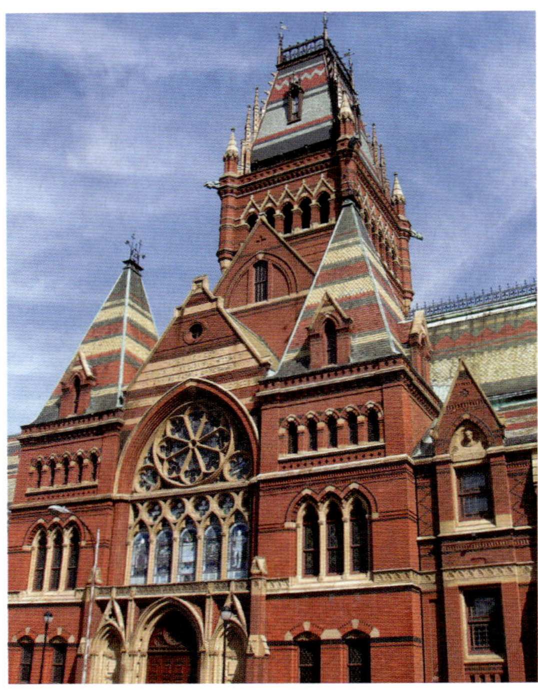

119 William Ware and Henry Van Brunt, Memorial Hall,
Harvard University, exterior, south transept, 1874.

South saw segregation imposed. Many African Americans moved north and, in the early years, they constituted most of the service staff in the hall. The building was of immense pride to the college, and a point of intersection between the institution and the public. Moses King praised the hall when it first opened in 1874, noting: 'At the west end (of the dining hall) is a great window 25 by 30 feet, filled with stained glass . . . Over a thousand persons can be accommodated at the tables.' He notes that the 'gallery at the east end of the dining hall is free to visitors, even at meal times'.[2] The building (illus. 119), in polychrome brick and with its original glass, reflects the prevailing aesthetic of Venetian Gothic. This can be attributed to the influence of John Ruskin (1819–1900), the eminent English cultural critic of this era. He praised the Venetian use of brick:

> In the ancient architecture of the clay districts of Italy, every
> possible adaptation of the material is found exemplified: from the
> coarsest and most brittle kinds, used in the mass of the structure,
> to bricks for arches and plinths, cast in the most perfect curves,
> and of almost every size, strength and hardness; and moulded
> bricks, wrought into flower-work and tracery as fine as raised

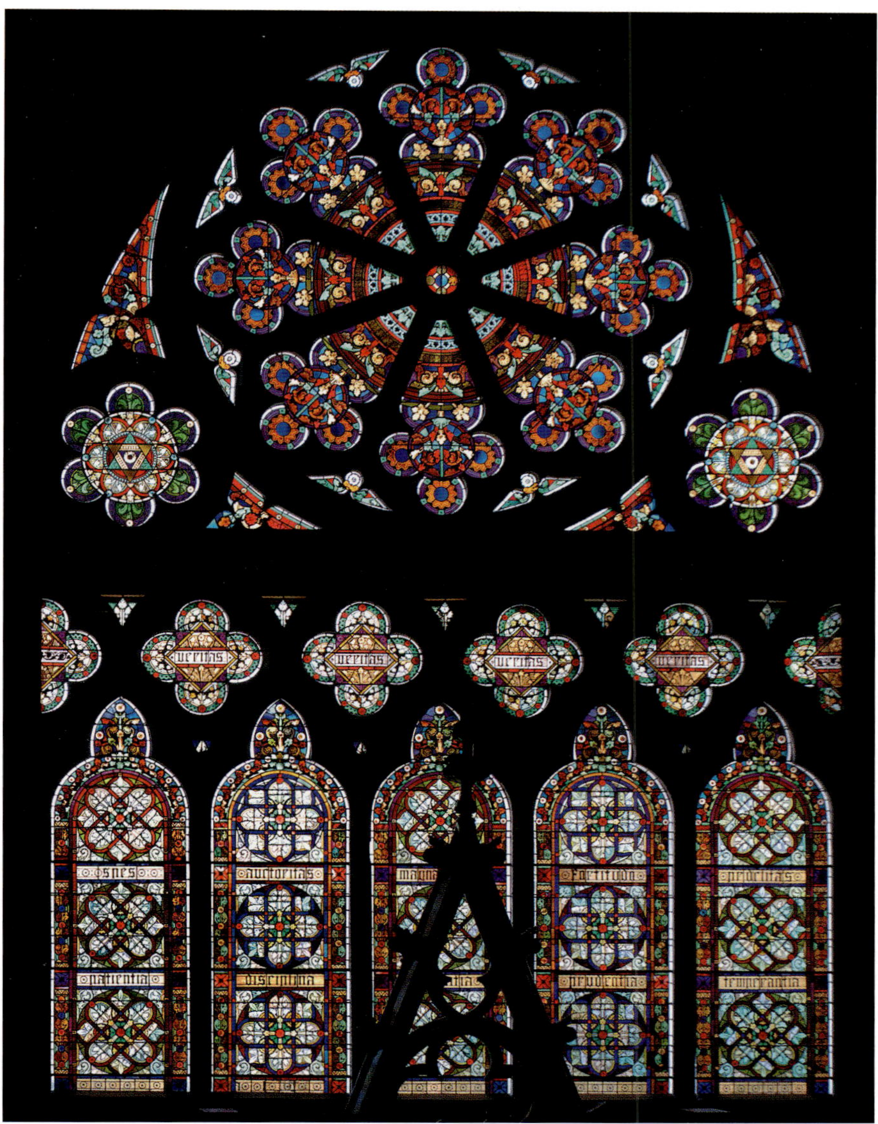

120 MacDonald and McPherson & Co., *Virtues Window*,
north transept (originally south transept), 1874.

patterns upon china . . . Many of the best thoughts of their
architects are expressed in brick . . . I believe that the best academy
for her [England's] architects, for some half century to come,
would be the brick-field.[3]

Ruskin illustrated his works with his own drawings. He delighted in the intricacies and varieties of form especially as repeated in arcades. This is reproduced

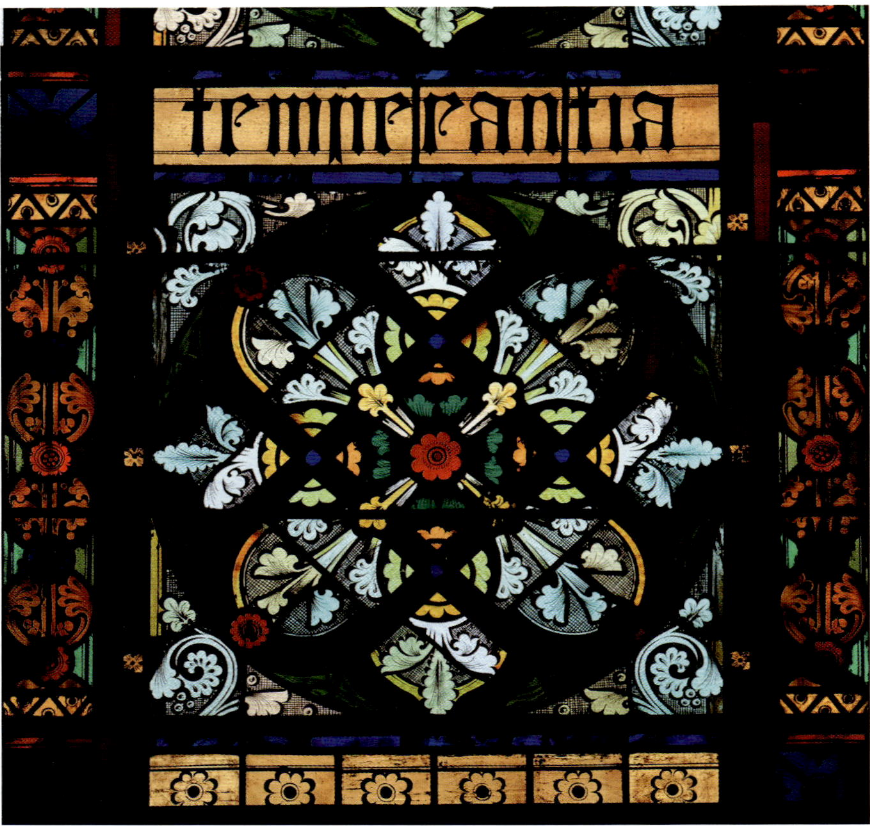

121 MacDonald and McPherson & Co., *Temperantia* (Temperance)
detail, *Virtues Window*, north transept, 1874.

in the arcade below Harvard's transept roses, showing a series of circles framing
quatrefoils, surmounting a row of pointed arches with trilobe cusps.

Memorial Hall's Ruskinian Gothic architecture is matched by the Gothic
Revival glazing patterns that appear in ornamental medallion designs of the windows of the north transept and west wall. These were produced by MacDonald
and McPherson & Co., Boston, in 1874. The present window in the north
transept (illus. 120) was originally in the south opening but was transferred
when the Brimmer window was shifted to the south. MacDonald exploited
clear, vigorous colours and stylized floral patterns to create shifting intensities
of light and hue. A huge rose of foliate pattern displays intense pot-metal glass,
uniform colours achieved during the manufacture of the glass itself. Above are
subtle interactions of turquoise, emerald, olive, purple, red and gold. The glass,
produced in Boston, is an extremely durable variety, a thick, richly coloured type,
with variegated surface texture. Restorers in the 1990s found no corrosion had

occurred during the century of exposure to New England weather and the more recent toxic atmosphere of urban environments. Below, the paler lancets carry a medallion design of quatrefoil patterns outlined in red and blue fillets over variegated grisaille grounds (illus. 121). Between the medallions are Latin inscriptions of ten virtues deemed essential to the scholar: *Spes* (Hope) *Patientia* (Patience), *Auctoritas* (Authority), *Disciplina* (Discipline), *Magnaminitas* (Generosity), *Constatia* (Constancy), *Fortitudo* (Strength), *Prudentia* (Prudence), *Proflitas* (apparently a misspelling of *Probitas*, or Probity) and *Temperantia* (Temperance). The west window was seen as a statement of the college. Its tracery depicts the authorities under which the hall took shape, the college, the state and the nation. To the left are the arms of the United States, a spread eagle carrying a shield with thirteen stars and thirteen red and white stripes on its breast. On the right is the shield of the Commonwealth of Massachusetts with inscriptions. In the centre is the red shield of Harvard with its three open books, but without the customary inscription VERITAS (truth).

Class Gifts of Windows

Figural windows added in the hall between 1879 and 1902 show a mingling of classical, medieval and Renaissance imagery memorializing not only Harvard's student-soldiers but the pictorial language of an entire generation. In contrast to the Gothic-inspired grisaille, the new windows exemplify America's preference for Renaissance three-dimensional form. The programme pairs figures that embody the virtues for scholar and soldier and, from the beginning, the college anticipated class gifts to fund the windows. The architects proposed the general format of two figures per opening and the Harvard Corporation specified a protocol: each window should consist of subjects from a time not later than Shakespeare's; two typical (symbolic) or historical figures, about life-size and celebrating the virtues of heroes and scholars. In the lower panels, characteristic ornamentation or incident connected to the figures should be present as well as borders in the same period style as the figures. There should also be an effort to provide as much illumination into the hall as the decorative purpose of the window would allow. These directions were generally followed. On the left, beginning on the west, we find *Sophocles and Shakespeare* (1883, Greek playwright/English Renaissance playwright and poet), *Charlemagne and Sir Thomas More* (1888, Holy Roman Emperor/Chancellor of England under Henry VIII), *Battle Window* (1881, generic ancient battle), *Sir Philip Sidney and Epaminondas* (1879, English Renaissance poet who died in battle in the Netherlands/statesman and soldier who liberated Thebes from Sparta and also died in battle), *Dante and Chaucer* (1897, Italian Renaissance poet/English medieval poet), *Columbus and Blake* (1880, Discoverer of America/English Renaissance admiral), *Cornelia the Mother of the Gracchi* (1891, mother of second-century BCE Roman statesmen, Tiberius and Gaius Gracchus) and *Honour and Peace* (1900, allegorical figures).

On the right (north), we view *La Salle and Marquette* (1895, French explorer of the Mississippi/French Jesuit missionary around the Great Lakes), *Bernard of Clairvaux and Godfrey of Bouillon* (after 1901, preacher of the Second Crusade/military commander of the First Crusade), *Student and Soldier* (1881, generic figures), *John Hampden and Leonidas* (1882, member of English Parliament who fought against the tyranny of Charles 1/Greek who died at the Battle of Thermopylae against the Persians), *The Parting of Hector and Andromache* (1888, scene from the Trojan War described by Homer), *Virgil and Homer* (1883, Roman and Greek classical epic poets), *Pericles and Leonardo da Vinci* (1882, artistic innovators in classical Athens and Renaissance Florence), *General Warren and John Eliot* (1889, Harvard graduate who died in the Battle of Bunker Hill/Congregational minister who preached to Native Americans), *Themistocles and Aristides* (1892, Athenian generals who reconciled to defeat the Persian invasion of 480 BCE).

Transition from European Traditional Glass to American Opalescent

Part of the fascination of the hall, arguably the most distinguished secular installation of stained glass in the United States, is the transition from traditional pot-metal glass, often called 'cathedral', to the American opalescent, first developed by John La Farge (1852–1910) but swiftly adopted and modified by many artists of the era. From the first, La Farge had been the artist of choice for the architects of the hall. Henry Van Brunt approached him as early as 1874, shortly after La Farge's return from Europe. The intent of the original plans would have seen most of the glass designed by La Farge. The initial commission, however, a design of Christopher Columbus and the Chevalier de Bayard, prompted the artist to experiment on a test panel with techniques of plating, 'that is to say placing one glass upon another, to enrich my stock of tones . . . superposing one colour on another so as to increase its depth and richness' as La Farge would recall. These innovations, carried out in a sample half-window viewed shortly before Harvard's commencement of 1875, pushed the projected price to more than twice the sum that the class had assumed. The project was abandoned and the class eventually chose the English artist Henry Holiday. In 1877, however, La Farge was offered another commission, for which he used traditional techniques, and the first version of the *Battle Window* was installed in 1879 (illus. 118).

Traditional glass can be seen in the windows of Daniel Cottier, who began his work in Glasgow and then expanded to London and in 1873 to New York. Cottier was frequently in the States to supervise the highly successful 'Cottier & Company: Upholsters, Fine Cabinet Makers, Glass and Tile Painters', which became a major force in developing American taste for Aesthetic Movement ware. He was also instrumental in supporting artists such as Albert Pinkham Ryder, Augustus St-Gaudens and La Farge himself. In 1878 the firm installed four windows on the ground level of the south transept for Trinity Church, Boston. The windows, especially the poignantly moving *Sower and Reaper*, display his

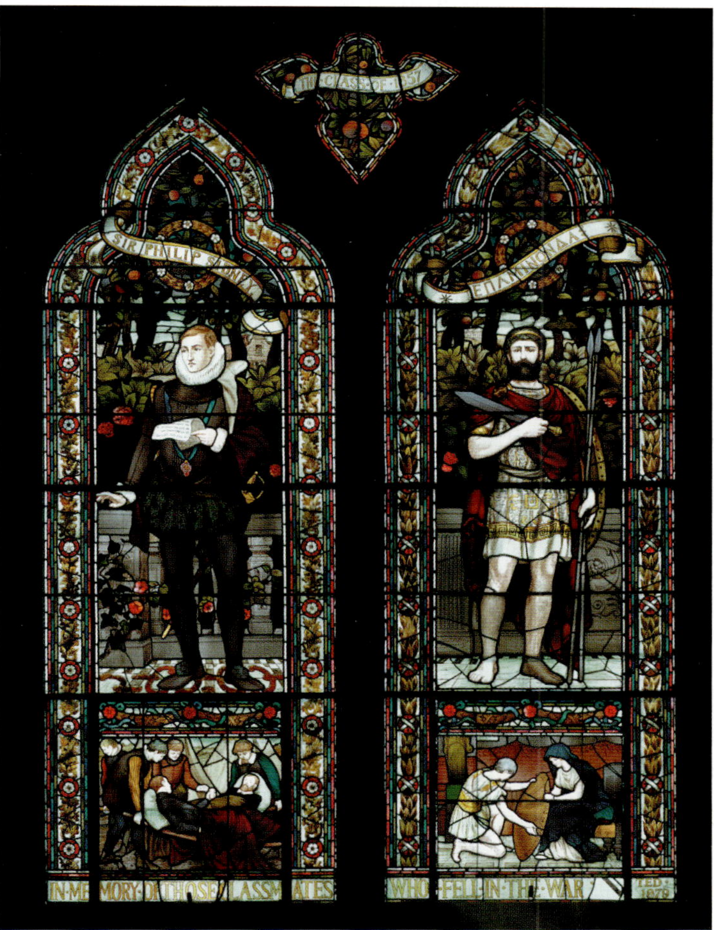

122 Daniel Cottier, *Sir Philip Sidney and Epaminondas*, donor class of 1857, 1879.

characteristic palette of olive, ochre, blue and gold as well as vigorous brush-work in the modelling of form. *Sir Philip Sidney* and *Epaminondas* (illus. 122), installed in the hall in 1879, shows a consistent clarity of form with the two figures silhouetted against a wooded vista with flowering laurel. They stand in front of a parapet, that for Sidney in Renaissance, and that for Epaminondas in classical Greek design. Each colour is a single tone, cut from uniformly tinted green, red, purple, yellow or uncoloured glass. Silver stain is used liberally as in Epaminondas' tunic and the borders.

During this time, however, La Farge had begun to experiment with innovative techniques for various smaller domestic commissions, especially the use of opalescent glass, for example *Peonies Blown in the Wind* (1879), for the house of Henry G. Marquand, Newport (Metropolitan Museum of Art, 30.50). La Farge's patent, filed 10 November 1879, explains:

This opal glass will be more or less opaque or milky in parts . . .
I am enabled by checking or graduating the amount of light in this
way, to gain effects as to depth, softness, and modulation of color
. . . These opalescent and iridescent effects may be enhanced by the
greater or less smoothness of one or both surfaces of the opalescent
glass, and by its thickness, and the glass may be waved, corrugated,
or roughened in molds, or be hammered or rolled or be stamped
or treated to accord with the design . . . In some instances I find it
very advantageous to back colored glass of ordinary construction
with independent pieces of opal glass, one or more layers of either
being used, according to the effect desired . . . On a cloudy or dark
day a window containing opal glass shows such a quality of color
and appears as if lighted by the sun. In the day time this opal-glass
window seen from outside, in variety of color, resembles mosaic
work and presents a highly ornamental effect.[4]

La Farge's Battle Window

By 1881 La Farge felt confident enough about the new processes that he had the *Battle Window* removed at his own expense and returned to his studio in Union Square, New York, where he reworked it using pot metal and opalescent glass, and plating (illus. 123). This must have been a heavy financial investment, but La Farge was convinced that the potential clients seeing the differences between his work and the traditional window would appreciate its value and justify the

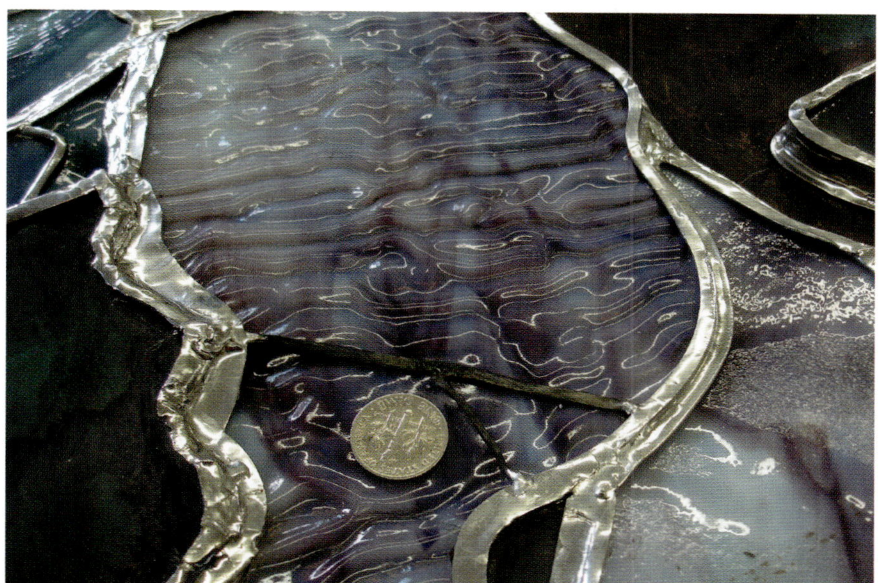

123 John La Farge, *Heavenly Jerusalem*, Trinity Church, Boston, 1884,
detail of opalescent glass in a ripple texture in restoration.

greater costs – especially for future Harvard classes. The reaction to the new version of the window was quite positive. An article in the *Newport Daily News* described it as 'now almost complete. As seen at Mr. La Farge's atelier, it is of exceptional beauty … The style of the work and its artistic treatment recalls the Italian school during the last half century.' La Farge himself would later describe his techniques to his biographer Cecilia Waern: 'I also painted the glass very much and carefully in certain places; so that in a rough way this window is an epitome of all the varieties of glass that I have seen used before or since.' The window attests to the artist's admiration for Raphael and Delacroix, and their works on the subject of Heliodorus driven from the Temple. The saturated colour and dramatic juxtapositions created by the torsion of the bodies bring the past into the present.[5]

Hector and Andromache

After the *Battle Window*, all the windows of the hall used opalescent glass, save *John Hampden and Leonidas* by Cottier of 1882. *The Parting of Hector and Andromache* (illus. 124) from Frederic Crowninshield (1845–1918) stands as an example. The artist graduated from Harvard in 1845, studied abroad and then opened a Boston studio, also teaching at the School of the Museum of Fine

Arts. Crowninshield was to later become influential as the first president of the National Society of Mural Painters between 1895 and 1899, president of the Fine Arts Federation from 1900 to 1909 and director of the American Academy in Rome between 1909 and 1912. The window was made in the artist's newly opened studio in New York. Opalescent glass in subtle hues of green, turquoise, salmon and chartreuse frame enamel colours used for the flesh areas. Crowninshield clearly embraced the innovative possibilities of the American glass. Unlike La Farge, however, he retains a mural flatness and subdued leadline interruption, inspired by his admiration for Italian Renaissance murals.

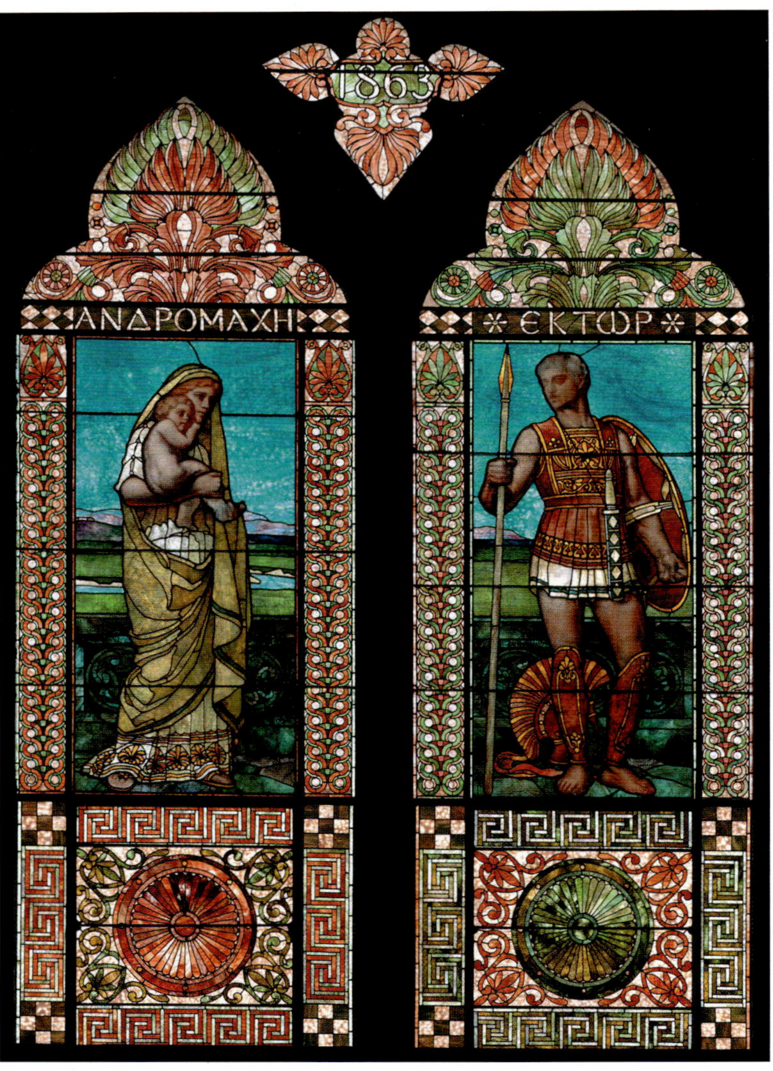

124 Frederic Crowninshield, *The Parting of Hector and Andromache*, donor class of 1863, 1888.

The artist submitted a long, erudite explanation to the class, justifying the need to 'abandon the idea of an historical restoration and to adopt the plan of handling the subject from what may be called the typical [classical] Greek standpoint'. The scene is Homer's account of the great Trojan taking leave of his wife Andromache. Their infant son Astyanax is frightened by his father's helmet, and Hector responds by placing his battle gear at his feet. The artist explained the exchange between Hector and Andromache where Hector delivers Astyanax into his mother's arms and instructs her to work at her loom. Hector will soon be killed by Achilles and Astyanax thrown to his death from the battlements

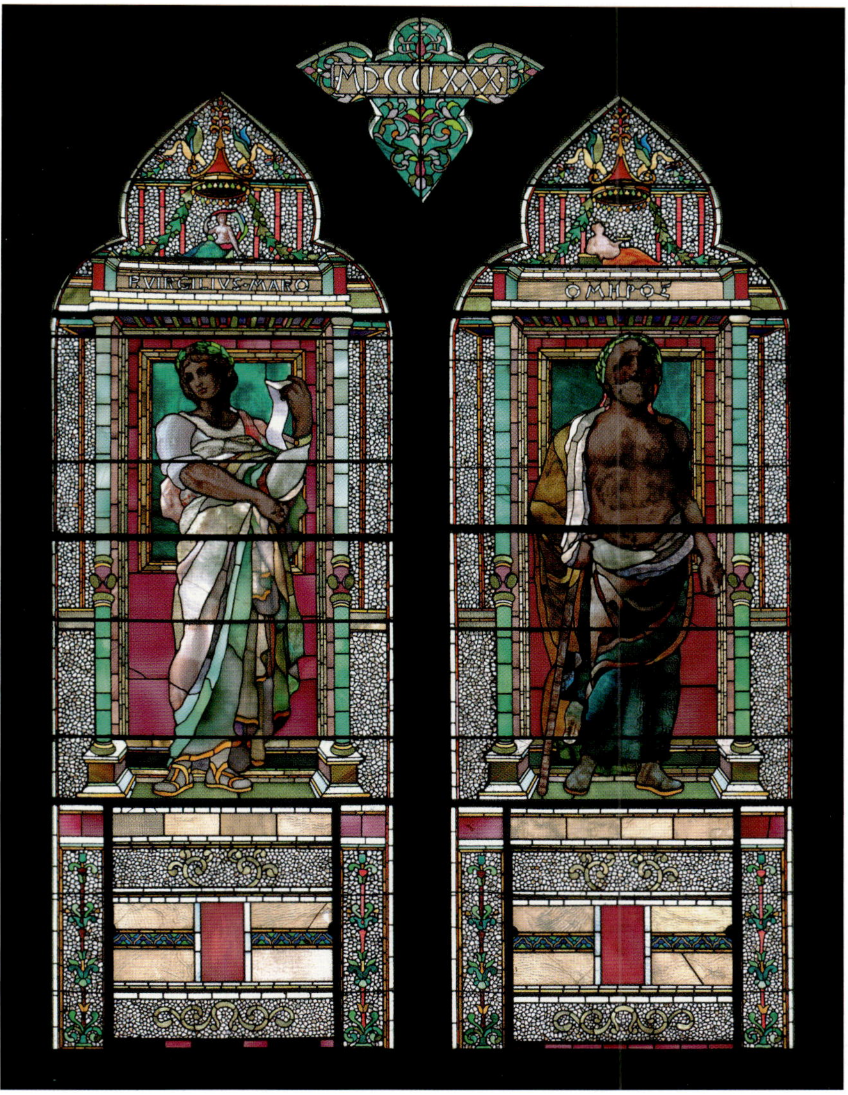

125 John La Farge, *Virgil and Homer*, donor class of 1880, 1883.

of Troy. Crowninshield, whose older brother Frank died from the effects of his service, comments specifically on the youthful, beardless Hector as a deliberate gesture to 'symbolize the uprising of college boys and their subsequent fate'. The poignancy of this moment has often been cited in literature and serves as a fitting memorial to the timeless moments of the soldier's farewell to his loved ones. Crowninshield unifies the separate panels via their common background on the green plain of Troy through which flows the Scamander river. He responds brilliantly to the fourth protocol from the corporation to design 'borders in the same period style as the figures'. The frame of the window is light green and rose set against the deeper green, blue, gold and russet of the central panels. A classical palmette fills the lancet head and, in a simpler form, terminates both side borders; a Greek key design frames the lower panels.

The skilful adherence to the protocol of framing with classical motifs has a precedent in La Farge's *Virgil and Homer* (illus. 125) of 1883, next to *The Parting of Hector and Andromache*. La Farge wrote that he created the window 'in accordance with certain types of Graeco-Roman design, which allows large open spaces and delicate architectural division'. The window shows a pebble border and segments of opalescent and cathedral glass that evoke classical inlay in architectural niches, as in the Pantheon in Rome. The recessed space framed by slender columns and projecting overhang, and the lower border of vertically thin leafy fronds and intertwining meanders, are typical of wall painting from Pompeii. A traveller to Italy could have seen these forms, but schematized renderings were also available in meticulously illustrated publications of historic ornament such as Owen Jones's *Grammar of Ornament* (1865) or Auguste Racinet's *L'Ornament polychrome* (1875).

Sarah Wyman Whitman: Artist and Community Leader

We may be able to understand the value of this complex monument by a deeper exploration of one of the window designers, Sarah Wyman Whitman (1846–1912). The artist belonged to a socially distinguished family and in her adult life was a leader in education, religion and art. Typical for women of her time, her early schooling by tutors was private, giving her a requisite fluency in French, the language of international relations and culture. She studied with William Morris Hunt, Boston's leading portrait and landscape painter, from 1868 to 1871. Whitman benefited financially from her marriage to Henry Whitman, who in 1888 achieved partnership in the wool company of Weston, Whitman & Co. Permitted the leisure of European travel, she studied in the studio of Thomas

Couture in France in the summer of 1877 and the winter of 1879. In the 1880s, while still pursuing painting, Whitman became a major designer of book covers for Houghton Mifflin publishers, Boston. She appears to have been highly valued by the firm, her name even appearing in their advertising. This interest in the art of printing and book design was aligned with the Arts and Crafts movement, the figurehead of which was William Morris. Whitman would also exert a strong influence on the founding of Radcliffe College, which would offer women education on a level comparable to Harvard's. She was a close friend of Elizabeth Cary Agassiz, Radcliffe's first president, who periodically solicited her services for the college. Whitman was also an active member of Trinity Episcopal Church, where she was a long-time leader of adult Bible classes, and a trusted friend of its charismatic rector, Phillips Brooks (1835–1893). Martin Brimmer (1829–1896), the founding director of the Museum of Fine Arts, was also a close friend as well as a member of Trinity's congregation. The original building of the Museum of Fine Arts, it must be remembered, was adjacent to Trinity in Copley Square and designed in a Ruskinian Gothic style similar to Memorial Hall.

Whitman's work in glass embodied the major artistic trends of Boston's most influential phase, often referred to as the American Renaissance. She believed that great art embodied values that could speak to the modern era, as explained in her book of 1886, *The Making of Pictures*. Typical for her time, she most valued Italian Renaissance figural painting and nineteenth-century landscape, including work by artists such as Guido Reni, Tintoretto, Michelangelo, Titian, Diego Velázquez, William Morris Hunt, Daubigny and Turner. Brimmer's own taste was similar. He owned landscapes by Constable, Corot and Diaz, portraits by Copley and Stuart, and figural works by Millet, Hunt and Vedder. Whitman and Brimmer articulated their generation's belief in the responsibility of the newly founded public institutions to teach; their authority, however, was based on their understanding of the past. Whitman had personally experienced the sensation of looking at the frescos of Michelangelo's Sistine Chapel, which Brimmer told her had given him a 'good moral shaking'. Charles Eliot Norton (1827–1908), an intimate of Ruskin, was also part of this influential circle. In 1875 Harvard created a chair in the new field of 'history of art' which Norton held until his retirement in 1898. Eliot's lectures centred on antiquity, Renaissance Florence and Ruskin's cherished Venetian architecture. The intersection of these articulate patrons and the receptive artist was at the heart of progress in opalescent glass design.

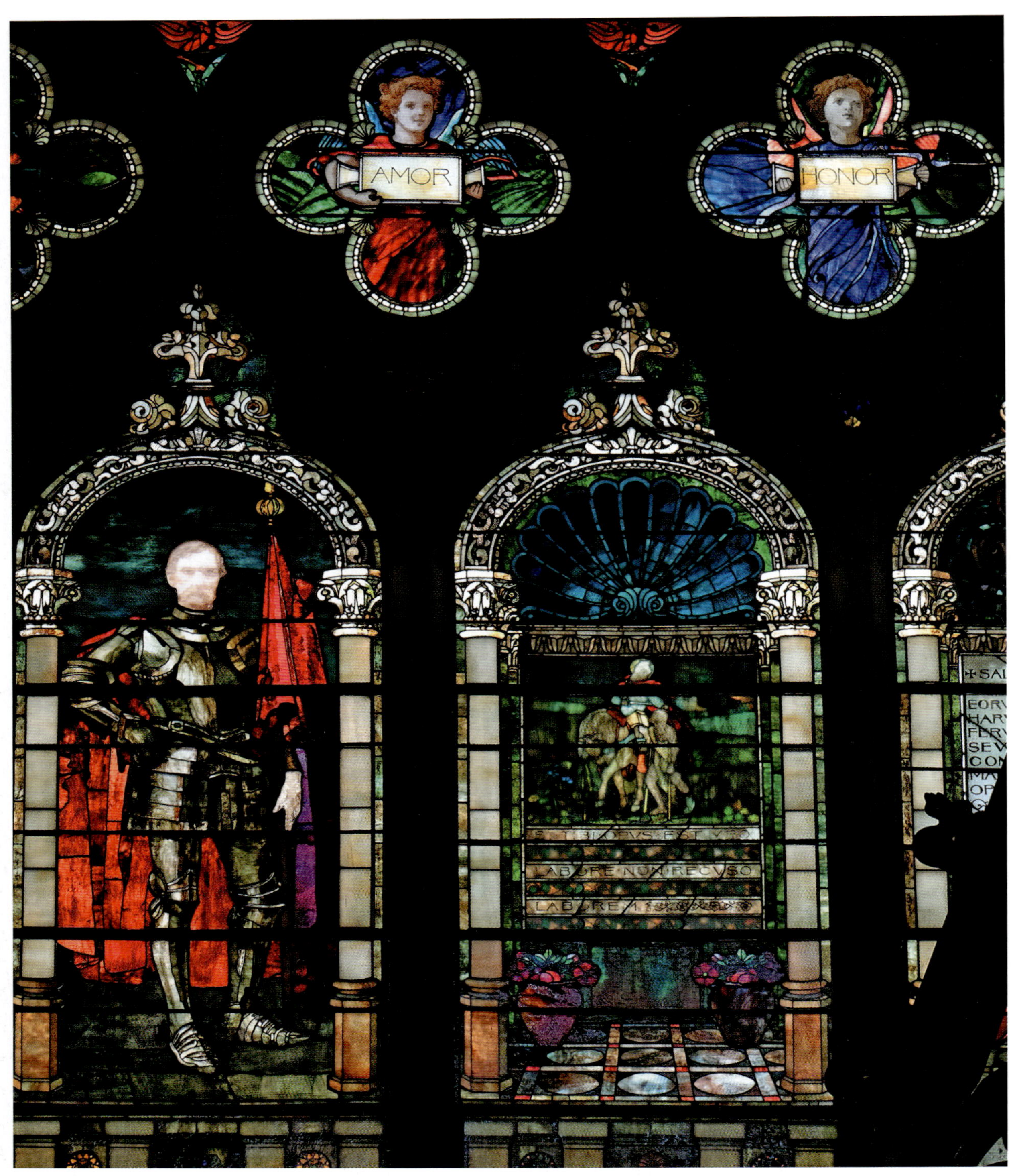

126 Sarah Wyman Whitman, *Brimmer Window*, detail Chevalier Bayard and St Martin, donor Martin Brimmer, 1898.

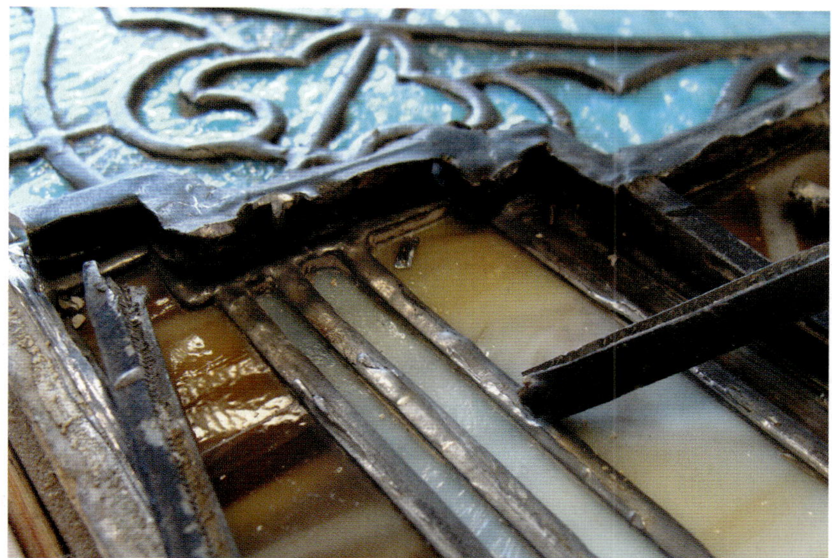

127 Sarah Wyman Whitman, north transept window, detail of plating
in restoration, First Parish of Brookline, Massachusetts, 1898–1901.

Whitman's Brimmer Window

Whitman's two windows for Harvard University are the most complex of her
stained-glass works. They display most completely not only her debt to La Farge,
borrowing from his technique and the theme of his original design, but her
ability to rival his work when given the kind of commission that would elicit a
major statement. As with the works of La Farge and Crowninshield, the model
of the oil and watercolour sketch dominates the effect. The interior surface is
also heavily painted both with applications fired during the initial construction
of the window and those applied as cold paint to the surface after the window
was assembled. The *Brimmer Window* (illus. 126 and see illus. 119), however, presented unusual structural and compositional challenges. It is divided between
a rose showing angels and five lancets that display imagery of the Chevalier
de Bayard, a soldier during the reign of the French king Francis I and of Sir
Philip Sidney, the Elizabethan poet and soldier. The window contains highly
sophisticated opalescent glazing techniques. The use of plating is particularly
developed; in some instances, the window contains as many as seven layers
of glass. There are never less than three. The window's subtlety in varying the
layers of different coloured glass, as seen in Whitman's work for First Parish of
Brookline, Massachusetts (illus. 127), achieves extraordinary control over the
varying clarity and opacity of the design. Richard C. Cabot, Harvard graduate

and physician responsible for reforms in healthcare delivery, addressed the graduating class at Radcliffe after the artist's death. He recalled Whitman's studio, where 'she built in layer upon layer the combinations of glass.' Cabot, a lifelong friend, confided that Whitman 'used to rejoice that, whereas in oil painting she had to try to imitate life by poor materials, through stained glass she had the real thing, she had light itself and did not have to make a visible imitation of it'.

The *Brimmer Window* was originally installed in the north face of the transept, positioned to allow students entering from Harvard Yard to confront the image before entering the dining area. The north exposure proved too dark, however, and the window was repositioned in the south face sometime in the early twentieth century. First unveiled on Commencement Day, on 29 June 1898, the window contains iconography that is an impressive testimony to the American ethos of its time. Its signature element appears in the first lancet: the Chevalier de Bayard standing in classical contrapposto pose, wearing steel-blue armour with a scarlet cape draped behind him. He is without helmet, as is Hector in his farewell to Andromache, the subject of Crowninshield's window in the hall. The second lancet shows St Martin of Tours in the gesture of sharing his cloak with a beggar. The selection of St Martin and the link with Sir Philip Sidney for the windows may have been suggested by the long and engaging description of Martin's charity in John Ruskin's *Bible of Amiens* (1884), a work that was well received in Brimmer and Whitman's circle. In 1880 Ruskin sent a copy of the first part of the *Bible of Amiens*, containing the reference to Martin and Sidney, to Harvard's Charles Eliot Norton, who would later act as his literary executor. In it he describes Martin as the traditional Roman mounted officer much as he is portrayed in the window. Martin debasing his rank by cutting off half of his cloak received special attention. Regarding the act, Ruskin writes: 'No ruinous gift, nor even enthusiastically generous: Sidney's cup of cold water, needed more self-denial.' Sidney was believed to have given his water to another soldier while he lay wounded. In this climate of shared ideas, Norton most likely passed Ruskin's work onto another good friend, Brimmer, and quite probably Whitman. A Latin inscription reads: 'If you need my labour, I do not withhold it.'

In the central lancet is the Harvard insignia followed by the Latin salutation: 'Greetings to whoever is present. You see the names of those men of Harvard who, fervent youths or men of more mature counsel, encountered death that the state/republic might remain whole.' Then follows an image of the mortally wounded Sidney, both soldier and poet, tending to a hurt soldier. The fifth lancet presents Sidney as a youthful scholar. The figures of both the soldier and the scholar are idealized portraits of Martin Brimmer, who was of French Huguenot (Protestant) descent. The French hero, the Chevalier de Bayard (*c.* 1473–1524), depicted with fair colouring, prominent cheekbones, a broad forehead and full drooping moustache, corresponds to published images of Brimmer. Verbal as well as visual eulogies constructed these analogies. The essayist John Jay Chapman (Harvard class of 1884) described him as 'the Old Knight Brimmer' and a poem at his death ascribed martial glory to him, ending with the lines 'Christ Militant, Thy soldier as he lies!' The window had been underway in 1895, and, after Brimmer's death in January, Whitman must have felt empowered to include a portrait as well as the ideological likeness.

While the hostilities between North and South raged, Brimmer had served in the Massachusetts House of Representatives (1859–61) and the Senate (1864). He also held many non-remunerative offices, as trustee of the Boston Athenaeum, trustee of Massachusetts General Hospital and fellow and later member of the Board of Overseers of Harvard College from 1877 to 1896, as noted in the window's inscription. He and Charles Eliot Norton were founding members and officers of the Archaeological Institute of America. As founding director of the Museum of Fine Arts, Boston, he had served 26 years in that post.

Whitman's Honour and Peace

Whitman's second window for the hall, *Honour and Peace* (illus. 128), donated by the class of 1865, shows continued sophistication in both theme and technique. Indeed, the relationship between the *Brimmer Window* and its follower suggests that Whitman's studio had developed a working system that was increasingly effective in meshing artistic vision with technical means. The use of plating is more consistent throughout the entire window. It is inevitable that a study of Whitman's major figural works raises questions about what was considered proper professional deportment in a woman. What served her well in social effectiveness, her gender and class, may have also restricted her total oeuvre to so few windows. She did not produce art out of commercial necessity. The novelist Sarah Orne Jewett stated in her introduction to the volume of Whitman letters that the artist lived 'for Love's sake'. What Whitman may have sacrificed to quantity, however, she certainly achieved in quality.

In *Honour and Peace*, large, pale, allegorical figures cradle the action of the youths, one who strides forwards, the other, bareheaded, who kneels to offer thanks. The warrior moving forwards recalls the leading figure in La Farge's *Battle Window* of some two decades earlier. The clear coloured glass in his shield approximates the high sheen of a polished metallic surface. The female

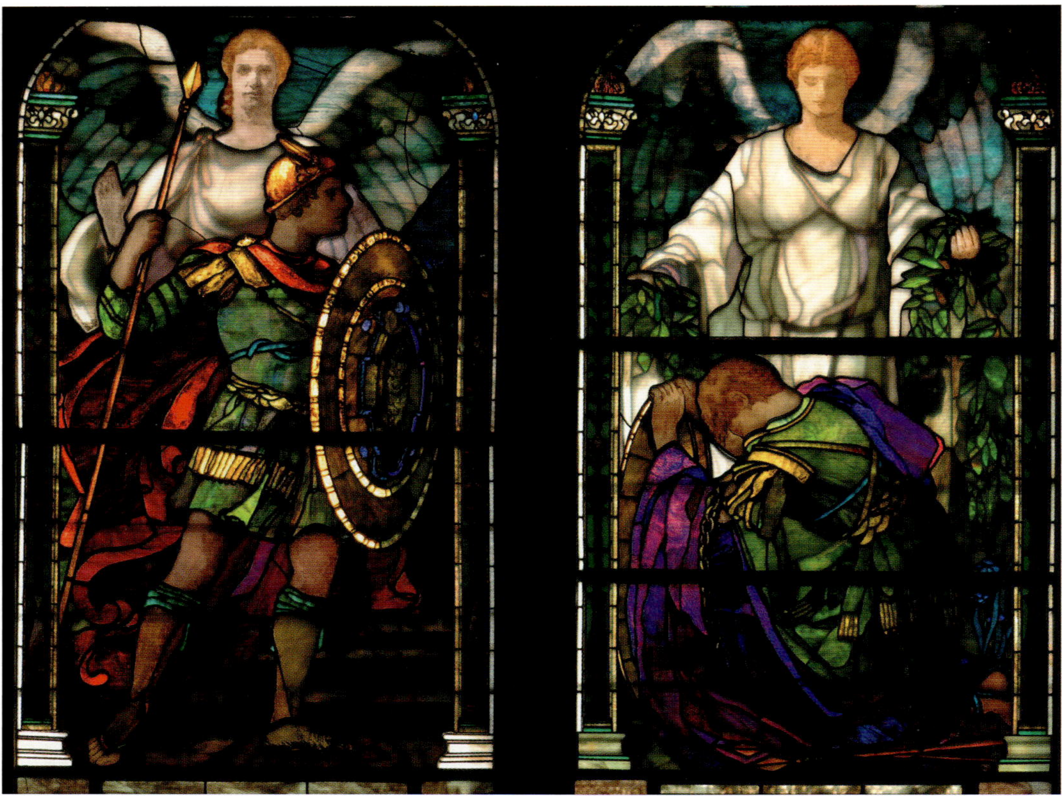

128 Sarah Wyman Whitman, *Honour and Peace*,
central scene, donor class of 1865, 1900.

figures are embodiments of the classical goddesses, Hera of the white arms or
grey-eyed Athena, dear to the tradition of education in the Greek and Roman
classics at Harvard. Visible even in subdued light, the plating achieves marvellous illusionary effects. The image of Peace, on the right, is constructed with a
large uniform plate over torso and waist. The multiple plating beneath creates
soft shadows revealing the contours of the female form. Segmented surface plating in the mauve mantle flowing over the arm of the kneeling soldier evokes the
undulations and folds of gathered drapery.

The Real and the Allegorical:
Photography and Self-Representation

The nineteenth century saw itself mirrored in the great events of the past.
Without abandoning symbolic depth, the identifiable portrait that was such
a part of nineteenth-century painting became a feature in glass. With the new

medium of photography, donor portraits often appeared in virtually photographic form, as demonstrated in the Brimmer window. A window in the hall, *Bernard of Clairvaux* and *Godfrey of Bouillon* (illus. 129), by Edward Peck Sperry (1850–1925), shows the Revd Phillips Brooks of Trinity Church, Boston, under the guise of Bernard of Clairvaux, the twelfth-century Cistercian monk and preacher of the Second Crusade. General Francis Channing Barlow, the highest-ranking Harvard soldier, appears under the guise of Godfrey of Bouillon, the military commander most emblematic of the First Crusade, which captured Jerusalem in 1099 and founded the Latin Kingdom of Jerusalem, which lasted for a century. Both individuals were members of Harvard's class of 1855 and

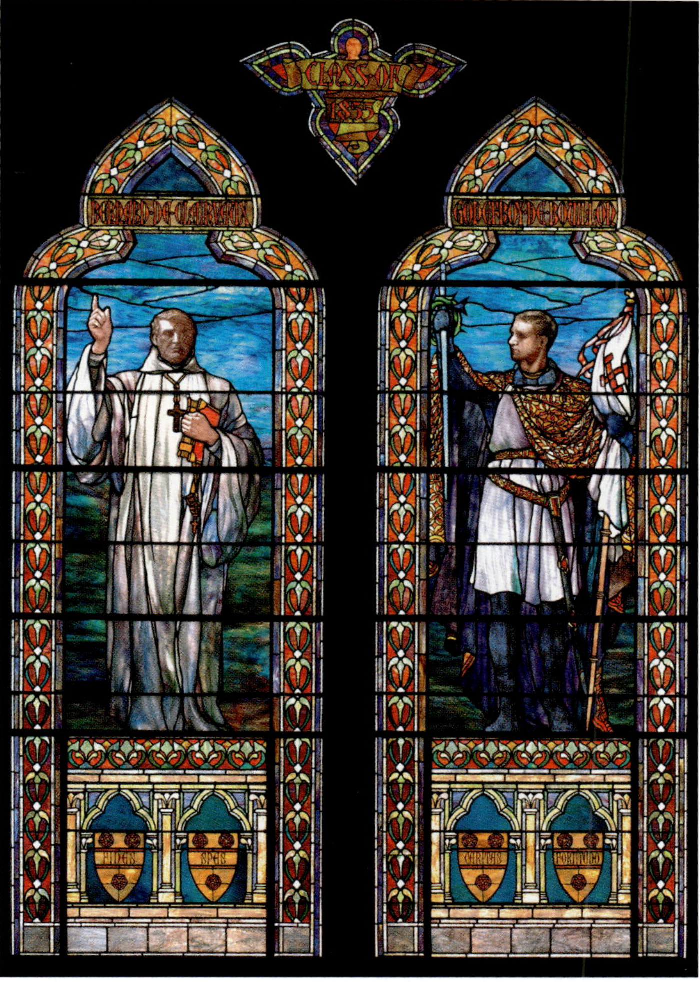

129 Edward Speck Perry, *Bernard of Clairvaux* and *Godfrey of Bouillon*, portrait likenesses of Phillips Brooks and Francis Channing Barlow, donor class of 1855, 1901.

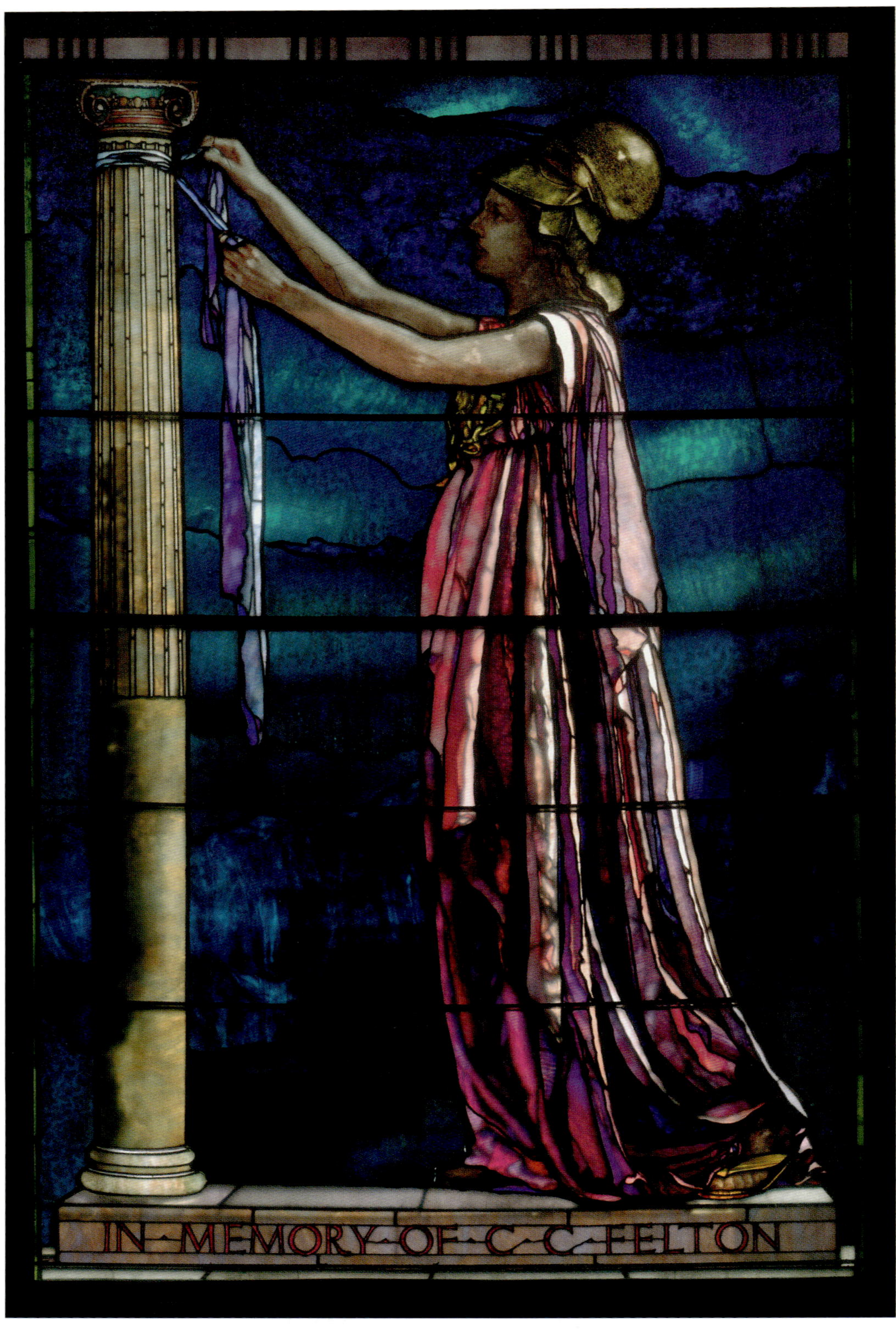

130 John La Farge, *Mourning Athena*, memorial to Cornelius Conway Felton, professor of Greek and Latin and Harvard president, donor Felton family, 1898.

were deceased by 1901, the date of the window. The broad swathes of opalescent glass in the sky and ground as well as the three-dimensional drapery in the garments demonstrate the triumph of the American innovation. Below the figures, on shields framed by Gothic arches, are inscribed the names *Fides* (Faith), *Spes* (Hope), *Caritas* (Love) and *Fortitudo* (Fortitude). Three rosettes appear in a two-over-one position like the books bearing the words VERITAS in Harvard's shield. The breadth of sources is impressive, as well as the freedom of a late nineteenth-century American Protestant patron – or set of patrons – to appropriate crusader, monk, knight and French history as part of their own personal tradition.

These reflections lead us to the sobering admission of class and privilege, yet recognizing a desire to create a visual language to unite all in a higher purpose. A single window installed in Sanders Theatre, on the opposite side of Memorial Hall, may sum up this tradition of classical learning and devotion aspired to by the Harvard programme. At this time, entrance to the college was based on proficiency in Greek and Latin. La Farge was called on to produce a window showing the *Mourning Athena* (illus. 130). It is dedicated to the memory of Cornelius Conway Felton (1807–1862), a professor of Greek and Latin who served two years as Harvard's president. At her birth, Athena sprang fully armed from the head of Zeus, and thus embodies virtues of both wisdom and courage, a reminder of the *Fortitudo* inscribed in the north transept and under *Godfrey of Bouillon*. As the patroness of Athens, she appealed to a classicist as the symbol of a golden age of Western culture. She wears the helmet of a warrior and the robe of a citizen, and with stately dignity ties a ribbon of mourning (in Greek, *tainia*, in Latin *taenia*) to a classical column.

Often, contemporary analysis of art focuses on the artist's differences, the things that distance him or her from the community, giving overwhelming focus to personalized vision. Such thoughts show a bias towards defining art as that which is produced self-consciously by an 'artist' in a society valorizing this function but essentially seeing fine art as separate from patron or social purpose. At best the patron becomes a passive purveyor of funds; at worst an interfering impediment. Harvard's programme contradicts this attitude. We see the tradition of art meeting the deep and broad needs of a society. These great works of glass, lead and iron, set within the noble frame of the architecture, are far more important than singular or personal statements; they have been produced by artists responding to the collective desires of a generation. That spiritual complexity, as well as their beauty, resonates even today.

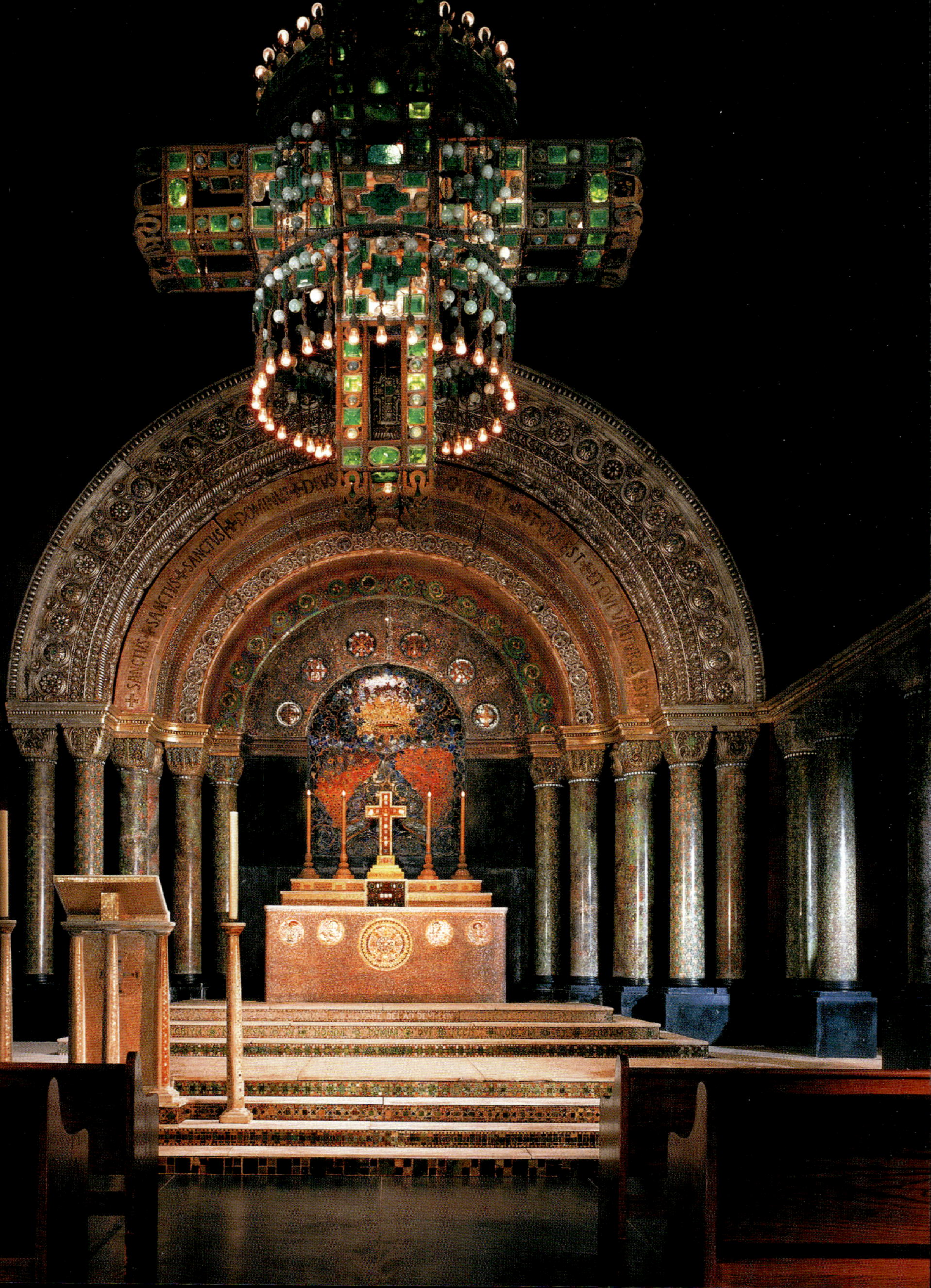

The Tiffany Chapel: World's Columbian Exposition

—

Louis Comfort Tiffany (1848–1933) was the son of Charles Lewis Tiffany, founder of the jewellery company Tiffany & Co. of New York. His innovations in materials and design of stained glass profoundly transformed the art of his time. Tiffany was a great entrepreneur, passionately convinced of his own capacity to meld diverse cultural traditions into a vibrant contemporary expression. Throughout his career he remained highly sensitive to the total environment and to blown and moulded glass objects as well as the leaded window. The three-dimensionality of cast and chiselled nuggets of glass that make up some of his most scintillating windows reflect the aesthetic of the vessels and the lamps also produced by the studio. In the second decade of the twentieth century, the taste for opalescent glass began to wane as simpler forms of Arts and Crafts and Art Deco began their ascendancy. The Second Gothic Revival, which began in the United States about 1910, championed medieval inspiration as the only appropriate style of windows. It challenged the appropriateness of the 'picture window', a window that incorporated three-dimensionality, and the variegated colour of opalescent glass for a religious edifice. Tiffany Studios began a gradual decline and in 1932 the firm filed for bankruptcy. The following year Tiffany died at the age of 84. The story of the chapel (illus. 131) demonstrates the rediscovery and appreciation of Tiffany's work some three generations later.

131 Louis Comfort Tiffany, Tiffany Glass and Decorating Company, Tiffany Chapel, 1893, reassembled at the Morse Museum of American Art, 1999.

The Complete Interior

Tiffany was motivated not only by window design, but the drive to develop a totally unified interior. An accomplished painter, in 1879 Tiffany was joined by Samuel Colman (1832–1920), a painter of landscapes, Lockwood de Forest II (1850–1932), painter and furniture designer, and Candace Wheeler (1827–1923), a designer of textiles, to work under the name of Louis C. Tiffany and Co., Associated Artists. The firm was dissolved in 1883, although Wheeler continued under the name of Associated Artists. Despite the short collaboration, this episode in Tiffany's career resulted in significant works. It was the crucible where four creative minds collaborated and shared their enthusiasm for a wide-ranging eclecticism that included inspiration from the Near East, North Africa, India and the European Middle Ages. In 1881–2, the firm designed the interior of the Veterans room of the Seventeenth Regiment Armory in New York, the Fifth Avenue mansions of Ogden Goelet and Cornelius Vanderbilt II and Mark Twain's sumptuous residence in Hartford, Connecticut. Eclectic combinations of Japanese, Chinese, Moorish and East Indian elements with the Italian Renaissance became an early signature of the firm. It was here that Tiffany began to use glass tiles to ornament fireplaces, a practice brought to stunning fruition in the New York Armory, one of the few of his surviving domestic interiors. Mosaic as well as almost every other lavish material combines in a kaleidoscopic display. The Armory's own description of the blue glass mosaic over the fireplace is apt: 'as if a bit of the Atlantic furthest from shore has been caught and pressed into service, with all the indigo held in hard, vitreous clutch'. In 2016 the room underwent a massive conservation campaign, bringing back the opulence on view in 1882.

World's Columbian Exposition

The artist astutely seized on contemporary developments to successfully reach a broad public as well as well-heeled patrons. The World's Columbian Exposition was a fair held in Chicago in 1893 to commemorate the 400th anniversary of Columbus's arrival in the New World. It became a defining moment in American cultural as well as industrial growth. A showcase for the arts, sciences and manufacturing, it employed the most distinguished architectural firms including Richard Morris Hunt, McKim, Mead & White, Peabody & Stearns and Adler & Sullivan. Sculptors included Augustus St-Gaudens, responsible for the *Monument to Robert Gould Shaw and the Massachusetts Fifty-Fourth Regiment* in Boston, and Daniel Chester French, famous for his 1875 *The Minute Man* in Concord, Massachusetts. Some 27 million people attended, setting national records. Tiffany took over space allotted to his father for Tiffany & Co. in the Manufactures and Liberal Arts Building. There, he displayed his own line of ecclesiastic furnishings and stained glass, including the chapel. In 1893, a reporter for the *American Architect and Building News* included a special section addressing the superiority of the American opalescent glass over European traditional glazing:

When we look at the production of Germany, England and France and then at our own, it is quite impossible for us not to imitate one of the notorious acts of 'Sir Joseph Porter, K. C. B.' for involuntarily we feel 'our bosoms swell with pride.' The chief point seems to be that our painted glass is not painted in the sense foreign glass is. Germany paints her figures, her draperies, her background with the most brilliant and often inharmonious colors. France and England treat their glass in much the same way, while we simply paint in clear brilliant coloring the flesh-tints and hair, having stained glass to fulfill the mission of background and drapery . . . [In] our stained glass there is much diversity of surface as well as thickness which leads to much more artistic results.[1]

The writer makes a special point of praising Tiffany's chapel (illus. 132) for its creation of a breathtaking atmosphere and noting that no other firm had devised a setting:

Of the work displayed at the fair, Tiffany's was noticeably the most artistic [sic] produced. It is to be regretted that the exhibit of glass as actual works of art was not larger, as it could not have failed to be exceedingly interesting. It certainly would have proved attractive to a great many people if one might judge by the crowds that even in the early part of the Fair season filled to more than overflowing Tiffany's pavilion. There was quite an extensive exhibit of what could more properly be called glass-mosaics which though having much beauty in themselves could not come under the exact head of painted or stained glass . . . The ecclesiastic glass either for windows or lamps was placed in a Romanesque chapel so perfect in its appointments that it was not an uncommon sight to see men

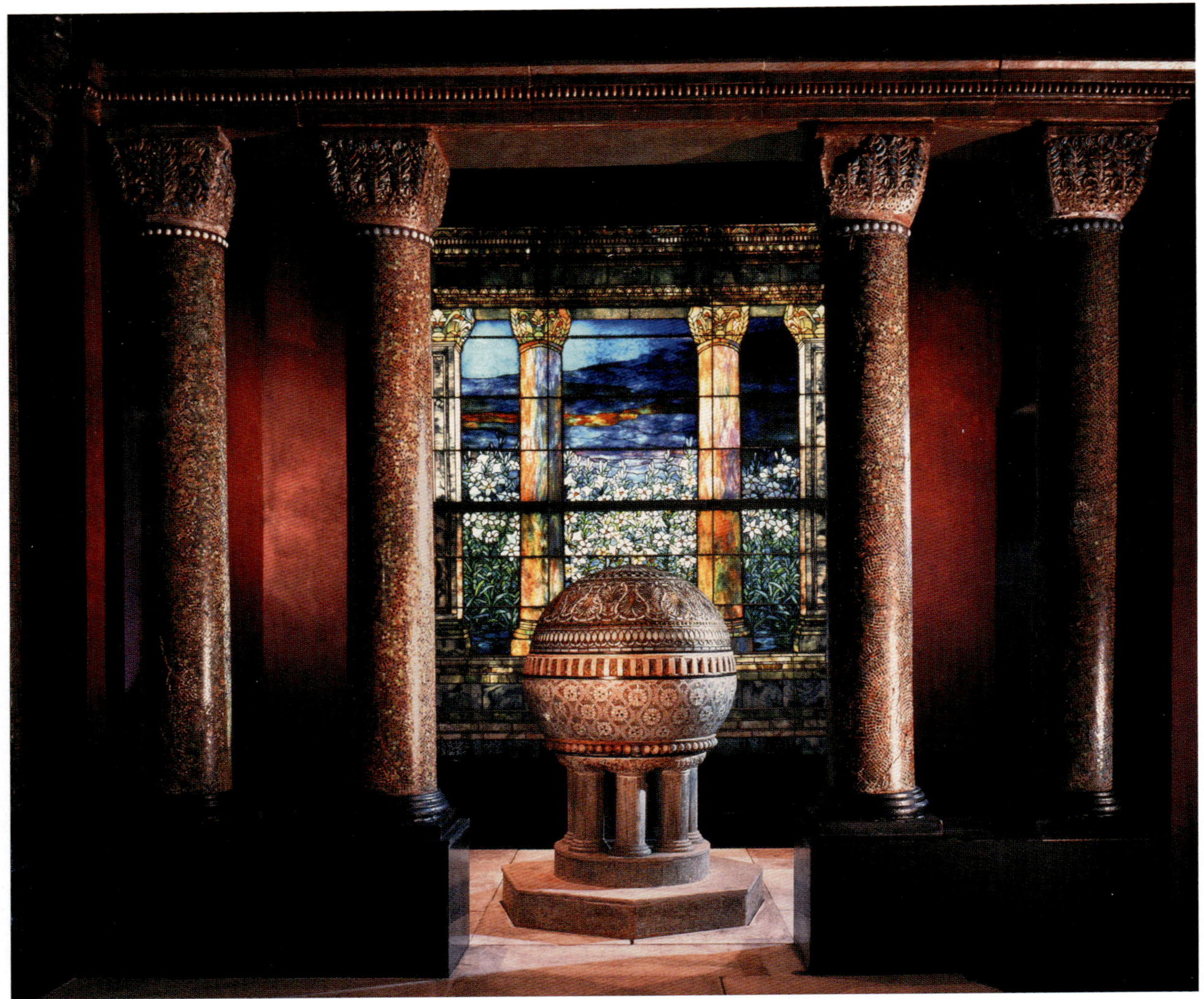

132 *Field of Lilies* window with baptismal font and columns sheathed in mosaics, Tiffany Chapel, 1893.

remove their hats upon entering the 'sacred' precincts. With the glass exhibit shown here the firm made a display of church furnishings, giving up to the altar and chancel nearly half of the space of the chapel. The Byzantine glass-lamps exhibited were very effective.[2]

In July 1894 most of the buildings were destroyed by a controlled burn; of the few remaining, one would become the Art Institute of Chicago. Tiffany had previously removed the chapel and brought it to his New York studio. In 1898, Mrs Celia Whipple Wallace purchased it as a gift to the Cathedral Church of

St John the Divine, in upper Manhattan. The firm of Heins and La Farge relegated the chapel to a basement crypt. Between 1899 and 1911 it was in use but was closed when the Gothic-style sanctuary above was completed for services. In 1916 Tiffany repossessed the chapel, transferring it to a freestanding building on his estate, Laurelton Hall, Oyster Bay, Long Island. In 1957 a fire devastated the abandoned estate. The chapel was spared and was rescued through the intervention of Hugh and Jeannette McKean. As a young artist, Hugh McKean had been granted a residency at the Tiffany foundation. The McKeans purchased all the leaded windows and the chapel, and later collected chapel furnishings that had been dispersed before the fire, bringing them to Winter Park, where the chapel was reinstalled in 1999.

Precedents

The installation of the chapel had been part of an effort to showcase the ecclesiastical designs of the firm. Tiffany himself named this a 'Romanesque' chapel, but we must be cautioned that art-historical labels for period styles today were far less precise a century ago. In 1896, Christopher Grant La Farge and Charles Louis Heins, St John the Divine's architects, referred to the chapel as 'Byzantine'. In 1896 Tiffany issued a promotional pamphlet entitled *Mosaics* where he explained that he had been deeply moved by the Byzantine churches that he had visited in his youth. We may be able to have a better understanding of Tiffany's accomplishments in the chapel if we look to the precedents he mentions. Hagia Sophia, Constantinople (Istanbul), built by the emperor Justinian I between 532 and 537, provides ample evidence (illus. 133). Polychrome marble revetment on the walls, mosaics, marble and carvings, despite losses over time, still dazzle the eye. Tiffany's enthusiasm for such materials was matched by chroniclers of the period. Procopius (*c.* 500–565), a historian in Justinian's service, wrote about the emperor's accomplishments in military campaigns and in building:

> [W]ho could recount the beauty of the columns and the stones with which the church is adorned? One might imagine that he had come upon a meadow with its flowers in full bloom. For he would surely marvel at the purple of some, the green tint of others, and at those on which the crimson glows and those from which the white flashes, and again at those which Nature, like some painter, varies with the most contrasting colours. And whenever anyone enters this church . . . his mind is lifted up toward God and exalted, feeling that

He cannot be far away, but must especially love to dwell in this place which He has chosen.[3]

Hagia Sophia's columns are indeed quite varied, including the imperial porphyry of a purple colour and other polychrome stone. The capitals are carved with acanthus and palm frond motifs in extremely low relief so that it almost seems as if the capital is wrapped in lace. In the chapel as now reconstructed in Winter Park, the sides are provided with freestanding columns that separate the main space from a side aisle. Tiffany was inspired by such precedents to sheath the columns in multicolour mosaics and keep the design of the capital's foliage as a tight sheath. The altar (illus. 134) is set against the wall and framed by rounded arches that are layered, the more complex and larger at the exterior supported by two columns. Three additional arches move towards the centre, each resting on a single column. The altar was carefully described in the *Synopsis of the Exhibit* as containing a table 'of Carrara marble resting upon a frontal of white glass mosaic, made of 150,000 pieces'.[4] It sits atop a stepped platform inlaid with tile. In the centre is a circular emblem with the Greek monogram of Christ, *Chi* (X) *Rho* (P) flanked by the *Alpha* and *Omega*, the first and last letters of the Greek alphabet, to signify Christ as the beginning and the end. The evangelists Matthew, Mark, Luke and John are shown under their symbols of winged beasts, man, lion, ox and eagle. The altar is decidedly Anglo-Catholic, having a tabernacle with glass cabochon inserts in the centre. On the sides, the Latin

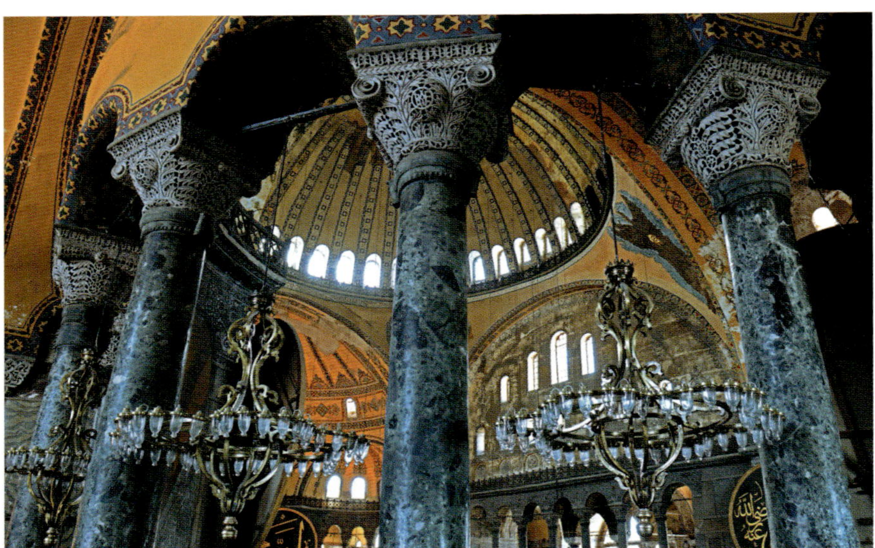

133 Basket capitals and antique marble columns,
537, Hagia Sophia, Constantinople (Istanbul).

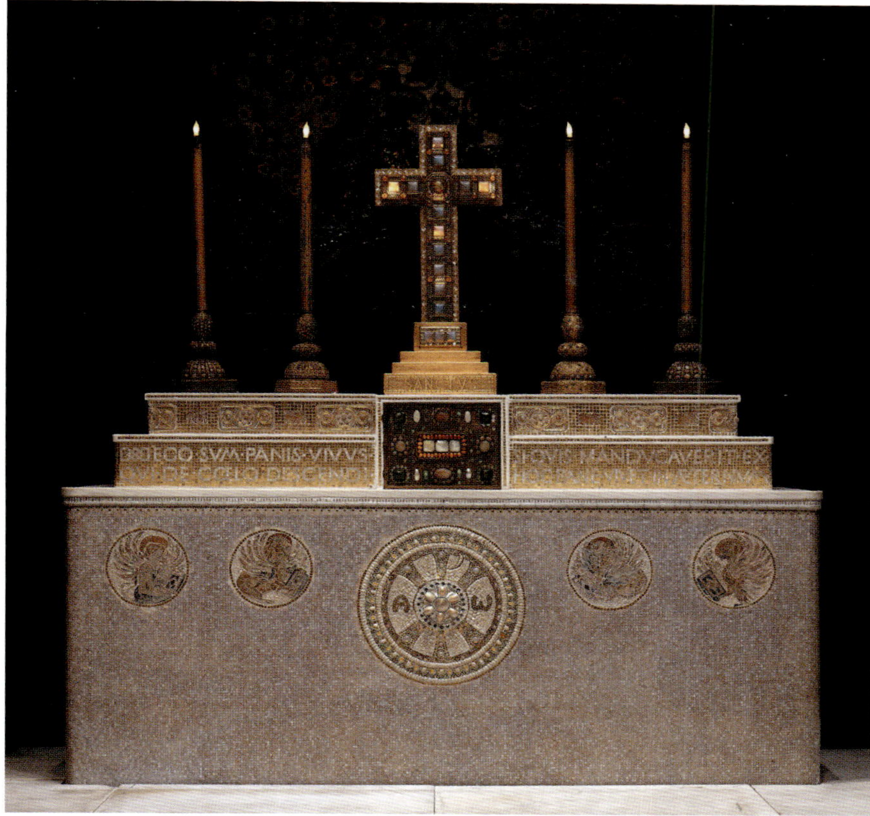

134 Tiffany Chapel altar, *c.* 1892.

text reads: 'I am the living bread which came down from heaven' (John 6:51).
Tiffany included a theological explanation of the mosaic behind the altar: 'The
design employed is the Vine, symbolical of the Sacrament of the Eucharist, and
among these vines there are portrayed peacocks, used here after the manner of
the Primitive Christians, as symbolizing immortality, for it was believed in the
early ages that the flesh of the peacock was incorruptible.'[5]

Tiffany had seen many historic mosaics on his travels, although the technique had been little exercised in Europe or the United States in the nineteenth
century. A detail of the eleventh-century mosaic of *Constantine IX* (illus. 135),
from Hagia Sophia, exemplifies the mesmerizing effect of the combination of
discrete elements: circular pieces of white onyx, red porphyry and green and
blue glass juxtaposed with gold leaf sandwiched between glass layers. The chapel's baptismal font (illus. 136) exemplifies Tiffany's response to these precedents.
The font's marble base is inset with opalescent glass and with marble mosaic.
Although enmeshed in repeating designs of palmettes, ovals and rectangles,

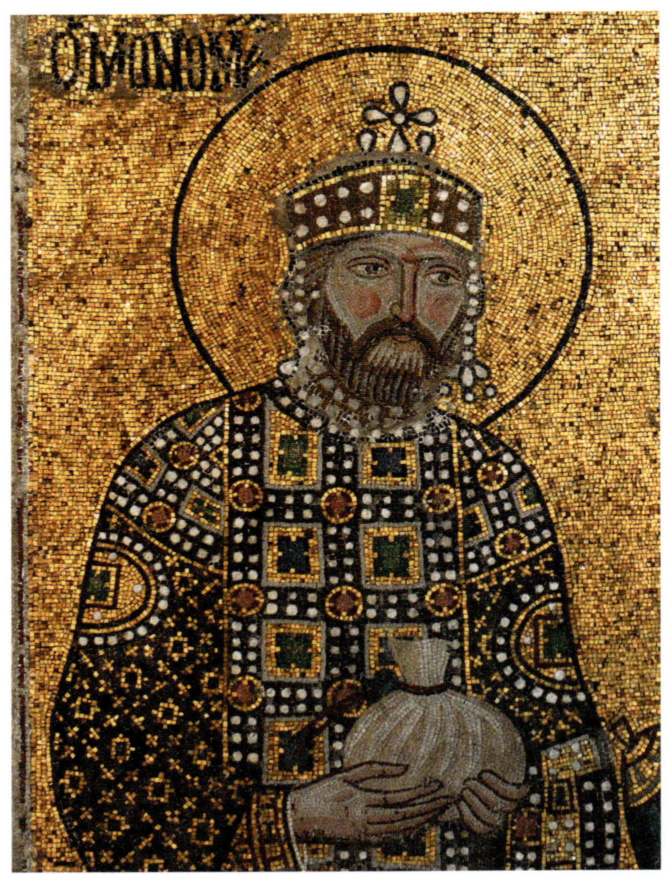

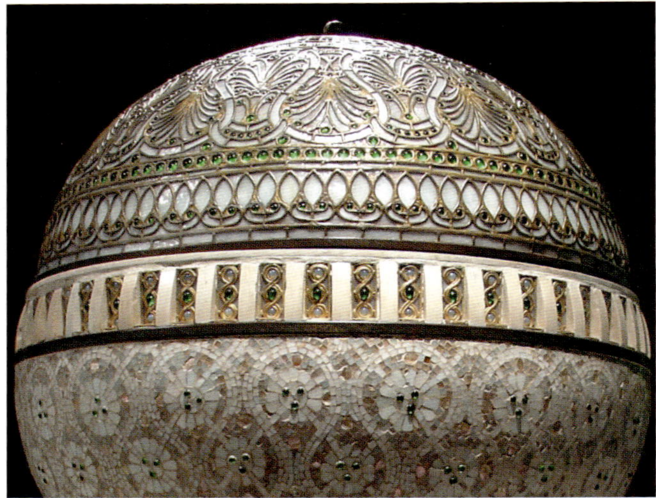

135 *Constantine IX*, Monomachos, husband of Empress Zoe, 1028–42, with alterations between 1042 and 1050, Hagia Sophia.

136 Tiffany Chapel, baptismal font, detail, *c.* 1892.

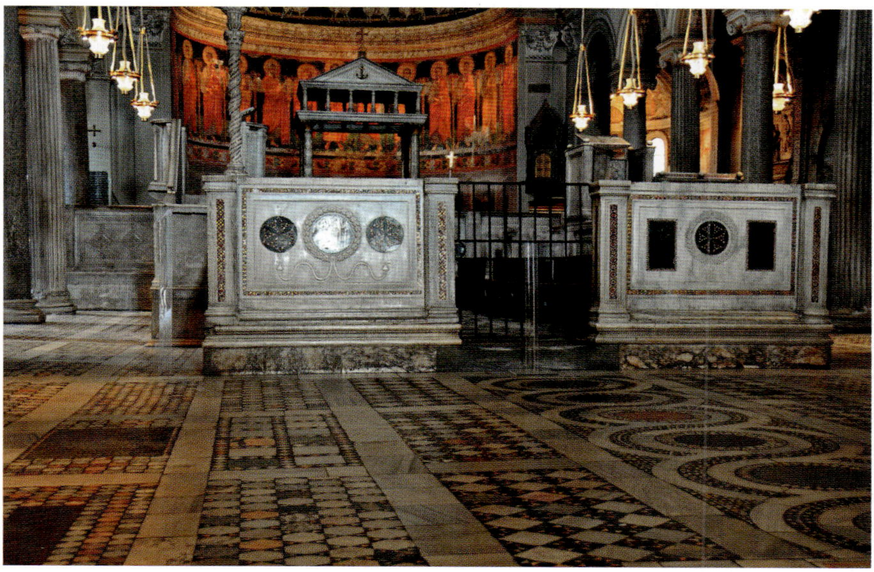

137 Basilica of San Clemente, Rome, rebuilt 1099–1119;
inlaid floor by the Cosmati brothers; choir stalls incorporate
5th-century elements from the 5th-century basilica beneath.

somehow each segment of glass or stone seems to achieve its own sensual independence. One is also drawn to a comparison with early Christian architecture. These churches of the fifth and sixth centuries, exemplified by the inlay stonework in the choir enclosure of San Clemente (illus. 137), Rome, find parallels in the chapel's juxtaposition of mosaic, cut stone and glass. Although Tiffany was a pioneer, his taste also found contemporary parallels. Austria's Secession movement, exemplified by the 1899 Karlsplatz station of Vienna, designed by Otto Wagner, was organized in 1897. Wagner's design for the church of St Leopold (1902–7), in a Viennese suburb, echoes the ethos of the Morse chapel. Like Tiffany, Wagner worked with other designers, especially the brilliant Koloman Moser (1868–1918) for stained-glass windows. The interior includes a mosaic showing Christ welcoming saints into heaven above an altar that is surmounted by an elaborate circular baldachin repeating the altar's gold accents.

Tiffany was an astute judge of his time and understood the desire of many Americans of the Gilded Age to surpass the Old World's hold on great culture. John Pierpont Morgan (1837–1913), the investment banker who dominated corporate finance on Wall Street, aggressively acquired outstanding examples of medieval metalwork, such as the *Lindau Gospels* (Pierpont Morgan Library, MS M.1), purchased in 1901. Its upper cover is arguably the most lavish of all surviving medieval jewelled bindings. Its centre displays a large gold repoussé figure of Christ crucified on a jewelled cross. Both the chapel's *Electrolier* and its *Altar Cross*, reconstructed in 1916, show the cabochon inserts that characterize the book cover. Whether cast glass or gemstones, for the original cross was decorated with white topazes, the inserts were shaped and polished, but not faceted. The three-dimensionality of the setting enables the stones to appear as if exuding an inner radiance. Morgan's equally renowned *Stavelot Triptych*, purchased in 1910, is composed of champlevé and cloisonné enamels, semi-precious stones and intaglio gems. The brilliance of the setting supporting the enamel pictorial work echoes the mingling of decorative surrounds and imagery in Tiffany's work.

Opalescent Glass

Windows from the Exposition stand as hallmarks of the Tiffany style. *Feeding the Flamingos* was exhibited in what Tiffany called the 'light room'. He explained that its construction 'has been obtained without the assistance of paints or enamels, solely by using opalescent glass in accordance with the principles that govern mosaic work'.[6] Enamel and vitreous paint, however, were used in the flesh areas. Other windows were included in the chapel: *Madonna and Child*, inspired by Italian Quattrocento paintings by artists such as Botticelli, and the *Story of the Cross*, in a more medieval form. The major window in the chapel contained an image of the Angel of the Resurrection flanked by columns against a background of lilies. Tiffany redesigned the window to eliminate the angel when he installed the chapel in Laurelton Hall in 1916; he then renamed it *Field of Lilies* (illus. 138). The variegated hues of blue, purple and green used for the sky and ground are achieved not only through a mixture of colours in the glass but by layering glass, as practised by La Farge and Whitman for Memorial Hall. In 1898, a popular writer on the arts of the period, Cecilia Waern (1853–after 1920), wrote on Tiffany's trademarked Favrile glass for *The International Studio*, a monthly arts magazine. She described in enthusiastic terms:

> Tiffany's Corona glassworks, Jamaica, New York, with its stock
> of 200 to 300 tons of glass stored in cases and on numbered
> racks bringing order to the selection of 5,000 colors. The machine-
> rolled glass sheets appeared remarkable for their varieties of color.
> A pane of dark blue and white, harsh and crude in reflected light,
> becomes suddenly glorious when seen in transmitted light, like a
> sunset all at once illuminating the sky in this land of rich effects . . .
> Other pieces suggest priceless onyx or lovely marbles, when seen

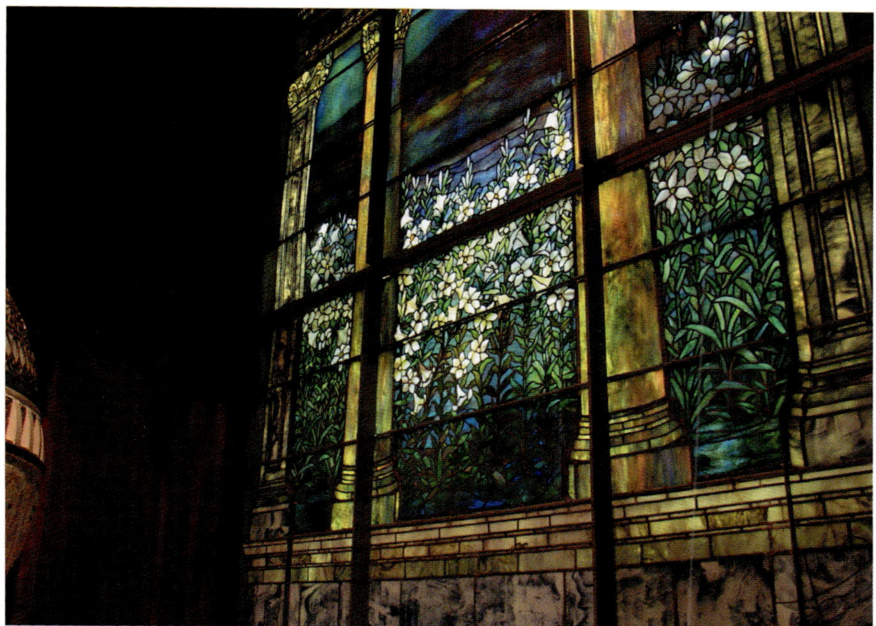

138 *Field of Lilies*, Morse Museum of American Art, 1893, altered by Tiffany 1916.

in reflected light, shot through with throbbing color when held up
to the window.[7]

The aesthetic range of Tiffany's glass from this era was later showcased in another
world's fair, the Exposition Universelle in Paris, 1900. Visitors entering the United
States pavilion were given a view of a large plated window where the colours
seem to flow, meld, fade, reappear and congeal in blotches. Depicting the theme
of Christ and the blessed in heaven (illus. 139), the window and accompanying
mosaics now grace the Wade Memorial Chapel, Lakeview Cemetery, Cleveland.

Despite the loss of many of Tiffany's interiors, the Church of the Covenant
in Boston testifies to the Chicago Exposition's legacy. The pioneer Gothic revival
architect Richard Upjohn designed the 1867 building. Its interior was then illuminated by stencilled translucent quarry glazing by an unidentified studio that
is still visible in the north transept. In 1893 the church began a complete reno-
vation that would include 42 windows, mosaics and a baptismal font, as well as
a coordinated painting scheme. The sanctuary light that Tiffany illustrated in
his *Synopsis* hangs before the altar. Designed by J. A. Holtzer, the light is a vertical structure with a circle of six angels holding globes standing atop a circular
element above a bejewelled basket. In 2013, Covenant was granted Landmark
status, based on Tiffany's success in ecclesiastical design and his cooperative

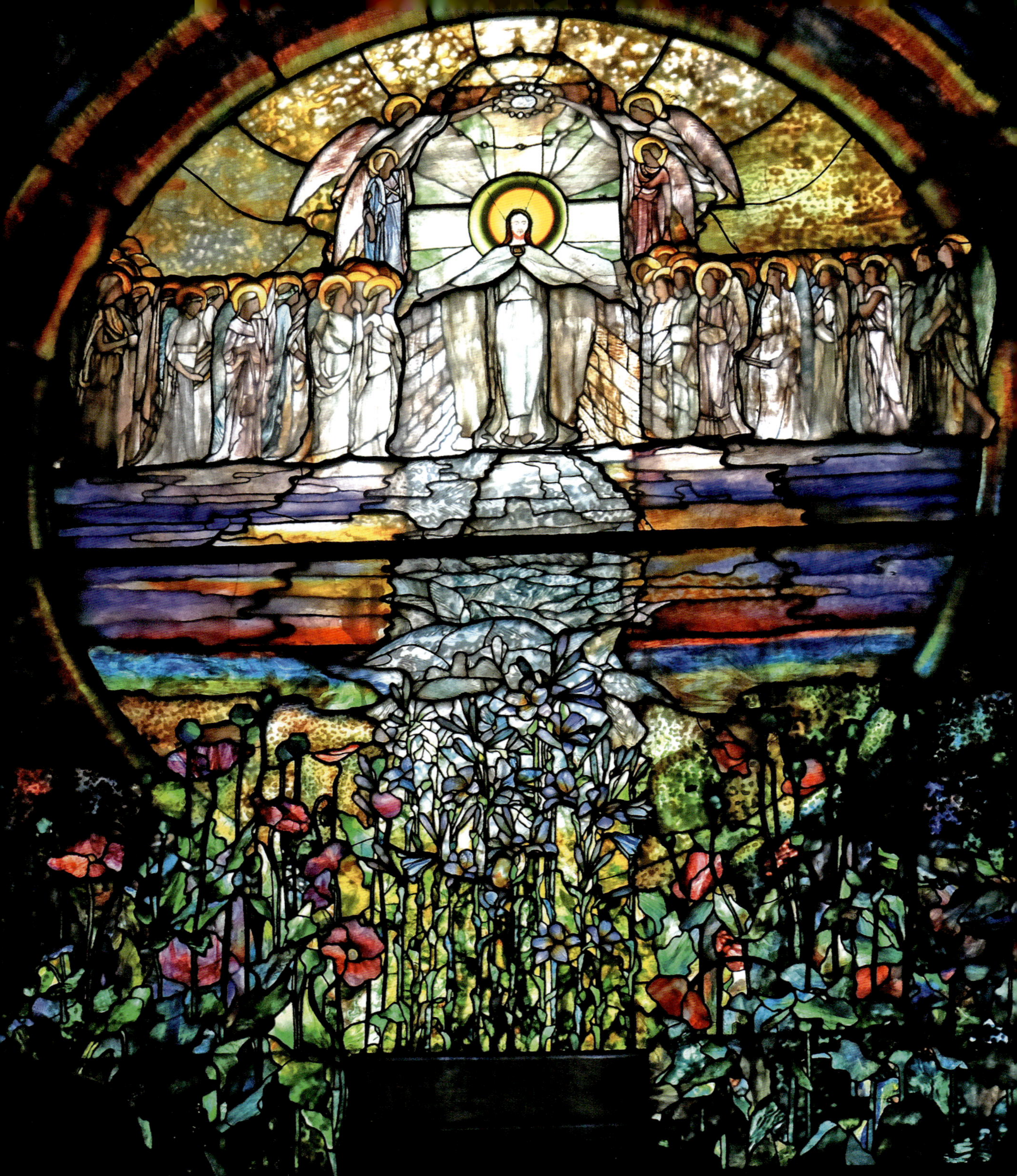

139 *Consummation of the Divine Promise*, originally United States pavilion, Exposition Universelle, Paris, 1900, now at Jeptha Wade Memorial Chapel, Lakeview Cemetery, Cleveland.

engagement with a series of artists. We note that before this commission Tiffany had already installed three windows for Harvard University's Memorial Hall designed by other artists: *Aristides and Themistocles* (1892) by Edward Emerson Simmons (1852–1931) and *Student and Soldier* and *General Joseph Warren and Reverend John Eliot* (both 1889) by Francis Davis Millet (1846–1912).

The first of Tiffany's designers at Covenant was J. A. Holzer. His sanctuary light produced for the World's Columbian Exhibition in Chicago of 1893 was acquired by the church. Holzer also designed Covenant's north aisle windows. Between 1895 and 1898, Edward Peck Sperry designed the windows of the *Nativity, Resurrection* and *Supper at Emmaus*. He also designed the *Four Evangelists* in the north transept. Tiffany's most frequently commissioned designer, Frederick Wilson, continued from 1898 to 1914, creating some of the most iconic windows of the firm. Wilson left Tiffany Studios in 1923, relocating to Los Angeles where he produced many designs for Judson Studios. At Covenant his windows include *St Augustine, Cornelius the Justified Centurion*, the *Madonna* (after Pascal Dagnan-Bouveret) and the series of *Four Biblical Women* in the south transept, representing the virtues of joy, courage, devotion and charity. These windows are particularly compelling for their brilliant use of three-dimensional glass, such as the drapery glass described by Cecilia Waern, used earlier in the *Field of Lilies* window of Tiffany's Chicago chapel. She described the hand-made glass that retained varying thickness, bubbles and imperfections from the process of the throwing:

> As many as seven different colours out of different ladles or spoons have been thrown together in this way . . . The throwing of certain masses and colour can be regulated, of course, and a definite design is often employed with a view to providing the glazier with 'useful' glass for obtaining certain effects of drapery, modeling or backgrounds . . . The famous Tiffany glass is made by manipulating the sheet while still hot, as one would do with pastry (with iron hooks, the hands cased in asbestos gloves) and pushing it together until it falls into folds.[8]

The upper windows present a series of triple arches framing varying tonalities of the sky achieved by a selection of streaky blue glass. Today, there are, happily, many opportunities to experience Tiffany windows and even the total aesthetic of Tiffany's vision.

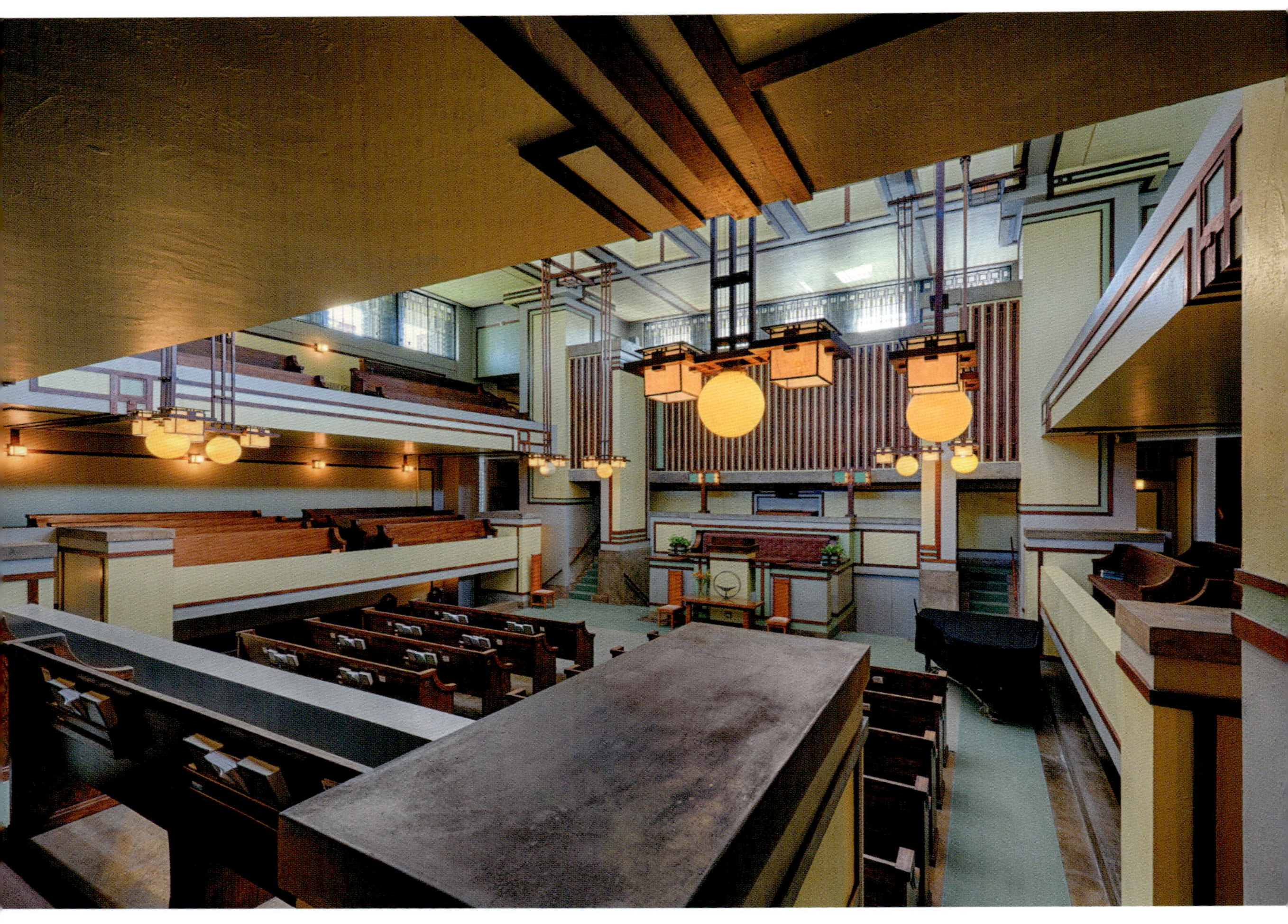

140 Frank Lloyd Wright, Unity Temple Sanctuary, Oak Park, Illinois, 1909.

I I

The Light Screens
of Frank Lloyd Wright

—

Frank Lloyd Wright (1867–1957) is regarded as the most distinguished American architect of the twentieth century. In a career spanning seven decades, he championed new concepts of spatial integration, innovative use of materials and a deep sensitivity to each building site. His early work focused on the domestic buildings where he rejected historicist references to embrace the juxtaposing of solids and planes inspired by geometry. Working with the horizontals and verticals of ground plan and structure, Wright needed windows that, in his words, would 'stay put'. He referred to his windows as 'light screens', which he organized through the geometric intersections of rectangles, trapezoids, parallelograms and circles.

At the time of Wright's development as an architect, a variety of movements were current, including the picturesque Queen Anne with its gables, rounded porches and turrets and the Beaux Arts with its classically inspired columns and pediments, often favoured for municipal buildings and train stations. Wright wanted change, but however he might have framed his contribution, his drive to construct the complete interior was paralleled in many contemporary movements. Art Nouveau was popular between 1890 and 1910, roughly the era dominated by Tiffany in the United States. Internationally, architects and designers such as Victor Horta in Belgium and Hector Guimard in France produced wall paintings, furniture, leaded glass windows and iron work, coordinated with the architectural design. The unified interior, indeed, is a principle frequently sought after by designers and their patrons, for example at the birth of the American nation with the Salem architect/cabinet maker Samuel McIntire.

Wright's work finds a parallel in the Palau de la Música Catalana, built between 1905 and 1908 (illus. 141). Its architect, Lluís Domènech i Montaner, was admired for both his sensitivity to place and function and his brilliant design in the Art Nouveau style. In 1997 UNESCO declared the Palace and Montaner's Hospital de Sant Pau World Heritage sites. Every inch of the building, much like its musical performances, is calculated to blend into a coordinated whole. At the stage level, relief sculpture depicts young women singing, while the proscenium arch is framed by sculptures, to the right the 'Ride of the Valkyries' from Wagner's opera *Die Walküre* and on the left a huge tree with leafy branches over the bust of the choir director Anselm Clavé, a major force in the revival of Catalan folk song. The windows at the side depict garlands of flowers, and the inverted dome of the skylight balances blues and golds, evoking the experience of sunlight. Indeed, the hall does not need artificial illumination during daylight hours.

Wright's Unity Temple, Oak Park, Illinois (illus. 140), built during the same period, also embraces the concept of total unity, but through a geometric, rather than organic, schema. Wright had a personal connection to Unity Church. The architect's father and uncle were Universalist preachers, and he was married to his wife Catherine in his uncle's church. In a groundbreaking decision for a religious edifice, Wright selected construction materials of reinforced cement. His forms were equally innovative, bold units with consistent repetition of horizontals, from the roof to the cornices, to the windows. The sanctuary is illuminated by 25 square skylights in the coffered ceiling. On the balcony level, continuing around the church, the windows display clear or delicately tinted glass in tones of green set in rectilinear patterns. Illumination is augmented by hanging lamps suspended by shafts of dark wood. Square or rectangular lamps in translucent white are juxtaposed with circular globes. Wright's description of windows can be applied to almost all his production:

> The windows usually are provided with characteristic straight line patterns absolutely in the flat and usually severe. The nature of the glass is taken into account in these designs as is also the metal bar used in their construction, and most of them are treated as metal 'grills' with glass inserted forming a simple rhythmic arrangement of straight lines as cunning as possible so long as the result is quiet. The aim is that the designs shall make the best of the technical contrivances that produced them. In the main the ornamentation is wrought in the warp and woof of the structure.[1]

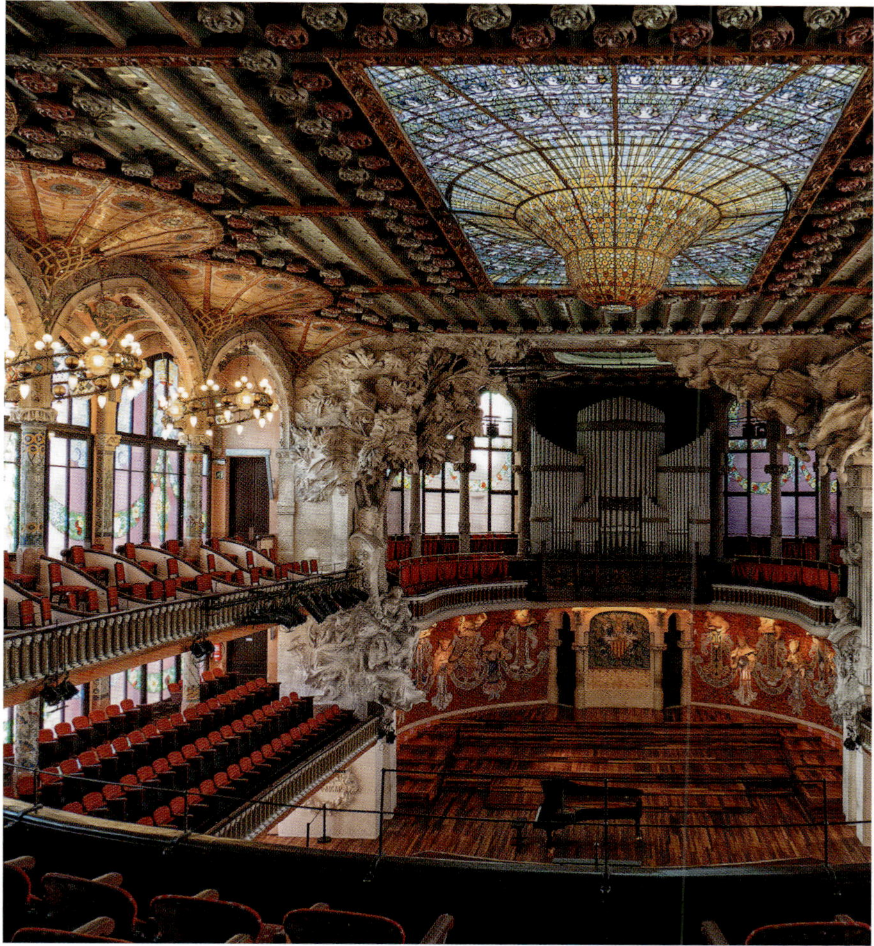

141 Lluís Domènech i Montaner, Palau de la Música Catalana
(Palace of Catalan Music), 1905–8.

Wright was concerned that the window be seen as a window, as well as an object
of unusually attractive decorative materials, stating that

> nothing is more annoying to me than any tendency toward realism
> of form in window glass, to get mixed up with the view outside.
> A window pattern should stay severely 'put' . . . The magnificent
> window-painting and plating [a reference to opalescent techniques]
> of the windows of the religious edifice is quite another matter.
> There the window becomes primarily a gorgeous painting –
> painting with light itself.[2]

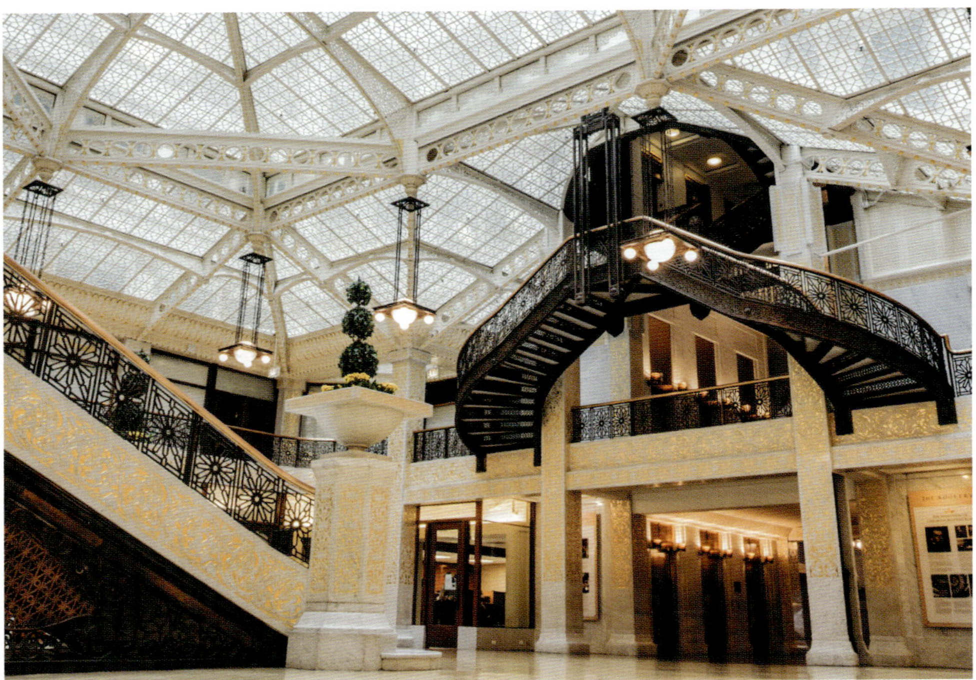

142 Frank Lloyd Wright, remodelling of the Rookery lobby,
Chicago, 1905, designed by Daniel Burnham and John Root, 1888.

Transition to the 'Wright Style'

Wright worked briefly at the firm of Joseph Lyman Silsbee (1848–1913). Early in 1888, at the age of twenty, he entered the firm of Adler & Sullivan in Chicago. Louis Sullivan (1856–1924), remembered as the individual who transformed the American skyscraper, proved to be an inspiration. Sullivan's respect for proportion and balance, natural materials and the relationship between form and function resonates through Wright's work. In 1893, Wright left his position as head draughtsman at Adler & Sullivan. As an independent architect, he gravitated to domestic architecture rather than the commercial and civic structures of his previous employer. He found opportunities in the suburbs of Chicago, beginning in 1893 with the Walter H. Gale House, added in 1973 to the U.S. National Register of Historic Places. It is a Queen Anne-style home, evident through the complexity of the massing, the dormer details, Palladian windows in the side gables and the varied textures of shingles, siding and brick as well as diamond-pane leaded glass. Yet, it announced the characteristic simplicity of forms that would later become Wright's signature.

The architect later looked back on this time, giving praise to his mentors:

This ideal of an organic architecture for America was touched
by Richardson and Root, and perhaps other men, but was
developing consciously twenty-eight years ago in the practice
of Adler & Sullivan, when I went to work in their office. This
ideal combination of Adler & Sullivan was when working to
produce what no other combination of architects nor any individual architect at that time dared even preach – a sentient, rational
building that would own its 'style' to the integrity with which it was
individually fashioned to serve its particular purpose – a 'thinking'
as well as 'feeling' process, requiring the independent work of a
true artist imagination.[3]

In 1905 the architect renovated and provided a glass ceiling for lobby of the
Rookery (illus. 142), a Chicago landmark set in the heart of the financial district.
Twelve storeys in height, the Rookery is considered the oldest standing high-rise
in Chicago. Designed by Daniel Burnham and John Root in 1888, its construction brought together traditional and new building techniques through exterior
load-bearing walls and an interior steel frame. The two-storey lobby displays
decorative ironwork, embossed columns and a projecting stairway balcony. The
ornament is restrained, with harmonies ranging from white, gold and cream, to
dark brown, in keeping with the Japanese juxtapositions that inspired Wright.
    Wright had a long-standing interest in Japanese art, which he cites in his
March 1908 essay for the *Architectural Record*, perhaps inspired by the examples
that his first employer, Joseph Silsbee, displayed in his home. He began to collect
seriously during a trip to Japan in 1905. In 1906 and 1908, at the Art Institute of
Chicago, he exhibited his own prints and helped organize a loan show. Buying
and selling prints lasted until 1938. Wright's early exposure to Japanese architecture had been through the Chicago World's Columbian Exposition of 1893,
where Tiffany had met such success. The Japanese pavilion was constructed to
reflect the Hō-ō-dō (Phoenix Hall) of the eleventh-century Buddhist Temple,
near Kyoto. The Chicago site, named Ho-o-Den (Phoenix Palace), grouped
three buildings, each representing a different era of Japanese tradition. Wright
was thus exposed to the Japanese emphasis on horizontality and openness, and
the architectural expression of the Buddhist philosophy of beauty in balanced
asymmetry, tranquillity and the elimination of clutter.

Prairie-Style Architecture

As Wright developed, he felt rooted in the structural simplicity of the early American home, especially with its central fireplace, the hearth. His work from 1899 to 1910 produced buildings emphasizing long, open spaces that became known as the Prairie Style, now regarded as a major contribution to American design. The Colonial Revival, popular since the 1890s, was dominant between 1910 and 1930, accounting for almost half of private homes. The style relied on recognizable citations referencing the American past from the domestic homes and English-inspired Georgian motifs. Wright was convinced that architecture needed to be derived from natural principles, rather than an inherited tradition of historic references. His writing frequently included the term 'truth.' 'Domestic architecture . . . will be likewise true; a natural, indigenous expression of modern life in its broader aspects and finer opportunities.'[4]

Wright was clear about the importance of glass to carry the design elements of a building:

> The element of pattern is made more cheaply and beautifully
> effective when introduced into the glass of the windows than in the
> use of any other medium that architecture has to offer. The metal
> divisions become a metal screen of any pattern – heavy or light,
> plated in any metal, even gold or silver – the glass a subordinate,
> rhythmical accent of any emotional significance whatever, or vice
> versa. The pattern may be calculated with reference to the scale
> of the interior and the scheme of decoration given by, or kept by,
> the motif of the glass pattern.[5]

The Dana-Thomas House

Designed in 1899 for Susan Lawrence Dana (1862–1942), the house is now managed by the Illinois Department of Natural Resources/Historic Sites. From 1943 to 1981 it was occupied by the Charles C. Thomas Publishing Company. Encompassing 35 rooms, the house displays the largest collection of original Wright art glass and furniture. After the deaths of both her father and her husband, Edwin Dana, Susan Lawrence Dana inherited a substantial fortune and, with it, responsibilities for its management. She made the decision to build a house that could be the centre of philanthropic and social meetings, as well as memorializing her father. Her influence was substantial in progressive causes

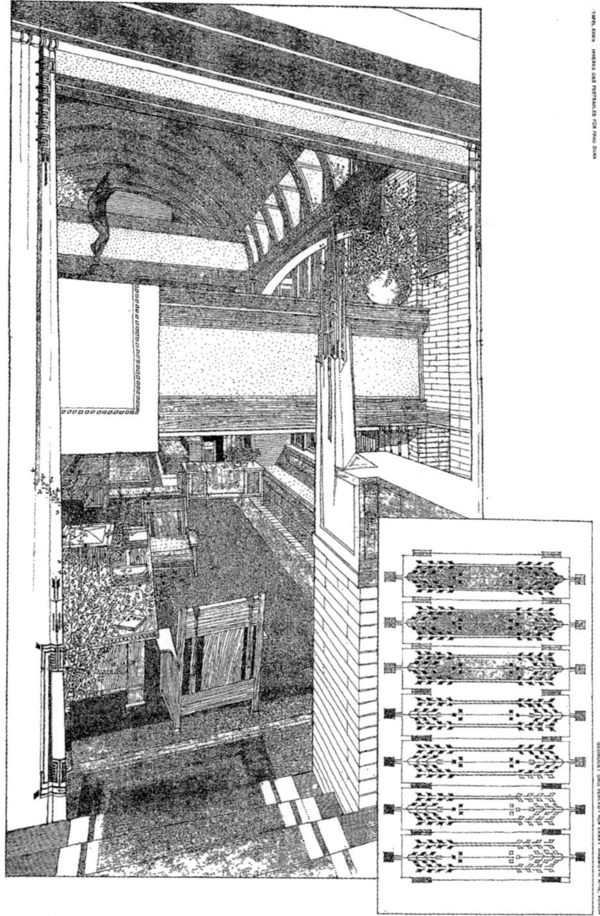

143 Dana House pl. XXXIb, from *Ausgefuhrte Bauten und Entwurfe von Frank Lloyd Wright*, 1910.

including equality for African Americans and voting rights for women; Illinois granted votes for women in 1913, the United States only in 1920.

Completely reworking an Italianate house built in the 1860s, Wright was free to innovate, such as repeating the brick of the exterior for interior walls. He incorporated many influences, including rounded arches in doorways, reminiscent of Henry Hobson Richardson. Some 250 windows, doors and panels exemplify Wright's ability to develop an interaction between interior and exterior forms through a screen of glass. Distinctive rounded transom lights and a vaulted glass dome mark the entrance. Four illustrations of the Dana-Thomas House (illus. 143) were included in the 1910 German publication *Ausgefuhrte Bauten und Entwurfe von Frank Lloyd Wright* by the Wasmuth Press, Berlin,

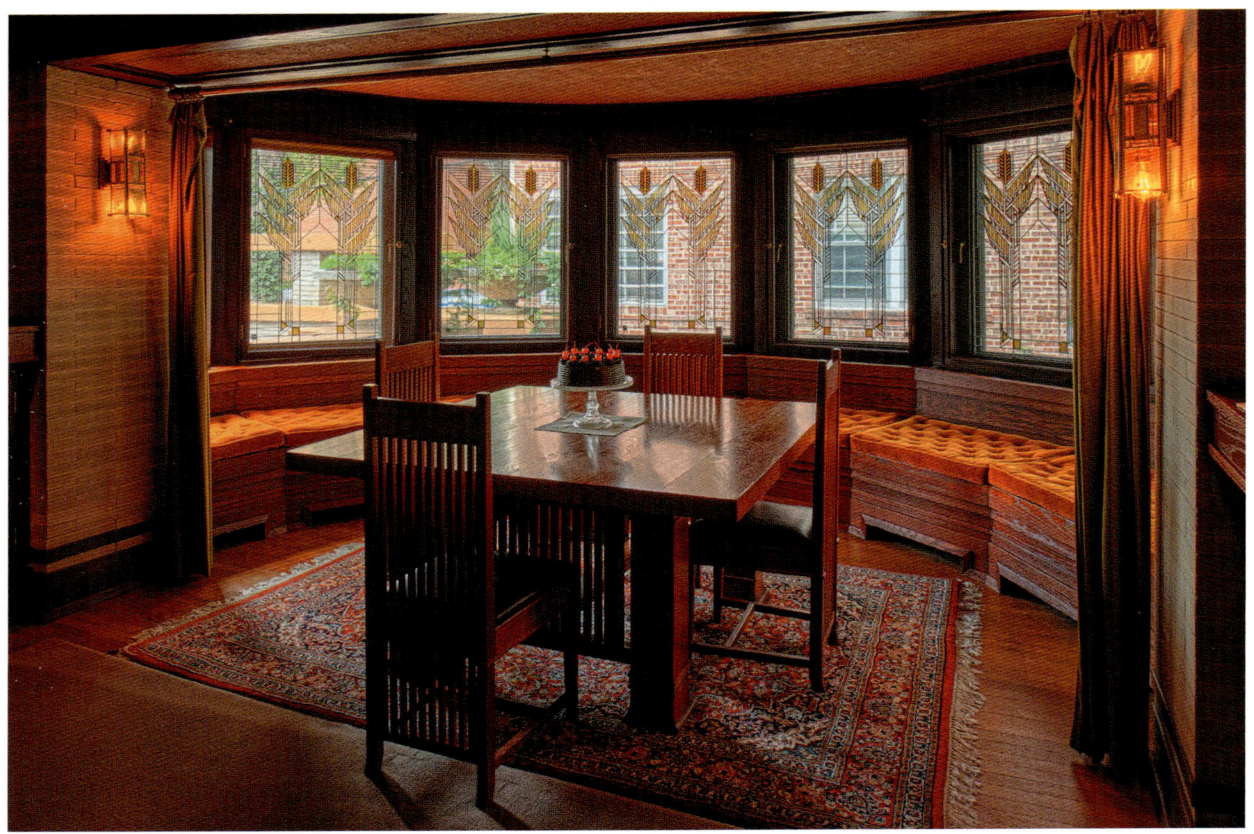

144 Dana House, Springfield, Illinois, breakfast nook, 1910.

founded in 1872 and specializing in architecture and related arts. Wright wrote an introduction. The large-scale folio of floor plans, elevations and other drawings deeply influenced a new generation of architects and designers from the Bauhaus school operating between 1919 and 1933 in Germany and those associated with the De Stijl movement, founded in 1917 in the Netherlands. In an unusual gesture, Wright commented on the Dana-Thomas House: 'Fixtures and furnishings designed with the furniture. Around the dining-room is a decoration of sumac (the plant motif for the decoration of the house proper). The woodwork is of freely marked red oak.' In the gallery, set in the public entertaining wing, a hanging tapestry of a freestanding series of glass panels in front of the east window resembles a Japanese gate. The tonalities of the windows are coordinated with the deep red stain in the woodwork. The breakfast nook (illus. 144) displays a bench against the wall and table and chairs designed by Wright, while the windows incorporate the stylized sumac motif. A bookcase door from the Dana-Thomas House is now in the Museum of Modern Art, New York.

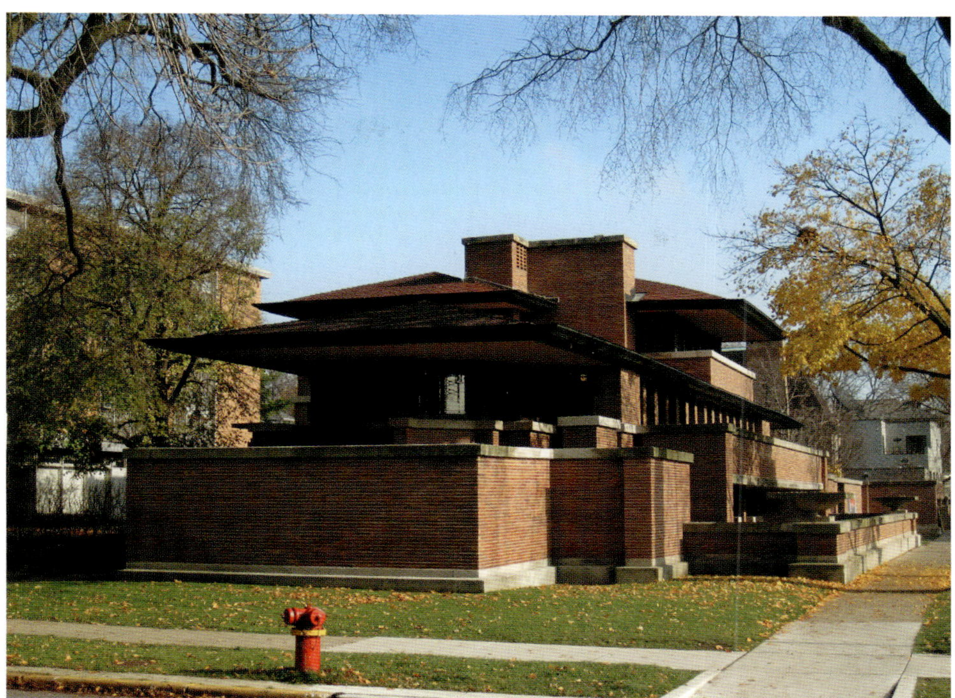

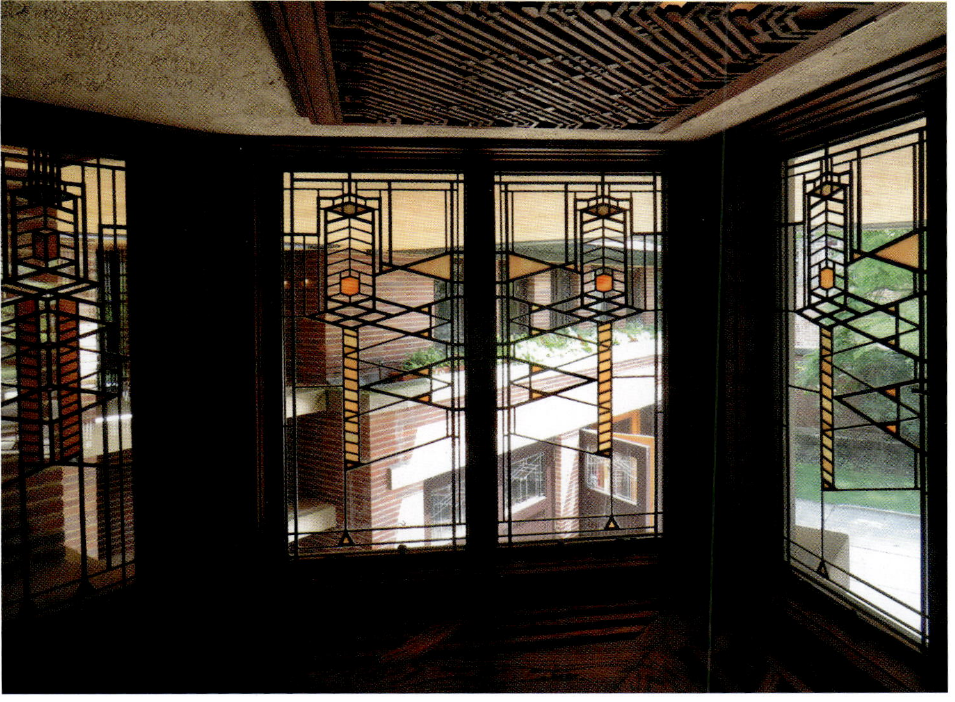

145 Frederick C. Robie House, exterior, 1908–10.

146 Frederick C. Robie House, windows, 1908–10.

Frederick C. Robie House

Built between 1908 and 1910, the Robie House (illus. 145) is frequently named as the finest example of Wright's Prairie Style designs. An exterior sketch and a ground plan were included in the Wasmuth publication. Designated a U.S. National Historic Landmark in 1963, it is now part of the University of Chicago. The clean lines of the Robie House are magisterial. Planar expanses of brick are framed by grey bands of stone. The levels, asymmetrically balanced, present as if they are natural layers of sedimentary rock. The windows show a transition in Wright's designs towards more asymmetrical patterns (illus. 146). The oblique angles used so effectively in the windows may be associated with patterns that are created through the intersection of roof pitches and walls as perceived from the exterior of the house. Tonality is warm, with varying hues of pale amber and frosted white. The copper-clad zinc came easily blends with these colours. Some elements of the window, unusually, were painted, not with the traditional vitreous paint that was fired on but cold paint, probably oil-based. It enhances the sepia tone of the windows. The home's first occupant, Frederick C. Robie, gave an interview in 1958 where he expressed almost the same kind of ethos as the architect. 'I wanted to be able to look out and down the street to my neighbours without having them invade *my* privacy. I certainly didn't want a lot of junk – a lot of fabrics, draperies, and what not, or old-fashioned roller shades with the brass fittings on the end – in my line of vision.'[6]

Avery Coonley House

The Coonley estate of 1907 is still largely intact, and its dining room displays the exquisite calibration of materials and forms in furniture, windows and architecture. The Playhouse added in 1912 functioned as a kindergarten operated by Mrs Coonley. It is now an independent residence. More than forty windows encircled the room to form a screen under the eaves. They take a playful direction, with densely coloured elements clustered at the upper portions of the window, above long rectangles formed by the vertical patterns of the zinc came. Circles of fully saturated red, yellow, blue and green float over chequered patterns of orange, red, green, white, yellow and black, creating an open intersection of solid and void, fully integrating the negative space of the clear glass, linear pattern of the cames and the almost opaque intensity of the coloured elements. The windows demanded a high level of craftsmanship to achieve the geometric precision of the design. Some of the windows have been dispersed; several are now in the Metropolitan Museum of Art and the Museum of Modern Art in New York.

Wright spoke of 'primitive color' in the Playhouse windows:

> I have used opalescent, opaque, white, and gold in the geometrical groups of spots fixed in glass. I have used, preferably, clear primary colors . . . believing that the clear emphasis of the primitive color interferes less with the function of the window and adds a higher architectural note to the effect of *light* itself. The kinder-symphony in the windows in the Coonley play house is a case in point. The sumac windows in the Dana dining room another.[7]

This ensemble has proved to be one of the most popular from Wright's oeuvre for reproduction. For example, a cotton blanket throw is sold by Pure Country Weavers, Lynn, North Carolina. Similar motifs are available on pillows, bags, coffee mugs and pencil holders, as well as clothing such as scarves and ties.

Museums have incorporated entire rooms as well as furniture designed by Wright. The Metropolitan Museum also exhibits the living room from the Francis W. Little House, originally in a suburb of Minneapolis, Minnesota, built between 1912 and 1914. The room displays two levels of windows amid ochre plaster walls and natural oak trim and flooring. In 1972 the museum purchased the house and portions of the interior were dismantled piece by piece. The library is now in the Allentown Art Museum, Pennsylvania, and a hallway in the Minneapolis Institute of Arts.

Hollyhock House

In 1919 Wright secured his first commission in Los Angeles, the Hollyhock House of the heiress Aline Barnsdall. The Millard (1923, which Wright called La Miniatura), Storer (1923), Freeman (1924) and Ennis (1924–6) residences followed, all showing similar use of concrete patterned blocks inspired by Mayan buildings of the pre-Columbian era. Judson Studios in Los Angeles, which fabricated the windows, has been responsible for several recent restorations.

The architect was deeply moved by the experience of California light and topography. Wright spoke of making the Hollyhock building 'a natural house . . . naturally built; native to the region of California . . . Suited to Miss Barnsdall and her purpose, such a house would be sure to be all that "poetry of form" could imply, because any house should be beautiful in California in a way that

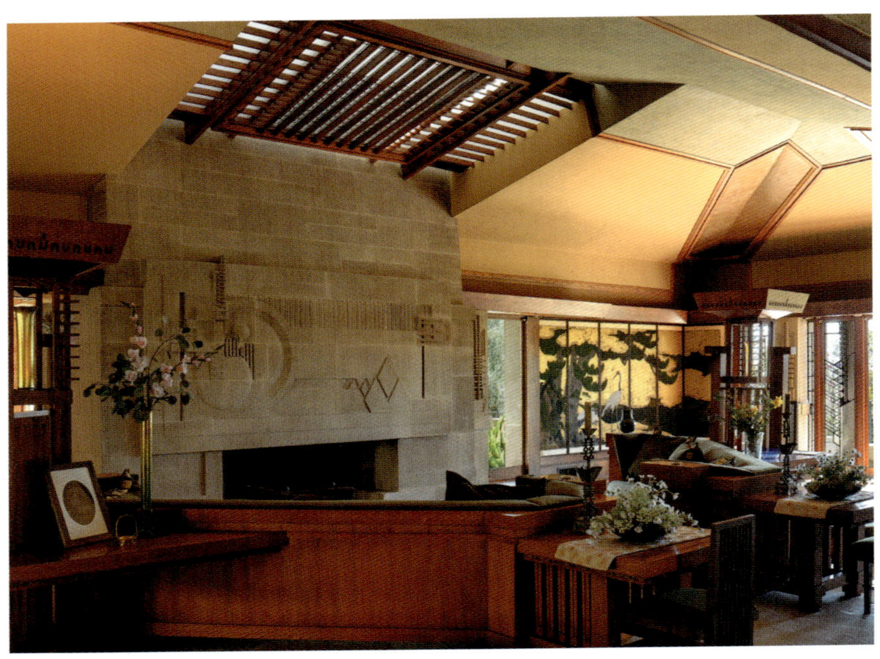

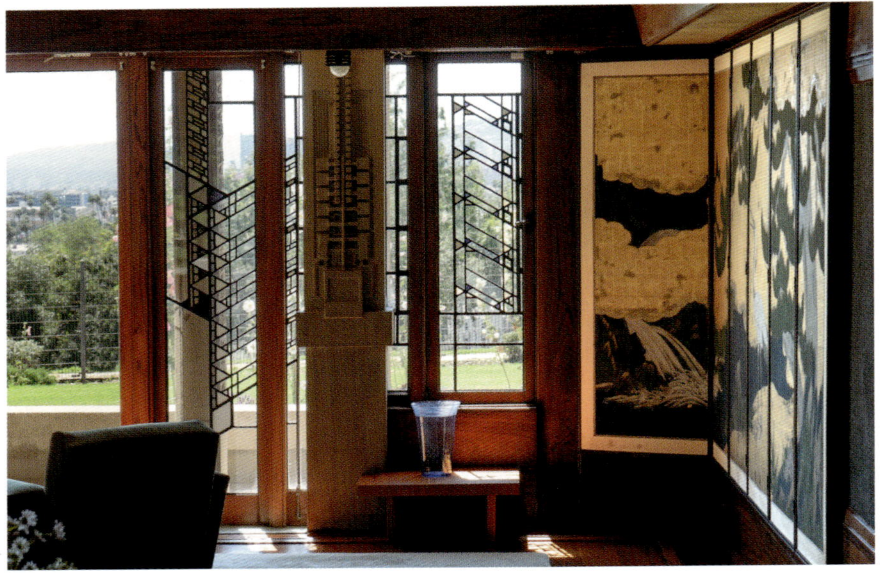

147 Hollyhock House, living room, 1919–21.

148 Hollyhock House, living room windows, 1919–21.

149 Ennis House, window and cast building stone, 1924–6.

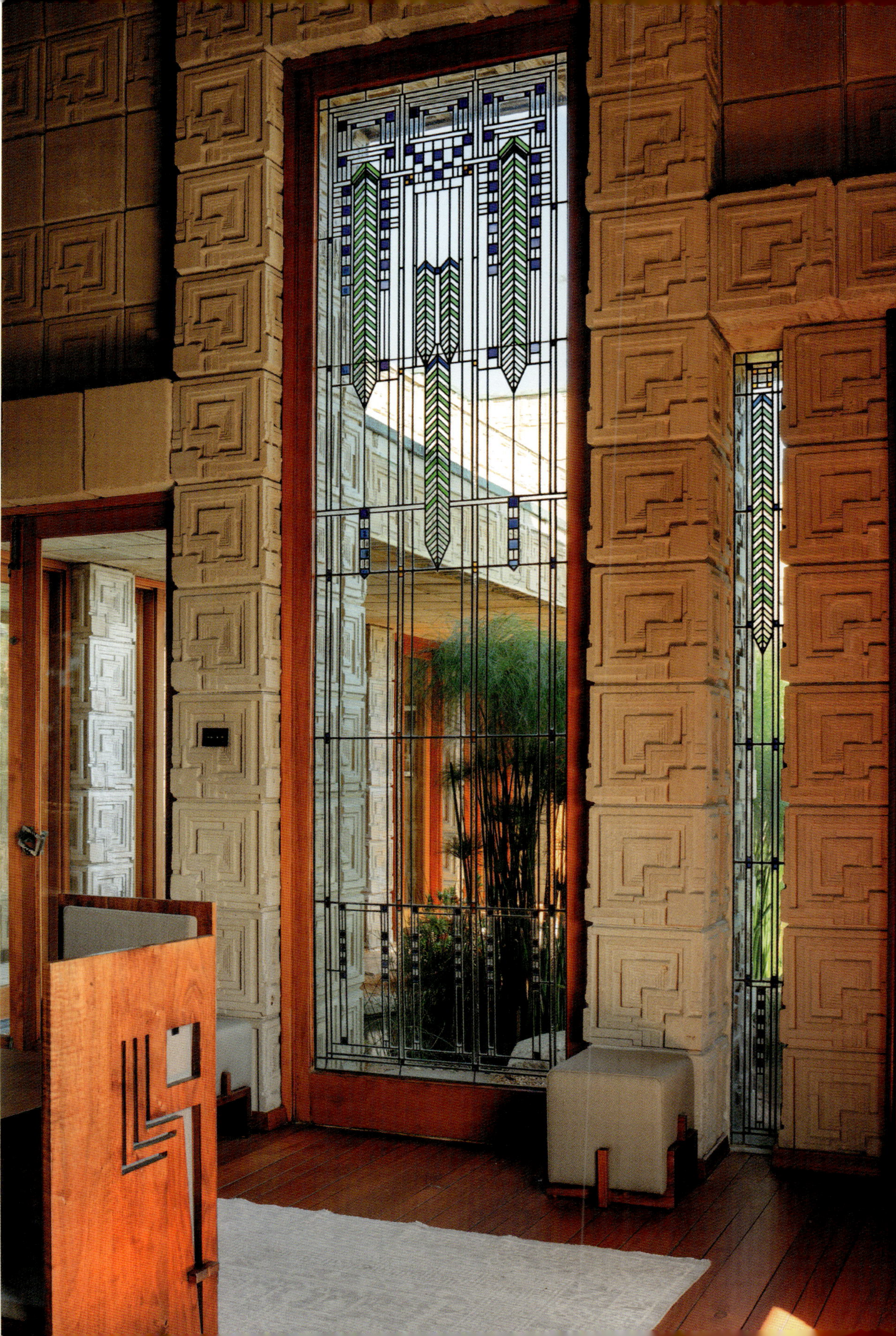

California herself is beautiful.'[8] We find the same exquisite harmony among furnishings, architecture and windows (illus. 147) as in the Dana-Thomas House. The architect, however, expressed a special commitment to the Los Angeles venue:

> The Olive Hill work in Los Angeles is a new type in California, a land of romance, a land that, as yet, has no characteristic building material and new type of building except this one carried there by Spanish missionaries in the early days, a version of the Italian church and convent – now foolishly regarded as an architectural 'Tradition.' I feel in the silhouette of the Olive Hill House a sense of the romance of the region when seen associated with its background and in the type as a whole thing adaptable to California conditions. This type may be made from the gravel of decayed granite of the hills easily obtained there and mixed with cement and cast in molds or forms to make a fairly solid mass either used as blocks to compose a 'unit-slab' system or monolithic in construction. This is the beginning of a constructive effort to produce a type that would fully utilize standardization and the repetition of easily man-handled units.[9]

The vista of Los Angeles provided by these homes illustrates the architect's understanding of space and form. We see the lines of the interior, in window design and wall relief, reiterated by the structure's external walls at Hollyhock and Ennis (illus. 148 and 149).

World Heritage Citation and the Conservator's Ethics

In 2019 eight buildings by Wright were grouped to constitute a single World Heritage inscription: 'The 20th-Century Architecture of Frank Lloyd Wright'. Judson Studios of Los Angeles has conserved several. The Studios' first reference to Frank Lloyd Wright is dated 28 April 1920 and reads: 'See Mr. Wright – Investment Bldg. Art glass, Chic Arch.' Wright apparently had temporary offices in the massive Los Angeles Investment Building at Broadway and Eighth Street. Wright later took more permanent space in the Homer Laughlin Building at 317 South Broadway. A month later, on 25 May, Judson Studios' logbook recorded an estimate of just over $2,000 for 'A. Barnsdall residence, Hollywood' and the name of Frank Lloyd Wright, architect. Judson fabricated a total of 130 windows for the Hollyhock House. As befitting so significant a part of the city's cultural heritage, the restoration of Hollyhock House was closely followed by many interested parties. David Judson worked with his brother Bill, who supervised the project, and remembers the studios' determination to retain as much original material as possible. The studio had also restored the windows of Unity Temple with the same goal. David reflects that the Hollyhock House project brought a memory of legacy, a reconnection with the work of his grandfather and great-grandfather and the early years of the studio. They were challenged to devise a means of reproducing the different finishes, copper among them, that Wright had used for the zinc came. They were also fascinated to find a mouth-blown purple glass used in the living room, in contrast to the machine-rolled glass more routinely used in other windows.

We look back on this list of eight buildings. They are Unity Temple (1905–9), Oak Park, Illinois; Frederick C. Robie House (1908–10), Chicago, Illinois; Taliesin (1912), Spring Green, Wisconsin; Hollyhock House (1919–21), Los Angeles, California; Herbert and Katherine Jacobs House (1936–7), Madison, Wisconsin; Taliesin West (1938), Scottsdale, Arizona; Fallingwater (1936–9), Mill Run, Pennsylvania; and the Solomon R. Guggenheim Museum (1956–9), New York. All these buildings are organized by design concepts linking furniture, architecture and windows in a coordinated whole. Wright's architecture was especially marked by his desire for formal unity and the integration of the landscape with both the exterior and interior design of the building. Thus the window, quintessentially linking outside to inside, drew his full attention.

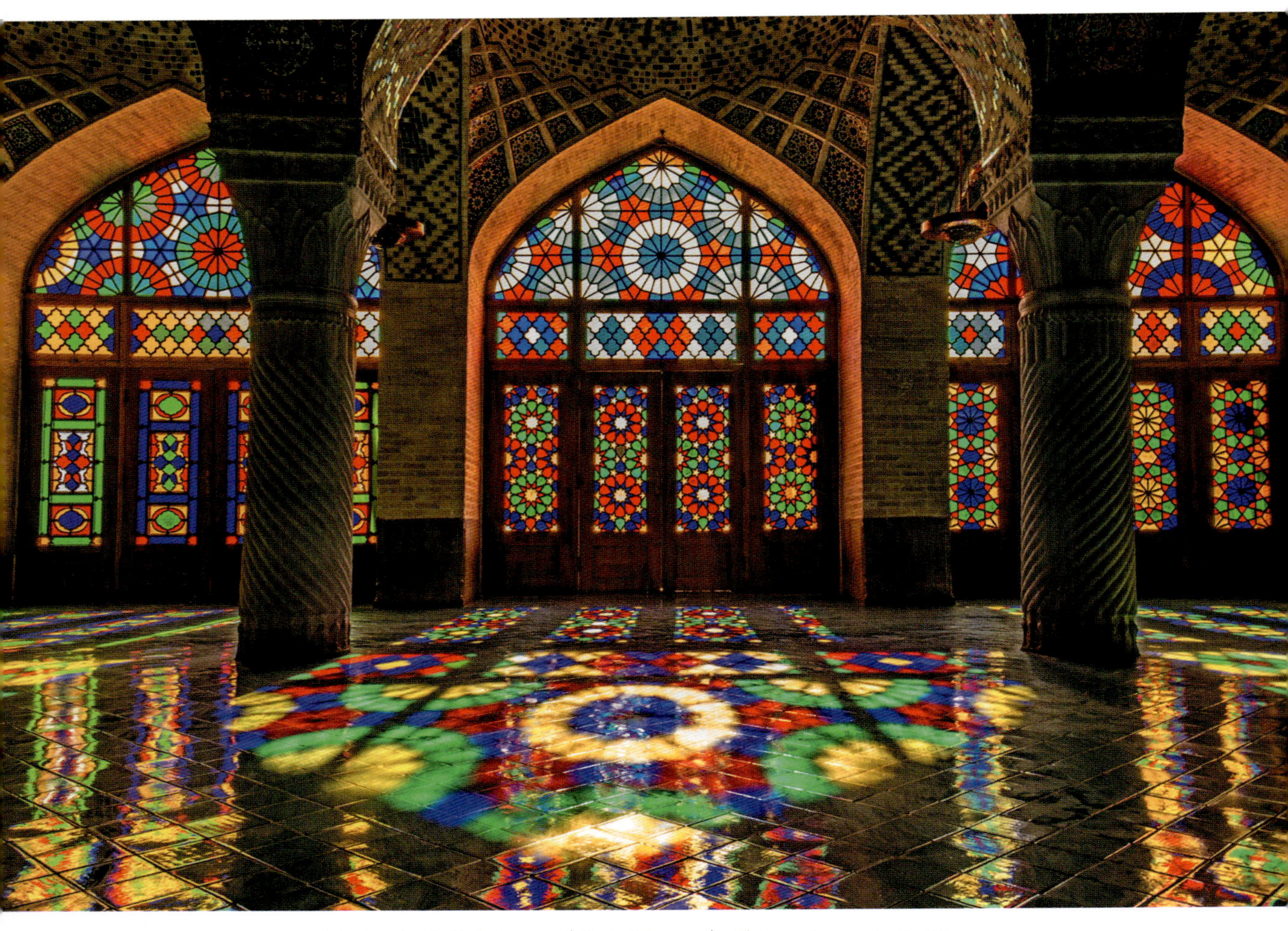

150 Nasir al-Mulk Mosque (Pink Mosque), Shiraz, Iran, 1876–88.

12

The Spirituality
of Abstraction

—

Art without identifiable images has thrived in religious settings over many ages. Pattern and colour were often believed to best embody God's ineffable perfection. Consider, for example, the symbolic form of the pyramid as an image of eternity. The sixth-century church of Hagia Sophia built by Justinian in Constantinople achieved its transcendent meaning primarily through geometry. The emperor selected a mathematician and a geometer and engineer to design the building. Figural mosaics were only added in the ninth to eleventh centuries. The repetitions, iterations and intersections of geometric forms mesmerize the viewer. Solid and void play with the light, with the result that the structure has a feeling of floating in space. Sacred geometry is clearly at play, inspired, certainly, by the Roman emperor Hadrian's Pantheon, dated about 126 CE, conceived both in height and in circumference as a perfect circle. The concept was inclusive, honouring all the gods, their perfection represented by an unchanging and encompassing form. Geometry inspired subsequent generations.

Medieval ideas of divine harmony saw the created world ordered by the four elements of earth, air, water and fire. In a quadratic order, each is an opposite, but each contains elements that link it to a complement. Earth is cold and dry, enabling it to link to Water, which is cold and wet. Air is both wet and hot, enabling it to link to the element of Fire, hot and dry, which returns to Earth, for it is also dry, although cold. Boethius' reflective *Consolation of Philosophy* (523), one of the most influential texts of the Middle Ages, was composed as the author awaited execution under the Ostrogothic king Theodoric the Great. In a poetic stanza in Book IV, Song VI he speaks of the overarching harmony of the universe: 'Thus, in wondrous amity, Warring elements agree; Hot and cold, and moist and dry, Lay their ancient quarrel by; High the flickering flame ascends, Downward earth forever tends.'

Pink Mosque, Shiraz, Iran

The Nasir al-Mulk Mosque, also known as the Pink Mosque, in Shiraz, Iran, was built between 1879 and 1888, and is still in use, supported by the Nasir al-Mulk Endowment Foundation. Elements that influenced the early development of Muslim art and architecture were outlined by the art historian Oleg Grabar: a ritual for prayer to be accomplished by preference in a mosque, a prototype for the mosque taken from the house of Mohammed in Medina, a reluctance concerning representation of living beings and the development of the Qur'an and the Arabic script as the vehicle for transmitting Mohammed's message.' Believed to be the precise words of the prophet Mohammed, under divine inspiration, the Qur'an takes central importance in the Muslim experience. Reciting, hearing or reading the Word of God is understood as the most direct way of coming closer to God. Prayer consists primarily of recitations of passages of the Qur'an while the faithful turn towards Mecca. The city of Mecca is revered as the birthplace of the prophet Muhammed and the site of the Kaaba, the cubic structure that is Islam's most sacred shrine.

Designing space conducive to both individual prayer and the recitation of the Qur'an long encouraged architectural embellishment. The Islamic oath, the *Shahadah*, constitutes the first of the Five Pillars of Islam: 'I bear witness that there is no deity but God, and I bear witness that Muhammad is the messenger of God.' Two of the following Pillars impact the construction of mosques: formal liturgical prayer five times daily, cited above, and the payment of an annual alms tithe. This obligation of charity can also be seen in the endowment by Nasir al-Mulk to enable the mosque to serve the community in perpetuity. Although the Qur'an makes no mention of the avoidance of imagery the Pink Mosque and many others are embellished primarily by geometric patterns. Floral designs appear in the domes and their supporting pendentives. Throughout, quotations from the Qur'an appear in elegant script.

In keeping with the Abrahamic faiths, Islam often describes the divine essence as light. The production of glass was well known in Islamic lands and was often a part of Islamic decor. As an example, the Blue Mosque (Sultan Ahmed Mosque) in Istanbul, Turkey, dated 1609–16, was illuminated by two hundred windows of Venetian glass, a gift of the city of Venice; today they hold largely modern replacements. In the Pink Mosque, coloured glass fills a series of

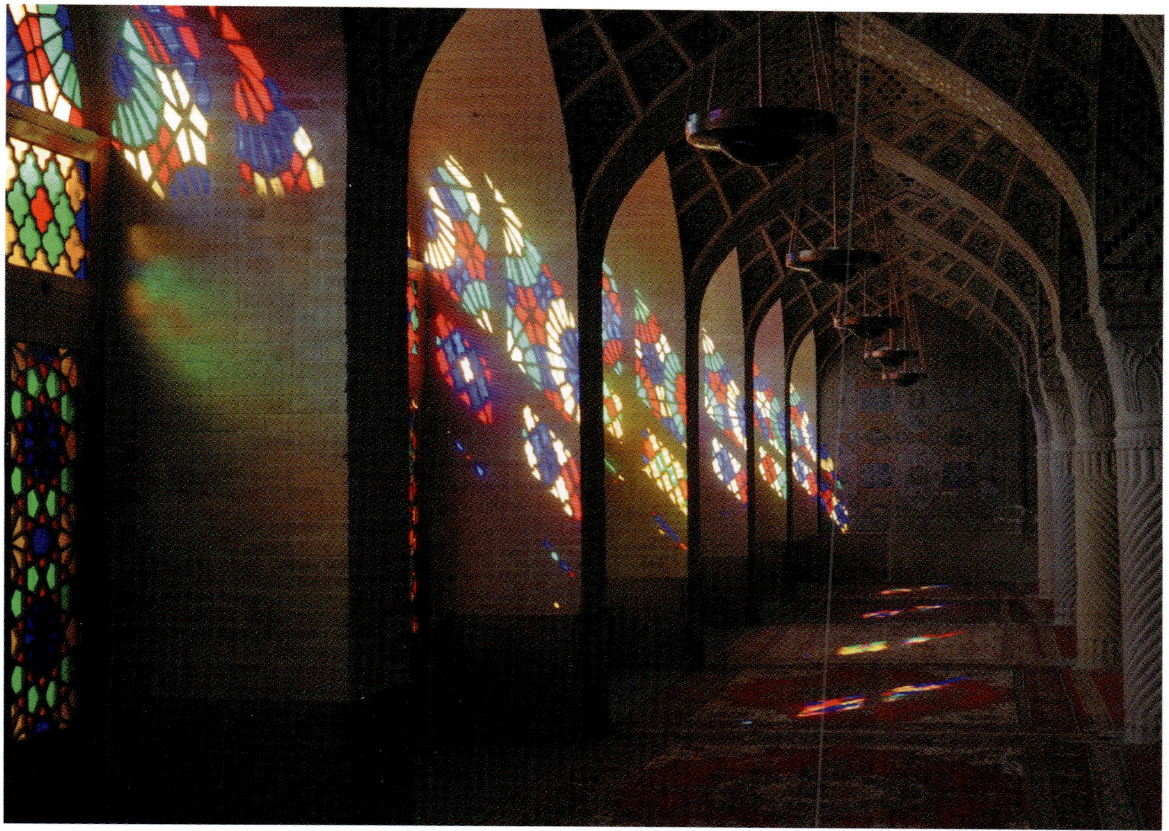

151 Nasir al-Mulk Mosqıe (Pink Mosque), Shiraz, Iran, 1876–88.

openings on the facade (illus. 151 and 152). The designs employ the concept of tessellation, a pattern of repeated shapes that fit together closely without gaps or overlapping. In tessellation, there is no background or foreground; each segment has its own identify within a pattern. The patterns operate independently yet coalesce in a harmonic whole. In the central parts of one wall, we at first see superposed circles composed of ten red elements surrounding a white centre with blue spokes. To the sides are a series of five-pointed stars, linked to green circles. The colouration is reversed in the flanking panels, where green becomes dominant and the red its complement. The reflection of the colour patterns on the glazed tile of the interior amplifies the harmonic ambiance of the space.

Sagrada Família: Architectural Space Fulfilled

The Basilica of the Holy Family, commonly referred to as the Sagrada Família, is one of the great attractions of Barcelona, Catalonia, Spain. Designed by

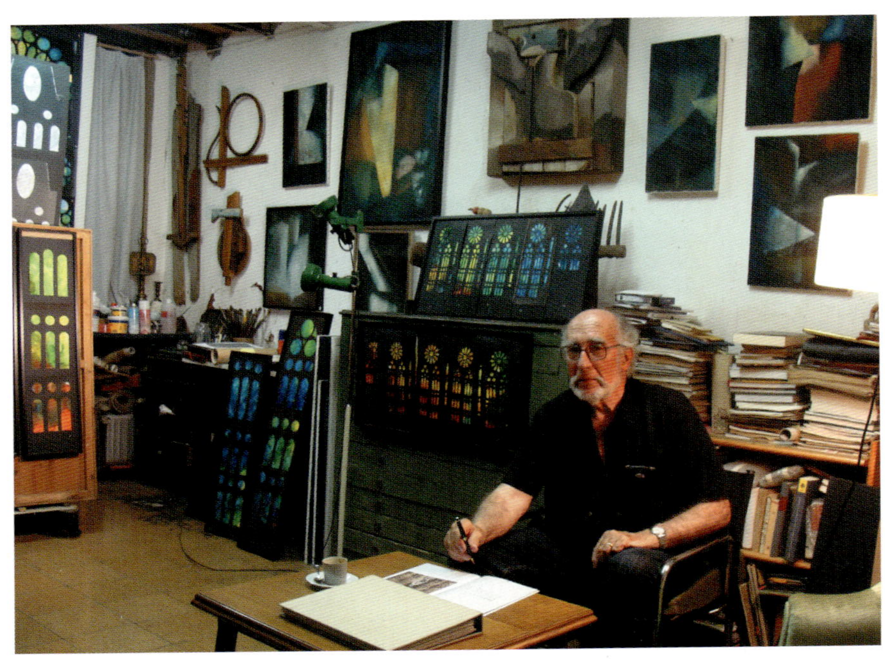

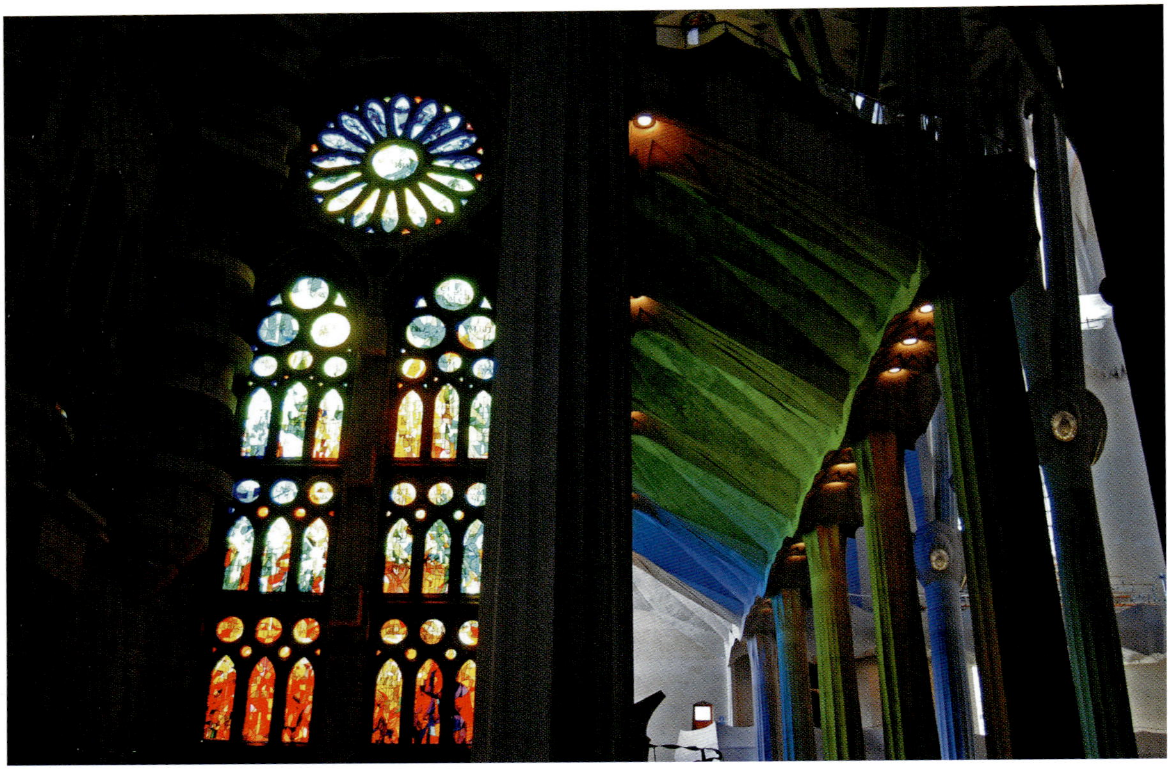

152 Joan Villa-Grau in his studio, Barcelona, 2009.

153 Joan Villa-Grau, Sagrada Familia, Barcelona, *Window of Life*, and aisle, 2010.

Antoni Gaudí (1852–1926), the building forms part of Barcelona's heritage of Modernism, known internationally as Art Nouveau. In 1883, barely five years after his degree, the young Gaudí became chief architect. Funding came from private donations. At his death, some forty years later, only a quarter of the building was completed but much enthusiasm remained for it to continue. Today, it is largely finished, with three complex sculpted facades. That of the east, depicting the Nativity, is closest to Gaudí's original conception. The Passion commands the west, and the Glory facade to the south, still in process, depicts the theme of the soul's ascension to God. Designed to have eighteen soaring spires resembling organic growth, nine have been built, four at the east and west facades and one over the choir.

Gaudí's reputation as an architect was solidified by his Barcelona creations in which he integrated ceramics, stained glass, wrought ironwork, woodwork and other craft materials in a seamless whole. Park Güell, a complex of buildings in the neighbourhood of Pedralbes, was an early creation, built between 1884 and 1887 and marked by sinuous ironwork and variegated brick. Casa Milà, dating between 1906 and 1912, with its extraordinary undulating facade and interior, was the last of his private residences. His successors supervising the Sagrada Família endeavoured to keep his vision, none more than the scholar and artist Joan Vila-Grau (1932–2022), who designed the windows installed from 1999 to 2018 (illus. 152 and 153). Awarded the *Creu de Sant Jordi* (St George Cross), one of the highest civil distinctions of Catalonia, Vila-Grau was a creator of painting, sculpture and stained glass, as well as a scholar of stained glass of the medieval and the contemporary era. He has a particular place in history as the discoverer of two medieval glazing tables related to a window in the cathedral of Girona dated to about 1340.

Vila-Grau's deliberation was long, and the search for appropriate hue and tone demanded contemplation on site and in the studio. He ultimately became absolutely convinced of the necessity for non-objective windows:

The spirituality of Gaudí is more in the rhythm of the colours and the architecture than in the iconography . . . The religious sensibility of Gaudí in the field of iconography is the sensibility of that epoch. But Gaudí is more than that epoch. For me a column of Gaudí's is more spiritual than putting 'Gloria in Excelsis Deo' [Glory to God in the Highest] on it . . . People can find in the Sagrada Família something that they can find in their own temples and churches. There are other buildings in the world where you can find this spirituality, for example, the Mosque at Cordoba. You can enter into another space, beyond the temple.[2]

We see this in the *Window of Life*, looking south, with its reds and earthy colours at the bottom, shifting to greens and finally to golds and blues at the top.

Vila-Grau's efforts to empathize with a preceding builder finds parallels with other artists, often designing new glass for revered historic structures. We have seen how, over eight centuries, the cathedral of Cologne was built, with success. The rapid evolution of urban sites and their surging population growth in the nineteenth century, however, challenged the preservation of historic structures. William Morris (1834–1896), a prolific writer and translator of ancient and medieval texts, and a designer of textiles, stained glass and book illustration, was England's greatest force in the Arts and Crafts movement. As a student at Oxford, he travelled to France, where he became enraptured by the architecture of northern French cathedrals, such as Amiens and Rouen. He subsequently began a short-lived apprenticeship with the Gothic Revival architect George Edmund Street. In 1877, appalled at the insensitive rebuilding and alterations of buildings he observed in England, he pioneered the founding of the Society for the Protection of Ancient Buildings. Its manifesto called for 'Protection in place of Restoration, to stave off decay by daily care . . . [and] to treat our ancient buildings as monuments of a bygone art, created by bygone manners, that modern art cannot meddle with without destroying'. The contemporary world has witnessed intersections of highly accomplished artists asked to design windows for historic sites, such as Gerhard Richter's south transept of 2007 in the cathedral at Cologne (see Chapter Four). These artists have all reflected on their keen desire to honour the space and the building.

St Foy Abbey Church, Conques, France

The practice of medieval pilgrimage supported commerce, international exchange and great innovations in architecture. St Faith of Agen had been martyred at the age of twelve for refusing to honour Roman gods. In 866, in the common practice of pious theft, monks transferred her body to Conques, a small town in a mountainous region to the east. We read in the twelfth-century *Pilgrim's Guide to Santiago de Compostela* that 'she was honourably buried . . . Above the tomb a magnificent basilica was erected by the faithful in which, for the glory of God, the rule of the Blessed Benedict has been till this very day observed with great punctiliousness.' The monastic building, begun in the mid-eleventh

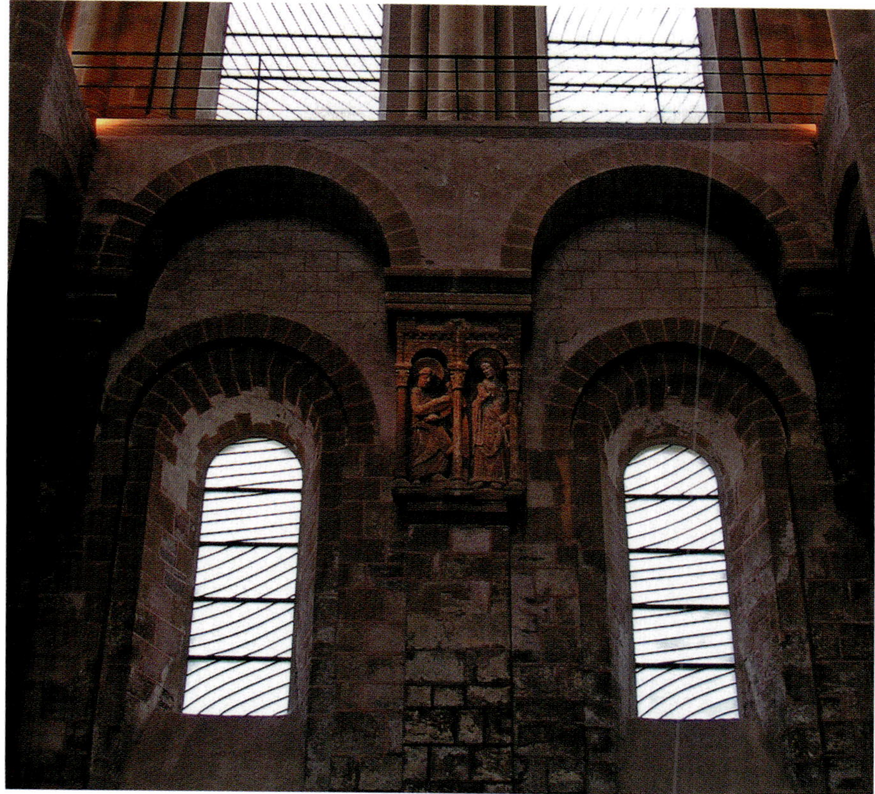

154 Pierre Soulages, upper window, St Foy Abbey Church,
Conques, France, 1994.

century, consists of a nave of six bays and transept of equal width with aisles that continue around the entire building. Pilgrims marvelled at the gem-encrusted reliquary statue of St Faith. The head was moulded over a Roman parade helmet and the statue bristles with gemstones and Roman cameos, in a manner very similar to the early descriptions of the shrine of Thomas Becket in Canterbury.

Renowned for its elegant simplicity and the soaring height of its rounded arches and barrel vaults, Conques has become an iconic example of the Romanesque style. Sculptural decoration is largely confined to capitals whose shape follows the form of the pillar. Abandoned after the French Revolution, in 1840 Conques became one of the first designated national monuments of France. The renowned author Prosper Mérimée, mesmerized by the site during his visit of 1838, was then inspector general of the Commission des Monuments Historiques (Historical Monuments Commission). Today, Conques' simplicity of form and the natural surface of the stone make the building feel at once a pow-erful monument to a past and a site of contemporary minimalist aesthetics. In

1986, the French government decided on a comprehensive glazing programme, commissioning Pierre Soulages (1919–2022), viewed as one of the most prestigious French artists of his time. The Louvre honoured him with a retrospective in 2019.

The artist spoke of his personal relationship to the area and to the church: 'I often visited Conques during my childhood – I was born in Rodez. It's in Conques that I experienced my first artistic emotions.'[3] Soulages has focused his mature work on the exploration of the colour black, explaining: *mon instrument n'est pas le noir mais la lumière réfléchie par le noir* (My subject is not the black, but the light reflected by the black).[4] Soulages, for this commission, needed light, but one sensitive to the space of the interior and texture of the stone. After many efforts, his material was found in security glass for doors produced by the Klinge Company, in Rheine, a small village north of Münster, Germany. Soulages installed a sample window in 1991. Working with the Jean-Dominque Fleury Studio he was able to design the spacing for the undulating lines by using black adhesive tape and viewing the cartoons from long distances. The 104 windows were completed in 1994 (illus. 154). In 2005, Pierre Soulages and his wife Colette donated 250 works and 250 documents to the community of Grand Rodez where he was born. In 2014, augmented by additional donations that profile his long career, the Musée Soulages was inaugurated. The museum exhibits the cartoons for the stained-glass windows created for Conques.

A Cathedral Receives a Peace Offering

The First World War initiated warfare of the modern era. The German bombardment of the city of Reims that began on 4 September 1914 profoundly shocked the European community. Additional shelling several days later set the cathedral on fire and caused irreparable losses of statuary and stained glass. Reims, founded in the fifth century, was revered as the baptismal site of Clovis, who first united the Frankish tribes. From the eleventh century it was the traditional site of coronations of the French monarch. Rebuilt in the thirteenth century as one of the most complex cathedrals of the Gothic era, it became a UNESCO World Heritage site in 1991. The French response to the German shelling was to declare that these actions revealed the true motivation of German barbarism, a desire to obliterate the cultural heritage of France. French intellectuals who previously had expressed admiration for German literature, music and art were horrified. Certainly, this memory became enmeshed in the cultural discourse of both France and Germany, even into the twenty-first century.

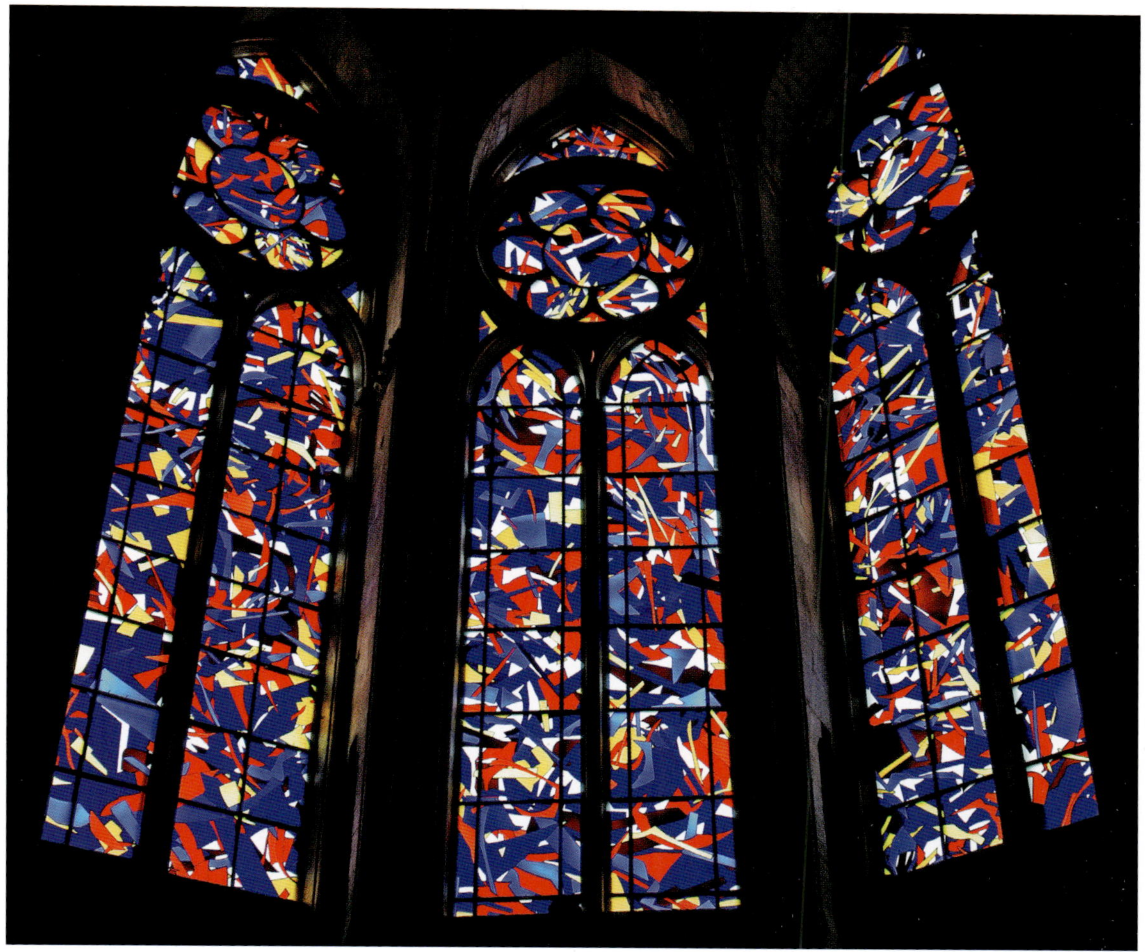

155 Imi Knoebel, Jeanne d'Arc chapel, Reims Cathedral, France, 2008–11.

Beginning in 2008, the Düsseldorf artist Imi Knoebel (1940–) donated his designs for windows in two radial chapels of Reims Cathedral (illus. 155). The fabrication was financed by the German Foreign Ministry. In the 1960s Knoebel had studied under the revolutionary Joseph Beuys at the Kunstakademie Düsseldorf. Encouraged by a climate that sought artistic relevance by engaging the viewer temporally and physically as well as mentally, he gravitated towards large-scale works heralded in international exhibitions. In the United States, the innovative site DIA Art Foundation acquired Knoebel's series in homage to his friend Blinky Palermo. His interest gravitated towards the abstract elements of art, colour and form that underpin all visual expression. The artist, like his mentor Beuys before him, is an activist. In 1988 he began the series 'Kinderstern' (Stars for Children), whose proceeds support projects for children in need.

The windows at Reims were fabricated in the glazing studios of Simon Marq of Reims and Duchemin of Paris, and later by Derix Glasstudios Taunusstein. The mouth-blown glass, of Lamberts manufacture, which had been employed for Richter's window at Cologne, juxtaposes 27 colours in a composition of ever-changing shapes. The windows were inaugurated in 2011 to celebrate the cathedral's 800th anniversary. While embodying pure abstraction in composition, the windows adopt a colour selection that echoes that of the original windows visible in the clerestory.

A Synagogue and a Century of History Revitalized

Built in 1887, Eldridge Street Synagogue, on New York's Lower East Side, is one of the first sites of worship in the United States erected by Eastern European Jews (Ashkenazim). This was a time of massive immigration, with the arrival of more than 25 million people, including more than 2.5 million Jews. Close to 85 per cent of Jewish immigrants from Eastern Europe came to New York. From its inception to the 1950s, the synagogue played a vital role in assimilation and in material as well as spiritual support for immigrants. One need only review period photographs or sites such as New York's Tenement Museum to understand the oppressive conditions of labour and of housing at this time. The synagogue must have been a transformative experience, colourful, open and spacious. Its elegant two-level sanctuary emphasizes rounded arches and circular reiterations in dome and windows. Its facade incorporates inspiration from Spanish Mudéjar art, a type of ornamentation and decoration used in medieval Spain, often associated with Jewish tradition.

In the 1950s the congregation that constructed the synagogue had moved into a lower level and the main sanctuary was unused. Roberta Brandes Gratz, a prominent author on urban issues and ardent preservationist, led a restoration effort to revitalize the historic structure. In 1986 Gratz formed the Eldridge Street Project (now the Museum at Eldridge Street) and in 1996 the synagogue secured a u.s. National Historic Landmark designation. With ground-roots efforts, the building was transformed from a deteriorating relic of a past to a cultural landmark of the present. In 2010, the artist Kiki Smith collaborated with the architect Deborah Gans to redesign the lost central window of the sanctuary (illus. 156). Smith came to prominence within the postmodern revolution of the 1990s centred on New York. Best known as a sculptor and printmaker, her work includes multifaceted references, not simply to contemporaries but historic art, including that of the Middle Ages. She is also the daughter of the sculptor

Tony Smith, who had trained as an architect and whose sculptural works are based on variations of geometric forms. Kiki Smith's work for the synagogue is at once geometric and figural.

There were precedents in the artist's past. Working with the Viennese architecture and design art firm Coop Himmelb(l)au, Kiki developed *Paradise Cage*, exhibited at the Museum of Contemporary Art, Los Angeles, in 1996. The large installation presaged the feeling of the window. Glass stars and animals, along with bronze scat, were strewn across a floor covered with blue hand-made Nepalese paper surmounted by a cage of metal cables and wooden stairs. Smith has spoken about religion, and her art, presenting transcendence and transmigration, something always moving from one state to another. In the synagogue, the window anchors a wall and repeats, in paler tone, the deep blue star-bedecked walls below and also the cupola above. The construction uses an innovative technique. Blue flashed glass is manipulated to remove the colour where the yellow silver-stained stars appear. Additional stars were added using gold leaf. The segments of glass are then laminated onto a transparent base.

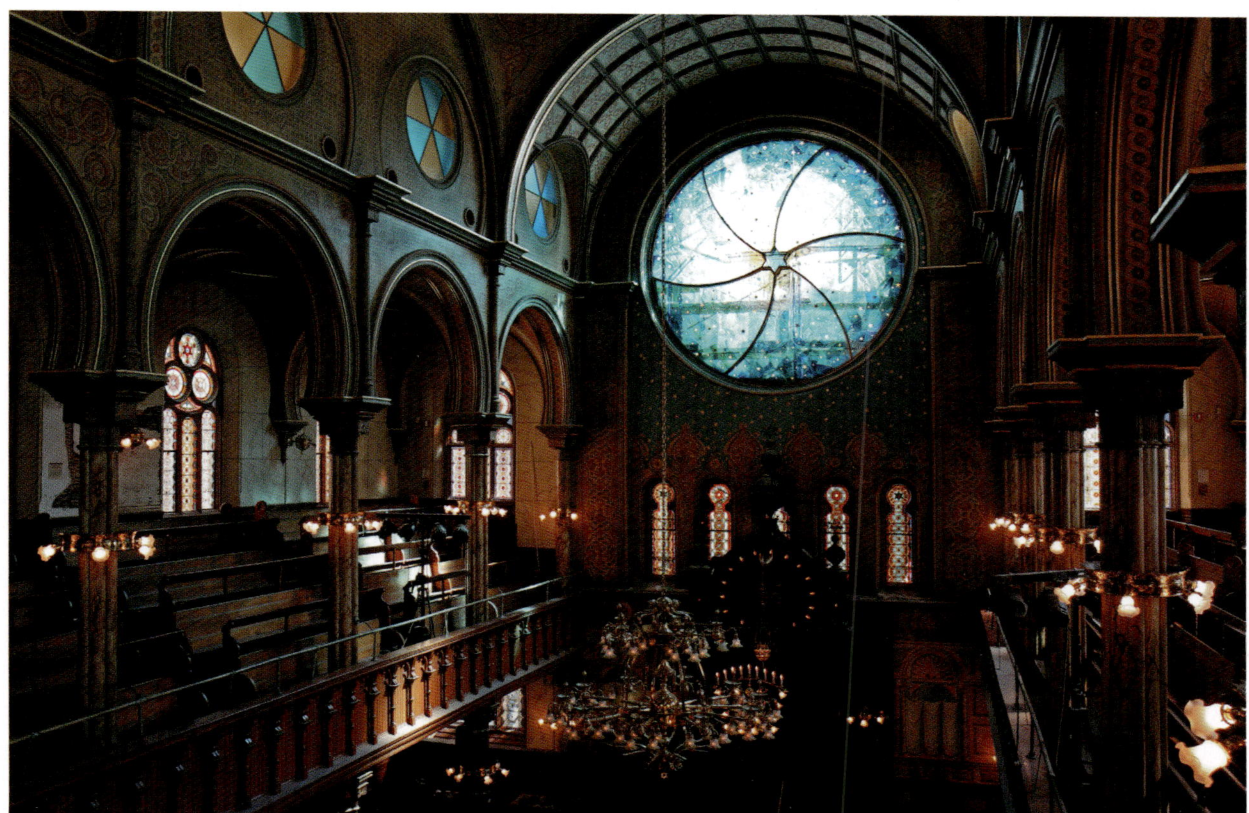

156 Kiki Smith, chancel window, Eldridge Street Synagogue, New York, 2010.

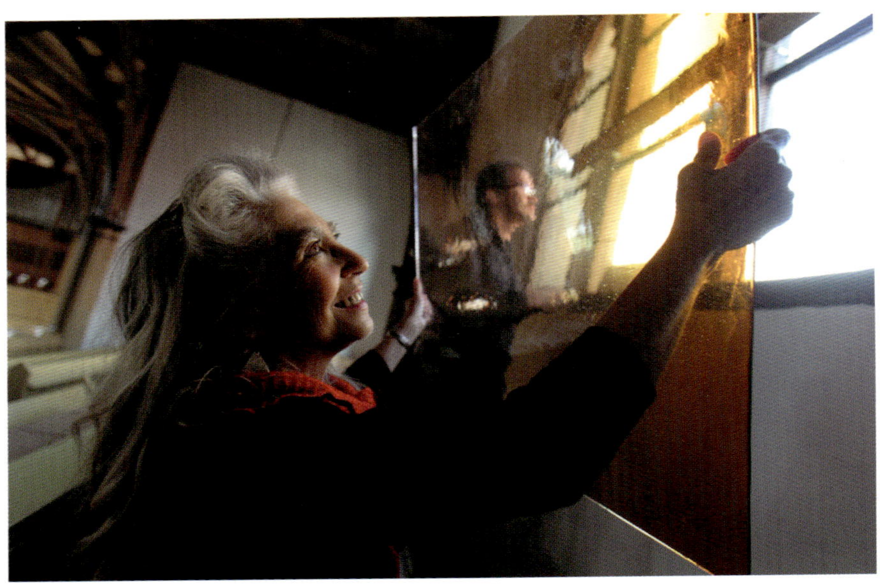

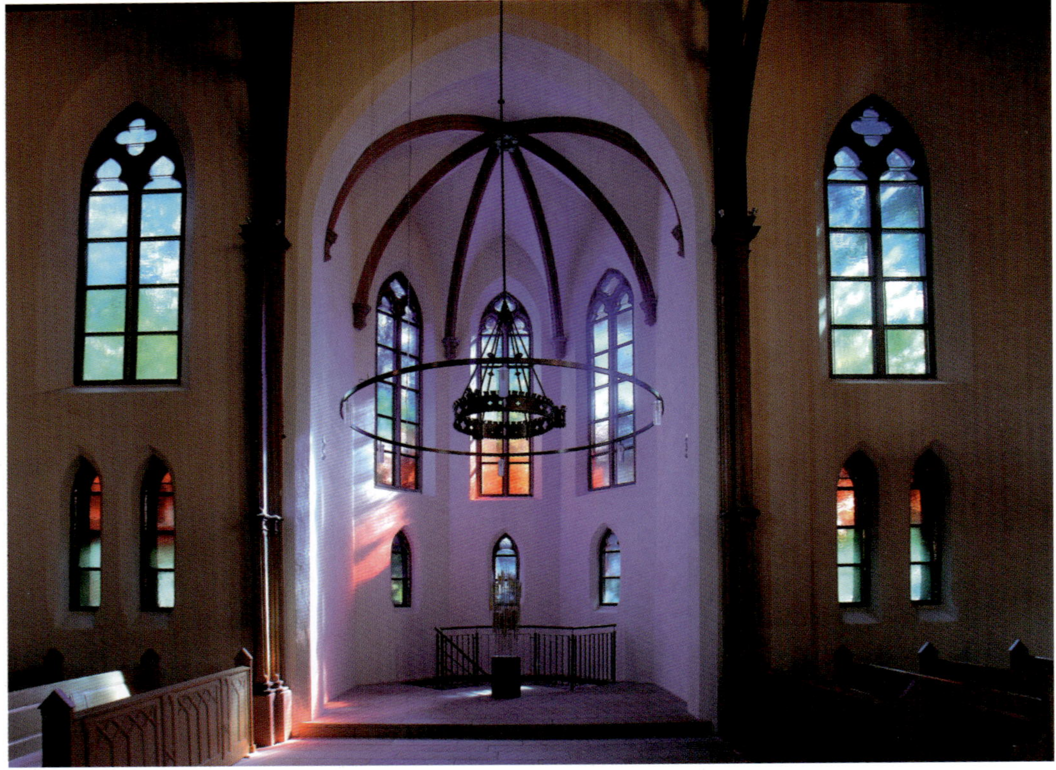

157 Romi Fisher examining a piece of glass in the process of designing
windows for the Lutheran church Kirche auf dem Damm.

158 Romi Fisher, east wall, Lutheran church, Kirche auf
dem Damm, Duisburg-Meiderich, Germany, 2007.

By this means, the fabricator avoids the traditional lead matrix. The artist and architect were keen on producing an uninterrupted sense of a transfigured night. Celestial elements appeared more frequently in her work after completion of the synagogue window. Her 'Blue Moon' series of metal relief sculpture around 2011 pondered circular mysteries. Her large star sculptures constructed of glass and metal were exhibited at the Pace Gallery, New York, in 2014.

Transformative Light for a Lutheran Church

The Kirche auf dem Damm is located in Duisburg's Mittel Meiderich district, about 72 kilometres (45 mi.) north of Cologne. The first church on the site dates to the mid-eleventh century but only the tower erected in 1502 has survived. In the Middle Ages, the church was associated with the female collegiate foundation (*Stift*) of St Margaret's in Gerresheim, a borough of the city of Düsseldorf, some 32 kilometres (20 mi.) to the south. In 1610, the church embraced the Lutheran confession. The present brick neo-Gothic building dates to 1862/3 and is credited to the architect C. Freyse, from Essen. Happily, the church survived the Second World War bombings that saturated this highly industrialized area of Germany.

In 2006, Romi Fischer, a Zurich artist, was asked to replace the blank glazing with a new programme, a process that lasted a decade (illus. 157). Fischer's work includes installations with structural steel sculptures, word and picture boards, film, light and sound. She accepted the commission with the goal of animating space. From its origins, Lutheran theology did not reject the image, but it did challenge the frequent abuse of the image as having an intrinsically spiritual power. Rather, the emphasis was to empower individuals by giving them the Christian sacred text in their own language, facilitating a personal communion with God. Fischer looked to finding a material that could transform experience at any time of day, facilitating meditation on God's unfathomable gift of creation as experienced in the passage of light. She selected glass produced by Lamberts Studio for all 43 windows of the church (illus. 158). The windows were fabricated in the Hein Derix Studios, Kevelaer. No surface paint was added; the colour and texture result from three to four layers of varied sheets of mouth-blown glass. At every stage over the ten-year installation, the artist worked on site with Herbert Janssen from Hein Derix. From the perspective of the studio, never had collaboration with an artist been so personal and intense. The artist designated areas for site-specific hues to meld with the condition of light from sunrise to evening. The chancel shows blues that flow into red and orange at the bottom of the upper windows as if they were catching the rays of the morning sun. The sides show blues and greens consonant with the filtering of cool light through verdant nature. The west window is the most intense; a brilliant yellow-orange at the top transitions down the window through cooler red to tranquil blue. The ensemble is transformative.

This meditation on the exploration of form and colour to transform architectural space brings us back to the origins of the medium. As a visual art, stained-glass windows employ the physical to evoke the immaterial. They use matter – glass, paint, lead and iron – to image deeply held convictions. As seen in the discussion of the window of Canterbury Cathedral in Chapter One, image is conveyed by form. Whether erudite discourse on sacred scriptures or eye-catching dramatic events such as cures and rescues, they depend on geometric and organic shapes. Their interplay of colour and pattern captures our attention, causing us to pause, to withdraw for a moment from the mundane, and hopefully, to see beyond.

References

—

Introduction

1 John G. Hawthorne and Cyril Stanley Smith, ed., *Theophilus On Divers Arts: The Foremost Medieval Treatise on Painting, Glassmaking, and Metalwork* [1963] (Chicago, IL, 1979), p. 64.

1 Canterbury: A Martyr's Tomb and Its Cathedral

1 Peter Brown, *The Cult of the Saints* (Chicago, IL, 1981), pp. 2 and 4.
2 J. N. Hillgarth, *Christianity and Paganism, 350–750: The Conversion of Western Europe* [1969] (Philadelphia, PA, 1986), pp. 23–7.
3 Bede, *A History of the English Church and Its People* (Book 1, 29), trans. Leo Sherley-Price (London, 1976), p. 85.
4 See the British Library: Harley MS 5102, f. 32.
5 See Amiens, Bibl. mun. MS. 0019, f. 008, Psalter S. Fuscian.
6 See the Morgan Library and Museum, New York, MS m.43, fol. 24v.
7 Author's modernization of the Old English.
8 Lynn Staley, ed. and trans., *The Book of Margery Kempe* (London, 2001), chs 28–9, esp. p. 50.

2 Chartres: Representations in an Iconic Gothic Programme

1 Arthur Kingsley Porter, *Chartres Cathedral: Norton Critical Studies in Art History*, ed. Robert Branner (New York, 1969), p. 93.
2 Ibid., p. 94.
3 Peter Brieger, *English Art, 1216–1307* (Oxford, 1968), p. 95.
4 Branner, ed., *Chartres Cathedral*, pp. 98–9.

3 Sainte-Chapelle, Paris: Propaganda for the Monarch

1 Robert Branner, *St Louis and the Court Style in Gothic Architecture* (London, 1964), pp. 56–7.
2 Ferdinand, baron de Guilhermy, *Description de la Sainte-Chapelle* (Paris, 1867), https://archive.org, accessed 15 January 2023.
3 Louis Grodecki, in *Les Vitraux de Notre-Dame et de la Sainte-Chapelle de Paris*, Corpus Vitrearum Medii Aevi France, 1 (Paris, 1959), p. 86.
4 *Annales archéologiques* (Paris, 1844).

5 All Saints, North Street, York: Instructing a Parish

1 Eamon Duffy, *The Stripping of the Altars: Traditional Religion in England, 1400–1580* (New Haven, CT, and London, 1992), p. 452.
2 Marguerite T. Harris, ed., *Birgitta of Sweden: Life and Selected Revelations*, trans. Albert R. Kezel (New York, 1990).
3 Edward H. Lanson, *A Manual of Councils of the Holy Catholick Church* (London, 1846).
4 Clifford Davidson, ed., *The York Corpus Christi Plays* (Kalamazoo, MI, 2011), play 2, ll. 89–92, https://d.lib.rochester.edu, accessed 15 January 2023.

5 Ibid., ll. 127–30.
6 Ibid., ll. 4770–75 (Book v, ll. 759–64).
7 Ibid., ll. 4798–801 (Book v, ll. 787–90).

6 St Mary's Parish Church, Fairford, Gloucestershire: Surviving Iconoclasm

1 William Strode, 'On Fayrford Windowes', in *The Poetical Works of William Strode*, ed. Bertram Dobell (London, 1907), pp. 26–7, https://babel.hathitrust.org, accessed 15 January 2023.
2 Ibid., p. 26.
3 Ibid., p. 28.

7 Renaissance Donors in Switzerland: An Art of Exchange

This chapter has been written with the kind cooperation of Rolf Hasler.
1 Voltaire, 'Helvetia', in *Voltaire's Philosophical Dictionary* (New York, 1900), p. 156.
2 *Luzernerchronik* [The Chronicle of Lucerne] (1513), www.e-codices.unifr.ch, accessed 15 January 2023.

8 Renaissance Roundels: The Transformation of European Image Making

1 The images cited but not illustrated in the chapter are accessible through their museum's online databases. Enter the accession number for direct access; enter the name of the artist for a larger view of the artist's works in the collection. Many museums have generously placed these images in the public domain: *The Triumph of Antwerp*, printed in 1550 by Pieter Coecke van Aelst (Metropolitan Museum of Art 20.43); *Joseph and His Brothers Feasting at Joseph's House*, print, dated 1549–50 (Rijksmuseum, Amsterdam, RP-P-BI-6477X); *Jacob in Transit with his Entire Household*, print (British Museum, 1868,0208.73); *The Ten Commandments* by Hendrik Goltzius, Antwerp, 1583 (British Museum, 1989,0722.39); Jan Pietersz. Saenredam's engraving after Abraham Bloemaert (*c.* 1600, National Gallery of Art, Washington DC, 2012.92.605); paintings by Hendrick Goltzius (1600–1603, Philadelphia Museum of Art, 1990-100-1); paintings by Peter Paul Rubens (1615, Koninklijk Museum voor Schone Kunsten, Antwerp); Simon Bening's miniature of the Way to Calvary from the *Prayer Book of Cardinal Albrecht of Brandenburg* (Bruges, *c.* 1525–30, J. Paul Getty Museum Ms. Ludwig ix 19, fol. 178v).

9 Harvard University's Memorial Hall: Honouring the Dead, the Nation and Art

1 Most of the information in this chapter has been sourced from material in the Harvard University Archives, including class reports and research by Mason Hammond (Harvard class of 1925), Professor of Classics.
2 Moses King and T. P. Ivy, *Harvard and Its Surroundings* (Cambridge, MA, 1878), pp. 37–9.
3 John Ruskin, *The Stones of Venice; with Illustrations* (New York, 1885), ch. 4, p. xxxviii.
4 At patents.google.com.
5 Virginia Raguin, 'John La Farge', in *American Paintings at Harvard*, ed. T. Stebbins, K. Orcutt and A. Anderson (Cambridge, MA, 2008), vol. ii, pp. 192–4. La Farge's patent can be accessed at patents.google.com.

10 The Tiffany Chapel: World's Columbian Exposition

1 *American Architect and Building News* (11 November 1893), pp. 74–5. Reference to Sir Joseph Porter, 'K.C.B.', from Gilbert and Sullivan's HMS *Pinafore*, and the song 'Ruler of the Queen's Navee', available online at https://victorianweb.org.
2 Ibid.
3 Procopius, *Buildings* (Book 1.i. 57–65), trans. Henry B. Dewing (Harvard, MA, 1914), p. 27.

4 See *A Synopsis of the Exhibit of the Tiffany Glass and Decorating Company in the American Section of the Manufactures and Liberal Arts Building of the World's Fair, Jackson Park, Chicago, IL, 1893, with an Appendix on Memorial Windows* (New York, 1893), p. 11.
5 Ibid., p. 12.
6 Ibid., p. 8.
7 *The International Studio*, 5 (1898), pp. 16–21, quoted on pp. 17–18.
8 Ibid.

11 The Light Screens of Frank Lloyd Wright

1 *Architectural Record* (March 1908), in Frederick Gutheim, ed., *In the Cause of Architecture: Essays by Frank Lloyd Wright for 'Architectural Record'* (New York, 1975), p. 59.
2 *Architectural Record* (July 1928), ibid., p. 201.
3 *Architectural Record* (May 1914), ibid., p. 122.
4 Frank Lloyd Wright, 'Third Dimension' [1925], in *The Work of Frank Lloyd Wright*, ed. Olgivanna Lloyd Wright (New York, 1965), p. 64.
5 *Architectural Record* (July 1928), in Gutheim, *In the Cause of Architecture*, p. 200.
6 Julie Sloan and David G. De Long, *Light Screens: The Leaded-Glass Windows of Frank Lloyd Wright* (New York, 2001), p. 215.
7 *Architectural Record* (July 1928), in Gutheim, *In the Cause of Architecture*, p. 200.
8 Frank Lloyd Wright, *An Autobiography* (New York, 1943), p. 226.
9 Frank Lloyd Wright, 'In the Cause of Architecture' [1925], in *The Work of Frank Lloyd Wright*, p. 59.

12 The Spirituality of Abstraction

1 Richard Ettinghausen, Oleg Grabar and Marilyn Jenkins-Madina, *Islamic Art and Architecture, 650–1250* (New Haven, CT, 2001).
2 Margaret Martlew, 'Glazing the Sagrada Família: Exclusive Interview with Joan Vila Grau', *Vidimus* (May 2010), www.vidimus.org.
3 Musée Soulanges, 'The Conquest Project', https://musee-soulages-rodez.fr, accessed 27 April 2023.
4 Musée Soulages, *Polyptyque*, 1 (1986), https://archive.org, accessed 15 January 2023.

Further Reading

Introduction

Hawthorne, John G., and Cyril Stanley Smith, ed., *Theophilus on Divers Arts: The Foremost Medieval Treatise on Painting, Glassmaking, and Metalwork* [1963] (New York, 1979)

1 Canterbury: A Martyr's Tomb and Its Cathedral

Bede, *A History of the English Church and Its People*, trans. Leo Sherley-Price (London, 1976)

Blick, Sarah, 'Comparing Pilgrim Souvenirs and Trinity Chapel Windows at Canterbury Cathedral: An Exploration of Context, Copying, and the Recovery of Lost Stained Glass', *Mirator* (2001), pp. 1–27

Caviness, Madeline H., *The Early Stained Glass of Canterbury Cathedral, circa 1175–1220* (Princeton, NJ, 1977)

——, *The Windows of Christ Church, Canterbury*, Corpus Vitrearum Medii Aevi, Great Britain 2 (London, 1981)

Hillgarth, J. N., *Christianity and Paganism, 350–750: The Conversion of Western Europe* [1969] (Philadelphia, PA, 1986)

2 Chartres: Representations in an Iconic Gothic Programme

Branner, Robert, ed., *Chartres Cathedral*, Norton Critical Studies in Art History (New York, 1969)

Kemp, Wolfgang, *The Narratives of Gothic Stained Glass* (Cambridge and New York, 1997)

Panofsky, Erwin, with Gerda Panofsky-Soergel, ed., *Abbot Suger on the Abbey Church of St.-Denis and Its Art Treasures* (Princeton, NJ, 1979)

Welch Williams, Jane, *Bread, Wine, and Money: The Windows of the Trades at Chartres Cathedral* (Chicago, IL, and London, 1993)

3 Sainte-Chapelle, Paris: Propaganda for the Monarch

Aubert, Marcel, Louis Grodecki, Jean Lafond and Jean Verrier, *Les Vitraux de Notre-Dame et de la Sainte-Chapelle de Paris*, Corpus Vitrearum Medii Aevi, France 1 (Paris, 1959)

Branner, Robert, *St Louis and the Court Style in Gothic Architecture* (London, 1964)

Durand, Jannic, and Marie-Pierre Laffitte, ed., *Le Trésor de la Sainte-Chapelle*, exh. cat., Musée du Louvre (Paris, 2001)

Ferdinand, baron de Guilhermy, *Description de la Sainte-Chapelle*, Paris, 1867 (98-page book digitized at https://archive.org/details/descriptiondelaooguilgoog)

Hedeman, Anne D., *The Royal Image: Illustrations of the Grandes Chroniques de France, 1274–1422* (Berkeley, CA, 1991)

Jordan, Alyce A., *Visualizing Kingship in the Windows of the Sainte-Chapelle* (Turnhout, 2002)

4 Cologne Cathedral: A Building over Time

Rode, Herbert, *Die mittelalerlichen Glasmalereinen des Kölner Domes*, Corpus Vitrearum Deutschland, IV/1 (Berlin, 1974)

Serota, Nicholas, and Mark Godfrey, ed., *Gerhard Richter: Panorama* [2011] (London, 2016)
Wolff, Arnold, *The Cologne Cathedral* (Cologne, 1990)

5 All Saints, North Street, York: Instructing a Parish

Davidson, Clifford, ed., *The York Corpus Christi Plays* (Kalamazoo, MI, 2011);
 see https://d.lib.rochester.edu
Duffy, Eamon, *The Stripping of the Altars: Traditional Religion in England, 1400–1580*
 (New Haven, CT, and London, 1992)
God Measuring the World with a Masons' Compass: First Master of the *Bible historiale*
 of Jean de Berry: Scenes of Creation, French, 1390–1400, J. Paul Getty Museum, Los Angeles,
 Ms. Ludwig XIII/3, leaf 1 (83.MP.146.1.recto)
Lanson, Edward H., *A Manual of Councils of the Holy Catholick Church* (London, 1846)
Rolle, Richard, *The Pricke of Conscience (Stimulus conscientiae)* (British Museum manuscript;
 Philological Society, London), ed. Richard Morris (Berlin, 1863)
Staley, Lynn, *The Book of Margery Kempe: A New Translation, Contexts, Criticism* (New York
 and London, 2001)
Twycross, Meg, 'Theatricality of Medieval English Plays', in *Cambridge Companion to
 Medieval English Theatre*, ed. Alan Beadle and Richard Fletcher (Cambridge and
 New York, 1994, 2008)

6 St Mary's Parish Church, Fairford, Gloucestershire: Surviving Iconoclasm

Barley, Keith, '"Man in a Red Hat": St Mary's Church, Fairford: The Creation of a Remarkable
 Late Medieval Glazing Scheme', MA thesis, University of York, 2015
Brown, Sarah, and Lindsay MacDonald, *Life, Death, and Art: The Medieval Stained Glass
 of Fairford Church* (Phoenix Mill, 1997), revised and augmented as *Fairford Parish Church:
 A Medieval Church and Its Stained Glass* (Stroud, 2007)
Henry, Avril, ed., *Biblia Pauperum: A Facsimile and Edition* (Ithaca, NY, 1987)
Love, Nicholas, *The Mirror of the Blessed Life of Jesus Christ: A Reading Text*, ed. Michael Sargent
 (Exeter, 2004)
Spraggon, Julie, *Puritan Iconoclasm during the English Civil War* (Woodbridge, Suffolk,
 and Rochester, NY, 2003)

7 Renaissance Donors in Switzerland: An Art of Exchange

Bergmann, Uta, *Die Freiburger Glasmalerei des 16. bis 18. Jahrhunderts, Le Vitrail fribourgeois
 du XVIe au XVIIIe siècle*, vol. VI (Corpus Vitrearum Schweiz, Reihe Neuzeit), 2 vols
 (Bern, 2014)
Giesicke, Barbara, and Mylène Ruoss, 'In Honor of Friendship: Function, Meaning, and
 Iconography in Civic Stained-Glass Donations in Switzerland and Southern Germany',
 in *Painting on Light: Drawings and Stained Glass in the Age of Dürer and Holbein*,
 ed. Barbara Butts, Lee Hendrix, exh. cat., The J. Paul Getty Museum (Los Angeles, CA,
 2000), pp. 43–55
Hasler, Rolf, *Glasmalerei im Kanton Aargau, Kreuzgang von Muri*, vol. II (Corpus Vitrearum
 Schweiz, Reihe Neuzeit), Buchs: Lehrmittelverlag des Kantons Argau, 2002
Hoegger, Peter, *Glasmalerei im Kanton Aargau: Kloster Wettingen*, vol I (Corpus Vitrearum
 Schweiz, Reihe Neuzeit), Buchs: Lehrmittelverlag des Kantons Argau, 2002
Meyer, Hermann, *Die schweizerische Sitte der Fenster- und Wappenschenkung vom XV. bis XVII.
 Jahrhundert* (Frauenfeld, 1884)

8 Renaissance Roundels: The Transformation of European Image Making

Cole, William, 'Glass Paintings after Heemskerck in England', *Antiquaries Journal*, 60, pt 2 (1980),
 pp. 247–67

Husband, Timothy, et al., *The Luminous Image: Painted Glass Roundels in the Lowlands, 1480–1560*, exh. cat., Metropolitan Museum of Art (New York, 1995)
Marrow, James H., *Passion Iconography in Northern European Art of the Late Middle Ages and Early Renaissance: A Study of the Transformation of Sacred Metaphor into Descriptive Narrative* (Kortrijk, Belgium, 1979)
Thornton, Peter, *Seventeenth-Century Interior Decoration in England, France and Holland* (New Haven, CT, 1981)

9 Harvard University's Memorial Hall: Honouring the Dead, the Nation and Art

Adams, Henry, et al., *John La Farge*, exh. cat., The Carnegie Museum of Art, Pittsburgh, and the National Museum of American Art, Smithsonian Institution, Washington, DC (New York, 1987)
Heller, Terry, ed., *Sarah Wyman Whitman, Letters* (Cambridge, MA, 1907)
Stebbins, Jr, Theodore E., et al., ed., *American Paintings at Harvard: Paintings, Watercolors, Pastels, and Stained Glass by Artists Born between 1826 and 1856* ('Stained Glass' by Virginia Raguin), vol. II (New Haven, CT, 2008)
Weinberg, H. Barbara, *The Decorative Work of John La Farge* (New York, 1977)

10 The Tiffany Chapel: World's Columbian Exposition

Duncan, Alastair, Martin Eidelberg and Neil Harris, *Masterworks of Louis Comfort Tiffany* (New York, 1989)
Long, Nancy, ed., *The Tiffany Chapel: Morse Museum* (Winter Park, FL, 2002)
McKean, Hugh F., *The 'Lost' Treasures of Louis Comfort Tiffany* (Atglen, PA, 2002)
Tiffany Glass and Decorating Company, *A Synopsis of the Exhibit of the Tiffany Glass and Decorating Company in the American Section of the Manufactures and Liberal Arts Building of the World's Fair, Jackson Park, Chicago, IL, 1893, with an Appendix on Memorial Windows* (New York, 1893)

11 The Light Screens of Frank Lloyd Wright

Gutheim, Frederick, ed., *In the Cause of Architecture: Essays by Frank Lloyd Wright for 'Architectural Record'* (New York, 1975)
Lloyd Wright, Frank, *An Autobiography* (New York, 1943)
Lloyd Wright, Olgivanna, ed., *The Work of Frank Lloyd Wright* (New York, 1965)
Sloan, Julie, and David G. De Long, *Light Screens: The Leaded-Glass Windows of Frank Lloyd Wright* (New York, 2001)
Studies and Executed Buildings by Frank Lloyd Wright, reissue of *Ausgefuhrte Bauten und Entwurfe von Frank Lloyd Wright* (Palos Park, IL, 1975)

12 The Spirituality of Abstraction

Ettinghausen, Richard, Oleg Grabar and Marilyn Jenkins-Madina, *Islamic Art and Architecture, 650–1250* (New Haven, CT, 2001)
Kunststiftung, NRH, ed., *Imi Knoebel: Reims* (Berlin, 2017)
Posner, Helaine, *Kiki Smith* (New York, 2005)
Raguin, Virginia, *Kiki Smith: Lodestar* (New York, 2010)
Sagrada Família, ed., *The Colors of Light: Vila-Grau's Stained Glass Windows in the Sagrada Família* (Barcelona, 2010)
Sweeney, James Johnson, *Soulages* (Greenwich, CT, 1972)

Acknowledgements

—

First, I am grateful to Reaktion Books and Vivian Constantinopoulos, Editorial Director, for having invited me to write this volume. I also extend gratitude to all of the researchers, librarians and preservationists who have dedicated their lives to ensure that these buildings would live on for future generations. Chief among them is the organization of the International Corpus Vitrearum founded in 1952. To Madeline Caviness, who wrote the Corpus Vitrearum volume on Canterbury, we owe the organization of the USA Checklist series which brought international colleagues together. This heroic service, aided by Marilyn Beavan and Ellen Shortell, enabled information to be disseminated to our European colleagues.

Invaluable aid has come from Daniel Parello of the Corpus Vitrearum, Freiburg, Elgin van Treeck-Vaassen and earlier from Ulrika Brinkman of Cologne Cathedral and Arnold Wolf, former Dombaumeister. In Switzerland, Rolf Hasler and Stefan Trümpler as well as the team at the Vitrocentre, Romont, Switzerland, Francine Geise, Sarah Keller and Uta Bergmann have provided long-term assistance. For help with English sites, I owe special thanks to Tim Ayers, Sarah Brown and Keith Barley. In Belgium and the Netherlands, the work could not have been accomplished without the assistance of Yvette Vanden Bemden, Isabelle Lecocq, Zsuzsanna van Ruyven-Zeman and Cornelis J. Berserik. I know I speak for an entire generation in expressing gratitude to Juan Vila-Grau for his windows of the Sagrada Família, a thanks that extends to the other artists mentioned here, Pierre Soulages, Imi Knoebel, Kiki Smith and Romi Fischer.

At the Los Angeles County Museum of Art, my research was aided by Rosie Chambers Mills, Marilyn B. and Calvin B. Gross, Associate Curator of Decorative Arts and Design, and at the J. Paul Getty Museum by Jeffrey Weaver, Associate Curator of Sculpture and Decorative Arts. Additional assistance was given by Jennifer Perry Thalheimer, Curator at the Charles Hosmer Morse Museum of American Art, and Enna Heller, Bruce A. Beal Director of the Cornell Fine Arts Museum at Rollins College. Peter J. Riley, Harvard University Real Estate, was the amazing facilitator for the restoration of the windows of Harvard's Memorial Hall.

Many others gave advice. Sarah Stanbury, with whom I collaborated on publications and classes at the College of the Holy Cross, provided insight on English medieval literature. Anne Heath, Hope College, helped with the chapters on Chartres and Canterbury, and Alyce Jordan, Northern Arizona University, Emeritus, reviewed the chapter on the Sainte-Chapelle. David Judson, CEO, Judson Studios, helped with insights on Frank Lloyd Wright's windows and Robert Christ of Glashütte Lamberts, Waldsassen, Germany, gave invaluable information on the production of glass. John Demers, a cherished former student, my sons- and daughters-in law, John and Janis Raguin and Daniel and Laura Raguin, read parts of the text.

Family and friends must be thanked for material as well as emotional support. While visiting many sites, I have benefited from 'in-kind' donation of lodging, food and energetic exchanges. In particular Jacqueline Drey, Paris, a college acquaintance who became a friend for life, and Chantal Bouchon, French Corpus Vitrearum colleague. Resonating through this entire publication, we find my husband's photography. Michel's work demonstrates the synergistic confluence of a software engineer and the digital camera, and we are the happy beneficiaries.

Photo Acknowledgements

—

The author and publishers wish to express their thanks to the below sources of illustrative material and/or permission to reproduce it.

Alamy: 91 (Nicholas Temple-Fry) 142 (Kim Karpeles); British Museum, London, Department of Prints & Drawings: 112 (No. 1949,0709.209); Bullseye Glass Co., Portland, Oregon: 3; © Doug Carr: 144 (courtesy of the Dana-Thomas House Foundation); Painton Cowen: 37, 81, 83, 84, 85, 86, 87, 88, 90; Romi Fischer: 157, 158; The Fitzwilliam Museum, Cambridge: 106 (No. 422); Flickr: 79 (Jules & Jenny), 80 (gailhampshire), 146 (Kyle Magnuson), 154 (jean-louis Zimmermann); University of Fribourg: 94 (www.e-codices. unifr.ch/en/kol/S0023-2/bindingA/0); J. Paul Getty Museum, Los Angeles, California: 5 (91.GG.69), 9 (2004.64), 97 (89.GG.18), 113 (2003.74), 115 (2003.59); Glashütte Lamberts, Waldsassen, Germany: 2, 4; Imaging Services, Harvard Library (Stephen Sylvester and Yosi A. R-Pozeilov, Photographers): 119, 120, 122, 124, 125, 128, 129, 130; © Historisches Museum, Basel, Switzerland: 98; Judson Studios, © 2017 Alexander Vertikoff for Judson Studios: 147, 148, 149; Los Angeles County Museum of Art, Los Angeles, California (William Randolph Hearst Collection): 36 (45.21.40), 96 (45.21.23), 105 (45.21.53), 108 (45.21.52); Metropolitan Museum of Art, New York: 12 (Gift of J. Pierpont Morgan, 1917/17.190.520/ Public Domain), 17 (Gift of Dr. and Mrs. W. Conte, 2001/2001.310/Public Domain), 41 (The Cloisters Collection, 1954/54.1.2, fol. 173v); The Morgan Library and Museum, New York: 24 (MS M.240); The Charles Hosmer Morse Museum of American Art, Winter Park, Florida, © Charles Hosmer Morse Foundation, Inc.: 131, 132, 134; Musées Royaux d'Art et d'Histoire, Brussels: 104 (Donor municipality of Lotzwil, given to Johannes Trachsel/Inv. I.A. 881); National Gallery of Art, London: 92 (Creative Commons, PD-Art/Yorck Project); Peyersche Tobias Stimmer-Stiftung, Sonnenburggut, Schaffhausen, Switzerland: 99; Philadelphia Museum of Art, Philadelphia, Pennsylvania: 46 (1930-24-3); Private Collection: 93 (with permission), 100 (with permission), 102 (with permission), 103 (with permission); Public Domain: 82; Daniel H. Raguin: 153; Michel M. Raguin: 10, 14, 15, 16, 18, 19, 20, 21, 25, 26, 29, 30, 31, 32, 33, 34, 35, 40, 42, 43, 44, 45, 47, 48, 49, 51, 53, 54, 55, 56, 58, 60, 61, 62, 63, 69, 70, 71, 72, 73, 75, 76, 77, 133, 135; Virginia Chieffo Raguin: 1, 6, 7, 8, 9 (Los Angeles County Museum of Art), 11, 13, 22, 23, 27, 28, 38, 39, 50, 57 (Wallraf-Richartz-Museum, Cologne/WRM 184), 59 (Neue Pinakothek, Munich), 64, 65, 66, 67, 68, 74, 78, 89 (Museum of Fine Arts, Boston), 109 (Museum of Fine Arts, Boston), 110 (Museum of Fine Arts, Boston), 118, 121, 126, 127, 136 (Morse Museum of American Art/75-025: A&B), 137, 138 (Morse Museum of American Art/75-025: A&B), 139, 152, 155; Rijksmuseum, Amsterdam: 107 (RP-P-1904-3279), 114 (BK-NM-10187), 116 (RP-P-BI-6261X), 117 (BK-1966-59); Roberto Rosa, Serpentino Studios: 123; Royal Museums of Arts and History, Brussels: 111 (2017-1111/with permission); Shutterstock: 140 (Nagel Photography), 141 (wonderlustpicstravel); Courtesy Kiki Smith: 156; U.S. National Archives (204903835): 52 (U.S. Department of Defense/Department of the Air Force/U.S. Air Force Number 72515AC); Vitromusée, Romont, Switzerland: 95 (Donors: Hans Felix Haller and Elisabeth Vogler/inv. nr. 444); Wasmuth Press, Berlin, 1910: 143; Wikimedia Commons: 141 (Tudoi61/CC BY-SA 4.0 International), 145 (Teemu08/ CC BY-SA 3.0 Unported), 150 (Hesam.montazeri/CC BY-SA 4.0 International), 151 (Gwen Fran from Nantes, France/CC BY-SA 2.0 Generic); Zentralbibliothek, Zürich, Switzerland: 101 (5.220/https:// doi.org/10.3931/e-rara-10598).

Index

—